Deficits, Debt, and the New Politics of Tax Policy

The Constitution grants Congress the power "to lay and collect taxes, duties, imposts, and excises." From the First Congress until today, conflicts over the size, role, and taxing power of government have been at the heart of national politics. This book provides a comprehensive historical account of federal tax policy that emphasizes the relationship between taxes and other components of the budget. It explains how wars, changing conceptions of the domestic role of government, and beliefs about deficits and debt have shaped the modern tax system.

The contemporary focus of this book is the partisan battle over budget policy that began in the 1960s and triggered the disconnect between taxes and spending that has plagued the budget ever since. With the federal government now facing its most serious deficit and debt challenge in the modern era, partisan debate over taxation is almost completely divorced from fiscal realities. Continuing to indulge the public about the true costs of government has served the electoral interests of the parties, but it precludes honest debate about the urgent task of reconnecting taxes and budgets.

Dennis S. Ippolito is Eugene McElvaney Professor of Political Science at Southern Methodist University. Among his previous books are *Why Budgets Matter: Budget Policy and American Politics, Uncertain Legacies: Federal Budget Policy from Roosevelt through Reagan, Hidden Spending: The Politics of Federal Credit Programs, Congressional Spending*, and *The Budget and National Politics*. He was awarded the 2010 Aaron B. Wildavsky Award for Lifetime Scholarly Achievement in the Field of Public Budgeting and Finance.

Deficits, Debt, and the New Politics of Tax Policy

DENNIS S. IPPOLITO
Southern Methodist University

CAMBRIDGE
UNIVERSITY PRESS

CAMBRIDGE UNIVERSITY PRESS
Cambridge, New York, Melbourne, Madrid, Cape Town,
Singapore, São Paulo, Delhi, Mexico City

Cambridge University Press
32 Avenue of the Americas, New York, NY 10013-2473, USA

www.cambridge.org
Information on this title: www.cambridge.org/9781107641402

First published 2012

Printed in the United States of America

A catalog record for this publication is available from the British Library.

Library of Congress Cataloging in Publication Data

Ippolito, Dennis S.
Deficits, debt, and the new politics of tax policy / Dennis S. Ippolito.
    p.   cm.
ISBN 978-1-107-01727-6 (hardback) – ISBN 978-1-107-64140-2 (paperback)
1. Fiscal policy – United States.   2. Finance, Public – United States.   3. Taxation –
United States – History.   I. Title.
HJ257.3.I67   2012
336.73–dc23   2012029079

ISBN 978-1-107-01727-6 Hardback
ISBN 978-1-107-64140-2 Paperback

To Melanie Kay

Contents

Figures and Tables

Preface

As a very important source of strength and security, cherish public credit. One method of preserving it is to use it as sparingly as possible... but remembering also that timely disbursements to prepare for danger frequently prevent much greater disbursements to repel it.... The execution of these maxims belongs to your representatives, but it is necessary that public opinion should co-operate. To facilitate to them the performance of their duty, it is essential that you should practically bear in mind that towards the payment of debts there must be revenue; that to have revenue there must be taxes; that no taxes can be devised which are not more or less inconvenient and unpleasant; that the intrinsic embarrassment, inseparable from the selection of the proper objects (which is always a choice of difficulties), ought to be a decisive motive for a candid construction of the conduct of the government in making it, and for a spirit of acquiescence in the measures for obtaining revenue, which the public exigencies may at any time dictate.

George Washington's Farewell Address, 1796

Tax policy provides illuminating perspectives on politics, particularly in the United States. Perhaps the most resonant protest leading to the American War for Independence was the colonists' denunciation of taxation without representation, and taxation has continued to spark political conflict ever since. From the early battles between Hamiltonians and Jeffersonians to the contemporary partisan clashes over taxes and "big government," tax policy has helped define American parties and shape American political development.

The economic stakes associated with taxes have likewise engaged interest groups throughout our history. Issues of fairness and economic impact have been repeatedly contested, with policymakers struggling to apply these and other prescriptive criteria to the complex provisions of an ever-expanding tax code. Because taxation continually engages the public in a way that few, if any, public policies do, the electoral salience of tax issues has often played an important part in presidential and congressional elections.

In the United States, the relationship between taxation and the other components of the budget – defense and domestic spending, along with deficits and debt – has also been an explicit and oftentimes contentious issue as well. A number of excellent studies have examined how major wars have ushered in lasting changes in the types of taxes that Americans pay and the amount of revenue that government demands. Indeed, with the exception of the recent wars in Iraq and Afghanistan, the decision to go to war has inevitably led to the enactment of new or special taxes. The individual income tax, for example, was first imposed during the Civil War, expanded into a major revenue source during World War I, and transformed into a mass tax in World War II. It has supplied the largest share of federal revenues ever since.

Wars do not provide the entire explanation, however, for long-term changes in tax policy. The Social Security Act of 1935 introduced payroll taxes to fund benefits for retired workers, and these and other social insurance taxes now provide more than one-third of the federal government's annual revenues. Social Security and Medicare are the largest of some two dozen social welfare entitlement programs that today account for more than half the federal budget and will likely absorb an even larger share in the future. With the federal government having taken on social welfare responsibilities for the elderly and the poor, taxation has become an important instrument of social policy and a critical part of the debate over the welfare state.

The purpose of this book is to analyze federal tax policy in this budget policy context. It provides a comprehensive historical account of how wars, changing conceptions of the domestic role of government, and attitudes toward deficits and debt created the modern tax system in the United States. It then focuses on the causes and consequences of the partisan disconnect between spending and revenue policy that has taken hold over the past several decades and remains firmly in place despite the unprecedented deficit and debt problems the nation now faces.

The revenue/spending/deficit-debt nexus explored in this book is not, in other words, simply a contemporary phenomenon. There was no federal budget as such in the 1790s, but there was nevertheless a remarkably comprehensive debate about the level and type of federal taxes, constitutionally permissible spending, the propriety of deficits, and the management of debt. For Thomas Jefferson and his followers, Federalist "High Finance" was anathema, and their political ascendancy after 1801 ushered in a very different fiscal vision for the federal government.

These early partisan battles over taxation (mainly tariffs and excises), spending (particularly "internal improvements"), and balanced budgets continued throughout the nineteenth and early twentieth centuries. Under the Republican Party that dominated the post–Civil War period, a new spending philosophy was introduced, funded by high protective tariffs and permanent excise taxes. As concerns grew about the fairness, economic distortions, and revenue capacity of this tax system, proponents of income taxation finally succeeded in passing the Sixteenth Amendment and reinstating the federal income tax.

Even under Republicans, however, federal spending remained extremely low by modern standards. When the federal government published its first comprehensive report on government finances in 1902, state and local spending was approximately 5 percent of gross domestic product (GDP), while the federal budget was well below 3 percent. From 1789 to 1930, moreover, balanced-budget principles generally ensured that national taxation satisfied its basic purpose – adequately funding the public programs that "provide for the common defense and general welfare of the United States." Federal budgets were usually balanced – the major exceptions being wars – and federal debt was usually quite low.

The era of modern budget policy began in the 1930s as budgets became much larger – spending was about 3 percent of GDP in 1930 and more than 15 percent two decades later. During the 1950s, with Cold War defense spending accounting for well over half of the budget, federal spending–GDP levels climbed to nearly 20 percent. And while Democratic versus Republican differences over tax policy certainly were evident, they were moderated by a strong bipartisan commitment to balanced budgets. In the fifteen-year period from the end of World War II through the Truman and Eisenhower administrations, budgets were balanced seven times, and deficits were tightly controlled. By 1961, the publicly held debt–GDP ratio had dropped to 45 percent, compared to nearly 110 percent after World War II.

As these figures suggest, revenue levels closely tracked spending over this period, while tax policy remained quite stable. The steeply progressive rate structure of World War II – 23 percent to 94 percent, with twenty-four income brackets and very low personal exemptions – remained largely in place for nearly two decades. Both the Truman and Eisenhower administrations resolutely subordinated tax policy to the financing requirements of an enormously costly Cold War defense program and a federal domestic role that preserved the New Deal's legacy.

The destabilizing of tax policy that began in the 1960s is the contemporary focus of this book. Over the past fifty years, the straightforward balanced-budget rule that had constrained tax policy change for much of our history has been modified to accommodate economic stimulus strategies, partisan spending priorities, and the electoral interests of increasingly competitive national parties. The disconnect between spending and revenues today is much larger than in recent decades and potentially much more damaging, but it is rooted in the very different partisan visions of federal budget policy that began to emerge in the wake of the Great Society.

Budgets were balanced only twice under the Kennedy and Johnson administrations, and deficit-GDP levels were about double the average for the 1950s. The Revenue Act of 1964, which cut income tax rates at all income levels, was an aggressive and largely successful effort to spur higher levels of economic growth, but when the Johnson administration launched the Vietnam War and insisted that the nation could also afford the Great Society, it sought to keep these tax cuts in place. In addition, Great Society initiatives were beginning to shift the spending side of the budget from defense to domestic programs even during the peak years of the Vietnam War. When congressional conservatives insisted on attaching domestic spending cuts to the temporary Vietnam War tax increase that was finally enacted in 1968, Lyndon Johnson fought doggedly to protect his spending priorities. By the end of Johnson's presidency, combined social welfare and other domestic spending accounted for nearly 50 percent of the budget, while the defense share was lower than it had been before the Vietnam War.

The disconnect between spending and revenues became even more pronounced during the 1970s as heavily Democratic Congresses steadily expanded the Great Society's domestic spending initiatives. Spending-GDP levels remained above 20 percent after the Vietnam War ended, with nearly half the budget devoted to social welfare programs. Congress attempted to pay for this "welfare shift" with defense cuts rather than tax increases, which seriously damaged important U.S. military capabilities and, at the same time, proved insufficient to offset the rapid rise in domestic spending. From 1970 to 1979, there were no balanced budgets, and deficit-GDP levels averaged almost 3 percent over the latter part of the decade. By the end of the Jimmy Carter presidency, Democratic hopes for a return to balanced budgets were predicated on revenue levels that exceeded those of World War II but somehow did not require the party to increase income taxes.

During the 1980s, deficit-GDP levels averaged more than 4 percent annually and the public debt rose from 26 percent of GDP to more than 40 percent. The Reagan tax cuts obviously contributed to this imbalance, but other budget policy dynamics also played an important role. In particular, social welfare entitlements continued to grow during the Reagan presidency. Increases in the defense budget – from 4.9 percent of GDP in 1980 to a peak of 6.2 percent in 1986 – were actually more than offset by cuts in nondefense discretionary spending, but overall spending-GDP remained high as retirement and healthcare entitlements expanded. During the 1960s and 1970s, entitlement growth had been financed largely through defense cuts. Under Ronald Reagan, these defense transfers were halted, and deficits quickly mounted.

Reagan-era spending dynamics had a dramatic impact on how Republicans and Democrats defined the balanced-budget problem. For Republicans, large deficits were caused by "excessive" domestic spending, and their stated goal was to balance budgets at low revenue levels (i.e., the 18-plus percent of GDP in Reagan's second term). Within this revenue level, moreover, individual income tax policy was their most important concern. The marginal rate cuts in 1981 (from a top rate of 70 percent to 50 percent) and 1986 (to 28 percent) were viewed by Reagan and most Republicans as the essential ingredient in long-term economic growth. In the face of large deficits, Reagan and congressional Republicans had agreed to corporate tax increases in 1982, 1984, and 1986 and to a significant increase in Social Security taxes in 1983, but Reagan repeatedly rejected efforts to raise marginal income tax rates, arguing that this would undermine economic growth.

Tax policy under Reagan, then, had a domestic retrenchment and economic growth rationale that have since become Republican orthodoxy. For Democrats, the deficit problem had very different implications for tax policy. First, Democrats needed to reduce deficits through higher revenue levels in order to protect the social welfare programs to which the party was committed. Second, this Democratic prescription for higher revenue levels was tied to individual income tax increases primarily for high-income taxpayers.

The paradigmatic budget battle of the Reagan years – whether to balance the budget at high or low revenue levels – was resolved in the 1990s with a heavy Democratic tilt. Individual income tax increases in 1990 and, especially, 1993 lifted revenue-GDP levels to nearly 21 percent by the end of the decade, with much but certainly not all of this additional revenue from high-income taxpayers. These were the highest revenue-GDP levels since World War II. As steep cutbacks in post–Cold War defense budgets reduced overall spending-GDP to its lowest level in more than three decades, the resulting fiscal turnaround was dramatic – from a $290 billion deficit in 1992 to a $236 billion surplus in 2000. The return of balanced budgets, however, actually exacerbated partisan divisions over budget policy and particularly over taxes. George H. W. Bush had been denounced by conservative Republicans for signing the 1990 tax increase, and congressional Republicans unanimously opposed the tax increase signed by Bill Clinton three years later.

When Republicans gained control of Congress in 1995, they tried to repeal these tax increases and to eliminate deficits solely through entitlement and other domestic spending cuts. Bill Clinton vetoed their initial attempt and then, as deficits quickly disappeared, blocked Republican efforts to restore the income tax policies of the Reagan years. With George W. Bush's victory in 2000, however, the Republican tax policy agenda was revived. A massive tax cut was passed in 2001, with additional tax reductions in 2002, 2003, and 2004. Spending for defense also surged during Bush's first term, with the wars in Afghanistan and Iraq, as did spending for entitlements and discretionary spending programs. This new disconnect between revenues and spending policy, amplified by an economic recession, rapidly erased the surplus that Bush had inherited and pushed the deficit to more than $400 billion by 2004.

As the economy recovered, deficits began to fall in Bush's second term, but the structural policy gap between revenues and spending remained. Bush and congressional Republicans never mounted a serious attempt to eliminate this structural deficit through domestic spending cuts, and they refused to consider a wartime tax program. Bush not only resurrected the "guns and butter" approach that Lyndon Johnson had taken during the Vietnam War but extended it to include tax cuts. For Bush and most congressional Republicans, "historical" deficit levels were an acceptable price for their low-tax program. Meanwhile, Democratic critics called for a return to the balanced budgets of the Clinton presidency but ignored the tax program that had made these balanced budgets possible. Rather than fighting to repeal the Bush tax cuts or simply allowing them to expire as scheduled in 2011, Democrats repeatedly promised to extend them for all but the wealthiest taxpayers.

The deep recession and extraordinary turmoil in financial markets that began at the end of 2008, however, abruptly transformed the nation's fiscal outlook. From fiscal years 2009 to 2012, deficits averaged more than 9 percent of GDP, while the publicly held debt in 2012 was nearly 75 percent of GDP. As the economy recovers, both parties have promised to bring deficits under control and to stabilize debt levels, but the partisan debate over deficit reduction has been intensely politicized and quite misleading. Republicans insist that tax increases will not be needed to fund the wartime defense budgets that they promise to continue or the Social Security, Medicare, and other domestic programs that their constituents demand. Democrats reassure voters that their expansive domestic agenda can be preserved through higher taxes for the very, very few. In fact, stabilizing future budgets without much higher revenue levels would require massive cuts in defense and domestic spending that neither party can be expected to support.

This budget policy deadlock might seem surprising, considering the United States has comparatively low tax burdens for individuals and businesses. Measured against GDP, federal revenues have averaged approximately 18 percent for the past half-century, while combined federal-state revenues have usually been less than 30 percent. Revenue levels in most advanced democracies have usually been higher, and in some larger economies, such as France and Germany, they have been significantly higher. Nevertheless, balancing the federal budget has been difficult for the past half-century and appears to be even more intractable today. As citizens and policymakers grapple with the fateful fiscal choices that lie ahead, an honest and informed debate about taxes and budget policy would undoubtedly be helpful. I hope that the historical and contemporary analysis presented in this book will contribute to that debate.

I am deeply grateful to colleagues and friends who have helped me with this project. I am particularly indebted to William R. Keech and Iwan Morgan, who encouraged me to extend and refine its treatment of contemporary tax policy issues. Their insights about the partisan and interest group dimension of the politics of tax policy have proved invaluable, as has their challenge to make the book more interesting and ambitious. While I wish that these qualities were more evident in the pages that follow, they likely would have been entirely absent otherwise. I would also like to acknowledge a long-standing intellectual debt to James D. Savage, whose work has encouraged me to integrate the history of budget policy into contemporary policy analysis.

Christine Carberry has brought her extraordinary meticulous standards to the preparation of this manuscript. From its earliest stage to its completion, she has truly been indispensable. Finally, Southern Methodist University provided a research leave that allowed me to work full time on this book. The university has also provided generous research support over the years. I am sincerely thankful to all.

A Brief History of Federal Taxation

The modern federal tax system is based on income taxation. This tax system, and the size and role of government it supports, is largely a creation of the New Deal and World War II. Although the U.S. Constitution granted Congress authority to levy many types of taxes, the first federal tax measure was a tariff bill, and the tariff remained the principal source of federal revenue until World War I.

Partisan conflicts over federal taxing power quickly emerged in the 1790s as Federalists proceeded to raise tariff rates and levy new excise taxes (notably an unpopular tax on whiskey) and direct taxes on land and property. Jeffersonian Republicans, in turn, denounced these "internal taxes" and the spending regime that they supported. As president, Thomas Jefferson proceeded to repeal internal taxes while pursuing balanced budgets and debt reduction exclusively through spending cuts. The War of 1812 then temporarily reinstated internal taxes, but tariffs and revenues from the sale of public lands largely funded the federal government for the next several decades. While tariff rates and protectionism continued to fuel partisan and sectional disputes over this period, federal budgets remained small and usually balanced.

The Civil War revived internal taxes and briefly introduced income taxes on individuals and businesses. With the growing federal budgets of the post–Civil War era, excise taxes remained in place, and protective tariffs became the focus of an escalating debate over fairness and economic distortions. Federal taxes and spending, however, remained relatively low. At the turn of the twentieth century, the federal budget was less than 3 percent of gross national product (GNP); state and local spending, by comparison, was nearly twice as high.[1]

---

[1] Dennis S. Ippolito, *Why Budgets Matter: Budget Policy and American Politics* (University Park: Pennsylvania State University Press, 2003), 84–85.

The constitutionality of the federal income tax was finally settled in 1913, and individual and corporate income taxes provided by far the largest share of federal revenues during World War I. These taxes remained in place at reduced levels during the 1920s, and the domestic policy initiatives of the New Deal and the enormous costs of World War II then completed the transition to the income-based federal tax system in place today. The development of federal tax policy, then, has been shaped by wars and also by competing visions of the size and role of government. The critical first step in that development, however, was the struggle to establish the federal government's power to tax.

Securing the Power to Tax

The Revolutionary War was fought by a national government that could not tax and had to resort to massive borrowing, paper currency, and even mass expropriation (impressment) of goods and services.[2] Once the war was over, the Confederation Congress was powerless to compel the states to raise revenues on its behalf and found itself unable to service the wartime debt or to fund an army or navy to protect the nation. Tax protests helped spark the movement toward independence, so the lack of a national revenue system during this period no doubt reflected widespread antitax sentiments. It can also be traced to colonial attitudes regarding "the authority to levy a tax, not over the tax itself."[3] The American colonies had, in fact, developed diverse systems of taxation that were far more important in terms of revenue than the taxes levied by England.[4] Because these taxes were imposed by the colonial governments, in particular by colonial legislative assemblies, they did not ordinarily raise the constitutional and representational issues that undermined the English government's efforts to tax the colonies.

Colonial Taxes

The taxes commonly used in the colonies affected property, goods, and people. Property taxes on land were levied, at one time or another, by most of the colonies, and "improvements, personal property, and inventories" were also taxed by several colonial governments.[5] Taxes on goods included excises (notably on domestic liquor), import duties (on rum, wine, finished goods, and slaves), and export duties (on commodities such as tobacco). Poll taxes were

---

[2] E. James Ferguson, *The Power of the Purse: A History of American Public Finance, 1776–1790* (Chapel Hill: University of North Carolina Press, 1961), 57–69.

[3] Steven A. Bank, Kirk J. Stark, and Joseph J. Thorndike, *War and Taxes* (Washington, D.C.: Urban Institute Press, 2008), 2.

[4] Glenn W. Fisher, *The Worst Tax? A History of the Property Tax in America* (Lawrence: University Press of Kansas, 1996), 12.

[5] Edwin J. Perkins, *The Economy of Colonial America* (New York: Columbia University Press, 1980), 125–126.

prevalent, in most cases with flat or graduated rates on adult males as well as slaves and servants.[6]

There were regional variations in the colonial tax system. The New England colonies "regularly used the property tax as a source of income and all accepted, at least nominally, the idea that taxation should be related to ability to pay."[7] Southern colonies relied on poll taxes and property taxes, but with considerably less concern for ability to pay. In the southern colonies, "men of landed and established wealth, who normally dominated the southern legislatures, erected a tax system that favored their interests."[8] Both direct and indirect taxes were found in the middle colonies.[9]

The New England colonies also used "faculty" taxes – precursors to the income tax – that applied to the earning capacity of various occupations or trades. These included special taxes on "merchants, moneylenders, artisans, lawyers, and others who did not live off the land."[10] In most cases, these levies were not directly applied to income but depended on the ability to earn. In Massachusetts, however, a specific tax rate was levied on incomes and profits from various business activities.[11]

While the types of taxes levied by the colonial governments were diverse, it is generally agreed that the overall level of taxation was relatively low. One study estimates that "British tax burdens were ten or more times heavier than those in the colonies."[12] In part, taxes were low because colonial governments provided few services beyond their administrative costs. County and town governments were usually responsible for whatever provision was made for the poor and were also called upon to help meet the expenses of locally organized militias.[13]

In addition, most of the cost for the military defense of the colonies was taken on by the English government. The French and Indian War, which lasted from 1756 to 1763, was the most expensive of the military campaigns fought on the North American mainland. England emerged from this war with undisputed control of Canada, Florida, and territory east of the Mississippi River, and with a very large wartime debt. The new taxes levied on the colonies by England, beginning with the Sugar Act of 1764 and the Stamp Act of 1765, were intended to defray some of these costs, but the response from the colonies was uniformly hostile. Boycotts of English goods, attacks on tax collectors, and a formal

---

[6] Ibid., 126.
[7] Fisher, *The Worst Tax?*, 15.
[8] Ibid., 16.
[9] Carolyn Webber and Aaron Wildavsky, *A History of Taxation and Expenditure in the Western World* (New York: Simon & Schuster, 1986), 364.
[10] Fisher, *The Worst Tax?*, 4.
[11] Perkins, *The Economy of Colonial America*, 127.
[12] Alvin Rabushka, *Taxation in Colonial America* (Princeton: Princeton University Press, 2008), 867.
[13] Davis Rich Dewey, *Financial History of the United States*, 6th ed. (New York: Longmans, Green, 1918), 8–9.

protest by the Stamp Act Congress that nine colonies organized in October 1765 led Parliament to repeal the Stamp Act the following year. Heavier import duties then were enacted, including the infamous tax on tea, and customs enforcement was strengthened as well. Thus, taxation continued to strain relations between the colonies and England until the Revolution.

The colonial period established some general views about taxation that would affect public finance for quite some time. The authority of colonial assemblies to levy taxes was widely accepted, but taxes were kept low by strictly limiting the types of expenditures for which the colonial governments were responsible. Colonial legislatures also resorted to borrowing, in the form of "bills of credit," to fund extraordinary expenses, such as war, and to promote commerce. The reliance on paper currency and borrowing, rather than taxation, to fund the Revolutionary War was a natural progression.[14] In addition, this legislative power of the purse was routinely used to prescribe "exactly what could and could not be done" with public funds.[15] While the administrative practices and capacities of the colonial governments were in many instances rudimentary, their understanding of the political importance of the taxing power was not.

Financing War without Taxes

The Continental Congress that operated as a "national government" until the Articles of Confederation were ratified in 1781 was never given the power to tax by the states, despite the repeated difficulties it encountered in financing a long and costly war. It first issued unsecured paper currency, with 2 million in Continental dollars printed in July 1775 and an additional 4 million by the end of the year.[16] The total climbed to $25 million in 1776, at which point this unsecured currency began to depreciate sharply in value. Congress had planned for the states to levy taxes in support of this currency, but the states were overwhelmed by their own wartime expenses and reluctant to impose heavier taxes. A requisition system that Congress adopted in November 1777 assigned financial quotas to each state, with an estimated $95 million apportioned over the next two years. Less than $13 million, however, was actually received and less than $1 million of this amount was in the form of specie payments.[17]

The Continental Congress also borrowed from domestic and foreign creditors. The first authorization for domestic loan certificates was issued in 1776. Foreign loans and subsidies began that same year, with an initial grant from

---

[14] James D. Savage, *Balanced Budgets and American Politics* (Ithaca: Cornell University Press, 1988), 65.

[15] Webber and Wildavsky, *A History of Taxation and Expenditure*, 365.

[16] Ferguson, *The Power of the Purse*, 26.

[17] Ibid., 33–34.

France. When the war ended in 1783, more than $6.3 million had been borrowed from France and nearly $1.5 million from Holland and Spain.[18]

The direction of wartime finance passed to the Articles of Confederation government in 1781. Like its Continental Congress predecessor, the Confederation Congress had no direct taxing power. Under Article VIII, expenses for the war and "all other expenses that shall be incurred for the common defence or general welfare, and allowed by the united states in congress assembled" were to be financed out of "a common treasury."[19] The mechanism for funding that treasury, however, depended on taxes "laid and levied" by the states. These taxes were to be apportioned among the states based on "the value of all land within each state," as well as buildings and improvements, but the states were then responsible for meeting their obligations.

The requisition system worked no more effectively under the Confederation government than it had previously. In an attempt to provide a more certain access to revenues, the Confederation Congress approved a national tariff in 1781 (an impost or import duty of 5 percent) that would be pledged to paying interest and principal on all wartime debt, foreign and domestic.[20] The states, however, rejected the constitutional change necessary to vest this power in Congress. A revised national tariff plan was submitted to the states in 1783, with stricter limits on its application and duration and with the further stipulation that state officials, rather than federal officers, would be responsible for its collection. It, too, failed to secure the unanimous agreement of the states required to amend the Articles. Federal taxes on land, poll taxes, and excises on liquor were also proposed, but none were approved by Congress.

The financial weaknesses of the Confederation government became even more glaring after the war ended in 1783. The wartime debt that the national government had incurred totaled nearly $40 million, while the states had an estimated $21 million in additional debt, most of which was directly or indirectly tied to wartime expenses.[21] For the national government debt, annual interest charges were estimated at almost $2 million, with roughly one-fifth of this amount needed to service foreign debt. Requisitions collected from the states had dwindled even further after 1783, so these obligations could not be met. In 1785, interest payments on the debt held by the French government were suspended, and a default on principal repayment occurred two years later. Private loans from Holland were rescheduled and interest continued to be paid, but principal repayment could not be postponed indefinitely, raising fears about another default.

[18] Dewey, *Financial History of the United States*, 47.
[19] Henry Steele Commager, ed., *Documents of American History*, 6th ed. (New York: Appleton-Century-Crofts, 1958), 113.
[20] Ferguson, *The Power of the Purse*, 117.
[21] Dewey, *Financial History of the United States*, 56.

As interest payments were delayed or suspended, the amount of outstanding debt increased. Between 1783 and 1789, arrears of interest on domestic debt totaled more than $8 million and arrears on foreign debt nearly $1.6 million.[22] The fiscal problems of the Confederation, and its political weakness, crippled its ability to maintain a military that could protect against external and internal threats. The Continental Army had been almost entirely disbanded after 1783, leaving a "pathetically small" force of 625 men.[23] Little could be done to enforce American territorial rights in disputes with England and Spain or to deal with frontier conflicts involving the Indian tribes. And without a navy, American commercial vessels had little protection against the Barbary pirates preying in the Mediterranean. When a rebellion broke out in western Massachusetts in 1786 over the state's tax and credit laws, Congress voted to raise troops and to collect requisitions from the states to support them.[24] Only one state, Virginia, complied. When the Massachusetts legislature refused to provide funds for a state militia, the governor and a group of bankers in Boston organized and privately funded a militia that ended Shays' Rebellion without any federal assistance. This episode had a "chilling effect on the thinking of prominent political leaders through the states [and] confirmed the widespread suspicion that the Confederacy was dangerously weak."[25] In 1787, Congress found itself "so destitute of funds and credit that it could neither pay its own civil officers nor borrow one penny from its own citizens."[26]

As the incapacities of the Confederation government deepened and apprehensions over foreign threats and internal disorder mounted, efforts to create a new national government gained widespread, if not universal, support. Led by such notables as George Washington, Alexander Hamilton, and James Madison, this movement persuaded a reluctant Congress to authorize the constitutional convention that met in Philadelphia in May 1787. Its stated purpose was to revise the Articles of Confederation through "alternations and amendments" that would "render them adequate to the preservation and support of the Union."[27] Shortly after the convention began, however, plans for a radically different national government began to take shape.

Taxation, Spending, and Borrowing

The deliberations of the Philadelphia Convention were concluded on September 15, 1787, and the proposed Constitution was submitted to Congress two days

---

[22] Ibid., 57.
[23] Bank, Stark, and Thorndike, *War and Taxes*, 5.
[24] Sheldon W. Pollack, *War, Revenue, and State Building* (Ithaca: Cornell University Press, 2009), 163.
[25] Ibid.
[26] Roger H. Brown, *Redeeming the Republic* (Baltimore: Johns Hopkins University Press, 1993), 27.
[27] Quoted in Pollack, *War, Revenue, and State Building*, 168.

later. On September 28, Congress approved a resolution submitting the Constitution to the states for ratification. The ratification debates that then took place revealed sharp divisions over the powers and structure of the new federal government. For its critics, the Constitution's transfer of power from the states to the federal government was unnecessary and even dangerous. The military was a major concern because the Constitution provided Congress with the authority "to raise and support Armies" and "to provide and maintain a Navy." Anti-Federalists were convinced that these provisions, and the power given to Congress over state militias, posed a serious threat to individual rights and liberties and, of course, to the states. The prospect of a federal standing army was particularly unsettling given the recent colonial experience.

Anti-Federalists also objected to the fiscal powers the Constitution conferred on Congress. The New York and Rhode Island statements of ratification, for example, included proposed constitutional amendments to restrict federal borrowing and debt by requiring two-thirds votes of the House and Senate.[28] Anti-Federalists also opposed the Constitution's prohibition on state-issued bills of credit and its related requirement for specie repayment of debt. The taxing power the federal government would exercise under the Constitution was especially troubling to those who wished to maintain the prerogatives the states had enjoyed under the Articles of Confederation. Their greatest concern was that the federal government would no longer be dependent on the states for revenue but rather would have an exclusive power over tariffs that would deprive the states of needed revenues. Finally, and "most abhorrent of all," the federal government would be able to levy "internal" taxes (such as excises) in addition to tariffs, or "external" taxes.[29]

That the Constitutional Convention would modify the requisition system was no great surprise. Edmund Randolph, who presented the Virginia Plan at the beginning of the Convention, explained that the Articles of Confederation had been drawn up when little was understood "of the science, of constitutions, and of confederacies."[30] As a result, the "inefficiency of requisitions was unknown – no commercial discord had arisen among any states . . . foreign debts had not become urgent – the havoc of paper money had not been foreseen." The competing New Jersey Plan, which envisioned only modest changes in the Articles of Confederation, nevertheless conceded the necessity for new revenue provisions. It authorized the Confederation Congress "to pass acts for raising a revenue" through tariffs and stamp taxes.[31] If additional revenues in the form of requisitions were needed, the New Jersey Plan provided that

---

[28] Savage, *Balanced Budgets and American Politics*, 83.

[29] Dewey, *Financial History of the United States*, 73.

[30] Max Farrand, ed., *The Records of the Federal Convention of 1787* (New Haven: Yale University Press, 1911), I–18.

[31] Commager, *Documents of American History*, 136.

Congress could apportion these among the states based on their population and "devise and pass acts" ensuring compliance.

When national tariffs had been proposed in 1781 and 1783, most states had been willing to amend the Articles of Confederation to authorize their use. The Constitutional Convention could have simply revived the tariff option but instead endorsed a comprehensive federal taxing power, completely eliminating the requisition system that had made the Confederation government dependent on the states. Thus, the language in Article I, Section 8 amounted to a sweeping change in the critical power of taxation:

The Congress shall have Power to lay and collect Taxes, Duties, Imposts and Excises, to pay the Debts and provide for the common Defence and general Welfare of the United States; but all Duties, Imposts and Excises shall be uniform throughout the United States.

The Constitution did place a restriction on "direct taxes" in Article I, Section 2, requiring that "Representatives and direct Taxes shall be apportioned among the several States, which may be included within this Union, according to their respective Numbers." During the colonial period, poll taxes and land taxes had been considered direct taxes, but the "precise meaning" of the term was not altogether clear when the Convention approved this language.[32] (The Supreme Court exploited this ambiguity in 1895, when it invalidated the federal income tax as a direct tax requiring apportionment. The Sixteenth Amendment in 1913 then removed the apportionment requirement for income taxes.)

The fiscal powers in Article I included broad grants of authority regarding borrowing and spending. No restriction was placed on federal deficits or debt, and both taxes and borrowing could be used to support spending. The spending power, in turn, extended to the "common Defence and general Welfare," the delegated powers assigned to Congress, and the "necessary and proper" clause that concludes Section 8.

The breadth of the federal government's power to tax, spend, and borrow was defended at length in Federalist Papers 30–36 by Alexander Hamilton. Hamilton had been one of the most ardent proponents of a strong national government at the Convention and was convinced that expansive and integrated fiscal powers were not only desirable but necessary. Federalist 30 contains Hamilton's classic statement that "Money is with propriety considered as the vital principle of the body politic; as that which sustains its life and motion and enables it to perform its most essential functions. A complete power to procure a regular and adequate supply of it . . . may be regarded as an indispensable ingredient in every constitution." For Hamilton, an "unfettered" power to tax and to borrow was needed so that the federal government could meet its foremost responsibility of defending the nation, but he argued that the

---

[32] Jack N. Rakove, *The Annotated U.S. Constitution and Declaration of Independence* (Cambridge: Harvard University Press, 2009), 110.

government's taxing power should be "requisite to the full accomplishment of the objects committed to its care and to the complete execution of the trusts for which it is responsible." Hamilton contended that this "indefinite power of taxation" should be "free from every other control, but a regard to the public good and to the sense of the people."

The Constitution had conferred on the federal government the broad powers to tax, spend, and borrow, so the checks on these powers were, as Hamilton understood, essentially political. Once the Constitution was ratified and the new government organized, the political contest over the actual size and role of the federal government began. As the nation's first Secretary of the Treasury, Hamilton set the initial course for federal financial policy, but he and his Federalist followers were challenged and ultimately defeated by a Republican Party that had very different views about taxation and the nation's finances.

Tariffs versus Internal Taxes

The fiscal history of the United States from the 1790s until the Civil War illustrates the important role that taxation played in national politics. The political majority for most of this era – the Jeffersonian Republicans, later the Democrats – was strongly opposed to internal taxes, especially excises. They had a correspondingly narrow view of federal spending, an intense commitment to balanced budgets, and an aversion to the accumulation of federal debt. The balanced-budget rule, as a prescription for limited government, thus became the operative principle for the federal government if not for the states. In addition, the legislative power of the purse, another Republican tenet, worked reasonably well during peacetime but was not well suited for emergencies, especially war.

The Federalist Vision
On September 2, 1789, Congress created the Department of the Treasury and assigned to its Secretary the responsibility for reporting to Congress on the administration of federal finances, including "plans for improving and managing the revenue and for support of the public credit."[33] Alexander Hamilton was appointed Secretary on September 11, and his first "Report Relative to a Provision for the Support of the Public Credit" was submitted to Congress on January 19, 1790. This report, which proposed that the federal government honor both its domestic and foreign debts at their original (or par) value and also assume the wartime debts contracted by the states, was extremely controversial. Hamilton's later proposals for a national bank and the use of tariffs and subsidies to promote domestic manufacturing and economic development further deepened the divisions with Thomas Jefferson and his followers in

---

[33] George T. Kurian, *A Historical Guide to the U.S. Government* (New York: Oxford University Press, 1998), 582.

Congress. Issues relating to taxation and debt became recurring themes in the struggle for political control between Hamilton's Federalists and Jefferson's Republicans during the 1790s.

The first national tariff was enacted shortly after Congress convened in 1789. The tariff act that became law on July 4, 1789, "provided for specific duties on over thirty kinds of commodities; for ad valorem rates, varying from $7\frac{1}{2}$ to 15 per cent, on a few specified articles, and for a 5 per cent duty on all articles not enumerated."[34] At Hamilton's urging, tariffs were increased the following year, and another tariff increase in 1791 was approved, as was a new excise tax on distilled spirits and stills. Other "internal taxes" soon followed, including a tax on carriages in 1794. These new taxes were not popular. Protests against the excise tax on whiskey culminated in the Whiskey Rebellion in 1794, which required the intervention of federal troops. The carriage tax was challenged by the state of Virginia but upheld by the Supreme Court in 1796. According to the Court, the carriage tax was not a direct tax and did not require apportionment among the states.

The following year, Congress passed a tax on land (including houses and slaves) that fell under the Court's definition of a direct tax and was accordingly apportioned among the states. This tax was needed to help fund a naval buildup that began during the late 1790s. Prior to that, the American "navy" consisted of a small fleet of revenue-cutters – armed sailing ships that patrolled American waters and helped enforce revenue laws – that Hamilton had established in 1790.[35] In 1798, Congress also authorized a payroll tax on seamen's wages to finance their medical care in the Marine Hospital Service.

The sweeping program of federal taxation enacted under Hamilton and Oliver Wolcott, who succeeded him in 1795, quickly restored the credit of the United States. Revenue from tariffs and other taxes were dedicated to payments on the nearly $80 million in consolidated debt that the federal government held in 1790, and the funding and servicing of the debt became routine. Between 1789 and 1801, interest on the public debt accounted for almost one-half of federal spending (see Table 1.1). Beginning in 1792, however, spending for the Army and, later, the Navy rose sharply in response to military threats involving Indians, Algerine pirates, England, and France, and other noninterest expenditures grew as well, averaging more than $1.2 million annually by the late 1790s. The total federal budget more than doubled over this period from less than $4.3 million in 1789–1791 to nearly $10.8 million in 1800. Despite the tariffs and internal taxes enacted by the Federalists, there were several deficits during the 1790s and a modest increase in the total debt.

For Republicans, the Federalists' accumulation of deficits and debt had to be reversed, but Republicans were also committed to restricting the use of internal taxes. Hamilton had wanted to establish the federal government's authority

[34] Dewey, *Financial History of the United States*, 81.
[35] Kurian, *A Historical Guide to the U.S. Government*, 584.

TABLE 1.1. *Federal Budgets, Fiscal Years 1789–1801 (in thousands of dollars)*

Fiscal Year	Total Revenues	Total Outlays	Deficit/Surplus	Debt
1789–1791	$4,419	$4,269	$150	$75,463
1792	3,670	5,080	− 1,410	77,228
1793	4,653	4,482	171	80,359
1794	5,432	6,991	− 1,559	78,427
1795	6,115	7,540	− 1,425	80,748
1796	8,378	5,727	2,651	83,762
1797	8,689	6,134	2,555	82,064
1798	7,900	7,677	223	79,229
1799	7,547	9,666	− 2,119	78,409
1800	10,849	10,786	63	82,976
1801	12,935	9,395	3,540	83,038
TOTAL	$80,587	$77,747		

Revenues, by Category (Cumulative, 1789–1801)

Tariffs	$70,152
Internal taxes	$5,489
Other	$4,942

Outlays, by Category (Cumulative, 1789–1801)

Interest	$35,524
Military	$29,924
Other	$12,297

Source: U.S. Bureau of the Census, *Historical Statistics of the United States, Colonial Times to 1970, Part 2* (Washington, D.C.: U.S. Bureau of the Census, 1975), 1106, 1115, 1118.

over internal taxation so that the states would not "beget an impression that it was never to be exercised, and next, that it ought not be exercised."[36] When Thomas Jefferson took office in 1801, he pledged to eliminate internal taxes and, at the same time, to balance budgets by cutting the size of the federal government and narrowly defining its constitutional responsibilities. Republican financial policy followed this prescription quite closely under Jefferson. The War of 1812 led to the revival of internal taxation, but the tariff-based system of federal finances quickly reemerged.

Republican Reaction

The balanced-budget principle was central to Jefferson's vision of republican government. As James D. Savage has explained, Jefferson associated federal deficits and debt with an expansive notion of political corruption:

[36] John C. Hamilton, ed., *The Works of Alexander Hamilton* (New York: Charles S. Francis, 1851), 4:256.

Jefferson's great fear was that a central government burdened by deficits and debt would undermine its republican and constitutional foundations while it promoted widespread social and economic inequality. While speculators, bankers, and the moneyed aristocracy would benefit from... financing the debt, the government would spend its added revenues by promoting an industrialized economy through Hamiltonian policies that resembled those of mercantilist and corrupted England.[37]

Once in office, Jefferson and his Secretary of the Treasury, Albert Gallatin, moved to cut spending, reduce taxes, and retire debt. While the heavy Republican majorities in the House and Senate did not always follow the administration's lead, the budget program that Gallatin advanced reduced the debt by $26 million, or nearly one-third, between 1801 and 1809.

Internal taxes yielded slightly more than $1 million in revenues in 1801. After the Republicans repealed excise taxes in 1802, internal tax revenues declined rapidly and virtually disappeared within several years. Part of this shortfall was offset by increased receipts from the sale of public lands, which totaled nearly $4 million from 1801 to 1809. Republicans also benefited from a substantial increase in tariff revenues. Until the Embargo of 1807 began to take effect, increased trade and higher duties on imports led to a surge in tariff revenues and a corresponding increase in total revenues (see Table 1.2).

The spending side of the budget initially fell under Jefferson but then rebounded and remained fairly stable. The administration sought to reduce military spending and civilian expenditures during its first term, but Army and Navy budgets reversed course after 1805. Jefferson's attitude toward domestic spending also became less restrictive, as the debt situation improved. In his second inaugural, Jefferson suggested that once revenues were no longer needed to retire the debt, the Constitution might be amended to allow federal funds to be distributed to the states for "rivers, canals, roads, arts, manufactures, education, and other great objects within each State."[38] Several years earlier, Congress had approved the limited use of proceeds from the sale of public lands for building public roads. Gallatin expanded this precedent into plans for a $20 million permanent revolving fund to build roads and canals.[39]

The constitutionality of federal support for "internal improvements" of this kind posed a problem for Republicans, which explains why Jefferson spoke to the necessity of amending the Constitution in order to distribute funds to the states. The constitutional issue would continue to cloud the debate over internal improvements in future administrations. For Jefferson, however, any expansive plans for a nation free from the burdens of debt were erased by the war buildup that began in the middle of his second term. That buildup, and

---

[37] Savage, *Balanced Budgets and American Politics*, 95.

[38] James D. Richardson, ed., *A Compilation of the Messages and Papers of the Presidents* (New York: Bureau of National Literature, 1917), I–367.

[39] Ippolito, *Why Budgets Matter*, 46.

TABLE 1.2. *Federal Budgets, Fiscal Years 1801–1809 (in millions of dollars)*

Fiscal Year	Total Revenues	Total Outlays	Deficit/Surplus	Debt
1801	$12.9	$9.4	$3.5	$83.0
1802	15.0	7.9	7.1	80.7
1803	11.1	7.9	3.2	77.1
1804	11.8	8.7	3.1	86.4
1805	13.6	10.5	3.1	82.3
1806	15.6	9.8	5.8	75.7
1807	16.4	8.4	8.0	69.2
1808	17.1	9.9	7.2	65.2
1809	7.8	10.3	− 2.5	57.0
TOTAL	$121.3	$82.8		

Revenues, by Category (Cumulative, 1801–1809)

Tariffs	$111.9
Internal taxes	$2.0
Other	$7.3

Outlays, by Category (Cumulative, 1801–1809)

Interest	$34.2
Military	$28.7
Other	$19.8

Source: U.S. Bureau of the Census, *Historical Statistics of the United States, Colonial Times to 1970, Part 2* (Washington, D.C.: U.S. Bureau of the Census, 1975), 1106, 1115, 1118.

the ensuing War of 1812, also revealed serious flaws in the revenue system the Republicans had put in place.

The War of 1812 In reporting to Congress in 1807, Secretary Gallatin stated that "should the United States, contrary to their expectation and desire, be involved in a war," revenues would not be affected immediately.[40] He went on to warn, however, that after 1808, revenues would "be considerably impaired" and recommended that additional funding sources "be selected for supplying the deficiency and defraying the extraordinary expenses."[41] Gallatin's plans for financing war, if war did occur, included borrowing and additional debt. He believed that loans should only be used, however, for the "extraordinary expenses" of war. All other spending, including interest payments on existing and new debt, was to be funded with tax revenues. If tariffs were not sufficient to cover these expenses once war began, new taxes would need to be considered.

---

[40] U.S. Department of the Treasury, *Reports of the Secretary of the Treasury of the United States* (Washington, D.C.: Government Printing Office, 1828), I-359.
[41] Ibid., I-360.

It was clear to Gallatin that taxes were needed to support the costs of new borrowing, but Congress remained unconvinced. When war was declared on June 18, 1812, Congress had authorized $11 million in borrowing, but new taxes had been rejected. Additional authorizations were passed in 1813 and 1814, but the Treasury found that its access to credit markets was woefully inadequate, a situation that had been exacerbated by Congress's refusal to recharter the Bank of the United States. Congress had rejected President James Madison's request to renew the Bank's charter in 1811, and Congress continued to block renewal after the war began.

Congress did raise tariffs several months after war was declared, but Republican opposition to new internal taxes was fierce. The Madison administration proposed new excise taxes and reinstatement of the direct property tax, but many congressional Republicans objected to what they viewed as Federalist taxation. Their intransigence finally gave way late in 1813 as federal finances continued to deteriorate and the military outlook became increasingly dire. A direct property tax was then enacted, along with numerous excises. When deficits and borrowing continued to increase, another round of tax increases was reluctantly approved in 1814. At the end of 1814, as additional taxes (including an income tax) were being considered, the war came to an official end with United States and English negotiators signing the Treaty of Ghent.

The public debt in 1815 was more than $127 million, nearly three times the prewar level, and the Treasury quickly began to retire that debt. Tariff duties were raised substantially in 1816, internal taxes levied during the war were kept in place for several years, and sales of public lands were stepped up as well. Budget surpluses in 1816 and 1817 were, by far, the largest yet recorded in the nation's three-decade history, and, in a further concession to the severity of the financial problems stemming from the war, the Second Bank of the United States was chartered by Congress in 1816.

Extinguishing Debt The balanced-budget principle that Jefferson had championed became institutionalized between 1815 and the Civil War. Every presidential administration during this period pledged its allegiance to fiscal prudence and debt retirement, and Jefferson's abhorrence of the political corruption stemming from deficits and debt was duly expanded into a broader critique of their economic and social effects. As summarized by Kimmel, this critique emphasized fairness and economic growth: "(1) interest on the public debt was a burden on the working classes; (2) interest payments involved a redistribution of income in favor of the well-to-do; and (3) the capital freed from unproductive employment through debt reduction would find its way into productive uses."[42]

---

[42] Lewis H. Kimmel, *Federal Budget and Fiscal Policy, 1789–1958* (Washington, D.C.: Brookings Institution, 1959), 19.

This aversion to federal debt produced a remarkable, if temporary, result. Two decades after the War of 1812, the federal debt had fallen to $38,000, and the nation was on the brink of what President Andrew Jackson termed "that memorable and happy event – the extinction of the public debt."[43] Moreover, this "happy event" had been achieved despite the repeal of almost all internal taxes in the 1820s. Tariff revenues supplied more than 85 percent of total revenues between 1820 and 1835, with most of the remainder provided by the sale of public lands. On the expenditure side, total spending remained low.

This dependence on high tariffs, however, was not without its problems. Rather, political conflicts over protective tariffs intensified as southern states fought to protect their economic interests against the protectionist designs of manufacturing and commercial interests in the North. In 1824 and 1828, tariff rates were raised on a wide range of imported finished goods and commodities. The so-called Tariff of Abominations in 1828 provoked an especially harsh response in the South, with South Carolina claiming the power to nullify federal laws and raising the threat of secession. Congress eased these tensions with tariff reforms in 1832, but the principle of protection still remained in place. The following year saw passage of a compromise tariff bill that established lower, uniform rates and defused the protective tariff issue for a time. The revenue consequences of these rapid changes in tariff policy were not necessarily well understood. In the debate over the 1824 tariff bill, Speaker of the House Henry Clay, an ardent protectionist, conceded that "estimates of the bills' effects on revenues were nothing but conjecture."[44] The 1824 tariff was, in this regard, unexceptional. Rather, Congress's "framing of the successive schedules" in this and other tariff legislation "was hardly a fiscal process."[45]

Fortunately, Congress could usually depend on a steady stream of tariff revenues to service and retire the debt and to fund other federal expenditures. The bulk of these expenditures were accounted for by Army and Navy appropriations and by veterans' pensions.[46] Direct federal spending for internal improvements was opposed by the Madison, Monroe, and Jackson administrations as unconstitutional, infringing on the reserved powers of the states. In one of the more prominent disputes over internal improvements, Andrew Jackson vetoed a series of bills in 1830 and 1831 providing funding for roads, harbors, and lighthouses. In addition to his constitutional objections, Jackson was intent on preventing what he called the "unnecessary accumulation of public revenue" by narrowly defining the spending for which the federal government was responsible.[47] This fiscal doctrine, which connected

---

[43] Ibid., 20.
[44] Dall W. Forsythe, *Taxation and Political Change in the Young Nation, 1781–1833* (New York: Columbia University Press, 1977), 77.
[45] Dewey, *Financial History of the United States*, 173.
[46] Ippolito, *Why Budgets Matter*, 54.
[47] Kimmel, *Federal Budget and Fiscal Policy*, 20–21.

limited peacetime taxation to balanced budgets and small government, was not universally accepted. Henry Clay and the nascent Whig movement, for example, provided an opposition of sorts. Nevertheless, Jackson's ideas about taxes and spending generally prevailed until the Civil War.

The Debt Restored Ironically, the economic well-being that was supposed to reward a nation free from debt did not materialize. Instead, the federal government found itself overwhelmed by financial turmoil resulting from unregulated state bank credit, speculation in public land sales and other ventures, and a collapse in stock and real estate values. Andrew Jackson's successful effort to kill the Second Bank of the United States in 1836 had weakened controls over currency and credit, and his successor, Martin Van Buren, failed in his attempts to restore financial stability. The Panic of 1837 turned into a severe depression that lasted until the early 1840s. A precipitous fall in revenues resulted in a $12.3 million deficit in 1837. Six years later, the public debt had risen to almost $33 million.

The sudden return of deficits and debt at least solved the problem of surplus revenues. In 1836, Congress had authorized the distribution of future surpluses to the states, but this scheme was "at best a makeshift expedient."[48] This surplus dilemma did not recur. The public debt was reduced by more than half from 1844 to 1846, but the Mexican-American War that began in May 1846 and the settlement that followed pushed the debt to more than $63 million in 1849. The wartime debt was then reduced until another financial panic in the late 1850s led to the largest peacetime deficits that had yet been incurred.

Tariff-Based Taxation

Despite the occasional volatility of tariff revenues, Congress did not seriously consider reviving internal taxation in the years leading up to the Civil War. During the 1840s and 1850s, tariffs supplied nearly 90 percent of total revenues, with the sale of public lands accounting for much of the remainder. The protectionism issue surfaced periodically over these years, and Congress continued to adjust and revise tariff schedules in response to the competing political demands for protection and free trade. By the 1850s, however, conflicts over tariffs had been eclipsed by the even more serious divisions over slavery.

The tariff-based tax system was, in terms of revenues, well suited to an era of limited government. Under normal circumstances, it could readily accommodate peacetime military requirements and modest federal domestic responsibilities, in addition to debt service and debt retirement. The federal government had fought the War of 1812 and the Mexican-American War and had been buffeted by the Panic of 1837 and other financial downturns, and yet the federal debt in 1859 was still $20 million less than it had been in 1789. In contrast,

[48] Ibid., 21.

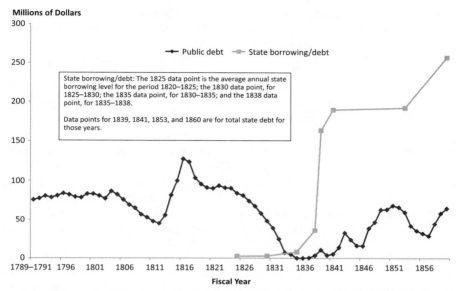

Millions of Dollars

State borrowing/debt: The 1825 data point is the average annual state borrowing level for the period 1820–1825; the 1830 data point, for 1825–1830; the 1835 data point, for 1830–1835; and the 1838 data point, for 1835–1838.

Data points for 1839, 1841, 1853, and 1860 are for total state debt for those years.

Fiscal Year

FIGURE 1.1. Public Debt and State Debt, Fiscal Years 1789–1860. *Sources:* Public Debt: U.S. Bureau of the Census, *Historical Statistics of the United States, Colonial Times to 1970, Part 2* (Washington, D.C.: U.S. Bureau of the Census, 1975), 1118; State Borrowing/Debt Levels: U.S. Bureau of the Census, *The Tenth Census (June 1, 1880),* vol. 7, *Valuation, Taxation, and Public Indebtedness* (Washington, D.C.: U.S. Bureau of the Census, 1884), 281, 523.

many states had encountered major financial difficulties related to their borrowing and debt (see Figure 1.1). After the federal government assumed the states' Revolutionary War debts in 1790, state debt levels remained low through the 1820s. A number of states then began to borrow heavily, and by 1860, collective state debt totaled almost $260 billion, more than four times the federal government's debt.

States had borrowed, moreover, to fund internal improvements that the federal government had largely ignored – roads, canals, bridges, and railroads – and to subsidize state banks.[49] The federal government had donated land to the states to help support capital projects and education, but its direct spending for internal improvements had been extremely limited. Because the states had taken on the financial responsibility for public works that contributed to the nation's economic development and even its defense capabilities, there was an effort in the early 1840s to have the federal government assume a portion of the debt that states had incurred.[50] This effort failed, but the federal government

[49] Savage, *Balanced Budgets and American Politics,* 111.
[50] Dewey, *Financial History of the United States,* 245.

did begin to spend more freely for projects the states could no longer afford. While the constitutional propriety of federal internal improvements continued to be debated, the practical necessity for a larger federal government role was growing, and post–Civil War budgets eventually grew to accommodate that role.

Tariffs and Internal Taxes

The Civil War was long, bloody, and enormously costly. Federal taxation during the war reached unprecedented levels. Because wartime taxation was delayed, however, much of the Civil War was financed by borrowing. The federal debt after the war was more than $2.7 billion, and annual interest payments to service that debt were roughly double total federal spending prior to the war. Larger federal budgets then remained in place even as these wartime obligations declined. With a Republican majority in place, tax policy was wedded to a more robust vision of the domestic role of the federal government. While the Civil War income tax disappeared in 1872, protective tariffs and excise taxes provided sufficient revenues to retire wartime debt, finance an ambitious program of internal improvements, and, for much of the postwar period, balance the budget.

The balanced-budget principle that Jeffersonians and Jacksonians had used to limit the size of the federal budget was, in the hands of Republicans, used to promote "Hamiltonian government."[51] In this recasting, the federal government used its tax, spending, and regulatory powers "to promote business . . . through direct and indirect government intervention, often by assuming the political and economic authority that once rested with lesser, decentralized governments." From internal improvements to the nation's first large-scale social welfare program, spending policy was used to expand the size and role of the federal government.

Civil War Taxation
The initial plan for financing the Civil War followed the general policies used in the War of 1812 and the Mexican-American War in 1846 – "extraordinary," or war, expenses were to be funded through borrowing; "ordinary" expenses, along with interest on existing and new debt, were to be covered through taxation. By the time that Congress convened on July 4, 1861, war had already broken out, and the Lincoln administration's Secretary of the Treasury, Salmon P. Chase, proposed to Congress that war-related appropriations for the next year, estimated at $240 million, be met by new borrowing. He also recommended higher tariffs and either excises or direct taxes to fund the estimated $80 million for "all ordinary demands, for the punctual payment of the interest on loans,

---

[51] Savage, *Balanced Budgets and American Politics*, 142.

and for the creation of a gradually increasing fund for the redemption of the principal."[52]

Congress quickly responded to the need for new taxes, prodded no doubt by the defeat Union forces suffered at the Battle of Bull Run that July. In August, Congress approved higher tariffs along with a direct tax on land and an income tax. The tariff increases, however, were limited, and the direct taxes and income tax had an even smaller impact on revenues. The direct tax, estimated at $20 million, was not assessed until April of the following year. The income tax, with an exemption of $800 and a 3 percent rate on income above this level, contained no assessment or enforcement provisions.[53] In addition, the Treasury was unenthusiastic about implementing income taxation, and in his December 1861 report to Congress, Chase again recommended that direct taxes and excise taxes be used instead.

The shortcomings in this hesitant approach soon became apparent. Spending for the war in fiscal year (FY) 1862 was much greater than had been estimated, revenues were much lower, and the deficit of $422.8 million was nearly double what Chase had forecast in 1861. The ratio of borrowing to taxes, which the administration had hoped would approximate 3:1, exceeded 8:1, and the government found itself unable to borrow the sums necessary to meet this shortfall. As a short-term expedient, the administration and Congress resorted to large issues of unsecured paper currency. The first of the legal-tender acts was enacted on February 25, 1862. Its initial authorization of $150 million was followed by additional authorizations totaling $300 million over the next year.

Congress also approved a wide-ranging set of tax increases that President Abraham Lincoln signed into law on July 1, 1862. A revised income tax, with a $600 exemption and graduated rates – a 3 percent rate on taxable income of less than $10,000 and a 5 percent rate on income of more than $10,000 – replaced the tax that had been provisionally approved the previous year. The 1862 measure also included numerous excise taxes, stamp taxes on legal and commercial documents, inheritance taxes, and gross receipts or dividend taxes on transportation and financial corporations.[54] The impact of these new taxes, however, was undercut by administrative shortcomings in assessing and collecting them. Moreover, war spending continued to exceed all estimates, so deficits and debt grew much more rapidly than anyone had anticipated, and the government's credit remained impaired.

Massive infusions of paper currency allowed the government to meet its immediate needs but created inflationary pressures during, and after, the war. In 1863, President Lincoln acknowledged to Congress his "sincere regret that

---

[52] Albert S. Bolles, *The Financial History of the United States from 1861 to 1865* (New York: D. Appleton, 1886), 6.

[53] Joseph A. Hill, "The Civil War Income Tax," *Quarterly Journal of Economics* 8 (1894): 420.

[54] Steven R. Weisman, *The Great Tax Wars* (New York: Simon & Schuster, 2002), 41–42.

TABLE 1.3. *Civil War Budgets, Fiscal Years 1861–1866 (in millions of dollars)*

Fiscal Year	Gross Debt	Deficit/ Surplus	Total Spending	Total Revenues	Percentage of Total Revenues		
					Tariffs	Internal Revenue	Other
1861	$90.6	−$25.0	$66.5	$41.5	95.4%	0.0%	4.6%
1862	524.2	−422.8	474.8	52.0	94.4	0.0	5.6
1863	1,119.8	−602.0	714.7	112.7	61.3	33.4	5.3
1864	1,815.8	−600.7	865.3	264.6	38.7	41.5	19.9
1865	2,677.9	−963.8	1,297.6	333.7	25.3	62.8	11.8
1866	2,755.8	37.2	520.8	558.0	32.1	55.4	12.5

Source: U.S. Bureau of the Census, *Historical Statistics of the United States, Colonial Times to 1970, Part 2* (Washington, D.C.: U.S. Bureau of the Census, 1975), 1104.

it has been found necessary to authorize so large an additional issue of United States notes" because paper currency had "become already so redundant as to increase prices beyond real values."[55] The administration accordingly recommended that Congress take the steps necessary to improve the government's ability to borrow, especially increased taxation. As Chase explained in his 1863 report to Congress, the new wartime financing required that taxation defray "the largest possible amount of extraordinary expenditures" as well as "ordinary expenditures and interest on the debt."[56] With sustained levels of higher tax revenues, Chase promised the "diminution of debt, the diminution of interest, and the improvement of credit."

In 1864, Congress passed much larger revenue increases, and it buttressed the government's credit by strengthening the national banking system that had been reestablished in 1863. Excise tax rates on alcohol and tobacco were more than doubled, income tax rates were raised, and gross receipts and dividend tax rates were increased. As these new taxes came into effect, and tax administration continued to improve, the yield from internal taxes rose sharply (see Table 1.3). In 1864 and 1865, excise and income taxes accounted for the largest share of total revenues. In 1865 and 1866, with an estimated 10 percent of households in the North subject to the income tax, approximately $110 million was collected.[57]

Budget Policy, 1865–1890

After a more than $960 million deficit in 1865, the budget moved into surplus for nearly three decades. The debt, which had climbed to more than

[55] *Congressional Globe*, 37th Cong., 3d sess., 392 (1863).
[56] Henry Carter Adams, *Public Debts: An Essay in the Science of Finance* (New York: D. Appleton, 1893), 128–129.
[57] Hill, "The Civil War Income Tax," 491.

$2.7 billion during the war, fell by approximately two-thirds over this period. The importance assigned to the retirement of wartime debt was unwavering, with the Treasury at times paying heavy premiums to purchase unmatured debt. This effort was reminiscent of the earlier attempts to retire Revolutionary War and War of 1812 debts, but the tax policies that supported it were, in fact, more far-reaching.

High protective tariffs were kept in place after the Civil War but were supplemented by internal taxes, primarily alcohol and tobacco excises, that accounted for a large share of this expanded revenue base. As the Democratic Party recovered from its Civil War nadir and began to challenge Republican dominance in the 1870s and 1880s, "sharply conflicting ideological views of the tariff and of taxation in general" emerged.[58] But the Republicans managed to keep their preferred version intact until the 1890s.

Tariff rates had been raised during the Civil War from an average of approximately 20 percent to nearly 50 percent in order to meet the demand for additional revenues. Disruptions in trade during the early years of the war lessened the revenue productivity of these rate increases; however, by 1864 and 1865, tariff revenues had climbed well above prewar levels. Moreover, once the war was over, the basic structure of the tariff system remained in place.[59] While tariff schedules were frequently revised, the "ratio between duties and the value of dutiable goods rarely dropped below 40 percent and was frequently close to 50 percent." The rates for manufactured items, where protectionist pressures were strongest, were especially high.

Some parts of the Civil War tax system were dismantled soon after the war ended. Except for alcohol, tobacco, and some luxury items, most excise taxes were repealed. Various business taxes levied during the war were sharply curtailed and, over time, virtually eliminated. Inheritance taxes did not survive for long, and more important in terms of tax policy, the income tax was reduced in 1867 and again in 1870 before being allowed to expire completely two years later.

As shown in Table 1.4, these postwar changes substantially altered the composition of federal revenues. By the early 1870s, tariffs had risen to more than one-half of total revenues, and that share remained quite stable for two decades. The alcohol and tobacco excises that had supplied approximately 10 percent of total receipts in 1865 subsequently rose to more than 30 percent. By the late 1880s, tariffs and excises were providing more than 90 percent of total revenues.

Spending Policy In 1865, the House of Representatives decided to improve its control over spending by creating a new appropriations committee. The Ways and Means Committee had, in the past, handled both revenue and

[58] W. Elliot Brownlee, *Federal Taxation in America: A Short History*, 2d ed. (Cambridge: Cambridge University Press, 2004), 43.
[59] Ibid., 37.

TABLE 1.4. *Composition of Federal Revenues, Fiscal Years 1866–1890*
(in millions of dollars)

| Fiscal Years | Total Revenues | Annual Average | | |
| | | Percentage of Total Revenues | | |
		Tariffs	Alcohol and Tobacco	Other
1866–1870	$447.3	40.0%	14.6%	45.4%
1871–1875	336.8	55.3	27.6	17.1
1876–1880	288.1	50.9	36.8	12.3
1881–1885	367.0	55.0	34.0	11.0
1886–1890	375.4	57.7	33.5	8.8

Source: U.S. Bureau of the Census, *Historical Statistics of the United States, Colonial Times to 1970, Part 2* (Washington, D.C.: U.S. Bureau of the Census, 1975), 1106, 1108.

appropriations legislation, and the 1865 change reflected the belief that this workload had grown too large and unwieldy, particularly given the fiscal problems stemming from the war. Two years later, the Senate followed the House lead, transferring spending responsibilities from its Finance Committee to the Appropriations Committee. The clear expectation at the time was that the new committees would provide the spending restraint needed to service the debt properly and retire it quickly.

The commitment to strict economy persisted for more than a decade. Between 1865 and 1870, total spending fell from nearly $1.3 billion to slightly more than $300 million. During the 1870s, total spending declined to less than $270 million. Interest on the debt accounted for the largest share of the budget over this period – approximately 40 percent. Spending for the Army, the Navy, and Civil War veterans' compensation and pensions accounted for most of the rest, and these noninterest expenditures were essentially flat during the 1870s.

Pressures to meet domestic needs were building, however, as was the need to justify continued high protective tariff levels even as debt-related expenditures declined. An early signal of the former was the House's decision in 1877 to curb the power of its Appropriations Committee by removing the rivers and harbors spending bill from its jurisdiction. In 1880, the agriculture bill was removed, and in 1885, six of the remaining fourteen appropriations bills were stripped from the committee. In each case, jurisdiction was transferred to the legislative, or authorizing, committee. The House's actions appear to have been rooted in widespread dissatisfaction with the independence and "excessive economy-mindedness" that the Appropriations Committee had demonstrated.[60] The jurisdictional changes meant that these spending bills, which accounted for about one-half of annual appropriations, would be reviewed by legislators

[60] Richard F. Fenno, Jr., *The Power of the Purse: Appropriations Politics in Congress* (Boston: Little, Brown, 1966), 43–44.

TABLE 1.5. *Composition of Federal Spending, Fiscal Years 1870–1890 (in millions of dollars)*

Fiscal Year	Total	Percentage of Total			
		Interest	War and Navy Departments[a]	Veterans' Pensions	Other
1870	$309.7	41.7%	25.6%	9.1%	23.4%
1875	274.6	37.5	22.8	10.7	29.0
1880	267.6	35.8	19.3	21.2	23.7
1885	260.2	19.8	22.6	21.6	36.1
1890	318.0	11.4	20.9	33.6	34.1

[a] Includes rivers and harbors spending.

Source: U.S. Bureau of the Census, *Historical Statistics of the United States, Colonial Times to 1970, Part 2* (Washington, D.C.: U.S. Bureau of the Census, 1975), 1114.

more sympathetic toward the programs being funded. With the rivers and harbors appropriations bill, the effects were predictable. During the 1880s, total spending for river improvement and harbor construction was more than $100 million, roughly double the amount from 1869 to 1879 and more than eight times the total for the three decades before the war.[61]

The growing support for federally funded internal improvements to promote commercial and economic development was demonstrated as well in the cash grants and land grants for building of the transcontinental railroad. In addition, the administrative capacity and regulatory reach of the federal government was expanded through new agencies and a growing bureaucracy. Executive branch civilian employment, for example, increased by 60 percent during the 1880s, to more than 150,000, with much of this increase in the Post Office.

The increased appetite for federal spending was especially evident in Congress's handling of Civil War veterans' benefits. In the early 1870s, veterans' compensation and pensions had risen to more than $30 million annually, but these costs were expected to decline unless, as one legislator warned, "our legislation should be unwarrantably extravagant."[62] Pension costs did, in fact, fall by almost 20 percent over the next few years. In 1879, however, Congress enacted the Arrears of Pension Act that reversed this decline and more than tripled annual spending over the next decade. The rise in veterans' pensions was part of a general increase in federal spending during the late 1880s (see Table 1.5). As interest costs fell and debt was retired, the "problem" of large surpluses could have been eased through revenue reductions. Instead, Congress raised spending, particularly for internal improvements, domestic services, and benefits.

[61] Savage, *Balanced Budgets and American Politics*, 131.
[62] Ippolito, *Why Budgets Matter*, 77.

The central role of tax policy in the partisan contest over the size and role of the federal government was freely acknowledged on both sides. The Democratic Party platforms of 1884 and 1888 pledged to reduce tariffs and "unnecessary taxation." The 1888 platform deplored the Republican record of channeling the surpluses from excessive revenues to "extravagant appropriations and expenses" and pledged to reduce these revenues and "enforce frugality in public expense" instead.[63] The Republican platform that year "uncompromisingly" reaffirmed "the American system of protection."[64] There was no "unnecessary taxation," because more spending was needed "for the early rebuilding of our navy, for the construction of coast fortifications...for the payment of just pensions to our soldiers, for necessary works of national importance in the improvement of harbors and the channels of internal, coastwise, and foreign commerce, for the encouragement of the shipping interests."[65] Republicans even proposed direct federal grants to help build a nationwide system of free public schools.[66]

Between 1870 and 1890, total federal spending was nearly flat, budgets were always in surplus, and debt was retired at an impressive rate. While the theme of "economy in expenditures" was constantly reiterated throughout this period, the fiscal reality was more complex. Total spending did not grow, but domestic spending increased rapidly. As military and debt interest expenditures fell, protective tariffs and excise taxes provided ample revenues to fund this spending. But when these spending transfers were no longer possible, and total spending began to climb, the revenue capacity of the tax system was strained to the breaking point.

Budget Policy, 1890–1915

By the 1890s, there was growing criticism of the fairness and economic effects of federal tax policy. Tariffs and excises were regressive, and these taxes also exempted rapidly growing forms of income and wealth. The economic distortions resulting from protective tariffs were troublesome, particularly because they exacerbated sectional cleavages that were already quite deep. During the 1890s, an additional problem emerged, as peacetime deficits became chronic. With new spending raising budgets ever higher, the revenue productivity of the tax system was proving less and less satisfactory. Eventually, the need for new revenue sources was acknowledged but only after a prolonged period of fiscal instability.

---

[63] Alexander D. Noyes, *Forty Years of American Finance* (New York: G. P. Putnam's Sons, 1898), 128–129.

[64] Congressional Quarterly, *National Party Conventions, 1831–1992* (Washington, D.C.: Congressional Quarterly, 1995), 56.

[65] Noyes, *Forty Years of American Finance*, 129.

[66] Kimmel, *Federal Budget and Fiscal Policy*, 79–81.

The Return of Deficits In 1890, congressional Republicans fulfilled their party's commitment to strengthen the protective tariff system. The McKinley Tariff Act of 1890 raised average tariff rates on most goods while revising the tariff schedules to exclude sugar and some less important imports. The revenue effects of this legislation were expected to be modest and, in any case, were incidental to the overriding goal of increased protection. In terms of budget policy, it was assumed the large surpluses of the late 1880s would continue indefinitely.

That optimism led Republicans to expand their domestic spending agenda. The 1890 Dependent Pension Act liberalized once again the Civil War pension program by extending benefits to any veteran with a physical or mental impairment, even if that impairment had not been incurred during the war. The number of newly eligible beneficiaries quickly swelled the pension rolls, and spending rose accordingly. In 1885, veterans' compensation and pensions accounted for 20 percent of a $260 million budget. In 1895, with a $356 million budget, the pension share was 40 percent.

General domestic appropriations, for rivers and harbors and other internal improvements, were also generously increased by what became known as the Billion Dollar Congress. Naval appropriations, which had been flat for nearly two decades, were nearly doubled from 1889 to 1893, and Army funding was raised as well. As one contemporary account of this spending largesse wryly noted, "A national legislature may be safely left to itself, if increased expenditure is desired, and nowhere is this principle more certain of application than in the United States."[67]

The revenue loss from the 1890 tariff act turned out to be much greater than expected, and with total spending increasing, the huge budget surpluses of the late 1880s evaporated. As the Economic Panic of 1893 took hold, tariff revenues plunged even further, and the fiscal 1894 deficit exceeded $60 million. The 1892 election had given the Democratic Party control of the House, Senate, and presidency. In response to the deficit problem they had inherited, Democrats determined to tighten controls over spending, and the resulting cuts in domestic and military spending were maintained for several years. In 1896, total spending was more than $50 million below the more than $380 million in 1893.

On the revenue side, Democrats lowered protective tariffs and enacted the nation's first peacetime income tax. The Wilson-Gorman Tariff Act of 1894 cut tariff rates and revised the tariff schedules that had been put in place in 1890. Its income tax provisions, however, fell short of many reformers' hopes. Although the income tax applied to both corporations and individuals and contained a reasonably broad definition of income – "dividends, interest, rents, sales of real estate and property, and gifts, as well as wages

---

[67] Noyes, *Forty Years of American Finance*, 133.

and salaries"[68] – the tax rate was a flat 2 percent. In addition, the exemption level was set at $4,000, sufficiently high to limit potential coverage to less than one-half of 1 percent of the population. The low rate and limited coverage of this income tax did not produce a massive infusion of new revenues. Raising rates and broadening coverage, however, would have allowed the federal government to reduce its reliance on tariffs. This possibility was quickly foreclosed, however, when the Supreme Court invalidated the income tax provisions of the Wilson-Gorman Act.

In its 1895 *Pollock v. Farmers' Loan and Trust Co.* decision, the Court held that certain types of income subject to federal taxation were direct taxes and therefore had to be apportioned among the states on the basis of population. It subsequently determined the entire scheme of income taxation Congress had adopted so violated the apportionment requirement as to be unconstitutional. Total revenues increased in 1895, despite the aborted effort to tax incomes, as tariff revenues rebounded. Nevertheless, tariffs remained well below the peak levels of the late 1880s, as did total revenues, and the budget remained in deficit for the remainder of the Cleveland administration.

The Republican Party recaptured control of the executive branch and Congress in 1896 and proceeded to change the tariff system yet again. The average rates under the Dingley Tariff Act of 1897 were even higher than those that had been in effect during the Civil War, but the expected revenue increases were not realized. The budget remained in deficit in fiscal years 1896 and 1897, and the Spanish-American War then further increased the deficit over the next two years.

Deficits during the Spanish-American War were moderated by a federal estate tax that was enacted in 1898 and by increased internal revenue collections. Between 1897 and 1900, tariff revenues increased by less than $60 million, to slightly more than $230 million. Over this same period, internal revenue collections went from $147 million to more than $295 million. The 1898 inheritance tax, which applied progressive rates to large estates, contributed only modestly to the rapid escalation in internal revenue collections.[69] Much more important were the higher alcohol and tobacco excises and, especially, the stamp and business taxes contained in the war revenue bill of June 13, 1898. The alacrity with which Congress acted on wartime taxation helped avoid the financing problems that had plagued earlier wars. With borrowing supported by new taxes, loans were quickly subscribed at low rates of interest. Deficit financing during the Spanish-American War averaged approximately 12 percent of total expenditures, well below the deficit-expenditure ratios for the War of 1812, Mexican-American War, and Civil War.

---

[68] John F. Witte, *The Politics and Development of the Federal Income Tax* (Madison: University of Wisconsin Press, 1985), 73.

[69] Dewey, *Financial History of the United States*, 466.

TABLE 1.6. *Federal Spending Trends, Fiscal Years 1890–1915* (in millions of dollars)

Fiscal Years	Annual Average				
	Total Spending	Interest	Military	Veterans' Pensions	Civil and Other
1890–1894	$356.0	$30.4	$76.7	$133.3	$115.5
1895–1899	424.5	36.3	137.3	141.7	109.1
1900–1904	526.3	31.0	209.1	139.9	146.3
1905–1909	613.9	23.3	268.1	147.5	175.0
1910–1914	703.0	22.2	326.7	164.2	190.0

Source: U.S. Bureau of the Census, *Historical Statistics of the United States, Colonial Times to 1970, Part 2* (Washington, D.C.: U.S. Bureau of the Census, 1975), 1114.

Once the war was over, the budget moved into surplus, as internal revenue collections remained high and tariff revenues finally rebounded. Spending, however, remained well above prewar levels, as the spending growth that had taken hold during the 1890s continued at a healthy rate (see Table 1.6). When "extraordinary" expenditures were necessary, as with the Panama Canal financing that began in 1904–1905, or the economy moved into prolonged recession, as it did from 1907 to 1910, the budget fell into deficit, but the underlying fiscal problem was more serious. Given the new spending needed for ongoing federal domestic programs and the military, a broader system of taxation was needed to keep budgets balanced under normal conditions. Where tax policy had, in effect, driven spending policy during the 1880s, this relationship was now reversed.

Republican opposition to the income tax began to wane during Theodore Roosevelt's presidency. In his 1906 message to Congress, Roosevelt stated that a "graduated income tax of the proper type would be a desirable feature of federal taxation, and it is to be hoped one may be devised which the supreme court will declare constitutional."[70] Roosevelt's successor, William Howard Taft, conceded that "should it be impossible to do so [secure sufficient revenue] from import duties, new kinds of taxation must be adopted," although Taft initially preferred a graduated inheritance tax.[71] An inheritance tax was part of the original Payne-Aldrich tariff bill introduced in 1909, but Congress instead approved a corporate income tax. Congress also proposed a constitutional amendment to allow an individual income tax.

The corporate income tax provisions in the Payne-Aldrich Tariff Act of 1909 levied a 1 percent tax on incomes of more than $5,000. In order to avoid potential problems with the *Pollock* decision, the new corporate levy was designated as an excise tax, and the Supreme Court subsequently accepted

[70] Edwin R. A. Seligman, *The Income Tax* (New York: Macmillan, 1914), 591.
[71] Ibid., 592.

this designation. The revenue yield from this tax was more than $20 million in 1910 and climbed to more than $35 million over the next three years.

The income tax amendment that Congress sent to the states for ratification eliminated the apportionment requirement. It provided that "The Congress shall have power to lay and collect taxes on incomes, from whatever source derived, without apportionment among the several states, and without regard to any census or enumeration." While some congressional Republicans who voted for the constitutional amendment hoped the ratification effort would fail, ratification was completed on February 3, 1913. With a new Democratic president and a Democratic-controlled Congress in power after the 1912 election, an immediate legislative priority was to lower tariffs and use the individual income tax to offset the revenue losses. The Underwood Tariff of 1913, which contained the individual income tax provisions, was easily passed in the House, survived major amendment efforts in the Senate, and became law on October 3.

The 1913 tariff law changes were extensive. Average rates were reduced by about one-fourth, with even greater reductions for some widely used manufactured goods, and the schedule of exempted items was substantially enlarged. In addition, the new law replaced the protective tariff scheme with a "competitive tariff" system, in which rates would "be fixed at a point where foreign competition may be effective, thereby preventing the growth of [domestic] monopoly."[72]

The 1913 income tax imposed a normal tax of 1 percent on income of more than $3,000 ($4,000 for a married couple) with an additional tax of up to 6 percent on income of more than $20,000. The top marginal rate of 7 percent applied to taxable income of more than $500,000. The high exemption and low rates of this initial income tax limited its revenue effects. In 1913 and 1914, the number of returns filed averaged slightly more than 355,000. The revenues collected over this two-year period totaled less than $70 million, compared to more than $80 million for the corporate income tax. In 1915, with these new income taxes, internal revenues climbed to more than $415 million, while tariffs provided less than $210 million. The growing reliance on income taxes became even more pronounced during and after World War I.

Income Taxation

The huge costs of World War I transformed federal tax policy. Wartime spending averaged more than $15 billion in 1918 and 1919. As was the case during the Civil War, an array of excise and special taxes was levied to help fund World War I, but income taxation was by far its dominant feature. And, unlike the Civil War, the individual and corporate income taxes of World War I were kept permanently in place as the core elements of a new, broader-based tax system.

---

[72] Dewey, *Financial History of the United States*, 489.

World War I Taxation

The United States did not enter World War I until April 6, 1917, some 30 months after war had broken out in Europe. While the program for wartime taxation did not fully emerge until 1917, Congress had passed war-related tax bills in 1914 and 1916. The Emergency Revenue Act of 1914 raised alcohol taxes and special excises to offset the expected decline in tariff revenues as trade with Europe was disrupted. The tariff shortfall was greater than anticipated, resulting in a FY 1915 deficit of more than $60 million. In FY 1916, with these additional excise taxes, the budget moved back into surplus.

As the United States moved closer to military involvement and increased funding for its Army and Navy, the Treasury Department proposed higher income taxes to Congress. The Revenue Act of 1916, which Congress passed on September 8, was an even larger and more progressive tax increase than the Treasury had initially proposed. Individual income tax rates were raised, with the normal or base rate doubled from 1 percent to 2 percent on taxable income up to $20,000. Surtax rates on income above that level were also raised, with a maximum tax rate of 15 percent on income of more than $2 million.

For corporations, the normal rate was set at 2 percent. Congress also levied an excess profits tax of 12.5 percent on armament manufacturers, similar to the munitions taxes adopted by the major belligerents in Europe.[73] Finally, an estate tax was enacted, with graduated rates from 1 percent to 10 percent, on estates valued at more than $50,000.

The revenue yield from these new taxes was substantial, but much larger revenue increases were soon needed to fund the military buildup. On March 3, 1917, Congress approved higher excess profits and estate taxes to fund military appropriations. One month later, after Congress declared war, the Wilson administration requested an additional $3.5 billion for the Army and Navy. President Woodrow Wilson was determined that "so far as practicable the burden of the war shall be borne by taxation."[74] He recommended that Congress repeal its March tax measure and replace it with a much larger package of tax increases, particularly for individuals and corporations.

The War Revenue Act of 1917 contained an estimated $2.5 billion in additional taxes, with the individual income tax provisions expected to raise $850 million of this total, and the excess profits provisions accounting for $1 billion. While both of these tax increases were controversial, business opposition to the expanded excess profits tax was especially intense, delaying congressional approval until October 3. In the end, Congress extended excess profits taxation to a wide range of businesses, with rates of up to 60 percent on profits above a

---

[73] Witte, *The Politics and Development of the Federal Income Tax*, 81.
[74] Charles Gilbert, *American Financing of World War I* (Westport, Conn.: Greenwood Press, 1970), 83.

specified percentage of invested capital. The normal rate for corporations was increased from 2 percent to 6 percent.

For individuals, the exemption level was cut from $3,000 to $1,000 for single persons and from $4,000 to $2,000 for married couples. The normal rate of 2 percent was applied to the first $2,000 of taxable income with graduated surtax rates above that amount. The progressivity in the rate structure was very steep, with a top marginal rate of 67 percent on taxable income of more than $2 million. The last component of the 1917 Revenue Act comprised new or increased excises and stamp taxes, but reliance on consumption taxes in World War I remained considerably less than it had been in the Civil War.

In the spring of 1918, with spending and deficits growing even faster than expected, the Wilson administration called upon Congress to raise taxes again. The Treasury plan focused on an integrated system of excess profits and war profits taxation to boost corporate income revenues and on higher marginal rates for wealthy individual taxpayers. With midterm elections looming, congressional Democrats were apprehensive about the political fallout from another tax increase, and there were added concerns that the complicated war profits proposal might not achieve the revenue gains the Treasury Department had promised. As it turned out, Congress failed to pass the tax bill before the November election, but Democrats still lost control of the Senate and saw their strength in the House drop to its lowest level since 1908.

As the lame-duck Congress was preparing for its postelection session, the war in Europe came to an abrupt end. After the armistice was signed on November 11, 1918, the Treasury Department reduced its pending revenue request, but Congress proceeded to enact the largest tax increase of the wartime period. The War Revenue Act of 1918 was finally passed on February 3, 1919, with its main revenue provisions aimed at individuals and corporations. For individuals, the normal rate was raised to 6 percent for the 1918 tax year, and the top marginal rate for 1918 was set at 77 percent for taxable income of more than $1 million. For the 1919 tax year, the normal and surtax rates were only slightly reduced. The corporate tax increases included higher normal rates and excess profits rates as well as strengthened war profits tax enforcement.

The revenue increases for World War I were substantial. During fiscal years 1915–1920, total annual receipts rose from $688 million to more than $6.6 billion. Wartime spending, however, grew at a much higher rate. In the peak years of 1918 and 1919, total spending was more than $31 billion – less than 30 percent of which was financed by taxes. Heavy borrowing was needed to finance World War I, but the several borrowing authorizations used by the Treasury were fully subscribed at favorable interest rates.[75] The institutional capabilities of the Treasury Department and Federal Reserve improved greatly over the course of the war, and they managed to coordinate short- and long-term borrowing with few major disruptions.

---

[75] Ibid., 223–231.

TABLE 1.7. *World War I Revenues by Category, Fiscal Years 1915–1920 (in millions of dollars)*

Fiscal Year	Income and Profits	Excise and Internal Taxes	Tariffs	Other Receipts	Total[a]
1915	$80.2	$335.5	$209.8	$72.5	$698.0
1916	124.9	387.8	213.2	56.6	782.5
1917	359.7	449.7	226.0	89.0	1,124.4
1918[b]	2,311.7	874.3	180.0	298.6	3,664.6
1919[b]	3,345.0	948.1	184.5	652.5	5,130.1
1920	3,956.9	1,450.6	322.9	966.6	6,697.0

[a] Excludes refunds, transfers, and interfund transactions.

[b] Incomes and profits taxes for 1918 and 1919 are estimates calculated from total receipts minus other revenue categories. Attribution of income and profits taxes for these tax years varies with official sources, in part because of reporting requirements associated with Treasury warrants and internal revenue collections.

Source: U.S. Bureau of the Census, *Historical Statistics of the United States, Colonial Times to 1970, Part 2* (Washington, D.C.: U.S. Bureau of the Census, 1975), 1106–1108.

Federal credit was also bolstered by the wartime tax program. Despite the high exemption levels in place during World War I, the revenue gains from the individual income tax were impressive. The corporate income tax, especially the broadened excess profits tax, was even more productive. By 1920, income and profits taxes, excises, and other internal taxes were supplying more than 80 percent of total revenues (see Table 1.7). Over the course of the war, by comparison, the contribution from tariff revenues was relatively small, and the tariff would never again regain the status it had enjoyed in the nineteenth century.

World War I established a revenue system that differed substantially from anything the nation had seen previously. The progressivity in rates, for individuals and corporations, was much greater than during the Civil War, firmly establishing fairness, or ability to pay, as a central principle in income taxation. While appeals to wartime sacrifice helped mute the opposition to steep progressivity during the war, the tax policy debates of the next two decades would reflect growing partisan divisions over fairness, over the economic and revenue effects of high tax rates, and over the size and role of government to be supported by taxation.

The 1920s

With the 1920 elections, the Republican Party captured the presidency and strengthened its control of the House and Senate. Over the next decade, with Secretary of the Treasury Andrew W. Mellon in the lead, income taxation was scaled back, spending was tightly controlled, and huge budget surpluses were committed to debt reduction. Balanced budgets remained a core belief for Republicans, but the displacement of tariffs by income taxation as the primary source of federal revenues required a recalibration of the relationship between taxation and spending.

Revenue Policy There was little question among policymakers that the high rates of wartime income taxation could not be sustained during peacetime. Mellon's Democratic predecessors as Treasury secretary, Carter Glass and David F. Houston, had previously warned that high rates were having an adverse effect on revenue collections. Wilson himself had expressed concerns about the continued revenue productivity of the wartime surtaxes and their potential impact on business activity. Mellon's program for cutting taxes, which was initiated in 1921 and extended in 1924, 1926, and 1928, was an elaboration of these themes but with a particular emphasis on the economic impact of high tax rates.

The economic issues that Mellon focused on were incentives and distortions. High tax rates, he argued, would inevitably discourage individuals (or businesses) from devoting themselves to the work, investment, and savings efforts upon which economic growth was based. In addition, high taxes could lead to a less efficient allocation of capital by channeling investments to tax-advantaged types of economic activity. With respect to revenues, Mellon worried that high rates would encourage avoidance or evasion, but he had a broader concern about the effect of high rates on economic growth and, therefore, on revenues. This "supply-side" element of Mellon's thinking did not mean, as some contemporary supply-side theorists allege, that cutting tax rates always generates more revenues. Rather, Mellon wanted to reduce rates in order to minimize economic disincentives and distortions but ensure that the government could still collect adequate revenues.

The corporate tax changes of the 1920s reflected this balancing of economic and revenue goals. The excess profits tax, which had been the heaviest wartime burden on corporations, was reduced in 1919 and completely repealed two years later. The Revenue Act of 1921 partially offset this by increasing the normal tax rate on corporations from 10 percent to 12.5 percent and retaining the low exemption level that had been in place since 1918. Tax rate changes over the next decade did not alter greatly this corporate tax structure. Normal tax rates fluctuated between 12 percent and 13.5 percent, while the exemption level was raised to $3,000 in 1928. Although the Revenue Act of 1926 contained a liberalized oil and gas depletion allowance, Congress otherwise avoided enacting major corporate tax preferences.

The tax cuts of the 1920s greatly reduced the tax burden on corporations but only when compared to wartime levels. In 1918 and 1919, corporate income and excess profits taxation was approximately 30 percent of net income.[76] From 1922 to 1930, the corresponding level was nearly two-thirds lower. Prior to the war, however, corporate income taxes had been less than 1 percent of net

---

[76] U.S. Bureau of the Census, *Historical Statistics of the United States, Colonial Times to 1970, Part 2* (Washington, D.C.: Government Printing Office, 1975), 1109.

income. The need for revenues to fund the interest payments, debt reduction, and other spending needs of the 1920s restrained Congress from whatever impulses it might have had to cut corporate taxes more drastically.

Individual income tax rates were lowered and exemption levels raised during the 1920s, but here again, revenue requirements and equity considerations moderated the scale and direction of change. The top marginal rate on taxable income had been cut to 73 percent in 1919 and was then lowered to 24 percent over the next decade. At the same time, however, the income bracket at which the top marginal rate was applied was reduced from $1 million to $100,000. Exemptions and dependent allowances were raised, eliminating tax liabilities for several million taxpayers. An earned-income credit along with lower first-bracket rates also helped maintain the progressivity of the individual income tax. Despite the reduced rates of the 1920s, the proportion of income tax revenues from the higher marginal brackets increased by nearly 50 percent.[77]

Tax preferences, however, began to proliferate as Congress enacted preferential rates on capital gains and exclusions for employer contributions to pensions.[78] The estate tax managed to survive repeal efforts, but rates were lowered and tax credits for state inheritance tax payments were expanded. Estate and gift tax revenues actually remained relatively high during the early 1920s but then declined sharply by the end of the decade.

The protectionist history of the Republican Party also resurfaced in the face of revenue losses from the repeal of wartime excises and the effective termination of alcohol excises because of Prohibition. The Fordney-McCumber Tariff Act of 1922 roughly doubled average tariff rates and had an immediate, positive impact on tariff revenues. From 1920 to 1922, customs duties averaged $330 million annually. Under Fordney-McCumber, revenues increased to $560 million and averaged more than $575 million annually through the end of the decade. The Smoot-Hawley Tariff Act of 1930 raised tariff rates even higher, but the projected revenue increases in this instance were not realized. Instead, Smoot-Hawley contributed to the worldwide economic downturn by depressing international trade still further, and customs duties plummeted. This ill-fated exercise effectively sealed the fate of protective tariffs, as the United States entered an era of free trade and reciprocal trade agreements. It also marked the end of the tariff as an important part of overall revenue policy.

By the end of the 1920s, individual and corporate income taxes had become the mainstays of federal finance, accounting for nearly 60 percent of total revenues. In addition, the revenue levels in place at that time remained relatively high, averaging nearly $4 billion annually from 1925 to 1930. The individual and corporate tax cuts enacted over the course of the decade were substantial, but they did not bring revenues anywhere close to what they had been prior to

---

[77] Ippolito, *Why Budgets Matter*, 118.
[78] Witte, *The Politics and Development of the Federal Income Tax*, 276–282.

TABLE 1.8. *Federal Outlays by Function, Fiscal Years 1920–1930 (in millions of dollars)*

Fiscal Year	National Security/ International	Veterans' Benefits	Interest	All Other	Total
1920	$4,432	$332	$1,024	$569	$6,357
1921	2,664	646	999	749	5,058
1922	939	686	991	669	3,285
1923	694	747	1,056	640	3,137
1924	662	676	941	611	2,890
1925	606	741	882	652	2,881
1926	603	772	832	681	2,888
1927	595	786	787	669	2,837
1928	668	806	731	728	2,933
1929	710	812	719	886	3,127
1930	748	821	697	1,054	3,320

Source: U.S. Bureau of the Census, *Historical Statistics of the United States, Colonial Times to 1970, Part 2* (Washington, D.C.: U.S. Bureau of the Census, 1975), 1115.

World War I or reduce the federal government's growing reliance on income taxation.

Spending Policy In 1920, the House restored exclusive jurisdiction over spending bills to its Appropriations Committee, and the Senate made a similar change in its rules two years later. Congress also agreed to confer on the president the authority to prepare an executive branch budget, a budget process reform it had staunchly resisted for decades. The Budget and Accounting Act of 1921 authorized the president to submit an annual budget to Congress containing his recommendations for appropriations to all executive departments and agencies, proposals for changes in revenue laws, and plans for handling the estimated surplus or deficit. It also established the Bureau of the Budget, in the Treasury Department, as the staff agency responsible for assisting the president in carrying out this new responsibility, along with a congressional staff agency, the General Accounting Office, to audit expenditures by executive branch departments and agencies. These changes were explicitly aimed at strengthening controls over spending, and the spending record of the 1920s demonstrated the effectiveness of these new controls when wedded to a narrowly defined set of federal responsibilities.

As shown in Table 1.8, total spending was stable from 1922 to 1930. Nevertheless, these spending budgets were higher by far than those for the years leading up to World War I, even excluding interest payments on the wartime debt. Much of this increased postwar spending was for the military. The active-duty force levels after demobilization were more than 250,000, approximately twice as high as the average for the 1900–1915 period, and the Army and Navy budgets were correspondingly greater. Veterans' compensation and pensions, along with expanded benefits for readjustment job training, medical services, and insurance, accounted for about one-fourth of total spending in the 1920s, and spending for these programs was also well above prewar levels.

Interest on the debt and domestic programs accounted for approximately one-half of total spending for fiscal years 1922–1930. What is noteworthy here is that spending for domestic programs was raised as declining interest payments provided a margin for additional spending. A portion of this new spending was used for federal capital spending grants to state and local governments. In 1930, for example, federal grants totaled $100 million, with highway funding accounting for more than three-fourths of the total and education grants virtually all of the remainder.[79] The spending philosophy of the 1920s allowed for the growing administrative costs of federal departments and agencies along with the internal improvements that Republicans had long championed. It also extended to the agricultural sector, with new federal credit and loan programs.[80] Republicans did not embrace, however, any significant federal responsibility for social welfare.

This controlled spending of the 1920s meant that taxes could be cut without endangering the large surpluses needed to retire wartime debt. When the economy began its steep decline in late 1929, however, this budgetary equilibrium quickly evaporated. The fiscal 1931 budget deficit was more than $460 million, and with an even larger deficit forecast for 1932, the Hoover administration called for a major tax increase to bring the budget into balance. The 1932 tax bill reversed much of the tax reduction that had been phased in during the 1920s. For individuals, exemption levels were cut and surtax rates increased. The top marginal rate for individuals was raised to 63 percent, the highest level since 1921, and the top estate tax rate was more than doubled from its previous level. The corporate income tax exemption was eliminated altogether, and the corporate tax rate was increased to 13.75 percent.

These higher rates did not yield increased revenues. Both individual and corporate income tax collections fell sharply in 1932 and 1933. Excise taxes, which had also been raised under the 1932 legislation, kept the plunge in total revenues from being even more severe, but the Hoover administration was paralyzed by the deficit. The traditional prescription for managing economic downturns – raise taxes, reduce spending, and balance the budget – was proving wholly inadequate for dealing with the Great Depression.

The New Deal

During the 1932 presidential race, Franklin D. Roosevelt sharply criticized Hoover's failure to balance the budget. The Democratic platform of 1932 pledged to restore the "national credit by a federal budget annually balanced on the basis of accurate executive estimates within revenues, raised by a system

[79] U.S. Bureau of the Census, *Historical Statistics of the United States*, 1125.
[80] Savage, *Balanced Budgets and American Politics*, 158.

of taxation levied on the principle of the ability to pay."[81] This balanced-budget orthodoxy was soon abandoned after Roosevelt took office, as his administration launched new spending programs and recast the politics of income taxation.

Revenue Policy and Progressivity Despite the tax increase that Congress had passed in 1932, individual income tax collections in 1933 and 1934 fell 60 percent below their 1930 level, and the drop in corporate income tax revenues was similarly sharp. During its first two years, the Roosevelt administration largely ignored the revenue problem, making only minor changes in tax policy, and instead concentrated on emergency spending programs. In 1933, the National Industrial Recovery Tax Act made limited changes in corporate taxation, including excess profits and dividends levies. That same year, the Agricultural Adjustment Act imposed new taxes on the processing of farm products. The Revenue Act of 1934 was primarily a structural reform designed to curb abuses of tax preferences by corporations and individuals. In fact, the most important revenue measure in this early period was the repeal of Prohibition. Alcohol excise taxes, which totaled less than $10,000 in 1932, climbed to more than $400 million in 1935. The alcohol, tobacco, and other excises actually generated more revenues than individual and corporate income taxation from 1933 to 1935.

Income taxation returned to center stage in 1935, with Roosevelt's special tax message to Congress on June 19. While progressivity had long been a prominent feature of income taxation, its rationale had traditionally rested on the ability-to-pay principle. Roosevelt, however, called for progressive income taxation to combat "an unjust concentration of wealth and economic power."[82] He recommended to Congress higher income tax rates for wealthy individuals, graduated rates for corporations, and a new inheritance tax, all with a view toward using taxation to achieve "a wider distribution of wealth."

The Wealth Tax of 1935 did not go as far as Roosevelt had hoped. Congress rejected the proposed inheritance tax and weakened the administration's original plan for taxing undistributed corporate profits. The top marginal rate for individuals, however, was raised to 79 percent, higher than the previous peak of 77 percent in World War I, although it applied only to taxable income of more than $5 million. Estate and gift tax rates were raised, and higher graduated rates were applied to corporate income. In 1936, Congress was persuaded to enact a new graduated tax on undistributed corporate profits with a top rate of 27 percent and to raise the tax rate on intercorporate dividends.

The individual income tax rates that were set under the 1935 law remained in place until 1940. Efforts were undertaken, however, to enforce these rates by closing loopholes that wealthy individuals and families were using to avoid taxes. Tax law changes in 1937 included reforms the Roosevelt administration

[81] Congressional Quarterly, *National Party Conventions*, 85.
[82] 79 Cong. Rec. 9657 (1935).

had proposed to cut back on tax avoidance in individual and estate taxation. The corporate tax increases of 1935 and 1936, however, were partially reversed in response to growing opposition by business interests. The tax on undistributed profits was first reduced and then replaced with a flat tax on net income. Tax rates for small businesses were lowered, and loss carryovers were reintroduced. In addition, capital gains taxation was lowered through revised asset classification schedules.

The cumulative effects of the peacetime New Deal's income tax initiatives were mixed, in part because individual and corporate income levels were continually buffeted by economic fluctuations. Individual income tax revenues, for example, more than doubled between 1935 and 1938 but then fell by 25 percent over the next two years. The individual income tax also remained limited in scope. In 1940, the individual income tax provided less than 15 percent of federal revenue and amounted to 1.3 percent of personal income, nearly the same level as in 1930.[83] The corporate tax was slightly more productive in terms of revenues than the individual income tax from 1935 to 1940, as the percentage of corporate profits paid in taxes increased from less than 2 percent in 1930 to 5.5 percent in 1940.[84]

In terms of tax policy, the most important New Deal innovation was the new Social Security payroll tax. The Social Security Act of 1935 established an old-age insurance program to provide cash benefits to retired workers. In his special message to Congress on January 17, 1935, President Roosevelt had insisted this new program "should be self-sustaining in the sense that funds for the payment of insurance benefits should not come from the proceeds of general taxation."[85] The legislation he signed on August 14, 1935, levied a 1 percent tax on wages for employees and a corresponding 1 percent tax on employers to be collected in an Old-Age Reserve Account to fund Social Security benefit payments. The tax was levied on the first $3,000 of wage income, with the tax rates scheduled to rise incrementally to 3 percent by 1949. Because it covered approximately 60 percent of the work force, the Social Security payroll tax generated substantial new revenues. Social Security taxes in 1940 totaled $725 million, nearly as much as the individual income tax that year.[86]

Nevertheless, the New Deal left a lasting imprint on income taxation. The Roosevelt administration explicitly connected progressivity to a broadly defined notion of equity – namely, the distribution of wealth in society – and its focus on redistribution has been an important part of tax policy debates ever since. In

[83] Congressional Budget Office, *Revising the Individual Income Tax* (Washington, D.C.: Congressional Budget Office, 1983), 8.
[84] Congressional Budget Office, *Revising the Corporate Income Tax* (Washington, D.C.: Congressional Budget Office, 1985), 28.
[85] Larry W. DeWitt, Daniel Béland, and Edward D. Berkowitz, *Social Security: A Documentary History* (Washington, D.C.: CQ Press, 2008), 56–57.
[86] Office of Management and Budget, *Historical Tables, Budget of the United States Government, Fiscal Year 2011* (Washington, D.C.: Government Printing Office, 2010), 30–36.

addition, the New Deal's spending policies created the need for higher income tax revenues.

Spending Policy During the 1920s, federal spending had stabilized at around 3 percent of gross domestic product (GDP), and more than 70 percent of this spending was for military and veterans' programs as well as for interest on the debt. By 1940, federal outlays had climbed to nearly 10 percent of GDP, and two-thirds of this spending was for domestic programs.[87] The federal government's expanding domestic role in the 1930s went well beyond the conventional budget. The New Deal's regulatory initiatives were unprecedented in their scope, extending to all major sectors of the economy, and in addition to direct spending, the Roosevelt administration freely utilized new credit and loan programs for agriculture, small business, housing, and transportation.

A substantial portion of New Deal domestic spending was for relief and recovery programs related to the Depression, but permanent additions to the budget represented a new philosophy regarding spending. According to Roosevelt, the federal government's "relatively minor role" had made possible the "relatively low and constant level of expenditures" during the 1920s.[88] The much larger budgets of his New Deal "mirrored the changing attitudes of the people toward the growing needs they expect their Government to meet." A permanent social welfare responsibility for the elderly and poor was, in terms of long-term budgetary effects, the New Deal's most important contribution, but the New Deal also redefined the federal government's responsibility for regional economic development, agriculture, transportation, housing policy, and aid to the states for capital projects and other purposes.

The full effects of this domestic expansion on tax policy did not emerge during the 1930s, because most of this spending was financed by deficits. And, of course, the use of deficits for fiscal stimulus was another New Deal innovation. Roosevelt's initial ambivalence about deficits never completely disappeared, and congressional criticism of Roosevelt's deficit record became especially heated during his second term. Toward the end of that second term, however, Roosevelt's defense of deficit spending became more forthright. His budget message in 1939 called for additional spending "to get enough capital and labor at work to give us . . . a total income of at least eighty billion dollars a year."[89] The following year's budget was a staunch defense of a fiscal policy "realistically adapted to the needs of the people" with "deliberate use of Government funds and of Government credit to energize private enterprise."[90] The fiscal policy approach "prior to 1933," Roosevelt stated, "was exceedingly

---

[87] Ibid., 47.
[88] 86 Cong. Rec. 47 (1940).
[89] Franklin D. Roosevelt, *The Public Papers and Addresses of Franklin D. Roosevelt, 1939*, comp. Samuel I. Rosenman (New York: Macmillan, 1941), 8.
[90] 86 Cong. Rec. 47 (1940).

simple in theory and disastrous in practice. It consisted in trying to keep expenditures as low as possible in the face of shrinking national income... [and] came near to bankrupting both our people and our Government."

The New Deal did not repeal the balanced-budget rule, but it certainly weakened that rule. The traditional connection between balanced budgets and limited government was also severed. With peacetime spending at much higher levels than at any time in the past, balanced budgets inevitably meant similarly high levels of taxation. Before that tax policy challenge fully developed, however, World War II intervened.

2

The Stable Era – World War II to the 1960s

During World War II, revenues climbed to more than 20 percent of GDP, by far the highest level in history at the time, with income taxes accounting for more than 75 percent of these revenues. After the war, high revenue levels remained in place, averaging 17 percent of GDP through the Truman and Eisenhower administrations, and income taxes continued to provide most of these revenues. The individual income tax was especially stable over this period, as its basic exemption levels and marginal rates went largely unchanged. As a mass tax covering most of the population, the individual income tax was the largest component of the post–World War II federal tax system.

This continuity in tax policy during the late 1940s and 1950s does not mean there were no important partisan differences over taxes. Democrats and Republicans clashed, as they had before and during World War II, over such issues as progressivity in tax burdens, corporate income taxation, and tax preferences. But these issues were typically subordinated to revenue considerations. Both the Truman and Eisenhower administrations resisted congressional efforts to cut taxes, insisting that adequate revenue levels be kept in place to fund the large Cold War defense budgets and the lesser, but still significant, domestic program responsibilities the federal government had assumed since the New Deal.

The singular importance of defense budgets over this period was rooted in a bipartisan consensus on Cold War defense strategy. Harry S. Truman launched the key initiatives of the Cold War in 1947 and forcefully advocated the massive and permanent defense budget commitments needed to counter the Soviet threat. Dwight D. Eisenhower then cemented Republican support for these commitments. During the 1950s, defense accounted for nearly 60 percent of all federal spending. Even more striking, defense-GDP levels averaged more than 10 percent over this period, roughly the same size as the entire federal government at the height of the New Deal.

On the domestic side, Republicans briefly controlled Congress from 1947 to 1948 but were unable to use tax cuts to force domestic retrenchments. This was the last serious effort to dismantle New Deal programs. Domestic spending was cut back during the Korean War but then grew at modest rates over the course of Eisenhower's presidency. Competition between defense and domestic needs was kept at politically manageable levels and with a clear priority assigned to defense. By keeping total spending within a fairly narrow range, budgets remained at or close to balance.

The fiscal approach of the Truman-Eisenhower period assigned great importance to balanced budgets. In line with the acknowledged need for fiscal policy stimulus during economic downturns, occasional deficits were tolerated. But Truman, Eisenhower, and most members of Congress were otherwise committed to keeping the budget balanced over the course of economic cycles. With permanent defense and domestic commitments firmly in place, high revenue levels had to be maintained and the political lure of tax cuts resisted. During this fiscal era, tax policy was effectively subordinated to spending policy.

World War II Finance

Despite aggressive efforts by the Roosevelt administration to promote military preparedness, the defense buildup to World War II developed slowly during the late 1930s. Even with the war in Europe well under way, American force levels and defense budgets remained quite low. In 1940, the combined strength of the Army, Navy, and Marine Corps was less than 400,000 active-duty personnel, and the defense budget of $1.7 billion represented less than one-fifth of total federal spending. Five years later, active-duty forces exceeded twelve million, and the $83 billion defense budget was 37.5 percent of GDP and 90 percent of total spending.

The tax program to fund World War II followed a similar course. The initial wartime tax bill, the Revenue Act of 1940, was enacted on June 25 and was expected to raise about $1 billion in its first full year of operation.[1] The Second Revenue Act of 1940, which passed Congress several months later, was even smaller. In combination, these tax bills reduced personal exemptions, raised individual and corporate income tax rates, increased excise taxes, and levied an excess profits tax on corporations. In addition, Congress authorized $4 billion in new borrowing and approved temporary tax increases to fund this borrowing over a five-year period.

In 1941, the Roosevelt administration called for much larger tax increases, with Secretary of the Treasury Henry Morgenthau, Jr. recommending that Congress agree to finance "at least two-thirds of the costs of defense from

---

[1] Roy G. Blakey and Gladys C. Blakey, "The Two Federal Revenue Acts of 1940," *American Economic Review* 30 (December 1940), 724.

taxes."[2] The Revenue Act of 1941, with an estimated annual revenue yield of nearly $4 billion, was the largest tax increase yet enacted. It was also viewed by some congressional leaders as having raised taxes to the limit of what the economy could bear and voters would tolerate.[3]

In fact, wartime taxation would climb to levels that few had foreseen, but the costs of World War II rose even faster. Not until 1944 and 1945 did taxes come close to covering 50 percent of spending, much less the two-thirds recommended in 1941. The Roosevelt administration repeatedly encountered strong congressional resistance to the tax policies and revenue increases it proposed. The individual income tax changes that Congress finally did approve were less progressive than Roosevelt had advocated, and Congress often spent an inordinate amount of time debating peripheral issues, such as whether married couples should be required to file joint returns. With corporate taxation, Congress proved more sympathetic than the administration to numerous technical relief provisions that eased the impact of high rates. In particular, the administration's efforts to fashion a strict wartime profits tax were at least partially undercut by the alternative calculations of excess profits that Congress allowed. Indeed, the Roosevelt administration's leverage on tax policy became arguably weaker after 1942, even as the case for revenue increases to finance the war and to control inflation became stronger.

Nevertheless, the World War II changes in both individual and corporate income taxation were profoundly important. The transformation of the individual income tax from a narrow to a mass system of taxation would have a lasting effect on the politics of tax policy and on federal budget policy generally. The changes in corporate taxation, while nearly as significant in terms of wartime revenue, would prove less enduring in terms of overall revenue policy. But World War II firmly established income taxation, rather than sales or consumption taxes, as the principal source of federal revenue over the ensuing decades.

The Wartime Tax System

The major changes in individual income taxation over the course of the war involved coverage, rates, and enforcement. Coverage was broadened by steadily lowering exemption levels and thereby making many more individuals subject to the individual income tax. Marginal rates were repeatedly increased; equally important were the downward adjustments in the income brackets at which these higher rates applied. In effect, as the taxable income base was expanded, the effective rates on taxable income were raised. Enforcement and compliance reforms were extensive, with tax withholding representing a key advance in revenue collection.

---

[2] Paul Studenski and Herman E. Kroos, *Financial History of the United States*, 2nd ed. (New York: McGraw-Hill, 1953), 438.

[3] Steven A. Bank, Kirk J. Stark, and Joseph J. Thorndike, *War and Taxes* (Washington, D.C.: Urban Institute Press, 2008), 92.

In World War I, the personal exemption had been $2,000 for a married couple ($1,000 for single persons). These exemption levels translated into taxable returns for approximately 10 percent of the labor force.[4] By the late 1930s, with similarly high exemption levels, an even smaller percentage of the labor force filed taxable returns. The Revenue Act of 1940 lowered the personal exemption from $2,500 to $2,000 for a married couple and also reduced the gross income level at which filing a return was required (see Table 2.1). Over the next several years, the personal exemption and gross income requirements were lowered still further, and with these successive changes, the size of the tax-paying population rose dramatically. From 1939 to 1945, the number of total returns filed climbed from 7.6 million to almost 50 million.[5] Whereas in 1939 nearly one-half of all filed returns were nontaxable, by 1944 the percentage of nontaxable returns had declined to less than 10 percent.

These new taxpayers were also confronted with much higher rates than in the past, even on very low levels of income. Here, again, the comparison with World War I is instructive. In 1918, the lowest income bracket, taxable income up to $4,000, was taxed at 6 percent. From 1940 to 1945, the lowest bracket was cut from $4,000 to $2,000, while the rate was raised from 4.4 percent to 23 percent. The top marginal rate in World War II was 94 percent, compared to 77 percent in World War I, and the taxable income level at which this top rate applied was also much lower – $200,000 in 1944–1945, compared to $1 million in 1918. In addition, income bracket adjustments from 1940 to 1945 steadily lowered the taxable income levels at which high marginal rates applied. In 1940, for example, taxpayers did not face marginal rates of more than 50 percent until their taxable income reached $60,000. In 1944–1945, the 50 percent rate applied when taxable income reached $14,000.

Congressional resistance to high taxation waned somewhat as the costs of war escalated, but there were strong disagreements with the administration over the distribution of tax burdens. In early 1942, Roosevelt had called for much higher taxes on individuals, but the administration also wanted to protect low-income workers by leaving exemption levels unchanged. Whether serious or symbolic, Roosevelt wanted to impose a surtax on wealthy taxpayers so that "no American citizen ought to have a net income, after he has paid his taxes, of more than $25,000 a year."[6] He was insistent that "discrepancies between low personal incomes and high personal incomes should be lessened" as wartime revenues were raised.

The Revenue Act of 1942 did not contain Roosevelt's 100 percent "war supertax," neither did it favor low-income workers. Instead, the personal

---

[4] John F. Witte, *The Politics and Development of the Federal Income Tax* (Madison: University of Wisconsin Press, 1985), 126.

[5] U.S. Bureau of the Census, *Historical Statistics of the United States, Colonial Times to 1970, Part 2* (Washington, D.C.: U.S. Bureau of the Census, 1975), 1110.

[6] Randolph E. Paul, *Taxation in the United States* (Boston: Little, Brown, 1954), 301.

TABLE 2.1. *World War II Individual Income Tax Changes*

	Income Year			
	1940	1941	1942–1943	1944–1945
Personal Exemptions (Married Couple)	$2,000	$1,500	$1,200	$1,000
Requirements for Filing (Gross Income, Married Couple)	$2,000	$1,500	$1,200	$500[a]
Tax Rates (Taxable Income)				
First Bracket (up to)	$4,000	$2,000	$2,000	$2,000
Rate	4.4%[b]	10.0%[b]	19.0%[b]	23.0%
Top Bracket (more than)	$5,000,000	$5,000,000	$200,000	$200,000[c]
Rate	81.1%	81.0%	88.0%	94.0%
Total Brackets	31	32	24	24
Number of Taxable Returns (millions)	7.5	17.6	27.7/40.3	42.4/42.7

[a] For each spouse.
[b] Earned-income credit equal to 10 percent of earned net income as a deduction.
[c] Subject to maximum effective rate of 90 percent.
Sources: U.S. Bureau of the Census, *Historical Statistics of the United States, Colonial Times to 1970, Part 2* (Washington, D.C.: U.S. Bureau of the Census, 1975), 1093, 1095; U.S. Department of the Treasury, *Statistics of Income for 1949, Part I* (Washington, D.C.: Government Printing Office, 1954), 196.

exemption level was reduced, as was the exemption for dependents, and a 5 percent "Victory Tax" was applied to gross income of more than $624 regardless of any income tax liability. Marginal rates were raised, but less steeply than the administration had hoped, with first-bracket rates more than doubled. As the House and Senate rejected outright some key administration proposals and substantially revised others, tax burdens for low- and middle-income taxpayers became heavier, and ability-to-pay principles were weakened.

A similar outcome was reached on excess profits taxation. The first excess profits tax of World War II was passed in 1940, with a top rate of 50 percent, but its impact was lessened by permitting firms to choose alternative ways to calculate excess profits. The administration succeeded in strengthening excess profits enforcement in 1941, but efforts to levy high effective rates on war profits were repeatedly stymied by Congress. Thus, the 1942 Revenue Act contained a 90 percent excess profits tax rate but included a multitude of relief provisions, including optional methods for calculating excess profits, and a maximum 80 percent rate on combined corporate income and excess profits taxes. The excess profits tax rate was raised to 95 percent in 1943, but again with countervailing relief provisions. The Revenue Act of 1943 was finally passed over Roosevelt's veto on February 25, 1944, and bore little resemblance to what the administration had initially proposed with respect to corporate taxation. With this setback, the administration abandoned its efforts to enforce strict, steep taxation on the wartime profits of corporations.

Roosevelt did succeed, however, in establishing income taxation as the key element in wartime finance. In 1942, Congress considered a national sales tax that would have lessened the need for higher income taxes and, at the same time, shifted tax burdens to low-income workers. Business groups were among the strongest proponents of the national sales tax, while organized labor was vehemently opposed to what it denounced as a highly regressive form of taxation. Despite strong support for the national sales tax in Congress's tax committees, the Roosevelt administration eventually persuaded Congress to discard the sales tax and to adopt a more progressive program of income taxation.

Congressional unease over income taxation did, however, complicate the introduction of tax withholding in 1943. With the expansion of the income tax to tens of millions of taxpayers in 1941 and 1942, tax collection became much more difficult. The administration duly introduced a plan for permanent tax withholding in 1943, but Congress insisted on granting relief to individuals with outstanding tax liabilities from the previous year. At one point, the Senate approved a 100 percent forgiveness plan recommended by its Finance Committee. The final version of the Current Tax Payment Act of 1943 provided a somewhat less generous forgiveness formula, and Roosevelt was forced to accept the resulting revenue loss in order to obtain this essential administrative reform.

In 1944, additional administrative reforms were approved with considerably less difficulty. The Individual Income Tax Act of 1944 provided for graduated withholding in order to improve revenue collection. It also introduced standard deductions, expanded tax tables, and integrated normal and surtax rate schedules that greatly simplified income tax calculations for millions of taxpayers. In 1944 and 1945, for example, the number of returns using the standard deduction was approximately five times greater than the number using itemized deductions.[7]

These efforts to simplify tax collection were viewed as a political as well as administrative necessity. As one contemporary observer noted, "While our tax system might safely, though not wisely, irritate 2 million citizens, it would run serious risks if it irritated 40 or 50 million."[8] Indeed, considerable irritation apparently had developed as income taxation became heavier and heavier over the course of the war, giving rise to a national movement advocating repeal of the Sixteenth Amendment and restrictions on the federal government's taxing power. This effort had, by 1944, gained the official support of seventeen state

---

[7] U.S. Department of the Treasury, *Statistics of Income for 1949, Part I* (Washington, D.C.: Government Printing Office, 1954), 216–217.

[8] Paul, *Taxation in the United States*, 381.

TABLE 2.2. *Revenue-GDP Levels, Fiscal Years 1940–1945 (as percentage of GDP)*

Fiscal Year	Individual Income Taxes	Corporation Income Taxes	Social Insurance Taxes	Excise Taxes	Other	Total
1940	0.9%	1.2%	1.8%	2.0%	0.7%	6.8%
1941	1.2	1.9	1.7	2.2	0.7	7.6
1942	2.3	3.3	1.7	2.4	0.6	10.1
1943	3.6	5.3	1.7	2.3	0.4	13.3
1944	9.4	7.1	1.7	2.3	0.5	20.9
1945	8.3	7.2	1.6	2.8	0.5	20.4

Source: Office of Management and Budget, *Historical Tables, Budget of the United States Government, Fiscal Year 2011* (Washington, D.C.: Government Printing Office, 2010), 34.

legislatures.[9] Business groups also continued to promote a national sales tax as either a full or partial replacement for the income tax.

The various attempts to limit income taxation, however, never progressed very far given the acknowledged need for massive revenues and the American public's evident embrace of wartime sacrifice. Both individual and corporate tax burdens became much heavier as the war progressed, and the changes in individual income taxation were particularly striking. Prior to World War II, individual income tax revenues had been about 1 percent of GDP, slightly below corporate income tax levels (see Table 2.2). With the tax increases in 1942 and 1943, individual income tax–GDP levels rose significantly, but the growth in 1944 and 1945 was even greater. At that point, the individual income tax averaged nearly 9 percent of GDP and had eclipsed the corporate income tax in terms of revenue productivity. The disparity between individual and corporate income tax revenues would become even more pronounced in the postwar period.

The actual progressivity of individual income taxation never matched its marginal rate structure, in part because effective tax rates for low- and middle-income groups were relatively high and, of course, the sheer number of tax-payers in these income groups was so large. In 1945, for example, more than 90 percent of all returns reported adjusted gross income of less than $5,000.[10] The share of adjusted gross income for this income class was 75 percent, and its share of income tax liabilities was more than 50 percent. For high-income groups, average tax rates went up sharply after 1940, but their share of federal income taxes still declined. For the very wealthy, their relative tax burden was actually lower at the end of World War II than it had been over the preceding

[9] Ibid., 380.
[10] U.S. Department of the Treasury, *Statistics of Income for 1951*, Part I (Washington, D.C.: Government Printing Office, 1955), 97.

three decades.[11] Moreover, wealthy taxpayers did not face significantly higher estate and gift taxes during the war. Total revenues from these taxes were less than $640 million in 1945, compared to slightly more than $350 million in 1940.[12]

At the same time, regressive taxes played a relatively minor role in wartime finance. The Roosevelt administration blocked a national sales tax, and consumption taxes provided a relatively small percentage of wartime revenues. Congress increased excise taxes on alcohol and tobacco and imposed new excises on numerous other goods and services, but the excise tax share of total revenues fell sharply over the course of the war. In 1940, excises accounted for more than 30 percent of federal revenues, about the same percentage as the individual and corporate income taxes combined. By 1945, excise taxes were 15 percent, approximately one-fifth the individual and corporate share. Further, on several occasions Congress delayed scheduled increases in Social Security tax rates, leaving in place the very low payroll taxes affecting manufacturing and industrial workers. The overall progressivity of the federal tax system in World War II was not as strong as Franklin Roosevelt had hoped, but it was considerably greater than his critics believed desirable.

Spending and Debt

In 1940, federal spending was less than $10 billion, the deficit was less than $3 billion, and the publicly held debt of $42.8 billion was less than 45 percent of GDP. Over the next several years, spending climbed to wartime heights of more than $90 billion in 1944 and 1945, deficits totaled more than $175 billion, and the publicly held debt rose to nearly 110 percent of GDP (see Table 2.3). In order to finance these deficits, Congress enacted six debt limit authorizations from 1940 to 1945, raising the statutory limits on federal debt from $49 billion in 1940 to $300 billion in 1945.

The wartime borrowing plan developed by the Treasury Department in 1941 envisioned a significant role for small investors. This voluntary borrowing program subsequently became more elaborate, with multiple types of low-denomination securities, payroll deduction options for purchasing securities, and sophisticated advertising campaigns to promote public participation. According to Treasury Secretary Morgenthau, large-scale voluntary borrowing was needed to curb inflationary pressures that posed a constant threat to economic stability throughout the war.[13] Because massive borrowing was going to be necessary even with large tax increases, broad public participation would

[11] Janet McCubbin and Fritz Scheuren, "Individual Income Tax Shares and Average Tax Rates, Tax Years 1951–1986," *Statistics of Income Bulletin* 8, no. 4 (1989), 45.

[12] Office of Management and Budget, *Historical Tables, Budget of the United States Government, Fiscal Year 2011* (Washington, D.C.: Government Printing Office, 2010), 45.

[13] Henry C. Murphy, *The National Debt in War and Transition* (New York: McGraw-Hill, 1950), 37.

TABLE 2.3. *Spending, Revenues, Deficits, and Debt, Fiscal Years 1940–1945 (in billions of dollars)*

Fiscal Year	Outlays	Revenues	Deficits	Publicly Held Debt	Publicly Held Debt (as percentage of GDP)
1940	$9.5	$6.5	$2.9	$42.8	44.2%
1941	13.7	8.7	4.9	48.2	42.3
1942	35.1	14.6	20.5	67.8	47.0
1943	78.6	24.0	54.6	127.8	70.9
1944	91.3	43.7	47.6	184.8	88.3
1945	92.7	45.2	47.6	235.2	106.2

Source: Office of Management and Budget, *Historical Tables, Budget of the United States Government, Fiscal Year 2011* (Washington, D.C.: Government Printing Office, 2010), 21, 133.

also make it easier to raise the necessary funds. Finally, Morgenthau viewed the national savings bond campaigns as a "powerful propaganda instrument" that would help unify the country during a time of extraordinary crisis.

The seven war loan drives that the Treasury Department launched, along with the Victory campaign at the end of the war, raised more than $150 billion.[14] The first campaign, which was conducted in 1942, was oversubscribed, as were all of the subsequent campaigns, and the individual sales targets that the Treasury set for these campaigns were usually met or exceeded. These bond sales succeeded, moreover, despite the low interest rates that the Treasury Department managed to keep in place throughout the war.

During the 1930s, President Roosevelt had prevailed on the Federal Reserve to help finance the New Deal's deficits by keeping interest rates low. While the Banking Act of 1935 had strengthened the Federal Reserve Board's powers and ostensibly affirmed its independence from political control, the Treasury Department insisted that monetary policy be coordinated with its borrowing requirements.[15] By working closely with Marriner S. Eccles, the Federal Reserve chairman he appointed, Roosevelt was able to maintain that coordination and ensure a stable supply of inexpensive credit.

With the transition to wartime borrowing, the Treasury Department was adamant that interest costs be controlled. The Federal Reserve, however, was concerned that very low interest rates might lead to excessive credit and make it more difficult to control inflation. The Treasury Department prevailed in the initial dispute over rates, and the Federal Reserve then agreed to support these rates for the duration of the war.[16] This February 1942 agreement, known as the "peg," also committed the Federal Reserve to purchasing securities in the event that loan campaigns were not fully subscribed. The latter proved

[14] Ibid., 135–155.
[15] Donald F. Kettl, *Leadership at the Fed* (New Haven: Yale University Press, 1986), 53–58.
[16] Ibid., 59.

largely unnecessary, but the interest rate support did minimize borrowing costs. In 1940, with a publicly held debt of $42 billion, net interest outlays were $899 million. In 1945, with a nearly eightfold increase in the size of the debt, interest costs had risen to only $3.1 billion.

For postwar budgets, however, debt service costs were likely to be much greater. In addition, nondefense spending had been controlled very tightly during the war, which meant that funding for social welfare and other domestic programs grew slowly if at all. The broadest classification of social welfare programs, "payments for individuals," totaled $2.2 billion in 1945, compared to $1.7 billion in 1940, a 30 percent increase over five years.[17] Nearly half of the increase was accounted for by veterans' service-connected compensation, and much of the rest was simply the result of more retired workers becoming eligible for Social Security benefits. Spending for education, training, employment, and social services programs was cut over this period, and only a few selected domestic sectors, such as transportation and agriculture, received significantly higher funding. As a percentage of GDP, nondefense programmatic spending fell from more than 7 percent in 1940 to 3 percent in 1945.

The large tax cut that took place immediately after World War I was made possible by a very rapid postwar demobilization that sharply reduced defense costs. Additional tax cuts over the next decade were routinely approved, because domestic spending growth was tightly controlled. As World War II came to a close, the prospects for equivalent postwar tax cuts were less certain. The relative size of the World War II debt was much greater, and its interest costs were likely to be much higher as well. In addition, funding for the New Deal's domestic programs had been stunted by the extraordinarily large budget shares absorbed by defense in World War II, which meant that Democrats were looking to strengthen and expand these programs as wartime spending fell. Congress had also increased the level and types of benefits available to World War II veterans, adding a costly, multiyear component to postwar spending budgets.

After World War II began, Congress quickly renewed the types of benefits that had been made available to veterans of previous wars. These included disability and death compensation, need-based pensions, hospital and medical care, vocational rehabilitation, and insurance. Then, in 1944, Congress enacted a readjustment benefit for veterans that went well beyond previous postwar programs. The Servicemen's Readjustment Act of 1944 (the GI Bill of Rights) provided job-placement and counseling services as well as education benefits covering tuition, books, and living expenses for up to four years of college. The maximum tuition benefit was set at $500 per year, and a living allowance of $75 per month was made available for veterans with families. A special unemployment compensation program was established that entitled veterans to up to fifty-two weeks of benefits if they could not find jobs, and loan guarantees

---

[17] Office of Management and Budget, *Historical Tables, Fiscal Year 2011*, 125.

were authorized to ensure access to credit when veterans purchased homes, farms, or businesses. One year later, Congress eased eligibility requirements for these benefits, provided more generous assistance for living allowances, and expanded the loan guarantee maximum for home purchases. The costs of these veterans' benefit programs were substantial. From 1946 to 1950, when the Korean War added a new cohort of beneficiaries, the service-connected compensation program, non–service-connected pensions, and insurance and death benefits totaled more than $14 billion.[18] The veterans' education benefit program outlays accounted for an additional $14 billion.

Harry Truman, who had succeeded to the presidency after Roosevelt's death on April 12, 1945, also had an ambitious postwar domestic agenda that did not leave room for large tax cuts. In a special message to Congress on September 6, Truman outlined his peacetime program, which included a new national health program, the expansion of existing social welfare entitlements, and a "transitional tax bill" that would provide "limited tax reductions for the calendar year."[19] Truman cautioned that "consideration of further tax reductions should have due regard to the level of governmental expenditures and the health and stability of our economy."[20] Congressional Republicans, however, were committed to large tax cuts and corresponding reductions in domestic programs. Once Truman's "limited" tax bill was passed, the partisan contest over taxes soon began in earnest.

The Battle over Postwar Tax Cuts

The Revenue Act of 1945 passed Congress on November 1 with strong bipartisan support. It repealed entirely the excess profits tax on corporations and reduced regular corporate income tax rates, with the top rate dropping from 40 percent to 38 percent. Individual income tax rates were lowered by three percentage points and 5 percent (e.g., the top marginal rate was cut from 94 percent to 86.45 percent). In addition, by extending exemptions for spouses and dependents to the normal tax, an estimated twelve million taxpayers were relieved from having to pay income taxes, at a revenue loss of $300 million.[21] The total reduction in calendar year 1946 tax liabilities for individuals and corporations, however, was estimated at less than $6 billion.[22]

The Truman administration was concerned that Congress had approved a slightly larger revenue reduction than had been recommended. There was also criticism from some congressional Democrats that the corporate tax cuts,

[18] Ibid., 225–226.
[19] Harry S. Truman, *Public Papers of the Presidents of the United States: Harry S. Truman, 1945* (Washington, D.C.: Government Printing Office, 1961), 294.
[20] Ibid., 295.
[21] Carl S. Shoup, "The Revenue Act of 1945," *Political Science Quarterly* 60, no. 4 (1945), 490.
[22] Ibid., 481.

particularly the repeal of excess profits taxation, had come at the expense of greater relief for low- and middle-income taxpayers. On the Republican side, the cuts in marginal rates for individuals fell well short of the larger, across-the-board reductions Republican leaders had advocated. All of these objections, however, were tempered by the widespread belief that immediate tax relief was a necessary first step in the transition from a wartime economy. Moreover, the 1945 act allowed the administration and Congress to put in place reduced withholding for individuals on January 1, 1946, without having to address the complicated equity issues arising from wartime taxation.[23]

The Truman Tax Program

The next step in tax policy change, however, was more contentious. In a combined State of the Union and Budget Message to Congress on January 21, 1946, Truman declared that he would not recommend further "tax reduction at this time."[24] Instead, he called for Congress to maintain the "large revenues" necessary to fund "anticipated expenditures" and "the volume of outstanding public debt" during FY 1947.

Truman was convinced that additional tax cuts would fuel inflation, particularly as wartime price and wage controls were removed and budget deficits continued. The estimated deficit for FY 1946 was more than $28 billion, and the administration's budget for FY 1947 projected a deficit of more than $4 billion. Congressional Republicans, however, decided that tax cuts could be a potent issue in the 1946 midterm elections. Like Truman, Republican leaders stressed the importance of cutting deficits and restoring balanced budgets, but they had very different ideas about how to accomplish that goal. In his budget message, Truman had spoken of the increased "domestic and international" responsibilities the federal government had taken on during the New Deal and World War II.[25] It was not possible, he declared, to "shrink the Government to prewar dimensions unless we slough off these new responsibilities – and we cannot do that without paying an excessive price in terms of our national welfare."

Republicans countered that massive spending cuts were not only feasible but also necessary. In the summer of 1946, senior Republicans on the Ways and Means and Appropriations committees agreed on a plan to cut income taxes by 20 percent and spending by 50 percent.[26] Despite more favorable deficit projections from his budget staff, Truman continued to oppose new tax cuts and to warn that tax increases might be needed to control inflation and retire wartime debt.

---

[23] Ibid., 486–487.

[24] Harry S. Truman, *Public Papers of the Presidents of the United States: Harry S. Truman, 1946* (Washington, D.C.: Government Printing Office, 1962), 72.

[25] Ibid., 86.

[26] Joseph J. Thorndike, "Out of (Re)alignment: Taxes and the Election of 1946," *Tax History Project*, December 14, 2006, Tax Analysts, http://www.taxhistory.org, 3.

The emerging conflict over tax cuts was part of a broader contest taking shape over the federal government's domestic role, in which many conservative southern Democrats joined Truman's Republican critics. In 1946, Congress rejected the administration's proposed new programs for national health insurance, low-income housing, and federal aid to education. The Employment Act of 1946 affirmed the federal government's responsibility for national economic management but did not include the full employment guarantees that liberal Democrats believed necessary. Congress agreed to authorize multiyear grants to states and localities for hospital and airport construction but then reduced funding for national transportation programs. Even with a Democratic-controlled Congress, Truman lacked a working majority on important domestic spending initiatives.

The 1946 elections made Truman's position even weaker. Republicans gained fifty-six seats in the House and thirteen in the Senate, putting them in control of both chambers for the first time in nearly two decades. Whether tax policy played a large role in this outcome is unclear. It is entirely possible that the electorate's pent-up frustrations with postwar strikes, food and consumer goods shortages, and various administration scandals made Democratic candidates unusually vulnerable. Regardless, Republicans interpreted their victory as a mandate for tax cuts and domestic spending cuts as the 80th Congress convened in 1947.

The Tax-Cut Vetoes

In foreign affairs, the Truman administration achieved some notable successes with the new Republican Congress. Senate Foreign Relations Committee chairman Arthur H. Vandenberg played a pivotal role in creating bipartisan support for the Truman Doctrine, Marshall Plan, and other Cold War initiatives that defined the new international responsibilities of the United States. On the domestic side, the contrast could not have been greater. Perhaps the single most controversial piece of legislation enacted in 1947 was the Taft-Hartley Labor-Management Relations Act, an antiunion measure that was passed over the president's veto. Truman and congressional Republicans also clashed often and bitterly over domestic policy, with Congress blocking Truman's attempts to extend the New Deal agenda, and Truman resisting Republican efforts to eviscerate that agenda.

The new Republican chairman of the Ways and Means Committee, Harold Knutson, introduced his party's tax-cut plan as H.R. 1, underlining the political importance attached to the measure. Knutson's original bill called for a 20 percent reduction in all income tax rates. As reported out of committee on March 24, the amended version provided for graduated reductions from 30 percent at the lowest income level to 10.5 percent for taxable incomes of more than $302,400, along with an additional exemption of $500 for taxpayers sixty-five years of age or older. Democratic members of the Ways and Means Committee had objected to the limited hearings conducted on the bill, and they sharply attacked the distribution of tax relief as the measure was debated on the House floor. Under the closed rule typically used by the House to govern debate on revenue bills, Democrats could not offer any amendments, and their motion to recommit the bill was rejected on a largely party-line vote. The House then passed the tax-cut measure by a comfortable margin, with forty Democrats crossing party lines to join with the Republicans.

In the Senate, the Finance Committee slightly modified the rate reductions in the House bill and also delayed its effective date for six months in order to eliminate any revenue loss for FY 1947. On the Senate floor, all Democratic amendments were rejected, and the vote for passage was supported by only seven Democrats. An expedited conference essentially ratified the Senate version of the tax-cut bill, and both chambers quickly approved the conference report. On June 16, the president vetoed the measure, and the House narrowly failed to override the veto.

Truman's veto was no surprise, because his budget message to Congress had reiterated his strong opposition to tax cuts. "High taxes," Truman stated, "contribute to the welfare and security of the country."[27] He went on to insist that when it finally came time to reduce taxes in future years, the "high priority" for tax relief should be the "millions of taxpayers with small incomes . . . called upon to pay high taxes" under the World War II tax system. Finally, to underscore the importance he assigned to deficit reduction and debt retirement, Truman recommended that Congress extend the special wartime excise taxes scheduled to expire in 1947.

Republicans responded to Truman by reviving the economic incentive and business investment claims attached to the Mellon tax cuts of the 1920s. They also were clear about their budget policy goal. As Ways and Means chairman Knutson conceded, Republicans intended to "cut off much of the government's income by reducing taxes and compelling the government to retrench, to live within its income."[28] The target of this Republican retrenchment was Truman's domestic spending agenda. His fiscal 1948 budget message, for example, called for increased spending in all domestic spending categories to address glaring deficiencies in social welfare, housing, and education programs. Truman went on to recommend that "Congress lay the legislative ground work now for the needed improvements, including general health insurance and a long-range housing program."[29] Republicans had no intention of laying this groundwork. Instead, they were intent on cutting back existing domestic spending commitments, and they attempted to utilize a new procedure, the legislative budget, to advance their spending-cut and tax-cut program.

[27] Harry S. Truman, *Public Papers of the Presidents of the United States: Harry S. Truman, 1947* (Washington, D.C.: Government Printing Office, 1963), 60.
[28] Witte, *The Politics and Development of the Federal Income Tax*, 132.
[29] Truman, *Public Papers of the Presidents of the United States: Harry S. Truman, 1947*, 58.

In the 1946 Legislative Reorganization Act, Congress had created the Joint Committee on the Legislative Budget, made up of members of the House and Senate revenue and appropriations committees, to review the president's budget and recommend overall spending levels that Congress would then adopt before acting on specific spending bills. This committee met for the first time in early 1947 and, on February 14, reported its proposed budget to the House and Senate. On February 20, the House adopted the committee's proposal on a party-line vote. The overall spending ceiling the House approved was $6 billion below the $37.5 billion in the president's budget; the appropriations ceiling was $24 billion, a cut of more than $7 billion below Truman's request.[30] More than half of the administration's budget was allocated to defense, veterans' services and benefits, and interest on the debt, so the impact of these congressional cuts on domestic programs would have been draconian. Whether House Republicans actually considered these cuts feasible, they hoped to strengthen the case for tax cuts by offsetting any revenue loss with future spending cuts.

In line with this strategy, House Republican leaders had delayed acting on H.R. 1, the tax-cut measure, until the spending limits in the legislative budget were in place. The Senate, however, then approved a higher spending ceiling than the House, and it also mandated that debt reduction and tax cuts be funded out of any projected surplus. House and Senate conferees were unable to resolve these differences, and there was no legislative budget in place when Congress considered the tax-cut measure. The House then approved H.R. 1, but the Senate delayed its effective date, which the House was forced to accept.

Truman's veto criticized what it called "the wrong kind of tax reduction, at the wrong time."[31] The tax relief provided under H.R. 1 was, in Truman's view, inequitable and unfair: "H.R. 1 reduces taxes in the high income brackets to a grossly disproportionate extent as compared to the reduction in the low income brackets."[32] The president also pointed out that "necessary expenditures for essential Government operations are still high" and that continued high revenues were needed to move the budget into balance and to reduce wartime debt.[33]

Truman's veto was barely sustained by the House; thirty-five Democrats joined all but two Republicans in the vote to override. Republicans then reintroduced the vetoed measure with one change that was designed to assuage concerns about its short-term budgetary impact. The effective date for the tax cut was delayed by an additional six months, to January 1, 1948, thereby postponing any revenue loss until the second half of FY 1948. The House and Senate promptly passed this measure, and Truman cast his second veto

---

[30] Congressional Quarterly, *Congress and the Nation, 1945–1964* (Washington, D.C.: Congressional Quarterly, 1965), 349.

[31] Truman, *Public Papers of the Presidents of the United States: Harry S. Truman, 1947*, 279.

[32] Ibid., 281.

[33] Ibid., 280.

on July 18, reiterating his earlier critique of "the wrong kind of tax reduction" at "the wrong time," and one that was "not consistent with sound fiscal policy."[34] The House immediately voted to override, as sixty-three Democrats deserted the president. In the Senate, the override vote fell five votes short of the required two-thirds, with thirty-three Democrats and three Republicans voting to sustain the veto.

Republicans finally passed a tax cut in 1948, as election-year worries prompted many congressional Democrats to support the override of a third Truman veto. In January, the president had proposed limited tax relief in the form of a $40 tax credit for individual taxpayers and their dependents but also insisted on an offsetting increase in corporate taxes. Despite an unexpected surplus in the FY 1947 budget and an even larger one projected for 1948 and 1949, Truman maintained that "total receipts should not be reduced" but rather that these surpluses "be used to decrease the national debt."[35]

Truman's tax-credit plan was ignored by the House Ways and Means Committee, which reported out an across-the-board tax cut on January 27. House Republicans had decided to grant a greater share of tax relief to low-income taxpayers in order to attract broader support from Democrats, and the Ways and Means proposal included an increase in personal exemptions from $500 to $600, an additional exemption for the aged and blind, and a 10 percent maximum rate reduction for taxable income of more than $4,000. The Ways and Means bill also eliminated a controversial tax advantage for married couples in community property states by allowing all couples filing returns to split their income. The calendar-year 1948 revenue loss under the Ways and Means bill was calculated at $6.5 billion, and the House passed it by a 297–120 margin on February 2.

The Senate Finance Committee then proceeded to redistribute an even greater share of tax relief to low-income taxpayers. The Finance Committee bill, which passed the Senate on a 78–11 vote, limited the rate reduction for high-income taxpayers to 5 percent while retaining the exemption increases the House had included in its bill. House Republican leaders then agreed to skip the conference stage by having the House vote directly on the Senate bill, which was passed on a 289–67 vote on March 24. Truman's veto, issued on April 2, was overridden the same day by large margins in both chambers.

The Revenue Act of 1948 had an estimated revenue loss in its first year of $4.7 billion, with nearly three-fourths of its tax reduction distributed to taxpayers with taxable incomes of $10,000 or less.[36] In addition, about half of the tax cut for taxpayers with taxable incomes of $10,000 or more was the

---

34 Ibid., 342.
35 Harry S. Truman, *Public Papers of the Presidents of the United States: Harry S. Truman, 1948* (Washington, D.C.: Government Printing Office, 1964), 22.
36 Stanley S. Surrey, "Federal Taxation of the Family: The Revenue Act of 1948," *Harvard Law Review* 61 (July 1948), 1106.

result of the new income-splitting provisions for married couples rather than marginal rate reductions. Indeed, the most important structural policy changes in the Revenue Act of 1948 were related to the income-splitting provision and related changes in gifts and estate taxation for families, which, according to a leading tax expert, "were barely considered by the Congress and practically ignored elsewhere except in initiated legal circles."[37]

What Republicans actually accomplished with the 1948 tax cut was, by most measures, considerably less than they had expected when H.R. 1 was first introduced. Marginal rates for high-income taxpayers remained extremely high, as did overall revenue levels. Republicans had also been forced to scale back their ambitious plans for cutting domestic spending. Congress did manage to pass a legislative budget in 1948 that contained a modest $2.5 billion reduction in the president's budget requests, but appropriators then could not agree on where to make these cuts. The appropriations bills that eventually passed were more than $6 billion above the spending ceiling in the legislative budget.[38]

In fiscal years 1947 and 1948, total spending did decline, but this reduction resulted entirely from defense cutbacks. In 1948, defense outlays were $9.1 billion, more than $32 billion less than in 1946, but domestic spending increased significantly. Excluding interest, nondefense outlays averaged approximately $17 billion in 1947 and 1948, more than double the level in 1946. When defense budgets began to increase after 1948, total spending began to rise as well.

The election of 1948 brought the tax-cut battles to a close. In addition to Truman's reelection, Democrats picked up seventy-five House seats and nine Senate seats. With Democratic control of both chambers restored, Truman called upon the 81st Congress to raise taxes. While Congress took no immediate action, the postwar tax cuts were largely canceled the following year.

The partisan debates over tax policy in 1947 and 1948 had an economic and fiscal dimension. Republicans rationalized their individual income tax cuts with reference to economic incentives, investment, and growth, and they claimed that budgets could be balanced at low revenue levels by cutting spending. They found it impossible, however, to translate their bold calls to reduce spending into specific program cuts. Given the domestic spending budgets in place at the time, the margin for massive cuts was, in fact, minimal, so it may have been that the focus on spending was really meant to foreclose new or expanded domestic spending.

For Truman and a majority of congressional Democrats, the economic and fiscal arguments against tax cuts were obviously quite different. As early fears about postwar deflation quickly were replaced by mounting apprehension over inflation, Truman advocated high revenue levels as a necessary fiscal brake on inflationary measures, and he continued to do so even as the budget moved

[37] Ibid., 1098.
[38] Dennis S. Ippolito, *Congressional Spending* (Ithaca: Cornell University Press, 1981), 48.

into surplus. In addition, Truman was trying to extend the New Deal domestic agenda, and surplus budgets provided the funding to support this expansion. While Truman's major social welfare initiatives were rejected by Congress, he was able to preserve the domestic program base the New Deal had established and to direct more generous funding to that base.

Given that strikingly similar tax-cut battles between Democrats and Republicans would resurface with a vengeance three decades later, it is helpful to recognize that both sides then, as later, professed an abiding commitment to balanced budgets. But as Randolph Paul, an influential Treasury official during World War II, pointed out, both parties sometimes used debates about balanced budgets and low debt "as instruments of criticism and useful arguments for doing what their advocates want to do for other reasons."[39] By the 1940s, both parties had in fact reversed their previous positions on deficits because other budget policy goals were more important:

In the thirties the desire of the Democrats to provide relief conquered their feebler desire to balance the budget. In the late forties the desire of the Republicans for tax relief proved stronger than their desire to balance the budget. Of course, each side rationalized the conclusion it preferred.... [T]he desirability of balancing the budget and the necessity of preventing an undue expansion of the public debt are not invariably the powerful political forces they are sometimes represented to be.

Korean War Tax Policy

The Korean War was much less costly than World War II. In 1953, total spending reached $76 billion, compared to the World War II peak of nearly $93 billion in 1945. In constant dollars, however, the disparity was considerably greater, and spending-GDP was less than half the World War II level. With the Truman administration firmly committed to "pay-as-you-go" financing for the war, and Congress initially supportive of tax increases, the tax program for Korea was unusually aggressive, and receipt-GDP levels were only slightly below those in World War II. As a result, the deficit effects of the war were very small (see Table 2.4). Publicly held debt grew by $10.2 billion between 1949 and 1954, and the debt-GDP level fell by nearly 25 percent.

The Korean War also had a decisive impact on spending policy. It catalyzed a massive military buildup that kept defense budgets elevated long after the war was over and halted the domestic spending growth of the late 1940s. With the spending side of the budget dominated by defense, high revenue levels were required to balance budgets even with continued tight control over domestic spending. The Korean War effectively imposed a partisan truce on budget policy. Republicans were forced to abandon their ambitious plans for tax cuts. Democrats were likewise forced to accept a more modest domestic role for the federal government.

---

[39] Paul, *Taxation in the United States*, 516.

TABLE 2.4. *Spending, Revenues, Surpluses/Deficits, and Debt, Fiscal Years 1949–1954 (in billions of dollars)*

Fiscal Year	Outlays	Revenues	Surplus/ Deficit	Publicly Held Debt	Publicly Held Debt (as percentage of GDP)
1949	$38.8	$39.4	+$0.6	$214.3	79.0%
1950	42.6	39.4	−3.1	219.0	80.2
1951	45.5	51.6	+6.1	214.3	66.9
1952	67.7	66.2	−1.5	214.8	61.6
1953	76.1	69.6	−6.5	218.4	58.6
1954	70.9	69.7	−1.2	224.5	59.5

Source: Office of Management and Budget, *Historical Tables, Budget of the United States Government, Fiscal Year 2011* (Washington, D.C.: Government Printing Office, 2010), 21, 133.

The Wartime Tax Bills

Three tax increases were passed to fund the Korean War. The Revenue Act of 1950 and the Excess Profits Tax Act of 1950 were passed quickly and with bipartisan support. The Revenue Act of 1951 was more contentious, and Congress wrestled with this legislation for months. In its final form, the Revenue Act of 1951 satisfied neither the administration nor congressional conservatives, and it illustrated the difficulty of balancing revenue needs against pressures for targeted tax relief. Although Truman called for additional tax increases in 1952, election-year politics doomed that effort.

The Revenue Act of 1950 The June 25, 1950, invasion of South Korea by North Korea abruptly changed the tax agenda in Congress. The year began with a modest administration proposal to reduce some World War II excise taxes that still remained in place and to replace the lost revenues with higher corporate taxes and tightened restrictions on tax preferences. Despite strong support for excise tax reductions in both parties, the offsetting corporate tax increases and tax preference reforms were divisive, and the House Ways and Means Committee spent almost five months putting together a compromise bill.

By the time the bill was brought to the House floor, war had broken out. The administration soon submitted a new revenue request for $5 billion, and Congress quickly agreed to a slightly larger increase. The Revenue Act of 1950, which was signed by the president on September 23, reinstated the individual income tax rates that had been in effect prior to the 1945 and 1948 rate reductions. The corporate income tax rate was also increased, again approximately in line with the highest rates in World War II. In a return to the World War II finance model, excise tax rates on alcohol, tobacco, gasoline, and automobiles were raised, and new excises on other goods and services were imposed.

While the administration had not originally requested an excess profits tax, Congress scheduled a postelection special session to consider reinstating excess profits taxation. As this special session was meeting, a surprise attack by Chinese forces extinguished hopes for a swift end to the war, and Treasury officials made clear that heavier taxation would be needed to meet the escalating costs of what was turning into an unexpectedly long and increasingly bloody war. With the president declaring a national emergency on December 15, the final version of the Excess Profits Tax Act of 1950 was quickly approved by voice votes in both chambers.

The political difficulties accompanying excess profits taxation, however, were reflected in the many exemptions and exceptions contained in the 1950 bill. As in World War II, the definition of excess profits was debated at length, and Congress again responded by providing corporations with alternative methods for calculating excess profits. In approving a 77 percent excess profits tax rate, Congress limited combined corporate income and excess profits taxes to 62 percent of net income. In signing the bill, Truman criticized its "excessive exemptions and relief provisions" that had "reduce[d] the Government's revenues needlessly."[40] Citing the need for "more and much heavier taxes," Truman promised to "canvass and recanvass every revenue possibility, including the new excess profits tax."

The Revenue Act of 1951 The president's fiscal 1952 budget message to Congress, submitted on January 15, 1951, renewed the call for higher taxes. In a special message to Congress on February 2, Truman called for immediate action on a $10 billion increase in individual and corporate income taxes as well as higher excise taxes. He also stated that a second increase, of an unspecified amount, would be needed later in the year to keep wartime funding "on a pay as we go basis."[41] When the new excess profits returns were filed in the spring, Truman expected to recommend "what changes in the excess profits tax law are desirable to obtain more revenue from that source."[42]

The Revenue Act of 1951 did not pass Congress until late October and contained temporary increases in individual and corporate income taxes as well as excises. Individual income tax rates were raised to a maximum of 92 percent on taxable income of more than $400,000 through December 31, 1953. The corporate tax increases in both normal and surtax rates were in effect for the twenty-four-month period ending March 31, 1954. Increased excise tax rates on alcohol, tobacco, gasoline, automobiles, and assorted other goods and services were extended through March 31, 1954, as well. The Revenue Act of 1951 also contained numerous tax preferences, including oil and mineral depletion allowances and capital gains and family partnership provisions.

These tax law changes differed significantly from those the administration had proposed, and their revenue yield was estimated at only $5.5 billion,

---

[40] Harry S. Truman, *Public Papers of the Presidents of the United States: Harry S. Truman, 1951* (Washington, D.C.: Government Printing Office, 1965), 1.

[41] Ibid., 136.

[42] Ibid., 137.

slightly more than half the amount that Truman had requested. In his signing statement, Truman criticized the bill as inadequate and unfair. The new tax preferences, in his view, "provide[d] additional means by which wealthy individuals can escape paying their proper share of the national tax load."[43] He was especially incensed about a rider the Senate had attached – the so-called Jenner amendment that permitted the states to open their welfare rolls to public inspection – and declared that "if we did not need the revenue from this act so badly, I would not have approved provisions such as these."[44]

Truman's leverage on tax policy, however, had greatly diminished. The 1950 midterm elections had reduced the Democratic margins in the House and Senate, giving Republicans and southern Democrats enhanced influence in the 82nd Congress. Popular support for the war and approval ratings for the president also declined in 1951, especially after Truman's controversial removal of the commanding general in Korea, Douglas MacArthur, in April. An improved budget outlook, including an unexpected surplus for the fiscal year that ended on June 30, further undermined the case for higher taxes, and the Revenue Act of 1951 marked the end of Korean War tax increases.

Revenues and Spending

The Korean War tax bills boosted revenues to nearly $70 billion in 1953 and 1954, $30 billion higher than the immediate prewar level and nearly $25 billion above the highest revenue level achieved in World War II. Individual and corporate income taxes had provided roughly equal revenue shares during World War II, but the individual income tax was by far the more important revenue source throughout the Korean conflict. With the automatic expiration of excess profits taxation after the war, the disparity between the individual and corporate income taxes became even greater. The individual income tax was, therefore, the chief target of congressional complaints about "high taxes." Republicans and conservative Democrats had managed to limit the 1951 tax increase, and they then turned their attention to domestic spending cuts in order to keep deficits under control. They were also looking ahead to the possibility of postwar tax cuts financed by reductions in domestic spending. In 1952, when Truman's request for another tax increase was simply ignored, Congress did cut several FY 1953 appropriations bills by significant amounts, but total spending still increased over the previous year, and the budget deficit climbed to $6.5 billion.

The battles over tax cuts in 1947 and 1948 had been part of a broader conflict about the domestic role of the federal government. Spending policy changes over the course of the Korean War, however, made it difficult to revive this conflict because the "permanent" defense budget had increased to a level that necessitated continued high revenues. After World War II, defense spending

---

43 Ibid., 590.
44 Ibid.

had dropped from $83 billion in 1945 to less than $10 billion in 1948. In 1955, two years after the end of the Korean War, the defense budget had fallen only by $10 billion, and it soon began to rise again. To put this in perspective, funding post-Korea defense budgets required revenue levels previously reached at the height of World War II.

The transition to Cold War defense budgets was also rapid. In 1949, the Departments of Defense and State had conducted the first comprehensive review of Cold War national military strategy and defense revenues. Their report, NSC-68, was submitted in the spring of 1950, and it called for major upgrades in U.S. conventional and strategic forces to counter the Soviet military threat. The budgetary cost estimates for NSC-68 were later calculated at approximately $40 billion annually, nearly three times the defense budget request that had originally been submitted for FY 1951.[45] With the outbreak of the Korean War, however, President Truman called for a comprehensive defense buildup "over and above the forces we need in Korea."[46]

Congress had shared Truman's pre-Korea belief that the economy could not support defense budgets of more than $15 billion. In presenting the original fiscal 1951 defense budget to the House, the chairman of the Defense Appropriations Subcommittee, George H. Mahon, warned his colleagues that "nothing would please a potential enemy better than to have us . . . destroy our economy by maintaining over a period of years complete readiness for armed conflict."[47] The Senate Appropriations Committee then proposed cuts in the defense budget passed by the House, explaining that "a nation which exhausts itself in enervating overpreparation . . . may well fall prey to a cunning and patient enemy who fully realizes the debilitating influences of a war-geared economy over a long period of time." This concern for what was "affordable" soon evaporated. On September 22, 1950, Congress passed a nearly $12 billion supplemental appropriation for the Department of Defense, along with $4 billion for military aid.[48] Several months later, a second supplemental of $17 billion was approved, and an additional $3 billion was provided for atomic energy and related procurement programs. Between 1950 and 1953, defense outlays increased from $13.7 billion to $52.8 billion. As a percentage of GDP, defense spending nearly tripled over this period, rising to more than 14 percent in 1953, and it remained at more than 10 percent for the rest of the decade.

Funding for domestic programs moved in the opposite direction. In 1950, Congress had raised Social Security benefits for the first time in more than a decade, and Social Security outlays increased by nearly $2 billion over the next

[45] Richard Smoke, "The Evolution of American Defense Policy," in *American Defense Policy*, 5th ed., eds. J. F. Reichart and S. R. Sturm (Baltimore: Johns Hopkins University Press, 1982), 107.

[46] Harry S. Truman, *Public Papers of the Presidents of the United States: Harry S. Truman, 1950* (Washington, D.C.: Government Printing Office, 1965), 611.

[47] Congressional Quarterly, *Congress and the Nation, 1945–1964*, 253–254.

[48] Dennis S. Ippolito, *Uncertain Legacies: Federal Budget Policy from Roosevelt through Reagan* (Charlottesville: University Press of Virginia, 1990), 102.

three years. Spending for other social welfare programs, however, dropped by more than $4 billion between 1950 and 1953. With very few exceptions, other domestic programs grew slowly, if at all, and the domestic share of the budget was reduced by more than half. The wartime cutbacks in domestic spending made it much easier for the administration to defend its tax program.

In 1948, after Congress had passed a large tax cut over Truman's veto, the Republican platform had pledged "to reduce the enormous burden of taxation" even further.[49] It also promised to enable state and local governments "to assume their separate responsibilities" by turning over to them revenue sources, such as excises and inheritance taxes, that the federal government had utilized. The Republican Party platform of 1952, which castigated the Truman administration for any number of domestic and foreign policy failures, was surprisingly muted when it came to taxes and spending. While deploring the Democrats' "wanton extravagance" and "confiscatory taxes," the platform did not offer much hope of immediate relief. Any "general tax reduction," it cautioned, would only be possible with the "elimination of waste and extravagance" that would balance the budget.[50]

The Eisenhower Years

Dwight D. Eisenhower's ascent to the presidency was swift. He resigned as Supreme Commander of the North Atlantic Treaty Organization (NATO) on April 2, 1952; received the Republican Party's nomination on July 11; and easily defeated the Democratic nominee, Adlai E. Stevenson, on November 4. During the campaign, Eisenhower had sharply criticized the Truman administration's management of the Korean War and pledged to end that war as quickly as possible. The Korean armistice was signed on July 27, 1953, the midpoint in Eisenhower's first year as president. The post-Korea budget program that then emerged set forth the fiscal themes that would define the rest of Eisenhower's presidency.

Like Truman, Eisenhower was strongly committed to balanced budgets. This commitment was reinforced, in both administrations, by the belief that deficits and debt would harm the economy by fueling inflationary pressures. While Eisenhower was perhaps more sympathetic to the view that high taxes stifled economic growth, he repeatedly opposed tax-cut stimulus as fiscally irresponsible. The fiscal conservatism that Eisenhower pursued placed great importance on spending control, but the defense and nondefense spending levels he supported were still extremely high, and the overriding issue for tax policy was how to finance that spending. Revenue levels, rather than equity

[49] American Presidency Project, "Republican Party Platform of 1948," http://www.presidency. ucsb.edu/ws/?pid=25836, 2.
[50] American Presidency Project, "Republican Party Platform of 1952," http://www.presidency. ucsb.edu/ws/?pid=25837, 4.

or economic growth, were the central priority during this stable era of tax policy.

The defense program that Eisenhower promoted was intentionally less costly than Truman's, and he "personally shaped the major strategic and budgetary aspects of defense policy" in order to control those costs.[51] Nevertheless, the defense budgets of the post-Korea period were enormous. On the domestic side of the budget, Truman had attempted to extend the New Deal, but Congress had blocked this effort. Eisenhower was not at all interested in extending the New Deal, but neither was he intent on dismantling it. As a result, social welfare and other domestic spending was stabilized at levels roughly comparable to those under Truman, the competition between defense and domestic needs was minimized, and the strong emphasis on balanced budgets precluded major tax reductions. The high tax system that had been put in place during the Korean War remained largely intact throughout Eisenhower's presidency. Neither the tax cuts demanded by conservative Republicans nor the tax relief advocated by liberal Democrats was allowed to disturb the fiscal consensus that prevailed.

Postwar Tax Policy

The issue of tax cuts led to an early confrontation between the Eisenhower administration and the Republican-controlled House Ways and Means Committee. In his February 2, 1953, State of the Union Address, the president announced that deficit reduction and a balanced budget would be his essential first step in fiscal reform. Emphasizing that any future tax cut would "be justified only as we show we can succeed in bringing the budget under control," Eisenhower stated that "until we can determine the extent to which expenditures can be reduced, it would not be wise to reduce our revenues."[52]

The Republican chairman of the Ways and Means Committee, Daniel A. Reed, had served in Congress since 1919, and he was determined to steer a tax cut through Congress. Under the Revenue Act of 1951, individual income tax rates had been temporarily increased through December 31, 1953. Reed's proposal, introduced as H.R. 1, advanced that scheduled reduction to July 1. In an unusual departure from committee procedures, Reed did not solicit the Treasury's views on his proposed tax cut, neither did he schedule any hearings.[53] Nevertheless, Ways and Means reported out H.R. 1 by a heavily bipartisan vote of 21–4 on February 17. The committee's stated rationale was that an immediate tax cut would force Congress to take action on cutting spending, and the committee report went on to oppose any increase in taxes, such as an extension of excess profits taxation, that would relax this pressure on Congress.

[51] Iwan W. Morgan, *Eisenhower versus the Spenders* (New York: St. Martin's Press, 1990), 22.
[52] Dwight D. Eisenhower, *Public Papers of the Presidents of the United States: Dwight D. Eisenhower, 1953* (Washington, D.C.: Government Printing Office, 1960), 21.
[53] Congressional Quarterly, *Congress and the Nation, 1945–1964*, 414.

Reed had made this same argument, if perhaps more colorfully, when denouncing the tax increases in 1951 as advancing the agenda of the "hard core of the Socialist planners within the Truman administration."[54] For conservative Republicans like Reed, the only acceptable path to a balanced budget was through spending cuts, particularly in the domestic programs that the New Deal had introduced. Tax increases, in their view, provided fiscal protection for these programs and, indeed, promoted their expansion. This calculation had featured prominently in the tax-cut debates between Truman and the Republican-controlled 80th Congress, so it was not surprising to see it resurrected when Republicans returned to power in 1953. The Eisenhower administration, however, persuaded House Republicans to block action on H.R. 1. The House Rules Committee refused to grant Reed's request for a rule that would have allowed H.R. 1 to move to the House floor, and Reed's attempt to circumvent the Rules Committee through a discharge petition was stymied as well.

Meanwhile, Eisenhower recommended an increase in taxes. In his May 20, 1953, Special Message to the Congress Recommending Tax Legislation, Eisenhower asked for a six-month extension of the excess profits tax that otherwise would expire on June 30, along with extensions of the increased corporate tax rates and excise tax rates that were to expire the following year. The only "tax cut" Eisenhower would accept was a one-year delay in increasing Social Security taxes during 1954, and the justification in this case was that the Social Security trust fund reserve was adequate to fund the expanded coverage the administration expected to propose.[55]

The excess profits tax extension was considered by the Ways and Means Committee in June. When hearings were concluded, with most major business groups registering their opposition to any extension, Reed determined that the committee would take no further action. House Republican leaders then threatened to bypass Ways and Means. Eventually, a majority of Ways and Means Committee members decided to defy Reed and report out the excess

---

[54] Ibid., 412.

[55] Congressional Democrats complained that the administration intended to limit the future growth of the Social Security plan by converting it to an entirely pay-as-you-go system (i.e., benefit increases would have to be matched by immediate tax increases). Eisenhower disavowed any such intent and in 1954 endorsed the existing Social Security financing system. Congress then approved an omnibus Social Security bill that extended coverage to an estimated 7.5 million workers and raised benefits for current retirees by more than 15 percent. As in 1950 and 1952, the benefit increases took effect in September, two months before federal elections. The corresponding Social Security tax increase to fund the 1954 benefit increase did not take effect until January 1955. Tufte later described this and similar manipulations of Social Security benefits (and other domestic transfer payments) and delayed or inadequate tax increases to fund these benefits as evidence of an "electoral-economic cycle." Edward R. Tufte, *Political Control of the Economy* (Princeton: Princeton University Press, 1978), ch. 2. See also William R. Keech, *Economic Politics* (New York: Cambridge University Press, 1995), 170–172.

profits tax extension. The House approved the extension by a 325–77 vote on July 10, and the Senate passed the House measure without amendment on July 14.

The Internal Revenue Code of 1954 With the scheduled expiration of the excess profits tax on December 31, 1953, and with the individual income tax rates reverting to their pre-1951 levels, the estimated revenue loss for 1954 was approximately $5 billion. The administration renewed its request for an excise tax rate extension that would leave in place the numerous temporary rate increases that were to expire in 1954. Congress agreed to a one-year extension for the alcohol and tobacco excise taxes but also included exceptions for reduced rates on various consumer goods such as household appliances and long-distance telephone service. The net effect of the Excise Tax Reduction Act of 1954 was estimated to reduce revenues by $1 billion, but the actual loss in excise tax collections turned out to be much lower.

These one-year extensions of "temporary" excise tax rates and of the higher corporation income tax rates from 1951 became an annual exercise for the remainder of Eisenhower's presidency, even with Democrats controlling the House and Senate after 1954. Partisan differences emerged, however, with the individual income tax changes in the Internal Revenue Code of 1954. These differences resurfaced the following year, as the new Democratic congressional leadership challenged the administration over tax relief for low-income taxpayers.

The Internal Revenue Code of 1954 was, in part, a comprehensive administrative revision of individual and corporate income tax laws. In response to widespread complaints about complexities and ambiguities that had accumulated with the tax law changes over the previous several decades and particularly during the 1940s, the Treasury Department launched a year-long review in 1953. Working with Congress's tax committee leaders and staff, the Treasury formulated a reform plan, the highlights of which were incorporated into the president's budget message to Congress on January 21, 1954. On March 9, the Ways and Means Committee reported out a nearly 900-page tax bill that conformed fairly closely to the administration's recommendations.

Most of the technical and structural policy provisions in the Ways and Means bill were not controversial. There was strong Democratic opposition, however, to the amount and distribution of tax relief it provided. The estimated revenue reduction in the Ways and Means measure was less than $1.5 billion, and most of this relief was accounted for by new or expanded tax preferences. For individuals, the important changes involved the tax treatment of medical expenses, charitable contributions, childcare costs, retirement income, and dependent children deductions. For corporations, the major tax relief provisions affected depreciation schedules for plants, equipment, and research and development costs as well as net operating loss accounting.

The focus of Democratic criticism, however, was a new exclusion and credit for dividend income received by individuals. The administration had recommended an even more generous credit than the Ways and Means Committee finally approved, but House Democrats attempted to delete this provision entirely and to substitute for it a $100 increase in the personal exemption. Democrats argued that increased personal exemptions would concentrate tax relief on low-income taxpayers and, unlike the dividend credit, result in a fairer distribution of tax burdens. In a national radio and television address on March 15, Eisenhower attacked the personal exemption proposal as too costly and "wrong."[56] In his view, it was unfair "to excuse millions of taxpayers from paying any income tax at all," and he called upon Congress to reject this "unsound tax proposal."[57] Three days later, the House narrowly defeated the Democratic substitute, and the Senate then defeated an amendment to the House-passed bill that would have reinstated the personal exemption increase. Final passage was not secured until July 29, after a prolonged Senate debate and House-Senate conference, and the dividend exclusion and credit was included in the bill the president signed on August 16.

Tax Cuts versus Tax Increases Tax relief for low-income taxpayers was blocked again in 1955. House Democrats included a $20 tax credit for all taxpayers and dependents in a corporate income and excise tax extension, but this provision was deleted in the Senate. The Eisenhower administration criticized the credit's cost, which it claimed would be more than $2 billion annually, and its potential for fueling inflation. The administration then made the case for debt reduction, rather than tax cuts, as the budget moved into surplus in fiscal years 1956 and 1957.

In 1956, Congress approved a Social Security tax increase and increased the excise tax on gasoline to fund the interstate highway program. In 1958, Social Security taxes were again increased, and Congress raised the gasoline excise tax in 1959. On those few occasions when the House managed to pass limited tax cuts, the Senate blocked action. Even with the increased Democratic congressional majorities after the 1958 midterm elections, Eisenhower continued to control the tax agenda.

In 1960, as Eisenhower entered his last year in office, the prospect of a $4.3 billion projected surplus for FY 1961 did not alter his opposition to tax cuts. Once again, he argued that debt reduction was more important but conceded that the next administration and Congress should decide "between reductions in the public debt and lightening of the tax burden, or both."[58] When another recession threatened to wipe out that surplus, Eisenhower insisted that

---

[56] Dwight D. Eisenhower, *Public Papers of the Presidents of the United States: Dwight D. Eisenhower, 1954* (Washington, D.C.: Government Printing Office, 1960), 316.

[57] Ibid., 317.

[58] Dwight D. Eisenhower, *Public Papers of the Presidents of the United States: Dwight D. Eisenhower, 1960–1961* (Washington, D.C.: Government Printing Office, 1961), 40.

TABLE 2.5. *Composition of Federal Revenues, Fiscal Years 1950–1961 (as percentage of GDP)*

Fiscal Year	Individual Income Taxes	Corporation Income Taxes	Social Insurance Taxes	Excise Taxes	Other	Total
1950	5.8%	3.8%	1.6%	2.8%	0.5%	14.4%
1951	6.8	4.4	1.8	2.7	0.5	16.1
1952	8.0	6.1	1.8	2.5	0.5	19.0
1953	8.0	5.7	1.8	2.7	0.5	18.7
1954	7.8	5.6	1.9	2.6	0.5	18.5
1955	7.3	4.5	2.0	2.3	0.5	16.5
1956	7.5	4.9	2.2	2.3	0.5	17.5
1957	7.9	4.7	2.2	2.3	0.6	17.7
1958	7.5	4.4	2.4	2.3	0.6	17.3
1959	7.5	3.5	2.4	2.2	0.6	16.2
1960	7.8	4.1	2.8	2.3	0.8	17.8
1961	7.8	4.0	3.1	2.2	0.7	17.8

Source: Office of Management and Budget, *Historical Tables, Budget of the United States Government, Fiscal Year 2011* (Washington, D.C.: Government Printing Office, 2010), 34.

the budget be brought back into balance. His FY 1962 budget, submitted to Congress days before he left office, called for "continuing present tax rates to maintain the revenues needed for a sound fiscal plan."[59]

The high-revenue system that remained in place throughout the Eisenhower presidency extended to all of the federal government's major revenue sources (see Table 2.5). Individual income tax–GDP levels, for example, declined slightly with the automatic expiration of the temporary wartime rate increases in 1955 but then rebounded and remained well above pre-Korea levels. In addition to the high marginal rates that continued in place, the individual income tax base was kept largely intact. In 1950, adjusted gross income was 79.2 percent of personal income; ten years later, it was 78.9 percent.[60]

The corporate income tax–GDP level fell after wartime excess profits taxes expired, but annual extensions of the high normal rates enacted during the war kept corporate taxes at historically high levels. Excise taxes, most of which were routinely extended as well, remained at more than 2 percent of GDP, and the Social Security tax increases in 1956 and 1958 helped to lift social insurance receipts to more than 3 percent of GDP by 1961. The year-to-year fluctuations in all these tax sources after 1955 were the result of economic factors rather than policy changes.

Eisenhower, like Truman, justified his opposition to tax cuts in terms of economic policy, specifically the importance of controlling inflation. Neither administration supported countercyclical tax cuts; instead, they relied on

[59] Ibid., 935.
[60] Ippolito, *Uncertain Legacies*, 39.

"automatic variations of the deficit or surplus" to stabilize the economy.[61] Both administrations also opposed financing major tax reductions out of budget surpluses, which they reserved for deficit reduction.

Initially, Eisenhower had taken a different position on this last point. His FY 1954 budget had declared "the determined purpose of this administration to make further reductions in taxes as rapidly as justified by prospective revenues and reductions in expenditures."[62] Three years later, with the budget in surplus, Eisenhower admitted that "tax rates are still too high" and promised "further tax reductions as soon as they can be accomplished within a sound budget policy."[63] He went on, however, to explain that "the reduction of tax rates must give way ... to the cost of meeting our urgent national responsibilities."

The most important responsibility, and largest component of the budget, was defense, but the Eisenhower budget program also had a "Modern Republicanism" domestic component.[64] While Eisenhower's determination to reduce federal spending never wavered, he did adjust his sights as the realities of defense and domestic budgetary needs became clearer. The high-revenue system that Eisenhower wound up defending was the fiscal trade-off for the spending program he ultimately embraced and promoted.

Defense Spending and Taxes

Partisan differences over spending policy during the Eisenhower presidency were blurred. For example, many Democrats complained that the administration's cuts in Truman's defense spending plan had been too severe, thereby underfunding both conventional and strategic forces. By comparison, strong objections about excessive defense costs came mostly from conservative Republicans, and even these were muted as the Cold War strategic consensus took hold. On domestic spending, the limited and selective growth that did occur was too much for many conservatives in both parties and too little for liberals seeking to expand and extend social welfare programs. With neither party united behind a meaningful spending retrenchment program, opposition to high revenue levels was scattered and ineffective.

The New Look The Eisenhower administration's FY 1955 budget unveiled "a new concept for planning and financing our national security program" with a heavy emphasis on controlling costs and ensuring long-term sustainability.[65] At the strategic level, the "New Look" sought to strengthen deterrence primarily through strategic airpower and nuclear weapons. At the budgetary level, the

[61] Herbert Stein, *Presidential Economics* (New York: Simon & Schuster, 1984), 80–81.
[62] Eisenhower, *Public Papers of the Presidents of the United States: Dwight D. Eisenhower, 1954,* 87.
[63] Dwight D. Eisenhower, *Public Papers of the Presidents of the United States: Dwight D. Eisenhower, 1957* (Washington, D.C.: Government Printing Office, 1958), 43.
[64] Morgan, *Eisenhower versus the Spenders,* 80.
[65] Eisenhower, *Public Papers of the Presidents of the United States: Dwight D. Eisenhower, 1954,* 117.

New Look envisioned cutbacks in costly conventional forces and substantial reductions in the defense planning levels that Truman had proposed in his final budget.

The defense buildup that Truman ultimately endorsed was striking. In 1949, Truman had proposed a 48-group Air Force, 10 Army divisions, 288 naval combat ships, and an active-duty force level for all the services of approximately 1.6 million.[66] Three years later, his goals were quite different: 143 Air Force wings, 21 Army divisions, 408 combat ships, and a 3.6 million active-duty force level.[67] Projected costs for these forces were expected to peak at more than $46 billion in FY 1954 and then decline "until they reach the level required to keep our armed forces in a state of readiness."[68] For Eisenhower, the long-term costs of Truman's defense program were too high, and he imposed budget ceilings or "directed verdicts" as a way to balance defense and domestic needs and to accommodate what he considered economic and social realities. Eisenhower was greatly concerned that excessive defense spending would weaken the economy, and he shared with some defense experts in Congress the view that the Soviet Union was intent on forcing the United States into a military buildup that would break its economy.

Eisenhower was also convinced that the United States could not "get this so-called adequate defense over a sustained period without drastically changing our whole way of life."[69] When other members of his National Security Council argued that larger defense budgets would not entail these social costs, Eisenhower insisted that the "American people [might] make these sacrifices voluntarily for a year or for two or for three years but . . . [not] for the indefinite future."[70] As post-Korea defense budget ceilings were unveiled in late 1953 and 1954, none of the services was satisfied with the result. While the Joint Chiefs of Staff nominally endorsed the president's program, the Army and Air Force managed to convey their misgivings to congressional supporters who then tried, but failed, to raise defense appropriations above the administration's requests. These interservice rivalries resurfaced with each year's defense budget, but there were only minor congressional changes in the budgets that Eisenhower submitted. From 1955 to 1961, the administration's requests for new budget authority totaled $289.6 billion; congressional appropriations were $287.6 billion.[71] In fiscal years 1955, 1956, 1958, and 1960, Congress cut the appropriations requests, with the average reduction slightly more than $1

[66] Harry S. Truman, *Public Papers of the Presidents of the United States: Harry S. Truman, 1949* (Washington, D.C.: Government Printing Office, 1964), 58–59.

[67] Harry S. Truman, *Public Papers of the Presidents of the United States: Harry S. Truman, 1952–1953* (Washington, D.C.: Government Printing Office, 1966), 1134–1135.

[68] Ibid., 1135.

[69] U.S. Department of State, *Foreign Relations of the United States, 1952–1954, vol. 2: National Security Affairs, Part 1* (Washington, D.C.: Government Printing Office, 1984), 520.

[70] Ibid., 521.

[71] Ippolito, *Uncertain Legacies*, 106.

billion. The fiscal 1957, 1959, and 1961 increases were of roughly the same magnitude.

Republican conservatives, who had hoped for dramatic defense cuts (and tax cuts), were not at all pleased with the New Look. The Senate majority leader in 1953, Robert A. Taft, had been Eisenhower's major opponent for the Republican presidential nomination in 1952, and he expressed his displeasure at a legislative leadership meeting with the president on April 30. Taft accused Eisenhower of "taking us down the same road Truman traveled" and called for a "complete reconsideration" of large defense cuts.[72] That reconsideration did not take place, and Taft died three months later, effectively bringing to a close whatever conservative challenge there might have been on defense.

The defense program that Eisenhower established in 1954 was heavily tilted toward strategic airpower and nuclear missiles. In 1950, the Air Force budget was $3.6 billion, approximately $400 million below the Army's budget and $500 million below the Navy's.[73] Ten years later, the Air Force budget was more than $19 billion, only slightly less than the combined Army and Navy budgets. Between 1955 and 1960, missile outlays increased from less than 5 percent of net procurement spending to more than 26 percent. This strategic air and missile buildup was the centerpiece of the "massive retaliation" deterrent concept that the administration first set forth in December 1953 and subsequently elaborated. Massive retaliation was enormously controversial, but one of its undeniable attractions was the cost advantage that strategic weapons had over conventional forces. Matching the Warsaw Pact's ground forces in Europe, for example, was viewed as prohibitively expensive. With atomic weapons in substantial quantities supporting U.S. and NATO forces, however, the United States hoped to deter a full-scale Soviet attack.

The Truman administration's NSC-68 defense plan assumed that the United States could spend as much as 20 percent of GNP to fund its conventional and strategic forces.[74] The NSC-162/2 plan that set the parameters for the Eisenhower administration's New Look program sought to achieve the same deterrent effect at roughly half that cost by rebalancing long-term conventional and strategic forces. And, in fact, the defense-GNP levels for fiscal years 1955–1961 averaged almost exactly 10 percent annually.

Critiques of the New Look and massive retaliation doctrine were wide ranging, but the major complaint in Congress was that defense spending was too low. These complaints became stronger and more widespread as the Soviet Union began to erase what had been a decided U.S. advantage in nuclear weapons and delivery systems. The successful launches of the Soviet Union's

---

[72] Morgan, *Eisenhower versus the Spenders*, 53.

[73] Ippolito, *Uncertain Legacies*, 107.

[74] Morgan, *Eisenhower versus the Spenders*, 55.

earth satellites in late 1957 were especially disquieting, because they demonstrated the dramatic progress the Soviet Union had made in long-range ballistic missile development. The Gaither Commission, which was appointed by Eisenhower to reassess U.S. deterrence capabilities, concluded that the defense budget needed to be increased immediately and significantly.[75] Similar conclusions were reached in reports that soon followed from a Rockefeller Brothers Fund defense study and from the Senate Armed Services Subcommittee on Preparedness.

Eisenhower's response fell well short of these recommendations. The fiscal 1959 budget request was less than $2 billion above the administration's original defense ceiling.[76] Increases in the fiscal 1960 budget were also modest. Congress made only minor changes in the administration's budget requests and force planning, but congressional Democrats repeatedly charged the administration had failed to address the numerous deficiencies in U.S. force levels and force structure the various defense panels had identified. Army and Navy supporters promoted "balanced forces," including limited-war forces. Advocates for the Air Force pointed to alleged inadequacies in U.S. strategic forces. John F. Kennedy's presidential campaign featured this "missile gap" charge, but the 1960 Democratic platform derided the entire military position of the United States as being "measured in terms of gaps – missile gap, space gap, limited-war gap."[77] The Democratic prescription was to strengthen both strategic and "balanced conventional military forces" and to ensure their "continuous modernization ... including essential programs now slowed down, terminated, suspended, or neglected for lack of budgetary support." In other words, a defense budget that already accounted for more than half of total federal spending would have to be increased. Because the Democratic Party was also committed to increased domestic spending and officially embraced balanced budgets, its platform did not propose any major changes in tax policy.

The Domestic Spending "Base"

Nondefense spending fell during the Korean War, but this decline was reversed after FY 1954. The spending-GDP level for payments for individuals, for example, had reached a peak of 5 percent under Truman. When the Eisenhower administration left office, the spending-GDP level was 5.2 percent. In terms of social welfare and other domestic programs, the "Modern Republicanism" that Eisenhower championed essentially "assimilated the New Deal legacy but drew the line against expanding federal responsibilities into new areas."[78] The one

---

[75] Ibid., 70.

[76] Ippolito, *Uncertain Legacies*, 107–108.

[77] American Presidency Project, "Democratic Party Platform of 1960," http://www.presidency. ucsb.edu/ws/index.php?pid=29602, 1.

[78] Iwan W. Morgan, *Deficit Government* (Chicago: Ivan R. Dee, 1995), 72.

area where Eisenhower attempted to reverse the New Deal was agriculture, but bipartisan backing for price supports and farm credit programs among rural legislators kept these spending commitments largely intact.[79]

The first, and arguably most important, sign that the Eisenhower administration would not attempt to reverse the New Deal was its January 14, 1954, special message recommending that Congress expand coverage and increase benefits for the Social Security program. There had earlier been mixed signals about the administration's intentions, but its 1954 proposal affirmed the social insurance principles that had been established in the Social Security Act of 1935. In addition to extending basic coverage to an estimated ten million new participants – self-employed farmers and professionals, along with farm and domestic workers – the administration proposed major new benefits.[80] Social Security protection for disabled workers was recommended, along with higher minimum and maximum benefit levels and a more generous benefit formula for current and future retirees.

The Social Security Act Amendments of 1954 did not include all of the coverage extensions the administration had recommended, but an estimated 7.5 million workers were brought into the system. Monthly benefits were raised by 16 percent for current beneficiaries, and the benefit formula for future retirees was liberalized. Benefit protection for disabled workers was implemented, and the earned-income penalty for Social Security was reduced. On the revenue side, the Social Security wage base was increased, and scheduled Social Security tax rate increases were extended through 1975. With its long-term financing greatly strengthened, the Social Security system was moving quickly toward comprehensive workforce coverage.

Additional Social Security expansions were adopted in 1956, 1958, and 1960, in some cases against administration opposition. Early retirement for women was permitted in 1956, and coverage for disabled workers was added in 1956 (for workers 50–64 years of age) and 1960 (for workers younger than 50). Scheduled tax increases were also accelerated. In 1960, the Social Security wage base was $4,800, and the tax rate was 3 percent for employers and employees, double the rate that had been in effect in 1950.

By 1960, Social Security was an important part of the federal budget, accounting for nearly one-half of the $24 billion in social welfare spending and more than 2 percent of GDP. It was also, given the programmatic changes that had been made over the preceding decade, a permanent and growing component. In the long-standing debate over the size and role of government, Social Security was no longer an issue.

Other components of the social welfare budget were also insulated from partisan politics. Federal civil and military retirement and various veterans'

---

[79] Ippolito, *Uncertain Legacies,* 208.
[80] Eisenhower, *Public Papers of the Presidents of the United States: Dwight D. Eisenhower, 1954,* 63–65.

benefits – medical care, education, non–service-connected pensions, insurance and burial benefits – accounted for nearly one-third of social welfare spending in 1960. Public assistance, food, and housing programs, by comparison, had much narrower bipartisan support, and public assistance program extensions during the 1950s were piecemeal and limited. Aid to the permanently and totally disabled was authorized in 1950, and federal support for rehabilitative services for public assistance beneficiaries was enacted in 1956. Federal reimbursement formulas for public assistance programs were made slightly more generous, and eligibility criteria were loosened, but only to a minor degree.

The most divisive social welfare issue of the late 1950s involved healthcare for the aged. Neither the Roosevelt nor Truman administrations had succeeded in adding a healthcare component to the Social Security system, and the Eisenhower administration, along with most congressional Republicans, strongly opposed extending social insurance to healthcare. In 1960, Congress approved federal matching grants to the states to subsidize healthcare expenses for the "medically needy" aged, and it also increased federal support for the existing program covering the indigent elderly. Universal Social Security–linked medical coverage for the elderly, however, was blocked by conservatives in both parties.

The New Deal model of social welfare coverage for the poor had given the states considerable leeway with respect to eligibility and benefits, and administration of public assistance programs was also reserved to the states. As a result, the types and amounts of benefits were more generous in some states than in others, but Congress was not prepared to eliminate these disparities through tighter federal control or to increase maximum federal grants significantly. The Eisenhower administration also wanted to limit and, in some cases, reduce the federal government's responsibility for the poor, so the public assistance share of social welfare spending remained quite low.

The New Deal had initiated numerous grant programs to the states for physical capital projects and had directly funded water and power projects that served multistate areas. There was typically strong bipartisan support for this type of spending, and its budget share remained fairly stable during the 1950s. The Eisenhower administration's attempts to cut back on large, multipurpose water projects were largely rebuffed by Congress, particularly after 1955. When Eisenhower left office, federal spending for these types of programs was roughly comparable to the levels under Truman.

The Federal-Aid Highway Act of 1944 had endorsed a national interstate highway system, but it took more than a decade to resolve funding issues. In this case, the Eisenhower administration took the lead, formally proposing a $50 billion program in 1954. Two years later, the Highway Act of 1956 authorized a multiyear program, at a projected federal cost of $26 billion, financed through earmarked taxes in a highway trust fund. The highway trust fund could not operate at a deficit, so future increases in fuel taxes and user fees were mandatory when costs exceeded projections, as they inevitably did.

Once the interstate and defense highway system was under way, however, the generous 90–10 federal matching ratio and the automatic distribution of benefits to all states reinforced congressional support for what was at the time the largest federal transportation program in the nation's history.

The several components of federal domestic policy had different spending trajectories during the 1950s. The increase in real dollar spending for social welfare entitlements from 1950 to 1960 was approximately 40 percent, with Social Security accounting for most of this increase. Grants to state and local governments for public assistance programs accounted for about 10 percent of payments for individual outlays in 1960, which was roughly the same share as in 1950. Grants to the states for transportation and other physical resource programs nearly tripled in terms of real spending between 1950 and 1960, but this spending accounted for less than 5 percent of the total budget in 1960. Real spending for other domestic programs actually fell by nearly 15 percent during this period.

Within this last category, which was controlled by the annual appropriations process, spending levels fluctuated from year to year, depending on administration and congressional pressures for economy in expenditures. While most programs received increases over prior-year funding, there were occasional appropriations reductions in some spending categories.[81] The budgetary process for the overwhelming number of domestic programs was, in Wildavsky's classic formulation, incremental: "The largest determining factor of the size and content of this year's budget is last year's budget. Most of the budget is a product of previous decisions."[82] It was also heavily influenced by general expectations about "the base" for a department – programs that "will be carried on at close to the going level of expenditures" and "fair share" – the apportionment of funding among a department's agencies and programs.[83]

In this budgetary environment, partisan conflict on the House and Senate Appropriations committees, and the subcommittees that handled the annual appropriations bills, was constrained. The federal government's "core" domestic responsibilities were generally accepted, and of equal importance, spending for these responsibilities was kept at levels that did not unduly strain bipartisan support. In effect, domestic spending–GDP that stayed at approximately 3 percent – and social welfare spending that remained at about 5 percent – did not fuel intense partisan debates about the size and role of government during the late 1950s. Those debates had occurred in the 1930s and 1940s, as the New Deal domestic expansion unfolded, and they would be resurrected with

---

[81] Ippolito, *Uncertain Legacies*, 204–205.
[82] Aaron Wildavsky, *The Politics of the Budgetary Process*, 4th ed. (Boston: Little, Brown, 1984), 13.
[83] Ibid., 16–17.

the ambitious domestic agenda ushered in by the Great Society. But the spending policy disputes of the Eisenhower presidency were conducted largely at the margins, not over major redefinitions of federal responsibility. The domestic spending commitments that were effectively ratified during the 1950s further buttressed the high-revenue system of the Eisenhower years.

3

Destabilizing Tax Policy – Vietnam and the 1970s

From 1949 to 1960, there were seven balanced budgets. Over the next two decades, the budget was balanced only once – in FY 1969 – and the relative size of deficits increased. In the late 1970s, deficits reached nearly 3 percent of GDP, just slightly below the average level for the 1930s. The gap between revenues and spending was amplified by the economic turmoil of the 1970s, but it was rooted in the expansion of domestic spending that began in the Kennedy and Johnson administrations and became even more pronounced in the 1970s.

By 1980, the defense share of the budget had dropped to less than 25 percent, yet total spending–GDP was at its highest level since World War II. As Democrats cut defense budgets and increased social welfare entitlements and discretionary domestic programs, partisan differences over spending policy became much greater, and the tax policy needed to support that spending became more politicized. As more revenue was directed toward the emerging welfare state, support for tax increases among Republicans and conservative Democrats evaporated.

The politics of tax policy over this period was complicated further by rising tax burdens for individuals. Despite a series of tax cuts, inflation-induced "bracket creep" forced many taxpayers into higher tax brackets; thus, taxes grew more rapidly than personal income. Social insurance taxes grew even faster, further undercutting the progressivity of the tax system. Finally, the size and number of tax preferences proliferated, as Congress was buffeted by mounting pressures for tax relief.

Adding to these policy disconnects, the institutional restraints that had stabilized budget policy in the late 1940s and 1950s became less effective. The growing acceptance of tax policy as a tool to regulate the economy encouraged President John F. Kennedy to promote an ambitious vision of presidential fiscal policy leadership. At one point, Kennedy proposed that Congress grant the president standby authority to adjust taxes in order to ensure timely action on fiscal policy changes. By the end of the Johnson presidency, that vision had disappeared. Congress took eighteen months to pass Johnson's wartime tax increase and repeatedly seized the initiative on tax policy during the 1970s. Presidential leadership on spending policy was likewise diminished by congressional budget process reforms that weakened those committees that had served as "guardians of the Treasury." In addition, both the president and Congress had to deal with a budget that was increasingly "uncontrollable" because of the growing share absorbed by mandatory spending for social welfare entitlements. With mounting dissensus over the size and priorities of government, repeated congressional challenges to presidential leadership, and diminished budget flexibility, the tax side of the budget was detached from balanced-budget principles.

The Kennedy Fiscal Program

The Kennedy administration's original tax program was conventional. In a special message to Congress on April 20, 1961, President Kennedy acknowledged the need for comprehensive tax reform but called for immediate action on limited proposals that were carryovers from the Eisenhower administration. Kennedy emphasized that "no net loss of revenue" was contemplated from the various policy and administrative changes being recommended.[1]

The 1961–1962 Agenda

The annual ritual of extending corporate income and excise tax rates continued in 1961. The most recent extension had continued these rates through June 30, 1961, and Kennedy declared that "our present revenue requirements make [another] such extension absolutely necessary again this year."[2] The House Ways and Means Committee reported out a one-year extension on June 5. The only serious challenge came from House Republicans who attempted, without success, to repeal the excise tax on passenger transportation. A similar effort was blocked by the Senate Finance Committee, and the Tax Rate Extension Act of 1961 was passed on June 22.

The other major tax initiative proposed by the administration was a tax credit for new business investment. Eisenhower's final budget message had endorsed "a better system of capital recovery allowances" to "foster long-term economic growth" and "strengthen the competitive position of American producers."[3] Kennedy called for an investment tax credit of 15 percent for "new plant and equipment investment expenditures in excess of current

[1] John F. Kennedy, *Public Papers of the Presidents of the United States: John F. Kennedy, 1961* (Washington, D.C.: Government Printing Office, 1962), 290.

[2] Ibid., 302.

[3] Congressional Quarterly, *Congress and the Nation, 1945–1964* (Washington, D.C.: Congressional Quarterly, 1965), 427.

depreciation allowances" and a lesser credit for expenditures below that level.[4] To offset the expected revenue loss, the administration recommended repeal of the controversial dividend credit and exclusion that had been enacted in 1954, limited deductibility for certain business expenses, and administrative reforms to boost revenue collections. The most important of these administrative reforms was a proposed withholding tax of 20 percent on corporate dividends and taxable interest received by individuals.

The administration's investment tax credit proposal did not make it to the House floor in 1961. The Ways and Means Committee reported out a more restrictive credit and a correspondingly narrower set of tax preference revisions on March 22, 1962, which the House passed by a largely party-line vote on March 29. Senate revisions in the House-passed bill were extensive, and many of these were incorporated into the conference measure that finally passed on October 16. The Revenue Act of 1962 included a 7 percent credit for certain types of business investment but limited the total credit that could be taken in a given year. Most of the "reforms" the administration had recommended were similarly scaled back by Congress. Required withholding of dividend and interest income was replaced with new reporting requirements for corporations and financial institutions, business expense deductibility was tightened only modestly, and foreign income tax rules for corporations continued to allow substantial leeway for tax deferral strategies. The dividend credit and exclusion for individuals survived intact.

The administration was able, on its own initiative, to resolve some long-standing complaints about depreciation schedules that had delayed congressional action on the investment tax credit. The Treasury Department issued a revised schedule, Revenue Procedure 62–21, that reduced the average depreciation period for manufacturing investments from nineteen years to twelve years and consolidated the depreciation rules for different types of assets.[5] These changes, which became effective in July 1962, were the first major revisions in equipment and machinery depreciation rules since 1942.

On June 27, 1962, Congress approved another extension of corporate income and excise tax rates. The Tax Rate Extension Act of 1962 continued the normal corporate income tax rate through June 30, 1963. Most excise tax rates were extended for the same period, but on this occasion, a number of passenger transportation taxes were repealed or reduced. The tax policy debate, however, was about to shift to a broader and more ambitious framework. The recovery from the 1960–1961 recession had stalled in mid-1962, prompting the administration to call for comprehensive tax reform that would promote sustained economic growth. In a speech to the Economic Club of New York on December 14, 1962, Kennedy had challenged the prevailing view about tax rates, tax revenues, and deficits. He advanced the "paradoxical truth that tax

---

[4] Kennedy, *Public Papers of the Presidents of the United States: John F. Kennedy, 1961*, 292.
[5] Congressional Quarterly, *Congress and the Nation, 1945–1964*, 432.

rates are too high today and tax revenues are too low and the soundest way to raise the revenues in the long run is to cut the rates now."[6] Kennedy stated that temporary deficits should not stand in the way of "a tax cut designed to boost the economy, increase tax revenues, and achieve . . . a budget surplus."[7]

The Revenue Act of 1964

Kennedy's budget message to Congress one month later was a sharp departure from the revenue philosophies of Truman and Eisenhower. For Kennedy, the choice was "not between a tax cut and a balanced budget."[8] Instead, it was a choice between "chronic deficits arising out of a slow rate of economic growth, and temporary deficits stemming from a tax program designed to promote fuller use of our resources and more rapid economic growth." The individual and corporate tax cuts being recommended to Congress, he asserted, were "sound fiscal policy" that would lead to "sharply increased budget revenues in future years."

With projected budget deficits for fiscal years 1963 and 1964 totaling nearly $20 billion, Kennedy's new tax program was attacked by congressional Republicans who repeatedly tried to make tax reduction contingent on spending cuts. There was also considerable dissatisfaction among liberal Democrats in Congress with Kennedy's emphasis on growth rather than equity as the administration made its case for across-the-board cuts in individual income tax rates. This opposition managed to delay, but not derail, congressional approval of the largest tax cut since World War II.

Rates and Reform The administration's January 24, 1963, Special Message to the Congress on Tax Reduction and Reform called for individual and corporate income tax rate reductions totaling $13.6 billion and tax preference reforms raising revenues by $3.4 billion.[9] The bulk of the income tax reduction ($11.2 billion) was reserved for individuals, with the first bracket rate cut from 21 percent to 14 percent and the top marginal rate lowered from 91 percent to 65 percent. For corporations, the maximum marginal rate reduction from 52 percent to 47 percent was complemented by income bracket adjustments designed to provide small businesses with a proportionally larger reduction. Both the individual and corporate cuts were to be phased in, becoming fully effective in the 1965 tax year.

The structural policy reforms in the administration's proposal addressed some equity concerns. A minimum standard deduction of $300 for couples, liberalized childcare deductions, and $300 tax credits for the elderly were

---

[6] John F. Kennedy, *Public Papers of the Presidents of the United States: John F. Kennedy, 1962* (Washington, D.C.: Government Printing Office, 1963), 879.

[7] Ibid., 880.

[8] John F. Kennedy, *Public Papers of the Presidents of the United States: John F. Kennedy, 1963* (Washington, D.C.: Government Printing Office, 1964), 29.

[9] Ibid., 75.

designed to provide additional tax relief for low-income individuals and families. The proposed limits on itemized deductions, repeal of the dividend credit and exclusion, and revisions in capital gains taxation were intended to improve equity by broadening the tax base for upper-income taxpayers. In order to highlight the equity trade-offs between lower rates and a broader base, the administration specified that failure to repeal the dividend credit and exclusion should be offset with lesser marginal rate reductions for middle- and upper-income taxpayers.

The House Ways and Means Committee opened hearings on the Kennedy tax program on February 6 and reported out a committee bill on September 10. The individual income tax rate reductions that the Ways and Means Committee approved were slightly less than the administration had recommended for all but the lowest taxable income bracket, with the top marginal rate set at 70 percent. The corporate income tax reduction was also slightly smaller. The more significant changes involved the tax preference reforms the administration had proposed, most of which were not included in the committee bill. According to John F. Witte's tally, "Of the nineteen administration proposals that would have increased taxes, only four were passed; of twenty-seven revenue-losing proposals, sixteen and a half were enacted."[10]

The basic issue that divided the Ways and Means Committee was the deficit effect of a large tax cut, regardless of how it was configured. The committee narrowly defeated Republican amendments that would have made the full implementation of the proposed tax cuts contingent on reductions in federal spending. During floor consideration of the Ways and Means bill, the House rejected, by a 199–226 vote, a Republican recommittal motion that would have imposed specific spending limits for fiscal years 1964 and 1965 as preconditions for the scheduled tax cuts.

The Senate Finance Committee began its consideration of the House-passed bill in mid-October and continued its work when the second session of the 88th Congress reconvened in January. After the assassination of President Kennedy on November 22, Lyndon B. Johnson made tax cuts a legislative priority, and the budget he submitted to Congress two months later contained spending cuts that eased congressional concerns about deficits. The Finance Committee bill, which essentially followed the measure passed by the House, was reported out on January 23. An extended debate on the Senate floor resulted in few substantive changes, with final approval of the bill by a 77–21 vote on February 7. The House-Senate conference was quickly concluded, and both chambers cleared the conference report by large margins later in the month.

The Revenue Act of 1964 reduced total tax liabilities for individuals by almost 20 percent.[11] The distribution of this tax reduction was progressive, ranging from 39 percent for taxpayers with adjusted gross incomes of less than

---

[10] John F. Witte, *The Politics and Development of the Federal Income Tax* (Madison: University of Wisconsin Press, 1985), 160.
[11] Congressional Quarterly, *Congress and the Nation, 1945–1964*, 438.

$3,000 to 13.2 percent for taxpayers with more than $50,000. For taxpayers in the lower income categories, rate reductions and new tax preferences, such as the minimum standard deduction, worked in tandem to reduce tax liabilities. For middle-income taxpayers, structural reforms offset a small portion of the reduced tax liability from lower marginal rates. The offset for high-income taxpayers was considerably larger. Nevertheless, upper-income taxpayers received a significant net reduction in their tax liability. The approximately 200,000 taxpayers with incomes of more than $50,000 had a $550 million share of the total tax cut under the 1964 act, compared to $565 million for the 9.7 million taxpayers with less than $3,000. This distribution of tax relief, however, was a secondary concern. The overarching goal was economic growth.

Budgetary Impact The Kennedy-Johnson tax cut had an immediate impact on economic growth, employment, and investment, and its deficit effects were less than expected, at least in the short term. Real GDP growth from 1964 to 1966 averaged more than 6 percent annually, nearly 50 percent higher than from 1960 to 1963.[12] By 1967, however, real growth dropped to 2.5 percent, roughly comparable to the levels at the end of Eisenhower's tenure. There is, as might be expected, disagreement about the relative contributions of tax policy, monetary policy, and other economic variables in generating the strong economic growth of the mid-1960s.[13] The same controversy, indeed a more heated one, would surround the 1981 Reagan tax cut, which posited an even stronger connection between low tax rates and economic growth. At the time, however, the tax-cut experiment was generally considered a success, particularly because the budgetary effects appeared to be benign. Deficits for fiscal years 1964 and 1965 totaled $7.3 billion, which was significantly less than initial projections. The fiscal 1965 deficit was 0.2 percent of GDP, the smallest in five years, and President Johnson's FY 1966 budget promised "continued progress toward a balanced budget."[14] Instead, the deficit increased in 1966 and grew to more than $25 billion in 1968.

The pivotal year in terms of the deficit was 1965. Individual income tax–GDP levels fell by nearly two percentage points as the 1965 tax cut became fully effective, while other revenues remained fairly stable. The sharp drop in the 1965 deficit was largely attributable to the spending cuts that Johnson had offered up in response to congressional fears that tax cuts would lead to unacceptably high deficits. Section 1 of the 1964 Revenue Act had incorporated "sense of Congress" language from the Ways and Means Committee that urged continuing efforts to hold down spending in order to control deficits.[15] The

---

[12] Harold W. Stanley and Richard G. Niemi, *Vital Statistics on American Politics, 2005–2006* (Washington, D.C.: CQ Press, 2006), 392.
[13] Herbert Stein, *Presidential Economics* (New York: Simon & Schuster, 1984), 101–113.
[14] Lyndon B. Johnson, *Public Papers of the Presidents of the United States: Lyndon B. Johnson, 1965* (Washington, D.C.: Government Printing Office, 1966), 84.
[15] Congressional Quarterly, *Congress and the Nation, 1945–1964,* 436.

problem was that Johnson's cuts in discretionary spending were entirely in defense, and these cuts could not be sustained once the Vietnam War began. In addition, Johnson was hoping to increase the budget share for domestic programs, and he was not willing to sacrifice that goal even as wartime spending rose.

This rebalancing of defense and domestic priorities had begun under Kennedy, who had pledged to remedy alleged inadequacies in the Eisenhower administration's defense program. Defense spending was raised in Kennedy's first year, but there was no real growth in defense spending from 1962 to 1964, and both the budget and GDP shares for defense fell well below the levels under Eisenhower. Nevertheless, in January 1964, Johnson informed Congress that the defense "buildup" could be halted, because the United States had built "the most formidable defense establishment the world has ever known."[16] The administration's FY 1965 budget called for a $3 billion reduction from FY 1962 levels in new obligational authority for strategic forces and did not include increases for the conventional or mobility forces that previous budgets had prominently featured.

Under Kennedy and Johnson, real spending for domestic discretionary programs rose by approximately $33 billion from 1962 to 1965, while defense fell by $23 billion. Both the budget and GDP shares for domestic programs grew, as the defense shares declined. With the launch of the Great Society under Johnson, even larger defense transfers were needed to keep spending and revenues reasonably close to balance, but the costs of the Vietnam War soon made these infeasible. Instead, total spending began to rise, as did deficits.

Johnson's Vietnam Transition

The military buildup in Vietnam did not begin in earnest until the summer of 1965 and had almost no impact on the FY 1965 budget. Defense outlays fell by more than $4 billion from 1964 to 1965, while nondefense spending rose by approximately the same amount, and total spending was essentially unchanged. The following year, however, spending surged in both categories, spending-GDP levels began to move sharply upward, and revenue growth could not keep pace. In FY 1968, with spending at 20.5 percent of GDP, the budget deficit was more than $25 billion – the largest since World War II.

Budget policy during Vietnam was very different from the Korean War model. On the revenue side, the Johnson administration did not propose a major tax increase until 1967, and Congress did not approve the administration's tax surcharge until mid-1968. On the spending side, the Johnson administration pursued its Great Society agenda as the Vietnam commitment escalated, and domestic spending climbed along with the defense budget. The

[16] Lyndon B. Johnson, *Public Papers of the Presidents of the United States: Lyndon B. Johnson, 1963–1964, Book I* (Washington, D.C.: Government Printing Office, 1965), 176.

long delay in enacting the tax surcharge contained in the Revenue and Expenditure Control Act of 1968 was, in fact, caused by disputes over domestic spending. The House Ways and Means Committee, under the leadership of Wilbur D. Mills, pushed aggressively for domestic spending cuts as a precondition for any tax increase. This effort succeeded but was more limited and less lasting than fiscal conservatives believed at the time. Over the next decade, as the trajectory for domestic spending moved inexorably higher, the disconnect with tax policy widened.

Wartime Taxation

Lyndon Johnson did not vacillate on a wartime tax increase. He strongly resisted it, even as his economic advisers became alarmed about the inflationary effects of wartime deficits. Congress had approved the Gulf of Tonkin Resolution by overwhelming margins on August 7, 1964, granting the administration broad authority to move from an advisory and supportive role to active participation in the decade-long conflict between South Vietnam and North Vietnam. By the end of 1964, there were more than 23,000 U.S. troops in Vietnam, but the scale of the eventual U.S. commitment remained unclear, at least outside the administration. Thus, the first post–Gulf of Tonkin tax bill was a tax cut.

Excise Taxes As the second stage of the 1964 individual income tax cuts went into effect in January 1965, the Johnson administration called for reducing the "emergency" federal excise taxes that had been levied during World War II and Korea. These had been repeatedly extended, and Congress had left the excise tax system in place when the Revenue Act of 1964 was taking shape. Johnson's proposed excise tax reductions were submitted to Congress on May 17, and economic growth was again at the forefront. With the "success of the 1964 tax cut," Johnson declared, "We must continually adjust our tax system to assure that it makes a maximum contribution to our economic growth."[17] The proposed excise tax reduction, to be phased in over four years, totaled nearly $4 billion, but with other revenues running well ahead of earlier projections, Johnson did not foresee any increase in deficits.

Congress acted quickly on an even larger $4.7 billion tax cut. The Excise Tax Reduction Act of 1965 reduced manufacturers' and retailers' excise taxes on more than two dozen items ranging from automobiles to home appliances to sporting goods and equipment. Excise taxes on liquor and tobacco, however, were renewed permanently. The automobile excise tax reduction that Congress approved was more costly than the administration's proposal, and Congress likewise rejected the offsetting "user charges," primarily on ground and air transportation, that had been recommended. Congress agreed, however, to phase in the cuts over several years, which made possible a delay in scheduled reductions as the deficit situation worsened.

[17] Johnson, *Public Papers of the Presidents of the United States: Lyndon B. Johnson, 1965*, 540.

The 1966 Tax Bills In his excise tax message to Congress in May 1965, Johnson had sidestepped the Vietnam issue. Acknowledging that it was "impossible to predict precisely what [defense] expenditures" might be in the future, Johnson saw "no present indication that expenditures will increase to an extent that would make these excise tax reductions inadvisable."[18] By the end of 1965, there were more than 184,000 troops in Vietnam, but the costs of the war were still being downplayed.

During 1965, the administration requested two supplemental appropriations for Vietnam, but these totaled less than $2.5 billion, and several senior Republicans on the House Defense Appropriations Subcommittee complained that the requested Vietnam funding was patently inadequate.[19] Republican complaints that the "phony budget" was simply a ruse to protect the administration's domestic program made little headway in a Congress with overwhelming Democratic majorities. In January 1966, however, the administration began to adjust course, requesting a $12.8 billion Vietnam supplemental for the current budget year and an additional $9.1 billion for the "special costs of Vietnam" in 1967.[20] It also called on Congress to approve "desirable reforms in tax collection procedures, having the effect of increasing revenues in the current and coming year" and to defer "certain scheduled excise tax reductions."[21]

The Tax Adjustment Act of 1966, enacted in March, established graduated withholding rates of 14 percent to 30 percent for individuals and required corporations with tax liabilities of more than $100,000 to pay these taxes during the calendar year when income was earned. The accelerated corporate tax payments were expected to raise $4.2 billion in the FY 1967 budget cycle.[22] An additional $1.3 billion, over two years, was estimated from suspending the automobile and telephone excise tax reductions scheduled to take effect in 1966.

In September, as deficit projections worsened and inflationary pressures mounted, the administration called for suspending the investment tax credit approved in 1962 and the accelerated depreciation schedule for buildings that had been in effect since 1954. The investment tax credit was repealed for fifteen months, through December 31, 1967. The credit was expanded for future years, however, and the carryover period for unused balances was extended as well. The accelerated depreciation schedules for industrial and commercial buildings were suspended for the same period.

---

[18] Ibid., 542.
[19] Congressional Quarterly, *Congress and the Nation, 1965–1968* (Washington, D.C.: Congressional Quarterly, 1969), 835.
[20] Lyndon B. Johnson, *Public Papers of the Presidents of the United States: Lyndon B. Johnson, 1966, Book I* (Washington, D.C.: Government Printing Office, 1967), 54.
[21] Ibid., 52.
[22] Congressional Quarterly, *Congress and the Nation, 1965–1968*, 153.

The final tax bill of 1966, widely derided as the "Christmas Tree Bill," was passed in December. This legislation had originated nearly two years earlier, with an administration proposal to encourage foreign investment in U.S. equity and bond markets to narrow the balance-of-payments deficit. The Foreign Investors Tax Act of 1966 reduced tax rates on dividend income, liberalized capital gains tax rules for nonresident foreigners, and also suspended income taxes on bank deposits in the United States through 1972. Other provisions, most of which were added by the Senate, included a new exclusion for self-employed individual retirement contributions, a special investment tax credit for machinery purchased for use in U.S. territories, more generous depletion allowances for mineral ore companies, a temporary suspension of capital gains taxes on "swap funds," and an excise tax cut for hearse manufacturers. A controversial rider attached to the bill, a Presidential Election Campaign Fund financed by voluntary contributions from taxpayers, was repealed the following year.

Missing from the congressional tax agenda in 1966, however, was any increase in individual or corporate tax rates. The administration did not recommend raising tax rates, and congressional Democrats were anxious to avoid the issue in an election year. In any case, Democrats lost forty-seven House seats and four Senate seats in the 1966 midterm election. While Democratic majorities in both chambers were retained, the liberal tilt of the 89th Congress had been moderated. As the deficit outlook worsened, the contest between the administration and the 90th Congress over tax increases and domestic spending cuts began in earnest.

The Revenue and Expenditure Control Act of 1968 In January 1967, President Johnson's budget message to Congress called for a limited tax increase. In recommending "a temporary 6% surcharge on both corporate and individual income taxes," Johnson warned against "a larger tax increase" or "large slashes in military or civilian programs."[23] Johnson explained that a "more restrictive" fiscal program might "depress economic activity, reduce the incomes of individuals and corporations, and thereby fail to secure the revenues it was designed to achieve."[24] The FY 1968 budget deficit was estimated at $8.1 billion, but delays in preparing a detailed tax surcharge program and an even longer congressional delay in enacting it left short-term revenues largely unchanged. With actual spending well above estimates, the FY 1968 deficit would exceed $25 billion.

Confusion over fiscal and economic policy also led to an abrupt reversal of the investment credit and accelerated depreciation suspension enacted the previous fall. On March 9, 1967, Johnson called on Congress to terminate the suspension immediately – it had been scheduled to end on December 31,

---

[23] Lyndon B. Johnson, *Public Papers of the Presidents of the United States: Lyndon B. Johnson, 1967, Book I* (Washington, D.C.: Government Printing Office 1968), 41–42.
[24] Ibid., 42.

1967 – because inflationary pressures on the costs of capital goods apparently had eased, as had "tight money and credit conditions."[25] Congress complied, although final agreement was not reached until late May because of a protracted Senate debate over repeal of the 1966 Presidential Election Campaign Fund Act.

Then, on August 3, Johnson presented Congress with a revised FY 1968 budget deficit estimate of $23.6 billion and called for a three-part tax program to combat "a spiral of ruinous inflation."[26] Accelerated corporate tax payment schedules would raise $800 million in FY 1968 revenues and slightly higher amounts in future years, while postponing scheduled excise tax reductions on automobiles and telephone service for two years was projected to raise $2.3 billion. Johnson's most important proposal was a "temporary surcharge" of 10 percent on corporate and individual income tax liabilities. This surcharge was higher than the administration had recommended in January, and its projected yield was "$6.3 billion in revenues for Fiscal 1968, and somewhat more in Fiscal 1969."[27]

The surcharge proposal triggered a prolonged confrontation with Congress over spending cuts. The chief congressional protagonist in this drama was Wilbur Mills, who had served as chairman of the House Ways and Means Committee since 1958 and had expressed strong reservations about Johnson's economic and fiscal policies. Mills was convinced that the administration's tax surcharge would aggravate rather than moderate inflationary pressures, and he was adamant about choosing between "guns or butter." Johnson had managed to avoid that choice as he steered the Vietnam War and Great Society along parallel tracks, and he finally concluded that a tax increase would protect the domestic expansion that he had worked so hard to achieve.

The debate over inflation was prominently featured in the extensive hearings conducted by Ways and Means in the fall of 1967. According to administration witnesses, "demand-pull" inflation was threatening the economy.[28] However, for Mills, the economic indicators pointed to "cost-push" inflation, with high labor costs leading to higher prices, and higher prices, in turn, leading consumers to press for higher wages that would further inflate labor costs. Mills argued that a reduction in government spending would curb demand without directly cutting personal and corporate incomes and bringing these cost-push factors into play. This inflation argument was no doubt important, but the fight over taxes and spending involved serious disagreements over long-term budget policy. As Zelizer has pointed out, "Mills was disturbed by his insight that the surcharge would not be temporary . . . Congress would use the additional

[25] Ibid., 302–303.
[26] Lyndon B. Johnson, *Public Papers of the Presidents of the United States: Lyndon B. Johnson, 1967, Book II* (Washington, D.C.: Government Printing Office 1968), 733.
[27] Ibid., 737.
[28] Congressional Quarterly, *Congress and the Nation, 1965–1968,* 158; Julian E. Zelizer, *Taxing America: Wilbur D. Mills, Congress, and the State, 1945–1975* (New York: Cambridge University Press, 1998), 268–269.

tax revenue as an excuse to finance domestic programs once the conflict in Vietnam subsided."[29] Bringing the budget into balance – or at least reducing deficits – through spending cuts would eliminate this margin and force future Congresses to raise taxes in order to finance new spending.

With strong bipartisan backing in his committee, Mills refused to consider the tax surcharge until the administration presented a credible plan for reducing current and future domestic spending. On October 3, the committee voted 20–5 to postpone action until the administration submitted such a plan. When the administration finally complied in late November, Mills rejected its proposed $4 billion expenditure reduction and demanded larger cuts to counter cost-push inflation. At that point, the Ways and Means Committee and the administration had reached an impasse that was not broken until the following spring. The committee did, however, report out an excise tax rate extension that passed the House on February 29, 1968, and allowed the Senate finally to weigh in on the tax surcharge issue. The Senate Finance Committee rejected attempts to add a tax surcharge amendment to the House-passed excise tax bill, but a combined tax surcharge and spending reduction was approved by a 53–35 margin during floor consideration. The key element in this compromise was a Republican-sponsored expenditure ceiling $6 billion below the administration's budget request and a limitation on federal civilian employment. The final version of the tax surcharge–spending limit bill passed the Senate on April 2.

House-Senate conference action was delayed for more than two months, while the administration and House Appropriations Committee worked on a detailed spending plan that would allow the conferees to proceed. Johnson, who had announced on March 31 that he would not seek reelection, continued to attack Mills and others who were blocking action on the tax increase. In a nationally televised news conference on May 3, Johnson declared that Congress was "courting danger by this continued procrastination," and he denounced those trying to "blackmail someone into getting your own personal viewpoint over on reductions."[30] Johnson reluctantly agreed to accept a $4 billion spending reduction for FY 1969 but continued to fight the $6 billion cut.

On May 6, Ways and Means conferees agreed to support an income tax surcharge and the spending-reduction plan approved by the House Appropriations Committee. The $6 billion FY 1969 appropriations cut and related spending provisions were then accepted by the conference committee on May 8. A final effort by administration supporters to limit the reduction to $4 billion was rejected on May 29, and the conference report was cleared by Congress on June 21.

[29] Zelizer, *Taxing America*, 263.
[30] Congressional Quarterly, *Congress and the Nation, 1965–1968*, 171–172.

The Revenue and Expenditure Control Act of 1968 included the excise tax increases and accelerated corporate tax payments that had been originally proposed. The 10 percent surcharge for individuals and corporations, with an exemption for low-income taxpayers, was levied but only for a limited period – January 1, 1968, through July 1, 1969, for corporations and April 1, 1968, through July 1, 1969, for individuals. Spending provisions included a $180.1 billion FY 1969 spending ceiling – $6 billion below the president's budget – a ceiling on new budget authority to be enacted in FY 1969, and a requirement for future rescissions of $8 billion in unspent budget authority. A federal employment ceiling was also enacted, with restrictions on future hiring of civilian employees.

The 1968 tax bill produced an immediate surge in individual and corporate income tax payments. Revenues-GDP for FY 1969 reached 19.7 percent – the highest level since Korea. The accompanying spending reductions failed to keep total outlays within the official ceiling but still lowered the rate of spending growth. As a result, the FY 1969 budget registered a $3.2 billion surplus – the first surplus since 1960 but, perhaps more telling, the last until 1997. The issue of domestic spending growth, which had delayed enactment of a tax increase for almost a year, had not been resolved. At the time, some liberals complained that the Great Society had been "gutted" by the 1968 spending cuts. In fact, it had been temporarily interrupted, because the domestic spending agenda that Johnson had put in place would prove to have enormous momentum.

Wartime Spending: Domestic versus Defense

The budget that Lyndon Johnson sent to Congress at the beginning of 1965 stressed that the "opportunities of the Great Society" should not be sacrificed because of Vietnam, but Johnson claimed that these "opportunities" would not have a major impact on spending. Instead, he informed Congress "that Government expenditures in the years ahead will grow more slowly than the gross national product, so that the ratio of Federal spending to our total output will continue to decline."[31] That decline did not occur, and the problem was not just Vietnam. During FY 1966, outlays increased by almost 14 percent, and spending-GDP rose accordingly. Of the $16.3 billion increase over FY 1965, about half was for defense; social welfare and other domestic spending programs accounted for the remainder. This rough balance between defense and domestic spending increases continued over the next several years, with the social welfare share of domestic spending expanding steadily.

Discretionary Domestic Programs An important turning point with respect to discretionary domestic spending was Johnson's abandonment of a federal revenue-sharing scheme in 1964. Instead, Johnson decided to expand and diversify categorical aid programs for states and cities. The Urban Mass Transportation Act of 1964 authorized federal grants and loans for mass transit

---

[31] Johnson, *Public Papers of the Presidents of the United States: Lyndon B. Johnson, 1965*, 84.

systems, and the Department of Transportation was established two years later to develop and coordinate a national transportation policy. Environmental initiatives included the Water Quality Act of 1965, the Clean Water Restoration Act of 1966, and the Air Quality Act of 1967, all of which authorized federal grants to the states for pollution control and abatement. The Appalachian Regional Development Act of 1965 and the Public Works and Development Act of 1965 provided federal grants to local governments and state agencies. With the establishment of the Department of Housing and Urban Development in 1965, the urban planning, model cities, and housing initiatives of the Great Society expanded federal support to cities.

Many of these Great Society grant programs were controversial, and appropriations for many of them lagged substantially behind their authorizations. In addition, older and more established programs continued to find broad support in Congress and to receive more generous funding. Despite the administration's plans for a national transportation policy, for example, the interstate highway program continued to absorb most of the transportation budget. Transportation funding, in turn, accounted for well over half of all physical resource spending from 1965 to 1969.[32] Despite the notoriety attached to many programs, community and regional development spending totaled less than $6.3 billion over this period, compared to more than $30 billion for transportation. As a percentage of GDP, moreover, physical resource outlays were 1.5 percent in 1960 and 1.5 percent a decade later.

Funding for education and employment programs, however, increased significantly under Johnson. Under the Elementary and Secondary Education Act of 1965, for example, federal outlays for education increased from less than $720 million in 1965 to $2.5 billion in 1969.[33] Spending for training and employment programs nearly tripled, reaching nearly $1.6 billion in 1969. Still, the growth in discretionary domestic outlays under Johnson was outpaced by the increase in social welfare spending. Over the next decade, however, the domestic program base that Johnson had put into place grew much more rapidly, as defense cutbacks created the budgetary margin to fund older and more established domestic programs along with the Great Society's innovations.

Social Welfare Programs Legislative additions to the federal government's social welfare responsibilities under Johnson were extensive in scope and enormously important in reshaping long-term spending policy. As with discretionary domestic programs, the full impact of the Great Society's social welfare initiatives was not immediately reflected in spending totals, in part because full implementation took some time. Still, by the end of Johnson's presidency, social welfare spending was rapidly approaching parity with defense and would eclipse it just a few years later.

[32] Office of Management and Budget, *Historical Tables, Budget of the United States Government, Fiscal Year 2011* (Washington, D.C.: Government Printing Office, 2010), 49–50.
[33] Ibid., 63.

The most important changes in social welfare spending resulted from the omnibus Social Security bills passed in 1965 and 1967. The Social Security Act Amendments of 1965 established the Medicare program, which provided medical care coverage for the aged, and the Medicaid program, which provided healthcare assistance for the poor. The Medicare program that Congress enacted was more comprehensive than the original Johnson administration proposal. It combined compulsory hospital insurance coverage (along with nursing home and diagnostic costs) financed by payroll taxes and administered under the Social Security program, and a supplementary plan covering physicians' services and other outpatient costs financed by premiums and general revenues.

The costs of the hospital insurance component, Part A, were to be covered by payroll taxes. Congress initially set the Medicare payroll tax, applied equally to employees and employers, at 0.35 percent for 1966, rising to 0.80 percent in 1987 and thereafter. As Part A costs rose more rapidly than expected, however, higher tax rates were needed. A similar problem occurred with Part B, the supplementary insurance plan, necessitating much larger contributions from general revenues.

The Medicaid program, Title XIX of the Social Security Act Amendments of 1965, replaced the limited federal-state program for the indigent aged that had been passed in 1960. Coverage was broadened to include needy persons in various public assistance programs, particularly the Aid to Families with Dependent Children (AFDC) program, with the federal share of total costs exceeding 80 percent for states with very low per capita incomes. Medicaid costs did not rise as rapidly as Medicare spending during the late 1960s, but the Medicaid program soon became a principal component of federal assistance to the poor.

The Social Security changes under Johnson included cash benefit increases of 7 percent in 1965 and 13 percent in 1967, along with less restrictive eligibility requirements and more generous coverage for disability. In order to fund the increased benefits, both the Social Security tax rate and wage base were raised immediately, and future increases were scheduled through 1987. Between 1960 and 1970, Social Security spending nearly tripled to more than $30 billion, and the Social Security–GDP level climbed to almost 3 percent. The share of federal revenues from social insurance receipts rose from 15.9 percent in 1960 to 23 percent in 1970, while the share from corporate income taxes fell by approximately the same amount. Under Johnson, social insurance taxes, primarily Social Security and Medicare, became the second-largest and fastest-growing source of federal revenues.

The Social Security legislation in 1965 increased cash assistance to the poor along with the new Medicaid benefits. The federal matching formulas for cash assistance were raised, and states were given incentives to liberalize their income-eligibility criteria in order to expand coverage. The 1967 legislation introduced work training requirements for AFDC recipients, but these restrictions did little to counter the rapidly rising caseloads and costs for public assistance programs in the late 1960s. Family support payments to the states roughly doubled during the 1960s, with more than two-thirds of this growth occurring after 1965.[34]

The Great Society's initiatives for the poor went well beyond cash assistance. The Economic Opportunity Act of 1964 authorized employment, training, and education programs administered by the Office of Economic Opportunity as the centerpiece of the administration's "war on poverty." The Food Stamp Act of 1964 created a permanent national program to provide food assistance to low-income households, while the Child Nutrition Act of 1967 established the school breakfast program for areas with large concentrations of low-income families. The Elementary and Secondary Education Act of 1965 authorized federal assistance to local school districts, again with funding disproportionately directed toward poorer districts. The Higher Education Act of 1965 authorized grants and subsidized loans for college students in financial need. Federal funding for urban improvement programs was authorized by the Demonstration Cities and Metropolitan Development Act of 1966, and new federal subsidy programs for housing assistance to the poor were incorporated into the Housing and Urban Development Act of 1968.

The philosophy of social welfare also changed during the Johnson presidency through administrative regulations and court decisions. Legal access to benefits was strengthened nationwide, and efforts were undertaken to reduce the social stigma attached to "welfare."[35] Entitlement program spending for the poor in 1960, excluding assistance to veterans, totaled less than $2.5 billion.[36] By 1970, the Medicaid program alone cost $2.7 billion; food, housing, and education assistance outlays were nearly $2 billion; and cash assistance was more than $4.1 billion.[37] Despite the disparities in congressional (and public) support for public assistance compared to Social Security, the Johnson administration was able to expand programs for the poor "to dimensions that would have been unimaginable in 1960."[38] Moreover, this expansion was accomplished during the peak years of Vietnam War funding. As shown in Table 3.1, the increase in defense outlays from 1965 to 1970 was almost exactly matched by the growth in social welfare spending. In addition, discretionary domestic spending increased steadily, with the exception of 1969 when the spending ceiling was in effect. During the Korean War, the defense budget share more than doubled, reaching nearly 70 percent in 1953. During Vietnam, the defense budget share was slightly lower than it had been prior to the war.

---

[34] Ibid., 229–233.
[35] James T. Patterson, *America's Struggle Against Poverty, 1900–1994* (Cambridge: Harvard University Press, 1994), 157–170.
[36] Office of Management and Budget, *Historical Tables, Fiscal Year 2011*, 229.
[37] Ibid., 233.
[38] Patterson, *America's Struggle Against Poverty*, 164.

TABLE 3.1. *Defense and Domestic Spending, Fiscal Years 1965–1970 (in billions of dollars)*

Fiscal Year	Defense	Domestic	
		Discretionary	Mandatory Programmatic[a]
1965	$51.0	$22.1	$31.8
1966	59.0	26.1	35.0
1967	72.0	29.1	40.7
1968	82.2	31.0	49.1
1969	82.7	30.5	53.6
1970	81.9	34.4	61.0

[a] Minus offsetting receipts.

Source: Congressional Budget Office, *The Budget and Economic Outlook: Fiscal Years 2007–2016* (Washington, D.C.: Congressional Budget Office, 2006), 146–148.

Peace Dividends and Tax Cuts: The Nixon and Ford Presidencies

The Revenue and Expenditure Control Act of 1968 attempted to coordinate tax policy and spending policy in order to control deficits. Over the next decade, that coordination largely disappeared. As domestic spending escalated, Congress refused to increase taxes, and budget deficits became a chronic and serious problem. The budget policy conflicts of the Nixon and Ford presidencies were particularly divisive, and the gap between revenues and spending was exacerbated by the economic turmoil over this period. By the end of the Carter presidency, partisan divisions over how to bring the budget into balance had hardened still further.

Defense versus Domestic Spending

For two decades after World War II, direct competition between defense and domestic programs was restrained by a bipartisan strategic consensus and congressional deference to presidential national security leadership. The Vietnam War weakened that consensus and undercut that deference. When Richard M. Nixon took office on January 20, 1969, he faced a heavily Democratic Congress with a large antidefense bloc eager to provide more generous funding for the Great Society's domestic programs. Public support for the war and for defense spending generally had greatly weakened over the course of Johnson's presidency, making the defense budget unusually vulnerable to congressional pressures for a "peace dividend" even as the war continued under Nixon.

The heightened competition between defense and domestic spending was played out in the annual appropriations process. Under Nixon and Ford, Congress routinely cut defense budget requests and repeatedly challenged executive control over defense policy. The peace dividend that Congress captured was substantial, as defense spending–GDP was cut nearly in half from 1968 to 1977. Much of the defense cutback was then transferred to discretionary domestic programs, as Congress regularly added to the funding requests from Nixon and Ford and created new domestic programs that required additional spending.

Congress's efforts to rebalance defense and domestic spending were part of a broader attempt to weaken presidential control over budget policy. In this institutional struggle, Nixon and Ford relied on spending ceilings, vetoes, and, in Nixon's case, outright refusals to spend funds appropriated by Congress. Congress finally curbed executive impoundments as part of the 1974 budget reforms that established budget committees and budget resolutions to provide congressional alternatives to the president's budget. By that point, however, Congress had already succeeded in taking control of discretionary appropriations, which still accounted for half the federal budget.

Defense and Domestic Appropriations In 1969, the debate over defense spending was overshadowed by clashes between the administration and Congress over weapons systems, including the antiballistic missile system, strategic deterrence and arms control negotiations, and reform of the selective service draft. Nixon had begun to strengthen budget controls in the Department of Defense through procurement reforms, reductions in support costs, and expanded force capabilities in anticipation of lower budgets, and his FY 1970 budget was $3 billion below Johnson's with respect to new obligational authority.[39] Congress then proceeded to cut an additional $5.9 billion, although the actual reduction in defense outlays from 1969 to 1970 was less than $1 billion.[40]

A similar pattern occurred the following year. The administration's defense budget request was below its FY 1970 recommendation, and Congress then cut appropriations by an additional $2 billion.[41] Outlays in FY 1971 were nearly $4 billion below FY 1969 spending, with disproportionately large cuts in procurement spending.[42] The administration's FY 1972 budget then called for an increase in defense spending, with an emphasis on long-term procurement programs. The same approach was taken in FY 1973. In both cases, Congress overrode Nixon's recommendations, and the cumulative effect of congressional cuts and inflation combined to drive real defense spending significantly lower. From 1969 to 1973, current dollar spending for defense fell by approximately 7 percent, while real defense spending dropped by 30 percent.[43]

As the conflict over defense spending mounted, the Nixon administration and Congress clashed over domestic appropriations. In 1970, Nixon vetoed three domestic appropriations bills and two domestic program authorizations.

---

[39] Congressional Quarterly, *Congress and the Nation, 1969–1972* (Washington, D.C.: Congressional Quarterly, 1973), 194.
[40] Office of Management and Budget, *Historical Tables, Fiscal Year 2011*, 50.
[41] Congressional Quarterly, *Congress and the Nation, 1969–1972*, 198.
[42] Office of Management and Budget, *Historical Tables, Fiscal Year 2011*, 56–57.
[43] Ibid., 127–128.

Two of the appropriations vetoes were overridden, but Congress was forced to cut the third vetoed bill to secure Nixon's signature. In 1971, three budget-related measures for domestic programs were vetoed, all of which were sustained. The 1972 congressional session produced a protracted contest over Nixon's spending ceiling, and a number of domestic authorizations and appropriations were again vetoed. The Labor–Health, Education and Welfare (HEW) appropriations bill was vetoed twice. A $24.7 billion authorization included in the Federal Water Pollution Control Act Amendments of 1972 was likewise vetoed for excessive spending, but Congress then overrode that veto. Nixon later pocket vetoed several other domestic authorizations, most notably a $3 billion authorization for public works programs.

Over his first term, Nixon frequently impounded funds that Congress had added to his domestic appropriations requests. The scale of Nixon's impoundments was unprecedented, and the preponderance of policy, as opposed to administrative, impoundments was also unusual. In 1971, for example, the administration impounded $12 billion in highway construction and urban program funding in an unsuccessful effort to replace categorical federal grants with block grants and revenue sharing.[44] The administration routinely used impoundments against congressional "overfunding" for public works programs, water and sewer grants, health research, and model cities and urban renewal grants. Great Society programs were targeted, as Nixon "relied on impoundment to move toward his own priorities."[45]

The controversy over impoundments and spending policy became even more heated after Nixon's landslide reelection in 1972. Nixon's FY 1974 budget message included a wide-ranging attack on the congressional budget process, decrying its fragmentation, complexity, and "momentum of extravagance."[46] Nixon insisted on "a rigid ceiling on spending, limiting total 1974 outlays to the $268.7 billion recommended in this budget."[47] FY 1974 spending was, in the end, only $700 million above Nixon's ceiling, but Congress continued to press for higher domestic spending. Then, as the Watergate investigations gained momentum during 1973 and Nixon's political standing eroded, the House and Senate passed bills to curb presidential impoundments. Even though the administration retreated on impoundments and spending ceilings, Congress pursued complementary budget process reforms to limit presidential influence over budget policy.

Less than a month before resigning from office, Richard Nixon signed into law the Congressional Budget and Impoundment Control Act of 1974,

---

[44] Louis Fisher, *Presidential Spending Power* (Princeton: Princeton University Press, 1975), 169–170.

[45] Ibid., 169.

[46] Richard Nixon, *Public Papers of the Presidents of the United States: Richard Nixon, 1973* (Washington, D.C.: Government Printing Office, 1975), 36.

[47] Ibid., 34.

TABLE 3.2. *Discretionary Real Spending Outlays, Fiscal Years 1969–1977 (in billions of FY 2005 dollars)*

Fiscal Year	Defense	Nondefense[a]	Total
1969	$494.1	$190.5	$684.7
1970	465.1	200.0	665.1
1971	423.6	211.0	634.6
1972	386.3	225.5	611.8
1973	348.4	233.3	581.7
1974	338.4	235.0	573.4
1975	331.0	263.4	594.4
1976	315.2	295.3	610.6
1977	312.3	315.6	627.9

[a] Approximately 10 percent of nondefense spending is for international programs.
Source: Office of Management and Budget, *Historical Tables, Budget of the United States Government, Fiscal Year 2012* (Washington, D.C.: Government Printing Office, 2011), 147.

which he deemed "the most significant reform of budget procedures since the Congress and this country began."[48] In fact, the new budget process that Nixon bequeathed to his successor simply reinforced the shift toward domestic spending priorities. Gerald Ford, like Nixon, attempted to block defense transfers to domestic programs but had even less success. Ford vetoed fourteen domestic appropriations and authorization bills for excessive spending, but Congress overrode eight of those. Discretionary domestic spending, which had increased by $18 billion from 1969 to 1973, grew by $43 billion over the next four years.[49] Ford managed to halt the decline in defense spending, but defense budget increases still lagged well behind the rate of inflation. As shown in Table 3.2, real defense spending dropped by almost 40 percent from 1969 to 1977, with the bulk of that decline during the latter stage of the Vietnam War. The nondefense real spending increase over this period was more than 65 percent, with especially steep growth after 1974. At the end of Ford's presidency, domestic discretionary spending–GDP was nearly 5 percent, considerably higher than Great Society levels and on a par with defense spending–GDP.

Domestic spending outcomes under Nixon and Ford were not entirely one-sided. Congress did approve, in 1972, the State and Local Fiscal Assistance Act that authorized federal revenue-sharing, but this was a much less ambitious program than Nixon had envisioned. In 1969, the administration had proposed a "New Federalism" program to transfer a fixed percentage of federal income tax revenues to the states with minimal restrictions on their use, except for the requirement that a portion of the funds be made available to local governments.

[48] Richard Nixon, *Public Papers of the Presidents of the United States: Richard Nixon, 1974* (Washington, D.C.: Government Printing Office, 1975), 586.
[49] Congressional Budget Office, *The Budget and Economic Outlook: Fiscal Years 2007–2016* (Washington, D.C.: Congressional Budget Office, 2006), 146.

TABLE 3.3. *Mandatory Programmatic Spending, Fiscal Years 1969–1977 (as percentage of GDP)*

Fiscal Year	Means-Tested Entitlements[a]	Social Security	Other[b]	Undistributed Offsetting Receipts	Total
1969	0.9%	2.8%	2.8%	−0.8%	5.7%
1970	1.0	2.9	3.0	−0.9	6.0
1971	1.2	3.3	3.2	−0.9	6.7
1972	1.4	3.3	3.4	−0.8	7.4
1973	1.3	3.7	3.6	−1.0	7.5
1974	1.4	3.8	3.6	−1.2	7.6
1975	1.6	4.1	4.8	−0.9	9.7
1976	1.8	4.2	4.7	−0.8	9.8
1977	1.7	4.2	4.2	−0.8	9.2

[a] Includes Medicaid, food stamps and nutrition programs, AFDC, SSI, veterans' pensions, education, and housing assistance.

[b] Includes deposit insurance (negative outlays).

Source: Office of Management and Budget, *Historical Tables, Budget of the United States Government, Fiscal Year 2012* (Washington, D.C.: Government Printing Office, 2011), 151.

Nixon's intent was to reallocate power and responsibility to the states by reversing "nearly 40 years of moving power from the states to Washington."[50]

The program that Congress authorized was a $30 billion multiyear appropriation that included a different revenue-sharing formula. More important, congressional revenue-sharing was a supplement to, rather than a replacement for, the numerous categorical grants-in-aid that had been established under the Great Society. Nixon and Ford also attempted, with limited success, to substitute block grants for categorical aid programs. The Comprehensive Employment and Training Act of 1973 consolidated various job training and placement categorical assistance programs into a block grant. The Housing and Community Development Act of 1974 did the same for a number of urban categorical aid programs, such as model cities and urban renewal. Most block grant initiatives, however, were not approved by Congress, and those that were approved generally increased federal funding while loosening restrictions on how these funds were used. The transfer of funds, power, and responsibility away from Washington that Nixon and Ford advocated so strongly found little support in the Democratic Congresses they faced.

Social Welfare Spending While the appropriations struggles during the Nixon-Ford era produced reasonably clear outcomes, the trends in social welfare policy were more complicated. The overall rise in social welfare spending was unmistakable – outlays climbed from 5.7 percent of GDP in 1969 to 9.2 percent in 1977 (see Table 3.3). By the end of the Ford presidency, mandatory

[50] Congressional Quarterly, *Congressional Quarterly Almanac, 1969* (Washington, D.C.: Congressional Quarterly, 1970), 77a.

programmatic spending accounted for approximately 45 percent of the budget, nearly double the budget share for defense.

A relatively small percentage of this social welfare expansion was accounted for by means-tested entitlements, but there were policy conflicts over many low-income assistance programs. The AFDC program was particularly contentious, as Congress rejected comprehensive reforms in cash assistance to the poor, notably Nixon's Family Assistance Plan (FAP). At the same time, Congress made numerous changes that liberalized eligibility and benefit levels for other public assistance entitlements, and spending for food and nutrition assistance, Medicaid, and a new Supplemental Security Income (SSI) program steadily grew under Nixon and Ford. The growth and budgetary impact of Social Security, Medicare, and other federal retirement programs were, by comparison, much greater, but these programs did not generate even remotely similar partisan and ideological disputes.

The Nixon administration's first social welfare initiative was, ironically, a guaranteed income program earlier deemed too ambitious by Great Society welfare planners.[51] The FAP that Nixon proposed in 1969 would have replaced the AFDC program with a basic federal payment of $1,600 a year for a family of four. Eligibility was extended to the working poor as well as unemployed adults, with job training and work requirements for the latter as a condition for receiving full benefits. An additional food stamp cash allowance was included, based on family size, as were federal grants for daycare services.

The House passed the FAP in 1970 with strong bipartisan support, and it approved a revised version of the program the following year. In both instances, the House-passed legislation failed to secure majority support in the Senate; liberals attacked the proposed benefits as too low, and conservatives criticized the program as too costly. Nixon eventually dropped welfare reform, and despite widespread dissatisfaction with the AFDC program, Congress refused to mandate stringent work requirements or to restrict eligibility. Congress was also unwilling, however, to make AFDC benefits more generous. The growth in AFDC spending therefore lagged behind other public assistance entitlements.

However, Congress did approve a major change in cash assistance programs for the indigent aged, blind, and disabled. These federal-state programs had been created by the Social Security Act of 1935, and, like cash assistance for poor families, there were wide disparities in benefits among the states. The Social Security Act Amendments of 1972 replaced these disparate programs with a new federal program setting uniform national standards for eligibility and benefits. Basic minimum benefits under the SSI program, which went into effect in 1974, were funded entirely by the federal government. The new benefit formula provided a generous increase for many recipients, and program spending grew accordingly. By 1975, SSI outlays were $4.3 billion, less than

[51] Leslie Lenkowsky, *Politics, Economics, and Welfare Reform* (Washington, D.C.: American Enterprise Institute, 1986), 67–69.

$800 million below AFDC spending, but nevertheless largely ignored by critics of "excessive" welfare spending.

In 1970, the administration and Congress agreed to provide free food stamps to families with very low incomes. In 1971, eligibility for food stamps was indexed to the official poverty level, and benefits were indexed to a "thrifty food plan."[52] Mandatory state coverage for the food stamp program was mandated in 1975. Congress also expanded, usually over Nixon administration objections, other nutrition assistance programs such as the school lunch program. As a result, spending for various federal food assistance programs nearly quintupled between 1973 and 1977.

The housing subsidy program initiated by the Great Society fared less well. House ownership subsidies were largely terminated in 1974, but Congress and the administration agreed to establish a new rental assistance program. A community development block grant was authorized that extended housing assistance to suburban areas and smaller cities, and overall funding for housing assistance continued to grow modestly.

For public assistance entitlements, Congress managed to extend the policy centralization and liberalization of the Great Society. The food stamp program was federalized, as was assistance to the indigent blind, disabled, and aged. Indexing was applied both to eligibility and benefits for food stamps in 1971, to eligibility for Medicaid in 1973, and to benefits for SSI in 1974. Congress rejected most attempts by the Nixon and Ford administrations to tighten eligibility standards for compensatory education and targeted food programs, and Congress also protected the Medicaid program against major changes, including a private national health insurance program advocated by both the Nixon and Ford administrations. Congress was strongly committed to categorical aid programs for specific diseases and beneficiary groups, fending off efforts by Nixon and Ford to consolidate or eliminate these programs. As healthcare cost inflation began to accelerate in the early 1970s, Medicaid and targeted health spending rose accordingly, but Congress refused to cut benefits or otherwise control healthcare costs.

For Social Security and Medicare, cost considerations were overwhelmed by bipartisan support for higher benefits. In 1969, the Nixon administration proposed an increase of 10 percent in Social Security benefits and the indexation of future benefit levels along with the Social Security taxable wage base. Congress ignored the indexing provisions and included a 15 percent across-the-board benefit increase in the Tax Reform Act of 1969. Congress did not increase either the Social Security wage base or tax rate but instead opted to fund the estimated $4.4 billion in additional spending from the retirement trust fund reserves. After failing to hold Congress to his recommended 10 percent increase or to gain approval for indexing, Nixon capitulated, stating that "the overriding consideration is that 25 million recipients of Social Security benefits

---

[52] R. Kent Weaver, *Automatic Government: The Politics of Indexation* (Washington, D.C.: Brookings Institution, 1988), 43.

have fallen behind financially, which makes my approval of this short-term revision necessary."[53]

In 1971, Congress approved a retroactive 10 percent increase in Social Security benefits and on this occasion raised the Social Security wage base and tax rate to fund the increase. These Social Security program changes were incorporated into legislation raising the public debt limit, and the same legislative vehicle was used in 1972, when Congress voted a 20 percent increase in Social Security benefits, raised once again the Social Security wage base and tax rate, and agreed to index future benefit increases. Later in the year, Congress increased minimum benefits under Social Security and the new SSI program.

In 1973, Congress approved a two-step increase of 11 percent in Social Security benefits for 1974 and also revised the cost-of-living adjustment schedule for future years to ensure more timely payment of benefit increases. Benefits under the SSI program were raised as well, effective with the program's implementation on January 1, 1974. When the benefits for the federal railroad retirement program were indexed in 1974, cost-of-living adjustments had been put in place for all federal retirement programs.[54]

The multiple increases in Social Security benefits from 1969 to 1977, including both legislative and automatic cost-of-living adjustments, roughly doubled Social Security outlays. Social Security–GDP spending, which had averaged approximately 2.7 percent during the Great Society, rose to 4.2 percent in 1977. The growth in average benefits for all beneficiary categories greatly exceeded the rate of inflation over this period, and the average replacement rate for Social Security climbed to more than 55 percent.[55] Even minor adjustments to restrain this growth found little support in Congress, despite the dwindling reserves in the Social Security trust funds. President Ford's proposal to cap the 1975 benefit increase at 5 percent was ignored by Congress, as was the Social Security Board of Trustees' request to correct a technical flaw in the Social Security benefit formula that was resulting in "unintended and excessively costly benefit payments."[56] Congress made this "decoupling" correction in 1977 but postponed its effective date until 1979.

Medicare spending was also growing rapidly, but Congress left its benefit structure and funding largely intact. In 1972, Congress extended Medicare coverage to Social Security disability recipients, adding an estimated 1.7 million new beneficiaries.[57] Coverage was also mandated for chronic kidney disease dialysis or transplants, regardless of age. Administrative efforts to control Medicare costs through regulation were ineffective, and Congress refused to consider legislative changes in healthcare provider reimbursements under the

[53] Congressional Quarterly, *Congress and the Nation, 1969–1972*, 611.

[54] Weaver, *Automatic Government*, 43.

[55] Daniel Béland, *Social Security: History and Politics from the New Deal* (Lawrence: University Press of Kansas, 2005), 139, 203.

[56] Congressional Quarterly, *Congress and the Nation, 1973–1976* (Washington, D.C.: Congressional Quarterly, 1977), 425.

[57] Congressional Quarterly, *Congress and the Nation, 1969–1972*, 620.

Part A and Part B programs. Like Social Security, Medicare spending growth was being driven by high inflation; however, in Medicare's case, the linkage was to healthcare cost inflation that usually exceeded the rate of increase in the overall cost of living.

The cumulative changes in entitlement programs over this period were expansionary, with the exception of AFDC cash assistance. For most programs, the number of beneficiaries increased, either through legislative changes in eligibility criteria or, in the case of Social Security, the growing number of retirees. In addition, the benefits per beneficiary in these programs were rising as well, through legislative and automatic indexing adjustments. As indexing was applied to more and more programs, annual control over their costs was obviously reduced. With mandatory programmatic spending, along with interest, accounting for more than half the total budget in the late 1970s, the year-to-year controllability of overall federal spending had been reduced as well.

The Revenue Problem

In 1969, Congress voted for a series of temporary and permanent tax increases. The income tax surcharge enacted in 1968 was extended at the 10 percent rate through December 31, 1969. Another six-month extension, at a reduced 5 percent rate, was then included in the Tax Reform Act of 1969, which also repealed the investment tax credit and postponed scheduled excise tax reductions. In addition, however, the Tax Reform Act of 1969 included an unfunded 15 percent Social Security benefit increase that offset most of its revenue gains. Despite growing deficits after 1969, Congress was reluctant to increase taxes. It rejected tax reforms proposed by the Nixon and Ford administrations and repeatedly cut individual and corporate taxes. The Social Security tax increases that Congress approved did not cover increased benefits. In 1976 and 1977, both on-budget and off-budget spending programs were in deficit, and unified budget deficits totaled nearly $130 billion.

The Tax Reform Act of 1969 The 1969 tax reform bill grew out of bipartisan concerns about the fairness and revenue productivity of the individual income tax. During 1968, the Johnson Treasury Department had focused attention on tax avoidance by wealthy individuals and recommended restrictions on tax shelters and other tax preferences to curb this practice. The Nixon administration then added its own reform proposals, including higher exemptions for low- and middle-income taxpayers and an investment credit repeal and excise tax extension to provide additional revenues.

The tax reforms that Nixon signed into law on December 30, 1969, affected corporations, financial institutions, and farms, as well as individual taxpayers. For individuals, the major changes included limits on exclusions and on the amount of capital gains taxed at preferential rates for high-income taxpayers and increased exemptions – from $600 to $750 over two years – and an increased standard deduction benefiting low-income taxpayers. The low-income tax relief for fiscal years 1970 and 1971 was estimated at $3.4 billion, but other provisions were expected to yield a net increase in revenues of $6.4 billion over two years.[58] Actual receipts in 1970 and 1971 fell well below estimates, but the combined shortfall of nearly $20 billion was more the result of an unexpected economic downturn than the legislated tax cut.

The Revenue Act of 1971 At the beginning of 1970, the Nixon administration proposed additional tax increases to balance the budget and control inflation. The recommended increases included higher Social Security taxes and another postponement of excise tax rate reductions, along with minor fees and user charges. Congress failed to act on Social Security taxes but did approve a two-year extension of excise taxes. By the time Congress completed action on the excise tax bill in December, however, growing concerns about recession prompted Nixon to embrace tax-cut stimulus and to defer efforts to balance the budget.

The economic recovery program that Nixon announced on August 15, 1971, included individual and business tax cuts, along with wage and price controls, an import surcharge, and an end to the gold standard. Earlier in the year, Nixon had taken administrative action to reduce business taxes by allowing accelerated depreciation write-offs by businesses. The Revenue Act of 1971 scaled back the business tax cuts that Nixon had requested and modified the asset depreciation schedule that Nixon had put in place, but several new business tax preferences were approved. The investment tax credit, which had been repealed in 1969, was reinstated; a tax credit of 20 percent was established for wages paid by businesses hiring former welfare recipients (the Work Incentive Program [WIN]); and a tax exemption was established for profits of businesses qualifying as Domestic International Sales Corporations. For individuals, scheduled increases in personal exemptions and standard deductions were moved up, and a new childcare deduction was created. The three-year cost of these business and individual tax cuts was estimated at the time at nearly $26 billion, but later calculations indicated that the actual revenue loss had been substantially higher.[59] In 1971, Congress also raised the Social Security taxable wage base beginning in 1972 and the Social Security tax rate in 1976, but these Social Security tax increases offset only a small portion of the decline in general revenues.

Tax Reform and Revenues The 1972 clashes between the Nixon administration and Congress over spending had clear implications for tax policy, at least on Nixon's part. His budget message singled out the "kind of spending that drives up taxes or drives up prices."[60] He claimed that the administration's

[58] Ibid., 83.
[59] Witte, *The Politics and Development of the Federal Income Tax*, 179.
[60] Richard Nixon, *Public Papers of the Presidents of the United States: Richard Nixon, 1972* (Washington, D.C.: Government Printing Office, 1974), 79.

proposed spending ceiling would "reduce the need for raising taxes so that the Federal Government plays a smaller, not a larger, role in the life of each of us."[61] But if Congress ignored his "recommendations for domestic spending as it did last year," Nixon warned that tax increases could not be avoided.[62] Congress ultimately prevailed in the battle over spending and managed to avoid individual or corporate tax increases.

In 1973, Congress held extensive hearings on tax reform, with particular attention to the curbing of tax preferences, and the administration proposed tighter restrictions on the use of tax shelters and a new minimum tax on investment income as part of its tax revision and tax simplification package. Congress failed to pass any tax reform, however, and in 1974 enacted pension law changes that greatly expanded tax-free retirement plans for self-employed individuals (and their employees) and created new tax-free individual retirement accounts (IRAs). After replacing Nixon in August, Gerald Ford called for an income tax surcharge to reduce the deficit and check inflation, but Congress did not seriously consider Ford's proposal.

With their gains in the 1974 midterm elections, congressional Democrats took firm control of tax policy. As signs of economic weakness mounted, Ford called on Congress to enact limited, temporary tax cuts to promote economic recovery. Congress took Ford's $16 billion one-time stimulus, expanded it to nearly $23 billion (with a $2 billion offsetting increase from changes in oil and gas depletion allowances), approved permanent new tax preferences, and added $1.9 billion in spending for $50 bonus payments to Social Security recipients and for emergency unemployment benefits.

In December, Congress extended the expiring provisions in its earlier tax-cut bill and fended off Ford's plea to match future tax cuts with equivalent cuts in federal spending. The tax bill that Congress then cleared on September 16, 1976, was quite different from a tax reform/tax increase package that the Ford administration had proposed. The reforms that Congress adopted totaled less than $1.6 billion for 1977, while individual income tax cuts and new tax preferences exceeded $17 billion.[63] Moreover, the spending cuts that Ford and congressional Republicans had hoped to extract never materialized. Instead, discretionary domestic spending continued to climb, as did entitlement outlays, and the FY 1977 deficit was more than $53 billion.

The 1968 Revenue and Expenditure Control Act linked spending cuts and tax increases, and the Tax Reform Act of 1969 combined structural tax changes to increase revenues and improve equity with a continued commitment to deficit reduction. The tax bills that were then enacted under Nixon and Ford were all tax cuts, either temporary or permanent. The number and scale of tax preferences increased, with the estimated revenue loss from tax preferences

[61] Ibid., 99.
[62] Ibid., 83.
[63] Congressional Quarterly, *Congress and the Nation, 1973–1976,* 105.

climbing from less than 25 percent in the early 1970s to more than 30 percent in 1977.[64] Despite individual tax cuts, tax burdens for many middle-income taxpayers increased as inflation pushed them into higher brackets, and Social Security taxes were raised to pay for more generous benefits. For low-income taxpayers, the steady rise in payroll taxes undercut efforts to improve income tax progressivity through higher exemptions and standard deductions. Finally, the connection between revenues and spending became weaker as Congress asserted greater control over budget policy.

The lack of discipline in tax policy during the mid-1970s was certainly not helped by the institutional weakening of the presidency after the Watergate scandal. The simultaneous loss of power and independence that the House Ways and Means Committee suffered as Wilbur Mills's career came to an ignominious end removed another fiscal constraint. But fiscal policy prescriptions had also become less clear-cut as the economy was buffeted by both inflation and slow growth. This uncertainty about fiscal policy reinforced Congress's reluctance to increase taxes and allowed it to justify repeated tax-cut stimulus. Congress was able to rely on the stimulus argument as well to protect its favored spending programs. The resulting deficits were unsettling to many, but Congress refused to adjust revenue and spending levels.

Carter versus Congressional Democrats

Jimmy Carter won the 1976 presidential election by only a narrow margin, but congressional Democrats maintained the large majorities they had gained in the post-Watergate 1974 midterm elections. With margins in the House and Senate almost identical to those of the Great Society's most productive legislative years, Democrats expected to extend the welfare state and expand the domestic role of the federal government. The one-term Carter presidency, however, failed to advance these lofty goals, as budget policy constraints drove a wedge between Carter and liberal Democrats in Congress.

The fiscal frustrations Democrats encountered grew out of their previous success. Social welfare spending had already risen so steeply that major expansions, such as national health insurance or welfare reform, could not be financed easily or painlessly. Post-Vietnam cutbacks in defense had been so large that rising concerns about eroding military capabilities made continued cuts less and less feasible. The abandonment of balanced-budget principles, in the guise of fiscal stimulus, had not delivered acceptable economic growth, and the persistence of high inflation further undermined support for new spending stimulus.

[64] Stanley S. Surrey and Paul R. McDaniel, *Tax Expenditures* (Cambridge: Harvard University Press, 1985), 35.

The Tax Policy Differences

The 1976 Democratic platform had promised that "a new Democratic President will work closely with the leaders of the Congress on a regular, systematic basis so that the people can see the results of unity."[65] The first test of this promise was the economic stimulus package that Carter sent to Congress shortly after his inauguration. His $31.2 billion proposal contained individual and corporate tax cuts, a one-time rebate of $50 for taxpayers and their dependents on taxes paid in 1976, a $50 payment to Social Security recipients and beneficiaries of low-income assistance programs, and increased funding for federal jobs programs and countercyclical revenue-sharing. Two months later, with the prospects for congressional approval still uncertain, Carter abruptly withdrew the rebate plan.

Carter's tax proposals also encountered strong opposition in Congress. The tax bill that was finally enacted included the increased standard deduction that the administration had recommended, but it created a business tax credit for new employees that the administration opposed and extended expiring individual and corporate tax cuts that had not been included in the original stimulus plan. In order to accommodate the estimated $34.2 billion cost of the 1977 Tax Reduction and Simplification Act within its FY 1977 budget resolution, Congress had been forced to revise its original budget plan, and administration efforts to lobby the House Budget Committee for additional changes had nearly derailed the already complicated and fractious process. The House Speaker, Thomas P. O'Neill, Jr., complained about administration representatives "not knowing the procedures of Congress."[66] The chairman of the House Budget Committee was less charitable, stating "This is the United States Congress where the Democratic majority is going to write the legislation. It is not the Georgia legislature."[67]

Whatever the economic impact of tax-cut stimulus might have been, it was largely dissipated by an even larger Social Security tax increase enacted by Congress. Here again, the Carter administration ran into difficulties. In May, the administration had proposed a temporary transfer of general revenues to avoid short-term deficits in the Social Security trust funds along with future Social Security tax increases to ensure long-term solvency. In legislation that finally passed in December, Congress rejected the use of general revenues for Social Security (or Medicare) and instead raised the Social Security tax rate and wage base above scheduled levels beginning in 1979. The administration's Social Security "rescue plan" had called for employers to pay Social Security taxes on all employee earnings after 1980, but

[65] Congressional Quarterly, *Congress and the Nation, 1973–1976*, 855.
[66] Ibid., 193.
[67] Ibid., 194.

Congress retained the taxable wage base maximum for both employers and employees.

Carter had promised to shield low-income earners from payroll tax increases, but the new tax rates and adjusted tax base meant higher taxes for all covered workers and, over a ten-year period, a tripling of the maximum tax on high-income earners. The projected increase in Social Security taxes from 1977 to 1987 was $227 billion, which was at the time "the largest peacetime tax increase in the nation's history."[68] By comparison, the tax cut that Congress had approved earlier in the year totaled less than $35 billion over three years.

In 1978, Social Security issues caused additional problems for Carter. In April, the House Democratic caucus voted overwhelmingly to rescind the Social Security tax increase that had been approved the previous December. A threatened veto helped convince the Ways and Means Committee not to report out rollback legislation.[69] The administration then informed Congress of new funding shortfalls despite the Social Security tax increase and proposed a number of benefit reductions to ensure continued solvency. Carter's Social Security reform package included partial taxation of benefits, tighter restrictions on early retirement and on disability eligibility, and new limits on survivors' benefits.[70] As congressional opposition predictably mounted, Carter retreated, and entitlement reform disappeared from the administration's agenda.

Finally, Carter's heralded tax reform program emerged from Congress in barely recognizable form. In January 1978, the administration proposed a $23.5 billion individual income tax cut and an $8.4 billion reduction in corporate income taxes. Net tax reduction, however, was considerably less, because the administration called on Congress to eliminate some major itemized deductions, such as sales taxes, reduce preferences for capital gains and tax-exempt interest, and restrict exclusions for fringe benefits. These individual income tax changes were expected to raise more than $8 billion, and corresponding cutbacks in business tax preferences would add an additional $1.1 billion in new revenues.

By lowering marginal rates by two percentage points in all brackets, adding a new tax credit, and restricting tax preferences, Carter's individual income tax plan would have distributed tax relief almost exclusively to individuals and families making less than $30,000 a year.[71] For business, the proposed changes were more limited. The major revision on the tax-cut side

---

[68] Congressional Quarterly, *Congress and the Nation, 1977–1980* (Washington, D.C.: Congressional Quarterly, 1981), 235.
[69] Iwan W. Morgan, *The Age of Deficits* (Lawrence: University Press of Kansas, 2009), 56.
[70] Ibid., 57.
[71] Congressional Quarterly, *Congress and the Nation, 1977–1980*, 239.

was an expanded investment tax credit, with revenue offsets from restricting business expense deductions and raising taxes on export firms and U.S. corporations with foreign subsidiaries. The tax cut that cleared Congress in October – and was reluctantly signed by Carter – contained little in the way of reform, and the distribution of tax relief did not strengthen progressivity.

Instead of cutting back the capital gains exclusion as Carter had advocated, Congress increased it from 50 percent to 60 percent, eased the rules on capital gains taxes from home sales, and reduced the amount of capital gains income subject to the minimum tax. The only individual tax preference that Congress agreed to repeal was the deduction for state and local gasoline taxes. Congress also left unchanged individual marginal tax rates but widened the brackets at which the rates applied. Low-income tax relief was provided in the form of higher exemptions and standard deductions and an expanded, permanent earned-income tax credit. For corporations, Congress lowered tax rates, approved a permanent investment tax credit, and rejected most of the administration's business tax reforms.

The distribution of tax relief in the Revenue Act of 1978 was heavily skewed to upper-income taxpayers. The capital gains tax changes, for example, affected an estimated 4.3 million returns, with the largest average reductions and largest share of the total reduction received by upper-income taxpayers.[72] The net effect of all individual income tax changes was to provide roughly proportional reductions for all but the lowest and highest income categories.[73] In addition, many low- and middle-income taxpayers actually faced higher tax burdens, as increased payroll taxes and "bracket creep" erased much of the income tax cut they received in 1979. With continued high deficits, however, neither the Carter administration nor Congress could address these rising tax burdens without cutting domestic spending. The Democratic dilemma was illustrated by an unusual provision of the 1978 Revenue Act that called for, but did not require, limits on future spending as a precondition for "significant tax reductions for individuals."[74]

The Revenue Act of 1978 was the last major tax bill of Carter's presidency, although the administration continued to press for structural tax reforms. It had no success, however, in persuading Congress to cut back individual tax preferences. In 1978, Congress barred the Treasury Department from issuing rules that would tax employee benefits as income unless they were explicitly excluded in the Internal Revenue Code. A windfall oil profits tax that passed in 1980 extended this prohibition for two years and repealed an inheritance tax rule governing capital gains that had been one of the major achievements in the Tax Reform Act of 1976.

[72] Ibid., 244.
[73] Ibid., 240.
[74] Ibid., 243.

The Spending Policy Deadlock

The Carter presidency began with expansive plans for new domestic programs and a continuing spending shift from defense to domestic priorities. The 1976 Democratic platform had called for "comprehensive national health insurance with universal and mandatory coverage" (financed by payroll taxes and general revenues) and a guaranteed "income floor both for the working poor and the poor not in the labor market."[75] The platform attacked the Nixon-Ford administration's "undue emphasis on the overall size of the defense budget," promised to "reduce present defense spending by about $5-billion to $7-billion," and pledged to commit these savings to discretionary domestic programs that had been neglected because of divided government.[76]

Democratic divisions over discretionary spending, however, surfaced almost immediately. Carter's plan to expand domestic spending margins by cutting "unnecessary" programs was derailed by a rancorous and damaging dispute with Congress over water projects. The amount of defense savings to be shifted to domestic programs found Carter and House Democrats at odds in the spring of 1977, and the defense issue proved even more troublesome once Carter came out in favor of defense increases the following year. The hope that unified government would somehow make it easier to direct discretionary spending policy faded very quickly.

In February 1977, Carter announced his intention to eliminate funding for 19 water projects that had been included in the Ford administration's last budget and to review an additional 300 projects for possible cancellation. The short-term savings were modest – "$500 million of the $2 billion allocated to water projects" – but signaled the administration's "intent to eradicate unnecessary spending in its drive to balance the budget."[77] Western-state Democrats, long accustomed to their pork-barrel prerogatives, were suitably outraged, and the House proceeded to pass a public works bill that restored eighteen of the projects. Carter threatened a veto but was persuaded by House leaders to accept a compromise that restored only half of the projects. This seemingly minor issue, however, caused lasting political damage. According to Iwan Morgan, Carter concluded that his concession "was accurately interpreted as a sign of weakness on my part and I came to regret it as much as any budget decision I made as President."[78] Moreover, nothing was really settled, as contests over water project rescissions, authorizations, and appropriations carried over into the 1978 and 1979 budget cycles.

The defense budget controversy began when Carter tried to limit congressional cuts. In marking up the first budget resolution for FY 1978, the House

---

[75] Congressional Quarterly, *Congressional Quarterly Almanac, 1976* (Washington, D.C.: Congressional Quarterly, 1976), 859–860.
[76] Ibid., 868.
[77] Morgan, *The Age of Deficits*, 50.
[78] Ibid., 50–51.

Budget Committee adopted a lower defense target than the administration had requested, and Carter officials then lobbied to rewrite the resolution when it reached the House floor. The amended resolution was then rejected by the House, and Democratic leaders proceeded to blame the administration for its alleged interference. Another compromise was reached, but Carter soon found himself embroiled in policy disputes with Congress over the B-1 bomber program, Minuteman III strategic missile production, and nuclear aircraft carriers.

In 1978, Carter changed course and called for "prudent real growth" in defense spending. In order to defuse Democratic opposition, particularly among House and Senate liberals, Carter coupled the defense increase to even larger increases in domestic programs. This tactic succeeded, but only temporarily. In 1979, Carter adopted a 3 percent real growth target for defense but rejected an equivalent increase in domestic programs. At that point, liberal Democrats deserted the administration, and Carter was simultaneously attacked by conservative Democrats and Republicans who were demanding a more aggressive defense buildup.

The politics of defense spending were changing very quickly in the late 1970s, and Democrats were struggling to respond. Among defense experts, assessments of U.S. military capabilities had become increasingly pessimistic as the post-Vietnam defense cuts took their toll. Comparisons of U.S. and Soviet military spending showed large and growing disparities, with the Carter administration estimating that by 1979 the Soviets had gained a 25 percent to 45 percent advantage in "relative defense spending, annual or cumulative, [which] is the best single crude measure of military capabilities."[79] The public's apprehensions about Soviet versus U.S. military power and its support for more defense spending were rising rapidly at this point, and the fear of U.S. military impotence escalated with the Iranian seizure of U.S. embassy personnel in November and the Soviet invasion of Afghanistan in December.

The Carter administration could not control this defense budget turnaround. In the fall, it was unable to block a Senate budget resolution that included 5 percent real growth in defense spending and failed to defend its own 3 percent target when the House acted. In December, after the Iranian seizure of U.S. embassy personnel, the administration raised its five-year defense targets to more than 5 percent, but Congress then proceeded to adopt even higher defense budget increases. In little more than a year, the administration had been forced to accept a defense spending plan that went well beyond what the president had previously claimed was financially prudent or necessary. At the same time, congressional Democrats rejected cutbacks in domestic programs to offset the defense buildup. In FY 1980, real defense spending was 6 percent higher than it had been before Carter took office, but discretionary domestic spending had risen by almost 20 percent. As a share

---

[79] U.S. Department of Defense, *Department of Defense Annual Report, Fiscal Year 1980* (Washington, D.C.: Government Printing Office, 1979), 5.

of the entire budget, defense was actually smaller in 1980 than it had been in 1976.

Social welfare spending proved similarly frustrating for Democrats. Congressional liberals, notably Senator Edward M. Kennedy, blocked the Carter administration's national health insurance initiative, but the huge costs associated with their own, more comprehensive proposals doomed their efforts as well. The signature Carter welfare reform for the poor – the Program for Better Jobs and Income – featured a new cash benefit to replace AFDC, SSI, and food stamps. The potential costs of this reform helped fuel conservative opposition, and liberals were unenthusiastic about the jobs and training programs associated with it. It, too, failed to pass in either the House or Senate.

Congress was also unwilling to curb benefits for existing programs, particularly Social Security and Medicare, in order to rebalance spending for the elderly and the poor. Congress routinely rejected administration proposals for targeting benefits and reducing costs. Instead, Congress raised benefits for retirees who continued to work and expanded eligibility for widowed and divorced beneficiaries. When Congress finally corrected a costly flaw in the Social Security benefit formula in 1977, it postponed the implementation of the new formula for two years. For Medicare, healthcare cost inflation was admittedly a serious problem, but Congress refused to tighten cost controls. In 1977, Congress agreed to increase legal penalties for fraud and abuse in the Medicare program but took no action to restrict hospital reimbursements. Medicare payment schedules were adjusted in 1980, but the savings were quite small. Congress then added new benefits for outpatient medical services.

The gap between federal assistance for the elderly and poor, which liberals had deplored during the Nixon-Ford era, became even greater in the late 1970s. Social Security and Medicare outlays were 5.2 percent of GDP in 1976 and 5.9 percent in 1981.[80] Over this same five-year period, Medicaid and income security spending for the poor dropped from 2.7 percent of GDP to 2.2 percent. Within the income security spending category, AFDC cash assistance fared considerably less well than did in-kind benefit programs like food stamps.[81]

Despite the high levels of domestic spending during the Carter presidency, Democrats were unable to pass national health insurance, welfare reform, or other major liberal initiatives. On the revenue side, the party's traditional commitment to tax reform disappeared, as individual and business tax cuts weakened the progressivity and revenue productivity of the income tax system. On Social Security, where taxes were increased, short-term solvency problems

---

[80] Congressional Budget Office, *The Budget and Economic Outlook: Fiscal Years 2010–2020* (Washington, D.C.: Government Printing Office, 2010), 135.

[81] Dennis S. Ippolito, *Uncertain Legacies: Federal Budget Policy from Roosevelt through Reagan* (Charlottesville: University Press of Virginia, 1990), 179.

were not resolved, because Congress failed to approve the even higher taxes or benefit reductions that were needed. In 1977, when Congress raised Social Security taxes, the trust funds were in deficit and remained in deficit through 1981.[82] This failure to balance spending and revenue extended to the rest of the federal budget, with annual deficit-GDP levels averaging nearly 2.5 percent from 1977 to 1981.

Restoring Balanced Budgets

The 1970s produced budget policy outcomes that satisfied neither liberals nor conservatives. Liberals had succeeded in funding the Great Society's domestic agenda at unprecedentedly generous levels but had failed to pass new programs that would have broadened that agenda. Conservatives had been unable to curb domestic spending growth or to maintain defense spending levels that adequately supported important U.S. military capabilities. On the revenue side, there was little appetite in Congress to raise taxes to fund the domestic programs already in place, much less the programmatic expansion that liberals envisioned. Efforts to link tax cuts and spending cuts within a balanced-budget framework made little headway as well.

The balanced-budget rule had not disappeared during the 1970s, but it had been reshaped to fit different partisan strategies. With the 1980 elections looming, the Carter administration and the Democratic leadership in Congress declared their commitment to balancing the budget. Balance would have to be achieved, however, at extremely high revenue levels, because the party had no intention of adjusting its domestic priorities. Carter's election-year budget, for example, projected a $25 billion surplus by 1983 but with revenue-GNP levels of more than 22 percent.[83] Revenues had never reached this level during World War II, and the administration admitted to being "extremely concerned about the significant rise in tax burdens implied in these [revenue] estimates."[84]

Carter also promised "continued real increases in defense" over this period "as a matter of fundamental policy."[85] The administration's budget program, however, did not change spending priorities. Carter's FY 1981 budget envisioned only a slight increase in the defense share of total spending – from 23.1 percent in 1980 to 24 percent in 1983 (see Table 3.4). As a result, the defense budget share during a second Carter term would have remained below the level that he inherited. In sum, the sharp domestic tilt of Democratic spending policy was to be maintained, and Carter's path to future balanced budgets was carefully tailored to preserve this tilt.

[82] Office of Management and Budget, *Historical Tables, Fiscal Year 2011*, 321.
[83] Office of Management and Budget, *The Budget of the United States Government, Fiscal Year 1981* (Washington, D.C.: Government Printing Office, 1980), M3, 32, 61.
[84] Ibid., 72.
[85] Ibid., M5, 41.

TABLE 3.4. *Defense and Nondefense Spending Budget Shares, Fiscal Years 1976–1983 (as percentage of total spending)*

	Actual Spending		
Fiscal Year	Defense	Nondefense	Net Interest
1976	24.4%	68.3%	7.3%
1977	24.2	68.4	7.4
1978	23.3	68.8	7.9
1979	23.8	67.5	8.6
	Carter Administration Fiscal Year 1981 Estimates		
Fiscal Year	Defense	Nondefense	Net Interest
1980	23.1%	67.7%	9.2%
1981	23.7	67.4	8.8
1982	24.1	68.0	7.9
1983	24.0	69.2	6.8

Source: Office of Management and Budget, *Budget of the United States Government, Fiscal Year 1981* (Washington, D.C.: Government Printing Office, 1980), 613.

In the contest against Carter, Ronald Reagan pledged his allegiance to balanced-budget principles, but Reagan was proposing a radically different fiscal path – tax cuts that would lower revenue levels, defense budgets that dwarfed Carter's, and a much narrower and costly domestic role for the federal government. The balanced-budget rule in Reagan's case was tied to a pre–Great Society version of spending policy. Republicans had been promoting a milder version of this linkage since the mid-1960s but arguing for simultaneous spending cuts and tax cuts. The Reagan approach was to cut taxes and to use lower revenue levels to impose spending cuts. With Reagan's victory over Carter, this fiscal strategy was tested almost immediately.

4

The Reagan Strategy – Balancing Low

The Reagan presidency began with a lofty fiscal agenda. The administration's March 1981 Budget Revisions vowed to "substantially alter the previous Administration's tax and spending policies" and to balance the budget in 1984 at precisely 19.3 percent of GNP – "significantly lower levels than under previous [Carter administration] policy."[1] The spending and tax components of the Reagan program marked a sharp departure not only from Carter policies but also from budget policy trends of the 1970s. Reagan's plan to revive the American economy featured large and permanent individual tax cuts that would reduce and stabilize revenue levels. His pledge to restore American military supremacy required much larger defense budgets, while the promise to cut the growth of government spending translated into even larger cutbacks in domestic spending. The Reagan version of a balanced budget began with a low revenue ceiling that would be matched by "the reduced size of the public sector."

Reagan's plan for balancing the budget proved to be wildly optimistic, and not just during 1984. Over Reagan's two terms, spending averaged more than 22 percent of GNP, while revenues averaged slightly more than 18 percent. Instead of balanced budgets, the Reagan years produced unusually large deficits and a near tripling of the publicly held debt. When Reagan took office, publicly held debt–GNP was approximately 25 percent. By the end of the decade, it had climbed to more than 40 percent.

The fiscal record of the Reagan presidency, however, was more complex than its liberal critics or conservative admirers have been willing to admit. The tax cutting, for example, was hardly unrestrained. The Economic Recovery Tax Act of 1981 (ERTA) remains, in terms of its relative size, the largest tax cut in the nation's history, but it was followed by three major tax increases in 1982–1984,

---

[1] Office of Management and Budget, *Fiscal Year 1982 Budget Revisions* (Washington, D.C.: Government Printing Office, 1981), 5–7.

a widely lauded and bipartisan tax reform in 1986, and another tax increase in 1987. The defense budget increases under Reagan were large by almost any standard, but they were offset by an even larger reduction in discretionary domestic spending. Combined defense and nondefense discretionary spending–GDP was 10 percent lower at the end of Reagan's presidency than it had been at the end of Carter's.

Entitlement spending, by comparison, remained high throughout the 1980s. The Reagan administration pioneered the use of budget reconciliation to trim entitlements, such as cash and in-kind assistance for the poor in 1981. Reconciliation was a special legislative procedure created in the 1974 Budget Act to provide expedited action – committee instructions and limitations on floor debate and amendments – on spending and revenue bills to enforce congressional budget resolutions.[2] It was used by congressional Republicans to circumvent Democratic opposition to Reagan's entitlement cuts in 1981, and this reconciliation precedent has since been used by every administration to effect major changes in budget policy.

Neither party in Congress, however, was eager to retrench the retirement and healthcare programs that accounted for the bulk of entitlement spending. Indeed, Congress soon reversed many of the cuts that it had approved in 1981, and the composition of the "social safety net" remained largely intact during the 1980s. Reagan's impact on social welfare spending was, in the end, quite modest.

As the administration's 1982 economic report conceded, Reagan's "strategy of reducing taxes in advance of spending cuts implies that it will take some time to achieve the desired level of deficits."[3] In fact, that strategy had been fatally undermined by faulty economic and political assumptions. The coherent fiscal program of early 1981 unraveled as the administration resorted to separate fiscal tracks for taxation and spending. Faced with a choice between large deficits and individual income tax increases, Reagan chose deficits and, for conservative Republicans, redefined the party's commitment to balanced budgets. For Democrats and many congressional Republicans, balancing the budget through entitlement cutbacks was equally unacceptable. Thus, the politics of budget policy during the 1980s produced partial victories for all sides but a collective result that was universally deplored. Moreover, given the policy changes under Reagan, future deficit reduction depended on individual income tax increases and reduced defense spending. In other words, Reagan budget priorities would continue to frame the fiscal policy debate long after he left office.

---

[2] See Walter J. Oleszek, *Congressional Procedures and the Policy Process*, 8th ed. (Washington, D.C.: CQ Press, 2011), 76–81.

[3] James Tobin and Murray Weidenbaum, eds., *Two Revolutions in Economic Policy: The First Economic Reports of Presidents Kennedy and Reagan* (Cambridge: Massachusetts Institute of Technology Press, 1988), 420.

Taxes and Spending: The Failed Linkage

Congressional Republicans made strong gains in the 1980 election, taking control of the Senate by a 53–47 margin and reducing the Democratic majority in the House by thirty-four seats to 243–192. The first test of the Reagan budget program took place with the adoption of the congressional budget resolution in the spring of 1981, and the administration secured a critical victory. A coalition of Republicans and conservative Democrats in the House managed to defeat the Democratic leadership's proposal and to adopt an alternative budget resolution that contained both the tax cuts and spending cuts the administration had requested. The budget resolution later adopted by both chambers in May provided for a $51.3 billion reduction in FY 1982 revenues and for additional tax cuts in 1983 and 1984. The spending cuts were incorporated into reconciliation instructions requiring more than two dozen House and Senate committees to report out legislation cutting spending in programs under their jurisdiction. Those cuts were to be packaged into a reconciliation bill that would be considered under expedited procedures in both chambers. The reconciliation instructions called for approximately $36 billion in FY 1982 savings and additional savings in future years from cuts in dozens of entitlements and other programs.

Once the budget resolution was in place, House and Senate committees began to work on the tax-cut bill and reconciliation proposals. The coalition of Republicans and conservative Democrats in the House once again prevailed, providing Reagan with major victories on the reconciliation bill that passed in June and the tax bill that passed in late July. The Senate Republican majority strongly supported the Reagan program, so the Senate versions of both bills passed without major challenges. The House-Senate conference on the reconciliation bill, which involved 250 conferees meeting in fifty-eight subconferences, was concluded on July 29, and the conference report easily passed both chambers on July 31. The House-Senate conference on the tax bill was also concluded on July 31, and after a brief delay, the House and Senate approved the measure several days later. Both bills were signed by Reagan on August 13, who praised them as "a turnaround of almost a half a century of a course this country's been on and mark an end to the excessive growth in government bureaucracy, government spending, government taxing."[4]

The Omnibus Budget Reconciliation Act of 1981 (OBRA 1981) and ERTA were remarkable legislative achievements, but their fiscal effects turned out to be quite different from what Reagan had envisioned. When the economy moved into recession in the fall of 1981, revenues fell more quickly and steeply than had been expected, and deficit projections soared. When the administration requested a second round of spending cuts to offset this revenue shortfall,

---

[4] Ronald Reagan, *Public Papers of the Presidents of the United States: Ronald Reagan, 1981* (Washington, D.C.: Government Printing Office, 1982), 706.

Congress balked. It soon became apparent that it was not feasible to erase this deficit gap solely with spending cuts, even if Congress had the political appetite to do so. The administration originally had planned for Congress to follow up the first round of spending cuts with even larger cutbacks for 1983–1986, but the promised incentive for doing so – a balanced budget in 1984 and thereafter – had been obliterated by the time that Reagan's second budget was sent to Congress. The second session of the 97th Congress not only rejected the administration's FY 1983 budget plan but moved to reverse part of the tax cut that it had passed in 1981 and to cancel some of the spending cuts as well. This same dynamic repeated itself in the annual budget cycles that followed, with the phrase "dead on arrival" usually applied to the president's budgets.

The fiscal "turnaround" that Reagan announced on August 13, 1981, was not just premature but completely inaccurate. The size of government would not be reduced under Reagan, neither would the disconnect between revenues and spending that had taken hold during the 1970s be erased. Instead of pressing a coordinated budget reform program as it had in 1981, the Reagan administration quickly found itself trying to defend specific policy priorities. The first of these was what Reagan considered the core of his economic recovery program – individual income tax cuts.

The Reagan presidency raised tax policy to the top of the political agenda. During what one expert called the "tax decade," there were "more frequent and detailed changes in federal tax law than ever before in [U.S.] history."[5] The starting point for these changes was ERTA, which sharpened partisan divisions over income taxation and generated revenue losses that constrained tax policy choices for the remainder of Reagan's tenure. The supply-side theory that shaped the final version of the 1981 tax bill had a great deal to do with both effects.

Taxes and Economic Recovery

In his final budget, Jimmy Carter emphatically opposed an income tax cut, arguing that it would increase the deficit and worsen already strong inflationary pressures. Several months earlier, he had raised the same objections to a $40 billion package of individual tax relief and business incentives approved by the Senate Finance Committee and persuaded Democratic leaders to keep the measure off the Senate floor. When Reagan took office, inflation was at nearly 12 percent, the prime lending rate was more than 20 percent, and unemployment was almost 7.5 percent. The unusual combination of low growth and high inflation – "stagflation" – did not offer a clear fiscal policy prescription, but Reagan's decision to focus on boosting economic growth through large, permanent tax cuts predictably heightened concerns about deficits and inflation.

---

[5] C. Eugene Steuerle, *The Tax Decade* (Washington, D.C.: Urban Institute Press, 1992), 1.

In addressing these concerns, the administration claimed that its plan for cutting spending would actually reduce deficits but acknowledged that it was ceding the responsibility for inflation control to the Federal Reserve. The administration's budget highlighted "a slower, steady, and predictable growth of the money supply set by the independent Federal Reserve System" to bring "runaway inflation" under control.[6] The Federal Reserve was, in fact, implementing a highly restrictive monetary policy during 1981 that would greatly reduce the rate of inflation, but congressional qualms about deficits and inflation threatened to limit the size of the Reagan tax cut. In the end, however, Congress approved an even larger tax cut than Reagan had proposed.

The Reagan tax-cut plan also met stiff resistance from Democrats, particularly in the House, for its favorable treatment of high-income taxpayers. From the outset, Reagan had insisted on across-the-board marginal rate reductions of 10 percent each year for three years. While the final reduction approved by Congress was 23 percent, the controversial across-the-board feature was retained. There was less Democratic opposition to the administration's business investment initiatives, because these were less costly and sidestepped the fairness issue that made the individual tax cuts so contentious. House Democrats offered an alternative to the accelerated cost recovery system the administration had devised for business, but the real battle in the House was over individual tax cuts.

Negotiating ERTA The income tax cuts that Reagan proposed in 1981 had first been promoted by congressional Republicans during the Carter presidency. Representative Jack F. Kemp and Senator William V. Roth had promoted a 30 percent marginal rate cut for individuals, phased in over three years, along with the indexing of tax brackets to prevent "bracket creep," and a smaller reduction in business taxes. The "Kemp-Roth plan" had been dismissed by congressional Democrats, and Republican support had been lukewarm as well. Reagan's endorsement of Kemp-Roth during his presidential campaign helped solidify Republican support, but the revenue costs of Kemp-Roth remained troublesome for many Republicans. Meanwhile, Democrats in Congress continued to object to the size of the Kemp-Roth tax cut and its distribution of tax relief.

The business cuts in the Reagan plan were based largely on liberalized depreciation rules. Business groups had been lobbying for accelerated depreciation for several years, and Reagan had endorsed this effort during his campaign. The formal proposal submitted to Congress in February 1981 included a "10-5-3 Accelerated Cost Recovery System" for investments in machinery, equipment, and buildings. While some Democrats favored alternative depreciation rules, there was broad congressional support for depreciation changes. Nevertheless, Reagan briefly considered trimming back business tax cuts in order to make

---

[6] Office of Management and Budget, *Fiscal Year 1982 Budget Revisions*, 1.

room for the individual tax cuts that were his first priority. Instead, the administration was persuaded by House Republicans to expand the business tax cuts and thus secure the support of conservative Democrats for Reagan's entire tax-cut package.

The Senate Finance Committee acted quickly on the tax-cut plan the administration submitted in early June. Democratic complaints about tax relief for the wealthy made little headway, as the committee approved a measure nearly identical to the Reagan plan by a 19–1 vote on June 25. The most important change the Finance Committee made was the inclusion of an indexing provision that the administration had concluded was too costly in terms of future revenues. The Finance Committee bill indexed tax brackets to changes in the consumer price index beginning in 1985. This provision was accepted by the Senate and then retained in the conference bill that went to the House and Senate on July 31. Other, less-costly Senate additions included a reduced windfall profits tax for oil producers and a temporary exclusion for interest income on savings certificates.

In the House, Ways and Means Democrats, led by chairman Daniel D. Rostenkowski, could not reach agreement with the administration on a bipartisan bill and decided to draft a Democratic version. With the backing of the House leadership, Rostenkowski announced that his committee would not consider a three-year across-the-board rate cut but would instead propose a two-year reduction targeted toward low- and middle-income groups. Committee Democrats also agreed to refashion the accelerated depreciation system the administration had proposed and to lower corporate tax rates. The individual income tax cuts in the Ways and Means bill were estimated at approximately $420 billion over five years, compared to $500 billion in the Senate Finance Committee bill; the revenue loss from the Ways and Means business tax changes was estimated at $485 billion through 1990, which was roughly equal to the administration's package but with a larger portion of the cut effective in later years.[7] In addition, a number of new and expanded business tax preferences were included in the Ways and Means bill to ensure support from conservative Democrats when the measure reached the House floor.

By late July, when Ways and Means reported out its bill, the administration had decided to revise its proposal. A number of the business tax preferences that Ways and Means was sponsoring were incorporated into the new administration package and added to the Senate Finance Committee bill that had finally been taken to the floor. The expanded Reagan tax package was then introduced by House Republicans as a substitute for the Ways and Means bill that had reached the House floor. On July 27, Reagan asked for public support of his tax plan in a nationally televised address, and the response was described by House Speaker Thomas P. O'Neill, Jr., as "a telephone blitz like this nation has

---

[7] Congressional Quarterly, *Congressional Quarterly Almanac, 1981* (Washington, D.C.: Congressional Quarterly, 1982), 99–100.

never seen. It's had a devastating effect."[8] When the House voted on July 29, the Republican substitute was adopted by a 238–195 margin, with forty-eight Democrats defecting to the Republican side.

The Senate approved the amended Finance Committee bill on July 29 by an 89–11 vote. This strong bipartisan support, however, came after nearly two weeks of debate, during which the Senate adopted eighty amendments, most of which were narrowly tailored tax preferences that added to the revenue loss from the main individual and business tax cuts. The rejected amendments featured Democratic proposals to limit the individual tax cuts to one year and to concentrate individual tax relief on those earning less than $50,000 per year. The House-Senate conference was concluded quickly, as Democrats conceded defeat on individual income tax cuts and joined Republicans in supporting the politically attractive "sweeteners" that had been added along the way. The bill that Reagan signed into law on August 13 cut individual and business taxes by an estimated $750 billion over five years (see Table 4.1). By far, the largest revenue losses from ERTA were the individual income tax rate cuts that lowered the bottom bracket from 14 percent to 11 percent, set a top marginal rate on earned and investment income of 50 percent, and indexed all income brackets (as well as the zero bracket amount and personal exemption) in 1985. The most important revenue change for business was the new accelerated cost recovery system that allowed corporations to write off capital investments more quickly and offered small businesses the option of "expensing" specified equipment costs immediately.

Revenue Losses and Deficits More than 80 percent of the projected revenue losses under ERTA were delayed until 1984–1986, a concession to congressional worries about short-term deficit effects. The severe recession that took hold in the latter part of 1981, however, multiplied immediate revenue losses and led to higher spending than had been expected. The impact on the budget was dramatic. In February 1981, the administration had forecast a $45 billion deficit for the 1982 fiscal year that began on October 1. When the administration submitted its next budget the following February, the FY 1982 deficit had been reestimated at $98.6 billion.[9] The actual deficit for FY 1982 turned out to be $128 billion. Of the approximately $80 billion deficit increase during 1982, more than $30 billion resulted from the unexpectedly sharp drop in revenues. Compared to the pre-ERTA revenue baseline, the revenue loss for 1982 was approximately $95 billion.

The deficit outlook after 1982 was also much worse, and Reagan proposed a modest tax increase of approximately $85 billion for fiscal years 1983–1987.[10]

---

[8] Ibid., 103.

[9] Office of Management and Budget, *Budget of the United States Government, Fiscal Year 1983* (Washington, D.C.: Government Printing Office, 1982), M5.

[10] Congressional Quarterly, *Congressional Quarterly Almanac, 1982* (Washington, D.C.: Congressional Quarterly, 1983), 32.

TABLE 4.1. *Economic Recovery Tax Act of 1981 (P.L. 97-34): Major Provisions and Estimated Revenue Effects, Fiscal Years 1982–1986*[a]

INDIVIDUAL INCOME TAXES	**(Revenue Loss: –$557 billion)**
Tax Rate	Marginal tax rates for individuals reduced by 23 percent for 1981–1983, beginning with a 5 percent reduction on Oct. 1, 1981.
Maximum Rate	The top marginal rate on investment ("unearned") income reduced from 70 percent to 50 percent, effective Jan. 1, 1982.
Capital Gains	The 60 percent exclusion of long-term capital gains maintained. The new 50 percent top marginal rate on investment income reduced the maximum effective tax rate on capital gains to 20 percent, effective June 10, 1981.
Deduction for Two-Earner Married Couples	Reduction of "marriage penalty," allowing couples to deduct 5 percent of first $30,000 earnings of spouse with lower earnings in 1982. Increased to 10 percent in 1983.
Indexing	The individual income tax brackets, zero bracket amount, and personal exemption adjusted annually for inflation (measured by the Consumer Price Index), beginning with calendar year 1985.
CORPORATE INCOME TAXES	**(Revenue Loss: –$151 billion)**
Accelerated Cost Recovery	Replaced depreciation rules for tangible property used in trade or business. Accelerated Cost Recovery System (ACRS) provided for faster write-off of capital expenditures under simplified and standardized rules.
Leasing	Liberalized rules allowing firms to transfer unused investment tax credits and depreciation deductions on new investments to profitable firms through leasing transactions.
ENERGY TAXES	**(Revenue Loss: –$12 billion)**
Oil Tax Reductions	Reduced windfall profits tax on newly discovered oil; exemption from windfall profits tax for small producers; tax credit against windfall profits tax for small royalty owners.
SAVINGS INCENTIVES	**(Revenue Loss: –$20 billion)**
IRAs	Increased exclusion for contributions to individual and spousal IRAs.
Self-Employed Retirement Plans	Increased exclusion for contributions to retirement plans.

(continued)

TABLE 4.1 *(continued)*

Savings Certificates	Temporary exclusion (Oct. 1, 1981–Dec. 31, 1982) of up to $1,000 in interest from special savings certificates.
ESTATE AND GIFT TAXES	(Revenue Loss: –$15 billion)
Marital Deductions	Surviving spouse permitted to inherit unlimited amount without paying tax.
Estate and Gift Tax Credits	Increased from $47,000 to $192,800 by 1987, exempting from tax all estates of $600,000 or less.
Rate Reduction	Maximum rate reduced from 70 percent to 50 percent over 1981–1985 period.
Gift Tax Exclusion	Increased from $3,000 to $10,000 per donee, effective Jan. 1, 1982.
MISCELLANEOUS PROVISIONS	(Revenue Gain: +$8.5 billion)

Administrative changes in corporate tax payment schedules.
Increased railroad retirement system tax rate.
Restricted tax shelters involving commodity futures.

a Revenue effects are for all provisions in each category, including the major provisions listed.
Source: Congressional Quarterly, *Congressional Quarterly Almanac, 1981* (Washington, D.C.: Congressional Quarterly, 1982), 92–95.

As the economy continued to weaken and the fiscal outlook deteriorated, the administration agreed that an even larger tax increase might be needed, but Reagan repeatedly insisted that no changes be made in the individual income tax cuts scheduled for 1982 and 1983. The administration instead called for higher business taxes, including a stricter minimum tax on corporations, along with cutbacks in tax preferences, and strengthened enforcement of tax laws. This tax package was then substantially rewritten by Congress, but the individual tax cuts survived intact in 1982, as they would in 1983 and 1984.

The notion that the Reagan tax cuts intentionally created large deficits in order to force Congress to cut domestic programs – the so-called starve the beast hypothesis – does not find much support in the actual congressional response. Among congressional Republicans, for example, enthusiasm for domestic cutbacks plummeted as the prospects for a balanced budget evaporated. As Morgan points out, Senate Republicans had been "remarkably united on budget votes in 1981 because of their shared belief that the new president's program should be given a chance, but ... [were] less willing to go along with the White House once the fiscal consequences were plain."[11]

[11] Iwan W. Morgan, *The Age of Deficits* (Lawrence: University Press of Kansas, 2009), 94.

The deficit miscalculation revealed a lack of understanding about the sensitivity of revenues to economic fluctuations. After the 1974 budget reforms, both Congress and the executive branch used multiyear budget planning and forecasts in order to gauge more accurately the long-term costs of spending and revenue bills. While this approach was, on the whole, beneficial, one drawback was the inherent uncertainty of budget forecasts tied to economic assumptions such as growth, productivity, and inflation. As the Congressional Budget Office (CBO) would later warn, accurate forecasts are especially difficult during "cyclical turning points" – that is, when the economy is moving quickly into or out of recession – and revenue forecasts are particularly uncertain under such conditions.[12] In the case of the 1981 tax cuts, the unexpected economic downturn completely upended the short-term revenue forecasts and made the long-term projections equally unreliable.

The Reagan-era revenue blunders were not unique. In the early 1990s, after the George H. W. Bush administration's tax increase, revenues fell well below estimates. Later in the decade, after the Clinton administration's 1993 tax increase, revenues followed a different trajectory, growing much more rapidly than expected. Then, in the early 2000s, after the George W. Bush tax cuts, revenue growth once again fell significantly below estimates. In Reagan's case, however, the search for what the administration called "revenue enhancements" began almost immediately, when revenue overestimates and spending underestimates began to inflate deficits.

Taxes and Deficit Reduction

From 1982 to 1984, Congress enacted three major tax increases, and two smaller ones, that offset approximately 35 percent of the estimated ERTA revenue losses in 1984 and 1985 and a slightly larger percentage thereafter.[13] Nevertheless, revenue-GDP levels continued to fall during Reagan's first term, hitting a low of 17.3 percent in 1984, two percentage points below the administration's original revenue target. For fiscal years 1982–1985, deficits averaged more than $180 billion annually, while the deficit-GDP level averaged nearly 5 percent. Although the tax policy adjustments after 1981 were substantial, deficits remained at extremely high levels.

TEFRA On September 3, 1982, President Reagan signed the Tax Equity and Fiscal Responsibility Act (TEFRA), a complicated package of tax preference reforms, payroll tax increases, higher excise taxes, and strengthened tax compliance provisions. Although Senate Republicans, particularly Finance Committee chairman Robert J. Dole, had taken the lead in putting together TEFRA, House Republicans were split over whether to support any tax increases at all. The

---

[12] Congressional Budget Office, *The Budget and Economic Outlook: Fiscal Years 2003–2012* (Washington, D.C.: Congressional Budget Office, 2002), 90–92.

[13] Dennis S. Ippolito, *Uncertain Legacies: Federal Budget Policy from Roosevelt through Reagan* (Charlottesville: University Press of Virginia, 1990), 74.

upcoming midterm elections were undoubtedly a concern, but a number of TEFRA critics in the House complained that the Republican low-tax message was being subverted under the guise of deficit reduction. Morgan reports, for example, a letter from sixty-one House Republicans to Reagan that warned "the Republican Party is in danger of making a U-turn back to its familiar role of tax collector for Democratic spending programs."[14] Newt Gingrich, a junior House Republican at the time who would become Speaker in 1995, later offered the famous characterization of Dole as "tax collector for the welfare state," and Gingrich would lead the House Republican revolt against George H. W. Bush's deficit-reduction tax increase in 1990 on the same grounds.

Even after Reagan called on both parties to support TEFRA, a majority of House Republicans deserted Reagan on three key procedural votes involving TEFRA, and only a bare majority voted for final passage. In order to placate the House Democratic leadership, Reagan had to promise personal letters thanking Democrats for backing the administration. Still, the final vote in the House was close, with 123 Democrats joining 104 Republicans to form a 227–206 majority, and the Republican Senate adopted TEFRA by a narrow 52–47 margin. Some Republicans were clearly upset that Reagan had reneged so quickly on his promise to oppose higher taxes. In his 1982 State of the Union Address, Reagan had pledged to "seek no tax increases this year" or to retreat from his "basic program of tax relief."[15] He maintained that the economic and deficit problems the nation had encountered had not been caused by the administration's program but rather were "the inheritance of decades of tax and tax and spend and spend" and was adamant that "higher taxes would not mean lower deficits."[16] In his budget message to Congress on February 8, however, Reagan announced a deficit-reduction program predicated largely on spending cuts but including $44 billion in additional revenues over three years from closing "unintended loopholes," repealing "obsolete tax incentives," strengthening the minimum corporate tax, and increasing user fees.[17] The proposed revenue increases, according to Reagan, "involve the collection of a tax that is owed now or that was intended by the Congress, or elimination of incentives that are no longer needed due to the sweeping reform of business taxation" enacted in 1981. The congressional response to Reagan's tax program was negative, and his proposed spending cuts found little support even among Republicans. The administration's budget program, which had dominated the congressional agenda in 1981, was dismissed outright in 1982.

The Senate Budget Committee voted 20–0 on May 5 to reject the administration's budget, and Republican leaders on the committee then discussed a three-year revenue increase nearly three times larger than Reagan had

[14] Morgan, *The Age of Deficits*, 99.
[15] Ronald Reagan, *Public Papers of the Presidents of the United States: Ronald Reagan, 1982, Book I* (Washington, D.C.: Government Printing Office, 1983), 74.
[16] Ibid., 73–74.
[17] Ibid., 131.

proposed.[18] The Budget Committee chairman, Pete V. Domenici, indicated that a "freeze on the third year of the scheduled [individual] tax cut" might be needed "if that is the final element that a compromise of this magnitude hinges upon." On the House side, the Budget Committee's plan contained an even larger tax increase – $147 billion over three years – that made the third-year freeze inevitable.

The administration and Senate Republicans finally settled on a $95 billion tax increase that preserved the third-year income tax cut, and the House agreed to accept the lower revenue target for the FY 1983 budget resolution. The Senate Finance Committee then took the lead in drafting the reconciliation tax bill mandated by the resolution, and its major "revenue enhancers" affected corporations and financial institutions. Senate Democrats attempted to amend the Finance Committee bill when it reached the floor by eliminating the third-year tax cut for high-income taxpayers, but this effort failed. A parallel effort by business interests to remove tax preference and compliance reforms was turned back as well. Banks and financial institutions, for example, strongly opposed the new withholding requirement for interest and dividend income in the Finance Committee bill, but the requirement survived on a 49–48 vote.[19]

On July 23, the Senate voted 50–47 to accept the tax-increase package. The House Ways and Means Committee, which had been unable to agree on its own tax-cut plan, decided to proceed straight to conference with the Senate. The Senate-passed bill emerged largely intact from the ensuing conference but still faced an uncertain fate in both chambers. Business lobbying against the conference bill was intense and reinforced by the American Conservative Union, which strongly denounced the bill, but President Reagan and the congressional leadership of both parties managed to secure a narrow victory in the House and Senate.

The three-year revenue increase under TEFRA totaled $98 billion, slightly more than the $95 billion required by the budget resolution, and the projected increase over five years was nearly $215 billion.[20] More than half of this long-term increase was accounted for by higher corporate taxes (see Table 4.2). The ERTA safe harbor leasing rules, one of the more costly "sweeteners" in the 1981 bill, were phased out, and some of the "unintended benefits" from the accelerated cost recovery system were scaled back. TEFRA effectively repealed a substantial portion of the business tax relief that had been conferred before the fiscal outlook turned negative, and it reduced other long-standing tax preferences as well.[21]

---

[18] Congressional Quarterly, *Congressional Quarterly Almanac, 1982*, 187.
[19] The Interest and Dividend Tax Compliance Act of 1983 repealed the withholding requirement. In this instance, financial institution lobbying overcame the opposition of the Reagan administration and the congressional leadership of both parties.
[20] Congressional Quarterly, *Congressional Quarterly Almanac, 1982*, 30.
[21] Ibid., 29–32.

TABLE 4.2. *Tax Equity and Fiscal Responsibility Act of 1982 (P.L. 97-248):
Major Provisions and Estimated Revenue Effects, Fiscal Years 1983–1987[a]*

INDIVIDUAL INCOME TAXES	**(Revenue Gain: +$13 billion)**
Exclusions	Strengthened minimum tax restrictions.
Deductions	Limited medical and casualty loss deductions.
CORPORATE INCOME TAXES	**(Revenue Gain: +$117 billion)**
Accelerated Cost Recovery	Modified 1981 ACRS depreciation rules.
Leasing	Repealed safe-harbor leasing.
Investment Tax Credit	Limited basis adjustments.
Miscellaneous Tax Preferences	Limited tax shelter and tax deferred accounting for life insurance companies, construction and aerospace firms, and corporate mergers.
SOCIAL INSURANCE TAXES	**(Revenue Gain: +$14 billion)**
Unemployment Tax	Increased tax rate and wage base.
Medicare	Extended Medicare Part A (Hospital Insurance) tax to federal employees.
EXCISE TAXES	**(Revenue Gain: +$15 billion)**
Airport and Airway	Increased passenger ticket tax, aviation fuel tax, and air freight tax.
Cigarettes	Increased per-pack tax rate.
Telephone	Increased telephone tax rate.
COMPLIANCE PROVISIONS	**(Revenue Gain: +$55 billion)**
Withholding	Required withholding for pension payments and 10 percent withholding of interest and dividend payments.
Reporting	Additional reporting requirements for tip income, independent contractor income.
Enforcement	Additional IRS personnel and strengthened enforcement.

[a] Revenue effects are for all provisions in each category, including the major provisions listed.
Source: Congressional Quarterly, *Congressional Quarterly Almanac, 1982* (Washington, D.C.:
Congressional Quarterly, 1983), 29–32.

The reluctant embrace of a major election-year tax increase by the administration and Congress was rooted in widespread fears that mounting deficits would stall economic recovery. In February, Federal Reserve chairman Paul A. Volcker had warned Congress that failure to hold down the deficit would lead to a "collision course" between monetary policy and fiscal policy.[22] The CBO had likewise alerted Congress to "the risk of an unprecedented clash between monetary and fiscal policy that could produce either a flat, no-growth economy ... [or] a spike in interest rates driving the economy into recession once again."

[22] Ibid., 176.

By the time Congress approved TEFRA, baseline deficit estimates had moved into the $200 billion range, interest rates remained extremely high, and the administration's forecast of a strong economic recovery in the latter half of 1982 had been dismissed by even its most optimistic supporters. In the face of these fiscal pressures, Reagan was forced to support increased taxes, but his policy compromise was still limited. The individual tax cuts of 1981, which had been attacked as too costly in terms of revenue loss and as unfair in the benefits afforded high-income taxpayers, were preserved in their entirety. The TEFRA business tax changes were of secondary concern to Reagan and were also less consequential with regard to revenues. Over the next two years, as the economy finally recovered, deficits still hovered around $200 billion, but the administration repeatedly rebuffed congressional entreaties to increase individual income taxes.

The political sensitivity of the tax issue for Republicans was underscored by an otherwise routine reauthorization for transportation programs in 1982. The Highway Revenue Act of 1982 authorized $71 billion for highway construction and repairs, as well as mass transit capital projects, for fiscal years 1984–1990. The interstate highway system was funded by the Highway Trust Fund, and the new authorization required additional revenues; Congress provided for this necessary increase in the gasoline tax and other highway taxes. Although Transportation Secretary Drew Lewis supported the construction program and related tax increase, Reagan refused to endorse it. On September 28, Reagan summarily dismissed a gas tax increase, stating, "Unless there's a palace coup and I'm overtaken or overthrown, no, I don't see the necessity for that."[23]

Two months later, Reagan announced that he would support higher gasoline taxes, explaining that his earlier statement had only applied to general revenues. A lame-duck session of Congress then took up the multiyear authorization, which included additional taxes on the sale of heavy trucks and on highway use by trucks. The Senate broke a filibuster by conservative Republicans who objected to the tax increase, and a conference committee bill was approved by both chambers in late December. During the protracted debate on the transportation bill, supporters argued that user fees were not technically taxes, but the projected revenue increases nevertheless averaged approximately $4.5 billion annually.

The 1983 and 1984 Tax Increases The 98th Congress renewed the contest over deficit reduction. Reagan remained determined to protect all of the individual tax cuts from 1981, while Congress refused to support the domestic spending cuts that Reagan continued to propose. The budget resolution that Congress adopted in 1983 mandated tax increases and spending cuts that never made it through the House and Senate. In 1984, the administration and Congress clashed once again over the appropriate balance between spending

[23] Ibid., 322.

cuts and tax increases, before agreement was reached on a modest deficit-reduction compromise.

In 1983, House Democrats renewed the battle over the ERTA individual tax cuts, passing a "cap" ($720 per family) on the maximum tax reduction scheduled to go into effect on July 1. The Senate then rejected the House-passed measure after Reagan warned the tax cap "must not and will not become law."[24] Democrats dropped this challenge, which was largely symbolic given the minor revenue gains involved. Serious deficit reduction required much larger revenue increases, but Democrats were not prepared to confront Reagan on the entire third-year tax cut.

The revenue increases that did pass in 1983 were divorced entirely from ERTA. The Social Security Act Amendments of 1983 increased the payroll tax rate for employers and employees and also levied a new tax on benefits for retirees whose incomes exceeded certain thresholds. These and related tax provisions were expected to increase revenues by an estimated $165 billion over seven years, restoring short-term solvency to the Social Security trust funds.[25] Other provisions, such as an increase in the normal retirement age from 65 to 66 years between 2004 and 2009 and from 66 to 67 years between 2022 and 2027, were designed to ensure long-term solvency.

The Social Security rescue plan passed quickly and with strong bipartisan support, but it came after nearly two years of intense partisan debates over benefits and taxes. In early 1981, the Reagan administration had proposed cutbacks in Social Security disability benefits, increased benefit penalties for early retirement, and mandated other benefit reductions that it claimed would maintain the solvency of the program's trust funds without raising taxes. Indeed, the administration claimed that the payroll tax rate could eventually be reduced if its recommendations were adopted. The Democratic reaction was swift and furious. On May 20, the House Democratic caucus unanimously adopted a resolution denouncing the Reagan plan as "an unconscionable breach of faith" that threatened to "destroy the program [and] a generation of retirees."[26] Senate Democrats promised to use "every rule in the book" to block Reagan's plan, and Senate Republicans quickly backed away as well. As part of a supplemental appropriations bill that Reagan had requested, the Senate unanimously agreed to an amendment that pledged congressional disapproval of any "immediate or inequitable" cuts in benefits.[27] The Democratic version of this amendment, which included the House Democrats' charge of a "breach of faith," was defeated by only one vote.

The administration officially withdrew its Social Security plan in the fall, even though its fate had been evident for months. Upon Reagan's

---

[24] Congressional Quarterly, *Congressional Quarterly Almanac, 1983* (Washington, D.C.: Congressional Quarterly, 1984), 250.

[25] Ibid., 219.

[26] Congressional Quarterly, *Congressional Quarterly Almanac, 1981*, 119.

[27] Ibid., 284.

recommendation, a bipartisan commission was then established to formulate a Social Security reform proposal. The National Commission on Social Security Reform issued its recommendations on January 15, 1983, and these proposals were then incorporated into the Social Security bill that cleared Congress on March 25. The tax increases that the Commission recommended and Congress approved were strongly criticized by some congressional Republicans and only grudgingly agreed to by the administration. There was virtually no support, however, for substantial benefit cuts, and Democrats were willing to stand up to the administration on Social Security much more aggressively than on tax cuts. On July 31, 1981, for example, Congress passed the Omnibus Budget Reconciliation Act, which cut spending for numerous entitlements and eliminated entirely the $122 minimum Social Security benefit. That same day, the House approved a Social Security financing bill that reinstated the minimum benefit. Reagan then went along with the House, stating, "It was never our intention to take this support away from those who truly need it."[28] On December 16, Congress restored the minimum benefit for three million recipients, funding it through a new payroll tax on sick pay for employees.

The administration also wound up supporting a payroll tax increase as part of a financial rescue plan for the railroad retirement program – a private pension plan administered by the federal government. On April 1, 1983, the Railroad Retirement Board reported to Congress that a 40 percent benefit cut for retirees would be needed to erase the shortfall between the employee and employer payroll taxes that funded the program and the scheduled benefit payments for the upcoming year. The Railroad Retirement Revenue Act of 1983, like the Social Security rescue plan, included some modest benefit cuts, but its primary component was increased taxes that, by the late 1980s, would exceed $1 billion annually.

In 1984, the Senate Republican leadership once again took the lead in attacking the deficit. Working with the administration, Senate Republicans formulated a multiyear deficit-reduction plan that included approximately $50 billion in tax increases for fiscal years 1985–1987. With the House accepting this revenue target and agreeing to leave individual income tax rate cuts and indexing in place, the Deficit Reduction Act of 1984 (DEFRA) was passed on June 27. The DEFRA tax increases included higher excise taxes on liquor and telephones and restrictions on numerous tax preferences for individuals and businesses. The largest revenue gains from individual tax preference changes were the repeal of the net interest exclusion and modification of income-averaging rules, which were expected to increase revenues by approximately $13 billion over three years.[29] Among the major changes affecting business were tighter restrictions on tax shelters, reduced depreciation for real estate, and stricter standards governing business leasing of equipment.

---

[28] Ibid., 117.
[29] Congressional Quarterly, *Congress and the Nation, 1981–1984* (Washington, D.C.: Congressional Quarterly, 1985), 144–145.

Bipartisan support for DEFRA was reinforced by a number of "sweeteners." Particularly important for conservatives was the reduction, from one year to six months, of the holding period needed to qualify for preferential capital gains tax treatment (the long-term capital gains tax rate was 20 percent, while the top marginal rate on ordinary income under ERTA was 50 percent). In acquiescing to the new capital gains tax break, Democrats insisted on increasing the maximum earned-income tax credit (EITC) for working-poor families and on raising the phase-out threshold as well.

The Reagan administration insisted that tax increases be accompanied by spending cuts as the DEFRA measure moved through Congress. Approximately $13 billion in spending cuts were included in DEFRA, primarily through reduced reimbursements for hospitals and physician services and higher premiums for Part B Medicare coverage. These savings estimates were no doubt inflated, especially given the potential cost of DEFRA provisions that expanded Medicaid, SSI, and AFDC benefits. The spending cutbacks that the administration had hoped to impose on other domestic programs were even less likely to be realized, because the House repeatedly rejected attempts to impose multiyear appropriations limits or "caps." At first, Reagan had insisted he would not sign any tax increase without enforceable spending ceilings, but he did not follow through on that threat. As a result, deficit reduction in 1984 came almost exclusively through tax increases.

The deficit issue dominated the budget policy debates during 1984, but the Reagan administration's defense of its core ERTA program did not waver. Indeed, that defense became even more aggressive as the economic recovery that began in 1983 gained strength, and Reagan's political standing rose accordingly. The economic recovery, however, did not remove the deficit challenge. In 1982 and 1983, approximately 40 percent of the more than $385 billion in deficits had been caused by a weak economy.[30] By 1984, the influence of cyclical economic factors on the deficit had almost disappeared. According to the CBO, nearly $160 billion of the $185 billion fiscal 1984 deficit was "structural" – the result of a basic imbalance between the spending and revenue laws then in effect.

Moreover, baseline deficit projections, which assumed no change in these laws, showed deficits steadily increasing to nearly $280 billion in fiscal 1989.[31] Much of this increase was due to the growing impact of the ERTA tax cuts that remained in place and that greatly exceeded the combined revenue effects of TEFRA, DEFRA, and other tax bills enacted from 1982 to 1984. According to the administration's own estimates, the tax legislation enacted during Reagan's first term reduced total net revenues for 1985–1989 by more than $740 billion

---

[30] Congressional Budget Office, *The Budget and Economic Outlook: Fiscal Years 2010–2020* (Washington, D.C.: Congressional Budget Office, 2010), 136.

[31] Congressional Budget Office, *Revising the Corporate Income Tax* (Washington, D.C.: Congressional Budget Office, 1985), 170.

compared to pre-1981 tax law, with individual income tax receipts falling by more than $785 billion.[32]

Nevertheless, Reagan was adamant that income taxes would not be increased, and the Republican Party platform in 1984 dutifully followed his lead. Indeed, Republicans promised to extend the philosophy behind ERTA by eliminating the "incentive-destroying effects of graduated rates" through a "modified flat tax."[33] On indexing, the platform pledged to "fight any effort to repeal, modify, or defer it." As for taxes in general, Republicans could "foresee no economic circumstances which would call for increased taxation" and warned that "tax reform must not be a guise for tax increases."

The Democratic response to this unequivocal stance was less than bold. In accepting the Democratic presidential nomination, Walter F. Mondale proclaimed that it was "time to tell the truth. It must be done, it must be done. Mr. Reagan will raise taxes, and so will I. He won't tell you. I just did. There's another difference. When he raises taxes, it won't be done fairly."[34] The Democratic platform, however, did not call for repealing the entire ERTA tax cut. Instead, it promised to reduce what it called "intolerable deficits" by raising "the revenues we need . . . without increasing the burden on average taxpayers."[35] This was to be accomplished by "limiting the benefits of the third year of the Reagan tax cuts to those with incomes of less than $60,000," a partial deferral of indexation, and unspecified tax reforms.

Neither the "intolerable deficits" caused by the Reagan tax cuts nor their alleged unfairness wound up having much resonance with the electorate. Reagan's landslide victory settled – at least for him – the debate over tax increases. The administration's tax reform initiative, which culminated in the passage of the Tax Reform Act of 1986, was intentionally divorced from deficit reduction. Despite serious congressional misgivings, Reagan imposed a revenue-neutral standard on second-term tax policy change.

The Second-Term Tax Policy Track

The Reagan administration's FY 1986 budget, submitted to Congress on February 4, 1985, did not challenge the need for reducing deficits. Rather, it proposed that "both the scope and scale of Federal spending be drastically cut back to reduce the deficit."[36] The only revenue increases in the president's budget were user fees, such as navigation and customs charges, that totaled an estimated $2.9 billion in FY 1986, and offsetting receipts, such as military

[32] Office of Management and Budget, *Budget of the United States Government, Fiscal Year 1987* (Washington, D.C.: Government Printing Office, 1986), 4-4–4-6.

[33] Congressional Quarterly, *Congress and the Nation, 1981–1984*, 42-B.

[34] Ibid., 70-B.

[35] Ibid., 78-B.

[36] Office of Management and Budget, *Budget of the United States Government, Fiscal Year 1986* (Washington, D.C.: Government Printing Office, 1985), M8.

retirement contributions, that added an additional $2.2 billion. These additional revenues were offset by proposed new tax incentives and tax credits, many of which Congress had failed to support in the past. In any case, the deficit reduction in the administration's program was based entirely on cuts in discretionary programs and entitlements, although the latter exempted Social Security.

The Last, Best Chance

Senate Republicans, notably the new majority leader Robert Dole and Budget Committee chairman Pete Domenici, were hopeful that a more ambitious (and more realistic) deficit-reduction plan could be negotiated with the administration and with House Democrats. Instead, the Senate plan – which included tax increases, suspension of the scheduled 1986 Social Security cost-of-living adjustment (COLA), a no-real-growth defense budget, and the elimination of thirteen domestic programs – was ultimately rejected. After a House-Senate conference committee was unable to reach agreement on a FY 1986 budget plan, Reagan decided to intervene. At a July 9 meeting with House and Senate leaders, Reagan made clear, once again, that he would not accept any deficit-reduction plan that included a tax increase.

The Senate plan was then supplanted by an agreement between Reagan and House Speaker O'Neill that protected their respective priorities but also ignored the deficit problem. O'Neill and House Democrats agreed to an inflation adjustment in the defense budget in exchange for scheduled Social Security benefit increases, and Reagan won assurance that House Democrats would not press for a tax increase. The budget resolution adopted on August 1 followed the Reagan-O'Neill agreement and, according to Reagan's Office of Management and Budget (OMB) director, David A. Stockman, scuttled the "last, best chance" for a serious attack on the deficit. Stockman, whose resignation became effective that same day, explained later that he realized there was no "rational possibility left of dealing with the irrationality that had descended on the nation."[37]

Congress passed legislation in December that mandated a balanced budget by FY 1991, but its enforcement provisions exempted Social Security spending and taxes. The nearly year-long struggle to deal with the deficit did not produce much in the way of tangible results. It did demonstrate, however, that Reagan would not compromise on tax increases, even if that meant siding with House Democrats rather than Senate Republicans. As a result, revenue-neutral tax reform became the only option available to Congress.

The Evolution of Tax Reform

The Reagan administration's tax program, later known as Treasury I, was officially released in November 1984. In line with Reagan's reform emphases – he

---

[37] Quoted in Morgan, *The Age of Deficits*, 109.

had focused on "fairness, simplicity, and incentives for growth" in his State of the Union Address earlier that year – Treasury I called for a sweeping overhaul of tax rates and the tax base. In exchange for lower rates – a top marginal rate of 35 percent for individuals and 33 percent for corporations – Treasury I proposed to repeal or reduce numerous tax preferences. These basic changes were complemented by more complicated reforms, such as the indexation of capital income gains and integration of individual and corporate income taxes. In order to achieve revenue neutrality, Treasury I shifted income tax burdens – from low-income to high-income taxpayers – and from individuals to corporations. While many of the specific recommendations in Treasury I would be changed over the next two years, revenue neutrality and these shifts in tax burdens managed to survive repeated challenges.

The economic policy case for Treasury I – reducing the distorting effects of tax preferences and thereby lowering rates – had reasonably widespread support among economists. The political case was problematic. Tax preferences had defenders in both parties. In addition, steeply progressive marginal rates had been part of the Democratic Party's catechism since the New Deal, and one of the main Democratic objections to ERTA had been the reduced rates for upper-income taxpayers. The even flatter rate structure in Treasury I therefore posed an obvious political difficulty. In 1982, however, Democratic Senator Bill Bradley and Representative Richard A. Gephardt had put forward a "Fair Tax" plan that emphasized progressive tax burdens rather than progressive marginal rates and recast the argument about trade-offs between an expanded tax base and lower marginal rates.[38] Similar proposals were promoted by members of both parties over the next two years, with another Jack Kemp tax initiative, the Kemp-Kasten bill, helping to strengthen Republican support for the low rate–broad base concept.

Treasury II On May 28, 1985, the administration's official tax reform proposal was unveiled, and it encountered stiff resistance in Congress to almost all of its key features. At a time of continued high deficits, revenue neutrality was a problem for members of both parties. In addition, Treasury II's top marginal rate for individuals was 35 percent, with a maximum effective rate for capital gains of 17.5 percent, and congressional Democrats focused much of their criticism on the potential tax savings for high-income taxpayers. Many Republicans were wary of the proposed business tax reforms, such as the repeal of investment tax credits and the lengthened depreciation schedules. Treasury II's recommendations for curtailing individual tax preferences – repealing deductions for state and local taxes, limiting interest deductions for home mortgages, and reducing exclusions for employee fringe benefits – were especially controversial.

As the Ways and Means and Finance committees took up Treasury II, these objections repeatedly threatened to stall comprehensive reform. In the

[38] Steuerle, *The Tax Decade*, 96.

House, the Ways and Means Committee struggled to put together a bill that could attract bipartisan support. A measure of the difficulty was the extended markup, beginning on September 18 and lasting until December 3, before Ways and Means could report a bill to the House. The Ways and Means chairman, Dan Rostenkowski, played a pivotal role in shaping the House bill, which finally passed in mid-December and only after Reagan had personally lobbied Republicans to support the measure.

Republican opposition to the Ways and Means proposal was largely aimed at its business tax provisions, which included a higher corporate tax rate than the Treasury II plan and a more extensive reduction of corporate tax preferences. The House bill's top marginal rate of 38 percent for individual taxpayers, its higher rate for capital gains, and the reduced tax relief for upper-income taxpayers added to the Republican disquiet. Reagan's assurance that he would veto the House version of tax reform unless it was substantially changed by the Senate persuaded 70 Republicans to vote with the Democrats on the rule that brought the measure to the floor, but 110 Republicans still voted against it.

The Senate's tax reform odyssey was even more protracted. The Finance Committee had held hearings on Treasury II in the summer of 1985 but waited until the House bill passed to begin work on an alternative that would hew more closely to the Treasury II framework. The deficit issue, however, soon complicated what was already a difficult political challenge. On February 7, 1986, a federal court invalidated the key enforcement provision of the balanced-budget legislation that Congress had passed the previous December. The Balanced Budget and Emergency Deficit Control Act of 1985 – popularly known as Gramm-Rudman-Hollings (GRH) after its Senate sponsors, Republicans Phil Gramm and Warren B. Rudman and Democrat Ernest F. Hollings – provided for automatic spending cuts (sequestration) if the president and Congress failed to meet annual deficit ceilings that would bring the budget into balance over six years. With the sequestration procedure deemed unconstitutional (a holding that was later affirmed by the Supreme Court), Senate leaders renewed their effort to enact a credible deficit-reduction program. On April 10, the Senate voted 72–24 for a nonbinding resolution that called for passage of a deficit-reduction plan as a precondition for considering tax reform.

Nonetheless, administration representatives and Finance Committee leaders continued to work on a revenue-neutral tax reform bill. That effort soon collapsed, however, because the committee found it impossible to agree on tax-law changes that would meet the revenue-neutral standard. The committee markup that had begun on March 19 was suspended by chairman Robert W. Packwood on April 18. The breakthrough came a week later as Packwood and the committee staff put together a new framework that reduced individual tax rates even further than the administration had proposed and, at the same time, greatly expanded the roster of repealed and reduced tax preferences. On May 7, the Finance Committee unanimously approved a bill that lowered the top marginal rate for individuals to 27 percent and the top corporate rate to 33 percent, eliminated the preferential treatment of capital gains income and the investment tax credit, and repealed or trimmed numerous other individual and corporate tax preferences. The committee bill reduced projected individual income tax revenues by more than $100 billion over five years, compared to existing law, but the net effect of its business tax provisions was to raise revenues by a similar amount.[39] In addition, substantial relief was provided for low- and middle-income taxpayers, with more than six million of the working poor relieved of all tax liability and an estimated 80 percent of all taxpayers benefiting from the 15 percent tax bracket.

Within the Finance Committee, a revenue-neutral rule had been applied to all proposed amendments.[40] That same requirement was enforced during the three weeks of floor debate on the Finance Committee bill. Efforts to restore two popular deductions – for full deductibility of state and local sales taxes and the $2,000 deduction for individual retirement accounts (IRAs) for all taxpayers regardless of income – were narrowly defeated. Perhaps the most important challenge to the central thrust of the Finance Committee plan was an amendment sponsored by Democrat George J. Mitchell to add a third marginal rate of 35 percent for high-income taxpayers and to provide additional tax relief for middle-income groups. In opposing the Mitchell amendment, Packwood argued that it was a "Trojan Horse" for groups to then say, "Please give us now our special exemption because you've raised the rates too high for us to invest in low-income housing or venture capital or contribute to charity, or whatever."[41] Only a bare majority of Democrats voted for the Mitchell amendment, and it was rejected by a 71–29 vote. Final Senate approval of the 1,489-page Finance Committee bill, with only minor amendments, took place on June 24 by a 97–3 vote.

The House-Senate conference began on July 17 and was concluded one month later. The resolution of major disputes over the individual income tax rate structure, tax preference changes, and individual versus corporate tax burdens generally followed the Senate-passed bill. The House managed to convince the Senate to reduce business depreciation write-offs in order to increase individual tax relief, and the House also managed to ease tax preference restrictions for middle-income taxpayers. A last-minute problem with the revenue-neutral rule – a budget and economic update in mid-August that estimated a $17 billion revenue loss from the conference bill[42] – was settled by raising the top

[39] Congressional Quarterly, *Congressional Quarterly Almanac, 1986* (Washington, D.C.: Congressional Quarterly, 1987), 510.
[40] Ibid., 511.
[41] Ibid., 513.
[42] Joseph White and Aaron Wildavsky, *The Deficit and the Public Interest* (Berkeley: University of California Press, 1989), 492.

individual and corporate tax rates by one percentage point. The conference committee bill was then reported out on August 16 and, after a lengthy redrafting process, approved by the House on a 292–136 vote on September 25 and by the Senate on a 74–23 vote two days later.

Despite these wide margins, serious questions remained about the economic and budgetary impact of the 2,000-page conference report. Republicans, in particular, were worried about the impact of business taxation changes on incentives for investment and growth. Republican John C. Danforth, who had helped draft the original Finance Committee bill but voted against the conference report, criticized the decision to "dump more and more taxes on our industrial sector, on research and development, on education, in order to placate this goal of low rates."[43] Even Packwood admitted that no one was certain whether the bill would "help the economy or hurt the economy." What was certain, however, was that the bill did not address the problem of large deficits. Senate Budget Committee chairman Domenici voted for the bill but warned that its five-year revenue neutrality masked immediate revenue losses that "will come back to haunt us."

The Tax Reform Act of 1986 The most noteworthy policy changes in 1986 were the new marginal rates (see Table 4.3). The steeply progressive rate structure that had defined the federal income tax since World War II was replaced by a 15 percent rate for most taxpayers, a 28 percent bracket, and for very high-income taxpayers, phase-out provisions that effectively applied the 28 percent rate to all taxable income. The near doubling of the personal exemption (from $1,080 to $2,000 by 1989) and higher standard deduction (from $3,670 to $5,000 for joint returns in 1988) eliminated all income tax liabilities for low-income families. Both the personal exemption and standard deduction were indexed beginning in 1990, ensuring that low-income tax relief would be maintained permanently. For high-income taxpayers, the personal exemption was partially or fully phased out through a surtax on taxable income above specified levels.

The Tax Reform Act of 1986 (TRA 1986) repealed or modified numerous tax preferences. The most important changes in terms of revenue effects were the repeal of preferential capital gains tax rates that had been in effect for decades and the investment tax credit for corporations. The revenue gains from these changes were estimated at approximately $95 billion in FY 1991.[44] Smaller but still significant revenue effects were expected from changes in the deductibility of state and local sales taxes and nonmortgage consumer interest and in the exclusions for pension contributions and private purpose tax-exempt bond interest. In addition, revenue losses from continuing tax preferences were

---

[43] Congressional Quarterly, *Congressional Quarterly Almanac, 1986*, 524.

[44] Congressional Budget Office, *The Effects of Tax Reform on Tax Expenditures* (Washington, D.C.: Congressional Budget Office, 1988), ix–x.

TABLE 4.3. *Comparisons of Tax Rates and Related Provisions, Existing Law through Tax Reform Act of 1986*

	Existing Law	Treasury II May 1985	House Bill Dec. 1985	Senate Bill June 1986	TRA 1986 Oct. 1986
Individual	11–50% (14 brackets)	15, 25, 35%	15, 25, 35, & 38%	15 & 27%/phase-out	15 & 28%/phase-out
Corporate	15–46%	15–33%	15–36%	15–33%	15–34%
Capital Gains	20% top effective rate	17.5% top effective rate	22% top effective rate	Same as regular income	Same as regular income
Minimum Tax (alternative or add-on)	20% individual/ 15% corporate	Revised/ expanded	Expanded/ 25%	Expanded/ 20%	Expanded/ 21% individual/ 20% corporate
Personal Exemption	$1,080	$2,000	$2,000/$1,500	$2,000/phase-out	$2,000/phase-out
State and Local Taxes	Deductible	Deduction eliminated	No change from existing law	Income, real estate and personal property taxes deductible; sales tax deduction limited to 60 percent of the amount in excess of state income taxes	Income, real estate and personal property taxes deductible; sales tax not deductible
Charitable Donations	Deductible	Full deductions for itemizers; none for non-itemizers	Full deduction for itemizers; non-itemizers could deduct amount above $100; appreciated value of charitable gifts subject to minimum tax	Full deductions for itemizers; none for non-itemizers	Full deductions for itemizers; none for non-itemizers; appreciated value of charitable gifts subject to minimum tax

(continued)

TABLE 4.3 (continued)

	Existing Law	Treasury II May 1985	House Bill Dec. 1985	Senate Bill June 1986	TRA 1986 Oct. 1986
Interest Deductions	Deductions for home mortgage and nonbusiness interest	Unlimited deduction for mortgages on primary residences; additional interest deductions capped at $5,000	Unlimited deduction for mortgages on first and second residences; additional deduction of $10,000 ($20,000 for joint returns) plus the value of a taxpayer's investment income	Unlimited deduction for mortgages on first and second residences; no consumer interest deduction; interest paid on borrowing to produce investment income deductible equal to the value of the investment earnings	Unlimited deduction for mortgages on first and second residences; limits on mortgage borrowing for unrelated purposes; no consumer interest deduction; interest paid on borrowing to produce investment income deductible equal to the value of the earnings
Retirement Benefits	Tax-deductible IRA contributions of $2,000 for each worker and $200 for each non-working spouse; employer-sponsored 401(k) tax-exempt savings plans with maximum contributions of $30,000 annually	Allow non-working spouse IRA contributions of $2,000; limit 401(k) contributions to $8,000 annually, less amounts contributed to IRAs	Continue existing law on tax-exempt IRA contributions; restrict 401(k) contributions to $7,000 annually; limit to $2,000 the total exemption for contributions by an individual to both an IRA and a 401(k) plan, to encourage 401(k) and discourage IRA contributions	Limit tax-exempt IRA contributions to persons not covered by pension plans; restrict 401(k) contributions to $7,000 annually; make sweeping changes to private pension plans to improve coverage and restrict benefits for high-income persons	Limit tax-exempt IRA contributions to persons not covered by pension plans or those below specified income levels; restrict 401(k) contributions to $7,000 annually; make sweeping changes in private pensions to improve coverage and restrict benefits for high-income persons

Investment Tax Credit	6–10 percent	Repealed	Repealed	Repealed retroactively to Jan. 1, 1986	Repealed retroactively to Jan. 1, 1986
Depreciation	Recovery periods of 3–19 years with accelerated writeoff	More generous writeoff over 4–28 years; value adjusted for inflation	Recovery periods of 3–30 years; partially indexed for inflation	Retain existing system of rapid writeoffs, permitting larger writeoffs for most property over longer periods	Retain system of rapid writeoffs similar to existing law; permit larger writeoffs for most property, but over longer periods
Business Expenses	Deductible	Deduction for entertainment repealed; limit on meals	Deduction of 80 percent of business meals and 80 percent of entertainment costs	Similar to House for meals and entertainment; most miscellaneous deductions eliminated	Deduction of 80 percent of business meals and entertainment costs; miscellaneous employee business expenses limited
Tax-Exempt Bonds	Bonds earning tax-free interest allowed for governmental and many nongovernmental purposes, such as sports arenas and mortgages	Effectively eliminate use of bonds for nongovernmental purposes	Cap use of nongovernmental bonds; reserve a portion for charitable organizations; some interest subject to minimum tax	Cap use of nongovernmental bonds, exclude multifamily rental housing and charitable organizations from the cap	Cap use of nongovernmental bonds, exclude charitable organizations from the cap; some interest subject to minimum tax

Source: Congressional Quarterly, *Congressional Quarterly Almanac, 1986* (Washington, D.C.: Congressional Quarterly, 1987), 492–493. Copyright 1987. Reproduced with permission of CQ Roll Call, Inc. via Copyright Clearance Center.

projected to decline because lower tax rates, along with higher standard deductions and personal exemptions, would lead fewer taxpayers to itemize deductions. Finally, TRA 1986 eliminated a widely used tax shelter by prohibiting losses from "passive" business activities from being used to offset other types of income.

TRA 1986 was ostensibly revenue-neutral when enacted, but there was considerable uncertainty about its actual revenue effects, particularly the tax preference changes. Later assessments showed net revenue losses after 1987 that were considerably greater than expected. For fiscal years 1987–1991, TRA 1986 reduced revenues by approximately $50 billion.[45] Tax measures in 1987 and 1988 compensated for some of these losses, but the impact on the deficit was modest. The most important of these measures was the Omnibus Budget Reconciliation Act of 1987 (OBRA 1987), adopted after an October 19, 1987, stock market crash that was widely blamed on the deficit. The merits of this claim were dubious, because the fiscal 1987 deficit was $150 billion, more than $70 billion less than the 1986 deficit and the lowest deficit since 1982. The administration and Congress nevertheless determined that tangible action was needed to calm investors, and a month-long "budget summit" led to an agreement on tax increases and spending cuts to reduce projected deficits for fiscal years 1988–1989 by more than $75 billion.[46] Approximately one-third of this total represented tax increases, including reduced corporate and individual tax deductions. The interest deduction for home mortgages, for example, was capped (the mortgage limit was set at $1 million), and various corporate tax preferences were curbed. But the bulk of new revenues came from excise taxes and from accounting and compliance reforms. Neither individual or corporate tax rates nor major tax preferences were affected.

For Reagan's entire second term, there was nothing even remotely comparable to the deficit-reduction tax increases from 1982 to 1984, despite the fact that second-term deficits were larger. Revenue losses from ERTA continued to be extremely high. For FY 1989, the net tax reduction from all tax bills enacted during Reagan's presidency exceeded $170 billion.[47] In addition, revenue-GDP levels averaged slightly more than 18 percent during the second term, well below the revenue "target" the administration had set in 1981. The heart of the Reagan tax program – large individual tax cuts and reduced revenue levels – remained in place when he left office.

---

[45] Office of Management and Budget, *Budget of the United States Government, Fiscal Year 1989* (Washington, D.C.: Government Printing Office, 1988), 4-4; Office of Management and Budget, *Budget of the United States Government, Fiscal Year 1990* (Washington, D.C.: Government Printing Office, 1989), 4-4.

[46] Congressional Quarterly, *Congressional Quarterly Almanac, 1987* (Washington, D.C.: Congressional Quarterly, 1988), 610.

[47] Office of Management and Budget, *Budget of the United States Government, Fiscal Year 1990*, 4-4.

Spending Policy: Reagan and the Great Society

The first budget that President Reagan sent to Congress called for "an immediate, substantial, and sustained reduction in the growth of Federal expenditures."[48] The administration's budget program recommended nearly $400 billion in outlay savings from 1981 to 1986, all from domestic programs, and stated that an additional $160 billion in additional savings would be proposed at a later time.[49] Years later, in the last budget he sent to Congress, Reagan complained, "Time and again I have proposed measures to help curb Federal domestic program spending. Time and again these proposals have been rejected by Congress."[50]

The extremely high spending levels that remained in place during the 1980s – annual spending-GDP averaging more than 22 percent, well above the "excessive" spending of the late 1970s that Reagan had criticized so strongly – obscured some important, albeit limited, progress in curbing spending growth. Discretionary domestic spending–GDP levels were sharply reduced, if not quite to pre–Great Society levels. This reduction offset the extremely large defense budget increases that Reagan managed to secure, often in the face of considerable opposition from Congress. When Reagan took office, total discretionary spending–GDP was slightly more than 10 percent; by FY 1989, it had fallen to a little more than 9 percent.

The level of mandatory programmatic spending, however, changed very little. Reagan did succeed in arresting what had been a two-decade-long expansion in the relative size of the social welfare budget. He was unable, however, to reverse that growth, particularly for the large retirement and healthcare entitlements. Reagan's impact was greater on the less costly but politically more vulnerable public assistance programs, especially cash assistance for the poor. But while some public assistance programs grew slowly if at all under Reagan, the "social safety net" remained intact.

Because the explicit goal of the Reagan program was to bring the budget into balance at reduced revenue levels, these spending outcomes were a measure of political feasibility. It might be argued that Reagan's failures with respect to domestic program spending were simply the result of divided government; the House was controlled by Democrats for his entire presidency, and the Senate was in Democratic hands after 1986. Republican opposition to aggressive cutbacks in domestic spending, however, came into play as well. Senate Republicans were especially protective of traditional domestic policy commitments after the initial round of budget cutting in Reagan's first year. Even at the height of his popularity in the mid-1980s, Reagan was unable to wield the same

---

[48] Office of Management and Budget, *Fiscal Year 1982 Budget Revisions*, 1.
[49] Ibid., 3.
[50] Office of Management and Budget, *Budget of the United States Government, Fiscal Year 1990*, 1-5.

influence over spending policy that he had on taxation, even among congressional Republicans.

Discretionary Spending

Reagan's most important achievement in terms of spending policy was the size and scale of his defense buildup. Ford and Carter had managed to halt the post-Vietnam decline in real defense spending, but other indicators – GDP shares and budget shares – remained at historically low levels. If Carter had won in 1980, there almost certainly would have been marginal improvements in each of these defense spending indices. Reagan, however, took the defense program that he inherited and greatly increased spending for every component of that program. He also added new and costly weapons systems. In his first three years, Reagan increased real defense spending by almost 25 percent. After 1983, the rate of increase slowed but never stopped. Real defense spending in FY 1989 was more than $480 billion (in constant 2005 dollars),[51] just below peak spending levels during the Korean War and Vietnam War. The Reagan buildup might have amounted to wartime spending but without wartime tax increases.

Protecting the Defense Buildup The Reagan administration's defense program had a strategic goal – restoring military parity with the Soviet Union – and a corresponding emphasis on long-term investment spending for procurement and research and development. The military parity criterion was obviously complicated, involving the quality and quantity of military forces (strategic, general purpose, and other) and their attendant capabilities. The administration boosted spending in all areas of the defense budget, but it targeted some areas, such as strategic modernization, for especially steep growth. Further, the size of the defense budget became a point of emphasis. From the outset, Reagan and his defense spokesmen maintained that defense spending levels demonstrated commitment and will. Reagan's first Secretary of Defense, Caspar W. Weinberger, would later explain that restoring "military parity with the Soviet Union" meant committing "roughly as much to our defense as our primary competitor invests in its forces."[52] Weinberger's successor, Frank C. Carlucci, was able to report that the "continued growth of U.S. outlays, primarily for procurement" had "virtually eliminated" the decade-long annual difference between U.S. and Soviet military spending.[53] He went on to warn, however, that "cumulative Soviet military procurement for the decade was higher than that of the United States . . . and expected to remain at levels high enough to allow for the continued modernization of the [Soviet] armed forces."

[51] Office of Management and Budget, *Historical Tables, Budget of the United States Government, Fiscal Year 2011* (Washington, D.C.: Government Printing Office, 2010), 130.

[52] U.S. Department of Defense, *Annual Report to the Congress, Fiscal Year 1987* (Washington, D.C.: Department of Defense, 1986), 18.

[53] U.S. Department of Defense, *Soviet Military Power: An Assessment of the Threat* (Washington, D.C.: Department of Defense, 1988), 32.

With domestic programs slated for deep retrenchments under the Reagan program, the U.S.-Soviet spending comparisons provided the administration with the rationale for separating defense from the rest of the budget. As deficits became more serious, the same rationale, reinforced by Reagan's unwavering commitment to defense priorities, shielded the defense budget against comprehensive deficit-reduction plans. On a practical level, the administration was able to protect defense by securing at the outset long-term budget authority commitments for weapons programs that ensured high spending in later years, regardless of congressional action.

In comparison to the Carter defense program, Reagan's budget authority requests were much higher and disproportionately concentrated in the investment accounts that funded procurement and research and development. For fiscal years 1981–1985, the Reagan administration's defense plans called for boosting investment outlays much more rapidly than readiness accounts (such as military personnel and operation and maintenance), and the budget authority differential was even greater. The defense budgets that Congress approved followed these spending priorities. Compared to FY 1980, investment account outlays in FY 1985 had increased by approximately 130 percent, and the budget authority increase was more than 160 percent.[54] During Reagan's second term, when Congress began to cut procurement budget authority, the earlier commitments for multiyear funding cushioned the impact on actual procurement spending.

The administration's attempt to separate defense from what was happening to the rest of the budget could not be sustained indefinitely. As shown in Table 4.4, the administration began to moderate its requests for defense spending increases after 1985, but Congress responded with even larger appropriations reductions. By the end of Reagan's first term, the three-stage defense budgeting process was becoming highly contentious. Debates over the congressional budget resolution allocations for defense and domestic programs were prolonged, disputes on defense authorizations were similarly protracted, and defense appropriations bills provided yet another opportunity for defense critics to attack the administration's program.

In 1985, a dispute between the House and Senate over defense funding limits in the budget resolution – "zero growth" on the House side versus "zero real growth" on the Senate side – delayed adoption of the FY 1986 budget resolution until August. When the budget resolution compromise favored the Senate, House Democrats rebelled and blocked action on the defense authorization bill. The defense appropriations bill was then delayed past the beginning of the fiscal year, necessitating a continuing resolution until the House-Senate differences could be resolved.

In 1987, Congress tried to tie the defense budget to a tax increase. A five-week-long conference on the FY 1988 budget resolution finally agreed on a

[54] Office of Management and Budget, *Historical Tables, Fiscal Year 2011*, 58–59, 90–91.

TABLE 4.4. *National Defense Budget Authority and Outlays, Fiscal Years 1981–1989 (in billions of dollars)*

Fiscal Year	Reagan Budget	Actual[a]	Change
Budget Authority			
1981	$180.7	$180.0	− $0.7
1982	226.3	216.5	− 9.8
1983	263.0	245.0	− 18.0
1984	280.5	265.2	− 15.3
1985	313.4	294.7	− 18.7
1986	322.2	289.1	− 33.1
1987	320.3	287.4	− 32.9
1988	312.0	292.0	− 20.0
1989	332.4	299.6	− 32.8
Budget Outlays			
1981	162.1	157.5	− 4.6
1982	188.8	185.3	− 3.5
1983	221.1	209.9	− 11.2
1984	245.3	227.4	− 17.9
1985	272.0	252.7	− 19.3
1986	285.7	273.4	− 12.3
1987	282.2	282.0	− 0.2
1988	297.5	290.4	− 7.1
1989	312.0	303.6	− 8.4

[a] The use of actual budget authority and outlay figures provides a reasonably accurate comparison, because supplemental funding enacted late in a fiscal year is included. The budget resolutions and initial appropriations bills would not reflect these adjustments.

Sources: Requests are based on the president's budgets for the years shown; see Dennis S. Ippolito, *Uncertain Legacies: Federal Budget Policy from Roosevelt through Reagan* (Charlottesville: University Press of Virginia, 1990), 142. Actual figures are from Office of Management and Budget, *Historical Tables, Budget of the United States Government, Fiscal Year 2011* (Washington, D.C.: Government Printing Office, 2010), 51–52, 90–91.

two-tier defense spending plan, with the higher figure contingent on Reagan's accepting a tax increase. While this measure was being debated, Congress was also working on a debt-limit extension and revision of the GRH deficit-reduction law. When the latter was finally approved in late September, it modified the budget resolution's tax-increase requirements, and the budget "summit agreement" that followed the October stock market crash eliminated the tax increase–defense increase linkage.

In addition to the issue of deficit reduction, congressional cuts in administration defense budgets involved substantive defense policy differences. Congress targeted several of the administration's more controversial strategic systems, such as the Strategic Defense Initiative and MX deployment program, for especially large reductions. Congress did not, however, seriously challenge the vast majority of weapons systems, conventional and strategic, that received accelerated funding under Reagan. It supported the administration's decision to renew the B-1 strategic bomber that Carter had canceled to build large-deck, nuclear-powered aircraft carriers and increase the number of carrier battle groups and to fund, at much higher levels, the weapons programs that were continued from the Carter administration.

Moreover, even as Congress slowed new procurement funding, readiness and sustainability initiatives continued to enjoy strong support. Most defense experts agreed that budget constraints in the 1970s had seriously eroded readiness and sustainability, and Congress remained sensitive to the need to prevent any recurrence. Unlike investment, readiness and sustainability funding was relatively immune to deficit-control considerations, which bolstered the administration's case for sustained defense budget increases.

The Reagan administration's original budget program called for increasing the defense share of total outlays from less than 25 percent to nearly 40 percent over five years.[55] It failed to do so, because Congress did not support the extremely large defense budget increases or the corresponding domestic spending cuts that comprised the Reagan program. The peak defense budget share under Reagan was 28.1 percent in FY 1987, and the highest defense-GDP share – 6.2 percent in FY 1986 – was also well below the administration's initial target.[56] The defense budget increases enacted under Reagan were nevertheless quite substantial, and the administration was able to reestablish the priority that defense budgets had enjoyed during the early stages of the Cold War. What was strikingly different during the 1980s was that this priority did not have a similar effect on the rest of the budget. It did not force the administration to increase taxes or require Congress to reverse the "welfare shift" that the Great Society had initiated. The trade-offs that did occur during the 1980s were largely confined to the limited category of discretionary domestic programs.

Discretionary Domestic Programs In the 1950s and early 1960s, spending for discretionary domestic programs lagged well behind defense. The Great Society increased the size and number of discretionary domestic programs, but funding for new programs was constrained during the early stages of the Vietnam War. Beginning in 1970, however, funding increases for domestic programs rose sharply. Real spending, for example, increased by more than 75 percent between 1970 and 1980, and the discretionary domestic–GDP share rose as well. By the late 1970s, the GDP shares for defense and for discretionary domestic programs were almost equal. In the case of defense, this represented

---

[55] Office of Management and Budget, *Fiscal Year 1982 Budget Revisions*, 124–125.
[56] Office of Management and Budget, *Historical Tables, Fiscal Year 2011*, 144–146.

a 50 percent cut from pre–Great Society levels, while the domestic program share was more than double what it had been in the 1950s and early 1960s.

The Reagan administration was determined to reduce funding for domestic programs and to define more narrowly the domestic role of the federal government. The first installment of the administration's program involved an FY 1981 supplemental appropriations bill. The administration's requests included additional funding of $23.5 billion, primarily for defense, and domestic rescissions (cancellation of prior appropriations) of approximately $15 billion. The latter were aimed at environmental and energy programs, along with the Department of Housing and Urban Development's subsidized housing program. The administration also proposed $3 billion in cuts for social programs administered by the Departments of Labor, Health and Human Services, and Education. The House and Senate modified the administration's proposal, but the supplemental appropriations bill that Congress approved on June 4, 1981, contained more than $14 billion in domestic rescissions.

The second, more extensive installment of the Reagan program was contained in revisions to the Carter administration's 1982 budget. The Reagan proposals included nearly $50 billion in domestic spending cuts affecting dozens of domestic programs, including some entitlements. Reagan's budget director, David Stockman, convinced Senate Republican leaders that the reconciliation process could be used to implement these cuts, and the Senate approved an FY 1982 budget resolution that instructed fourteen Senate committees to cut $36.9 billion in fiscal 1982 spending.

The House Democratic leadership failed to block this reconciliation initiative. More than sixty Democrats joined House Republicans in passing the administration-backed substitute for the budget resolution reported out by the Budget Committee. The same coalition prevailed when the House adopted the reconciliation bill containing cuts made by House and Senate committees in accordance with the reconciliation instructions. OBRA 1981 was passed on July 31. It was described at the time as "the deepest and most widespread package of budget cuts in the history of Congress," with an estimated reduction of more than $35 billion in FY 1982 and cumulative savings of more than $130 billion for fiscal years 1982–1984.[57]

OBRA 1981 eliminated or retrenched numerous discretionary domestic programs. The Johnson administration had established a number of federal job training and employment programs that were later brought together under the Comprehensive Employment and Training Act (CETA) of 1973. The two main public service jobs programs under CETA were terminated by OBRA 1981, as were the regional planning commissions of the Economic Development Administration, another Great Society creation. The Community Services Administration, a successor agency to the War on Poverty's Office of Economic Opportunity, was abolished by OBRA 1981, although Congress did provide

[57] Congressional Quarterly, *Congressional Quarterly Almanac, 1981*, 257.

funding for a new community services block grant to the states. New block grants also replaced various health and grant programs for states and localities. With many of the block grant consolidations, funding levels were sharply reduced, and spending cutbacks were extended to other domestic programs that were reauthorized and extended.

In the fall of 1981, Reagan announced another round of multiyear cuts, including $13 billion in additional FY 1982 savings. Reagan cautioned that "this cannot be the last round of cuts. Holding down spending must be a continuing battle for several years to come."[58] For most discretionary domestic programs, the administration's new proposals represented a 12 percent cut from the spending levels in its March budget. In this case, however, the administration did not ask Congress to use reconciliation, with budget director Stockman explaining that it would instead use vetoes and veto threats "to contest [the cuts] one bill at a time." The veto threat was soon carried out. There was much less congressional support for the administration's spending program in the fall than there had been in the spring, particularly as the economic and deficit outlook worsened, and the congressional appropriations process ground to a halt. On October 1, when the 1982 fiscal year began, none of the thirteen appropriations bills had been enacted, and Congress adopted a last-minute continuing resolution that funded agencies through November 20. When that resolution expired, twelve bills still had not been enacted, and Congress proceeded to clear another continuing resolution for the remainder of the fiscal year. Reagan had demanded larger domestic cuts than contained in this resolution, and his November 23 veto triggered a one-day government shutdown. Congress then approved a temporary extension through December 15, which Reagan signed. A third continuing resolution, which at that point covered ten appropriations bills, was enacted on December 15. It included only a fraction of the savings that Reagan had insisted on, but he signed this measure. As the remaining regular domestic appropriations bills moved toward passage, veto threats recurred, but Congress approved only minor cuts.

In 1982, Reagan again called on Congress to terminate domestic "Federal activities that overstep the proper sphere of Federal Government responsibilities."[59] Reagan also announced a "New Federalism" program that would reapportion federal-state social welfare responsibilities and consolidate further what he called the "jungle of grants-in-aid" that remained in place.[60] According to the administration, categorical grant programs had increased nearly fourfold in two decades – from 132 in 1960 to more than 500 in 1980 – with funding climbing from $7 billion to nearly $100 billion. The New Federalism proposal involved giving the states the responsibility for continuing many

[58] Ibid., 267.
[59] Office of Management and Budget, *Budget of the United States Government, Fiscal Year 1983*, M4.
[60] Congressional Quarterly, *Congressional Quarterly Almanac, 1982*, 5-E.

of these programs along with dedicated funding from certain excise taxes that the states could use at their discretion.

Congress rejected the New Federalism's program transfers but agreed to the broader use of block grants, while allowing the states greater leeway under a number of continuing categorical aid programs. In addition, the administration managed to curtail spending for federal grants-in-aid, particularly for the types of Great Society programs that had flourished during the 1970s. Traditional capital investment grant programs increased by nearly $3 billion during the 1980s, but nonentitlement grant programs declined by more than $7 billion. In constant dollars, these latter programs were cut by more than half.[61]

The Reagan administration never could replicate the sweeping domestic cuts in OBRA 1981, but the annual domestic appropriations cycles allowed it to repeatedly challenge the programs that it opposed. Outright terminations were rare after 1981, but funding levels were severely constrained for numerous energy, housing, economic development, and nonhighway transportation programs. The alternative energy supply programs that Carter had enthusiastically promoted, for example, were eviscerated under Reagan, who was committed instead to "minimum Government intervention in the operation of energy markets."[62] Energy supply and conservation outlays totaled nearly $9 billion in 1980 but less than $1.6 billion in 1989.[63] Community and regional development dropped from $9.2 billion to $5.6 billion over the same period.[64] Federal training and employment programs averaged more than $10 billion annually during the late 1970s. A decade later, spending had been cut in half.

In FY 1982, total domestic discretionary spending dropped by approximately $9 billion. After 1982, current dollar spending rose but at a very slow rate (see Table 4.5). Real spending, GDP shares, and budget shares, however, all continued to fall over the course of the Reagan presidency. Reagan did not bring discretionary domestic spending back to Great Society levels, but he came surprisingly close. These cutbacks kept the Reagan-era deficits from being even larger, but they did not, and could not, bring the budget anywhere near balance. Neither Reagan nor his most ardent supporters in Congress ever contemplated abolishing all discretionary domestic spending, and even that extreme option would not have eliminated the large deficits during Reagan's tenure.

Social Welfare Entitlements

The Reagan budget program called for limiting the federal government's social welfare responsibilities to "those programs, mostly begun in the 1930s, that now constitute an agreed-upon core of protection for the elderly, the

---

[61] Office of Management and Budget *Historical Tables, Fiscal Year 2011*, 249.
[62] Office of Management and Budget, *Budget of the United States Government, Fiscal Year 1989*, 5-35.
[63] Office of Management and Budget, *Historical Tables, Fiscal Year 2011*, 58.
[64] Ibid., 65–66.

TABLE 4.5. *Discretionary Domestic Outlays, Fiscal Years 1980–1989 (in billions of dollars)*

Fiscal Year	Current Dollars	Constant (FY 2000) Dollars	Percentage of GDP	Percentage of Total Outlays
1980	$128.9	$268.9	4.7%	21.8%
1981	136.3	256.7	4.5	20.1
1982	127.1	223.9	3.9	17.0
1983	129.8	218.5	3.8	16.1
1984	135.1	218.4	3.5	15.9
1985	145.3	227.2	3.5	15.4
1986	147.0	223.4	3.3	14.8
1987	146.5	215.0	3.1	14.6
1988	157.8	223.9	3.1	14.8
1989	168.2	231.7	3.1	14.7

Source: Office of Management and Budget, *Historical Tables, Budget of the United States Government, Fiscal Year 2005* (Washington, D.C.: Government Printing Office, 2004), 125–128.

unemployed, and the poor, and those programs that fulfill our basic commitment to the people who fought for this country in times of war."[65] The administration proposed two major changes in the social welfare programs that it had inherited. The first was the elimination of "unintended benefits" in the "newer Federal entitlement programs and related income security programs that have undergone rapid growth during the last 20 years." Proposed retrenchments in these programs would mostly affect the poor. The second change was aimed at non–means-tested entitlements that provided "benefits for people with middle to upper incomes," a category that included Medicare, Social Security, and other retirement programs and some federal credit programs.

The Poor: Public Assistance Programs OBRA 1981 narrowed eligibility and benefits for numerous public assistance programs. The most important and controversial changes affected the AFDC and food stamp programs, but new restrictions on housing assistance, child nutrition, and low-income energy assistance programs also were designed to target assistance for the demonstrably poor. OBRA 1981 provided greater flexibility to the states in administering most public assistance programs, and it permitted states to establish "workfare" requirements for welfare recipients.

The AFDC eligibility changes, which involved the income and property tests needed to qualify for benefits, were expected to remove approximately 10 percent of the 3.9 million households that had previously been covered.[66] The benefit reductions, again according to Department of Health and Human Services estimates, were expected to affect another 279,000 households. The benefit reductions primarily involved low "income disregards" – the amounts

[65] Office of Management and Budget, *Fiscal Year 1982 Budget Revisions*, 8.
[66] Congressional Quarterly, *Congressional Quarterly Almanac, 1981*, 473.

subtracted from earned income for various expenses in calculating cash assistance benefits. In addition, benefits that families received in the form of food stamps or housing assistance could be treated by the states as income, as could EITCs. According to the CBO, the estimated savings from these AFDC changes were $1.2 billion in fiscal 1982 and an additional $2.8 billion over the next two years.[67]

The food stamp program's basic eligibility standard was lowered to 130 percent of the federal government's official poverty standard. Families with total household income below this level qualified for benefits, but there were stricter administrative requirements for measuring and reporting income and a reduced income disregard allowance for calculating benefits. The reconciliation bill also stretched out the schedule for applying inflation adjustments to the "thrifty food plan" that was used to determine actual benefits. Food stamp savings were estimated at $6 billion for fiscal years 1982–1984, with benefits eliminated entirely for more than one million of the approximately twenty-three million people previously covered and reduced benefits for most of the remainder.[68] In the case of food stamps, the spending cuts that Congress approved were larger than the administration had requested, and Congress then adopted annual authorization limits to ensure that these savings were realized.

When the administration called for a second round of public assistance "reforms" in the fall of 1981, Congress was much less supportive. It refused to make additional changes in the food stamp program and rejected proposed restrictions on Medicaid spending. The administration's 1982 New Federalism plan to give the states full responsibility for the AFDC and food stamp programs, in exchange for full federal funding of Medicaid, made no headway in Congress and quickly disappeared. Congress then began to ease some of the public assistance restrictions that it had made in 1981, beginning with the reinstatement of unemployment compensation extended benefits in the Tax Equity and Fiscal Responsibility Act of 1982. Two years later, AFDC eligibility was liberalized. In 1985, food stamp eligibility was expanded, and benefit levels were increased.

With Medicaid – one of the fastest-growing public assistance programs during the 1970s – the administration never achieved major savings. Reagan's proposed "cap" on Medicaid spending in 1981 involved limiting federal reimbursements to the states to 5 percent over the previous year's total. At the time, the federal share of Medicaid costs for covering the nearly twenty million beneficiaries was approximately 55 percent, and the proposed change would have required the states to manage their programs within the capped amount or to absorb the additional spending. Congress approved modest savings in 1981 and 1982, primarily through administrative reforms, but Medicaid spending

[67] Ibid.
[68] Ibid., 466–467.

continued to grow. Then, in 1984, Congress passed the Child Health Assistance Program, which required states to provide prenatal and pediatric care under their Medicaid programs at an estimated cost of $270 million over three years.[69] The program was expanded in 1987, with states being allowed to provide coverage for families that did not qualify for AFDC but which had incomes below the poverty level. In 1988, coverage was made mandatory for women and infants whose family incomes were below certain poverty thresholds but nevertheless too high to qualify for Medicaid.

The problem of the working poor also led to expansions of the EITC during the mid-1980s. The EITC was created as a temporary program in 1975 to provide a refundable credit to low-income taxpayers. The maximum credit of $400 per year was raised to $500 in 1978, when the program was made permanent, with the eligibility income level increased to $10,000. In 1984, the maximum credit and eligibility level were raised again by approximately 10 percent. The Tax Reform Act of 1986 then utterly transformed the EITC. The maximum credit was increased by 45 percent and automatically adjusted for inflation by indexing the program's phase-out income level and maximum earned income level. From 1986 until 1990, when the EITC was again increased, the number of recipients grew by nearly 7.4 million, the average credit more than doubled, and the cost of the EITC went from $2 billion to $7.5 billion.[70]

Another important welfare reform was also enacted during Reagan's second term, in this case with the administration taking the lead. Reagan was intent on extending the workfare concept to include mandatory job training and work requirements, while congressional Democrats wanted to extend nationwide AFDC coverage to two-parent families with an unemployed principal wage earner (AFDC-UP). With a strong assist from the National Governors Association, which called for linking the two initiatives, agreement was finally reached on the Family Support Act of 1988. States were required to participate in the AFDC-UP program, to offer a Job Opportunities and Basic Skills (JOBS) Training Program for AFDC recipients, and to enforce standardized work rules for certain recipients. In addition, Medicaid and childcare benefits were extended for twelve months in cases where families had increased earnings that made them ineligible for public assistance benefits. The immediate impact of the 1988 work requirement was limited, but it eventually led to a major change in welfare policy. With the 1996 welfare reform act, the recasting of public assistance from permanent to temporary income support was extended much further, and the corollary job training and work requirements were made more stringent.

The Reagan administration's impact on public assistance spending was, in the end, more modest than its supporters hoped or critics feared. Current dollar spending for all means-tested entitlements nearly doubled over fiscal

[69] Congressional Quarterly, *Congress and the Nation, 1981–1984*, 546.
[70] Christine Scott, *The Earned Income Tax Credit (EITC): An Overview* (CRS Report for Congress, January 10, 2007), 9.

TABLE 4.6. *Public Assistance Outlays, Fiscal Years 1980–1989 (in billions of dollars)*

Fiscal Year	Current Dollars	Constant (FY 2000 Dollars	Percentage of GDP	Percentage of Total Outlays
1980	$45.0	$88.1	1.6%	7.6%
1981	52.2	93.2	1.7	7.7
1982	52.2	87.8	1.6	7.0
1983	57.3	92.1	1.7	7.1
1984	58.6	90.8	1.5	6.9
1985	62.9	94.2	1.5	6.6
1986	66.9	97.6	1.5	6.8
1987	70.8	100.1	1.5	7.0
1988	78.1	106.3	1.6	7.3
1989	85.4	111.3	1.6	7.5

Source: Office of Management and Budget, *Historical Tables, Budget of the United States Government, Fiscal Year 2005* (Washington, D.C.: Government Printing Office, 2004), 125–128.

years 1980–1989, real spending stabilized after the 1981 cutbacks and then began to grow, and the spending-GDP level was fairly stable over the period (see Table 4.6). Of course, public assistance spending had grown at a much faster rate during the 1970s, but even then it accounted for only about 10 percent of total domestic spending and an even smaller portion of the overall budget.

Social Security and Medicare, by comparison, offered a much larger pool of potential savings. Along with other non–means-tested entitlements, spending for these programs soared during the 1970s, and they accounted for more than 55 percent of total domestic spending when Reagan took office. Reducing the relative size of the budget, while shifting its composition toward defense, could not be accomplished without substantial cutbacks in these programs, but the Reagan administration quickly learned that even minor retrenchments were politically explosive.

The Non-Poor: Social Benefits The Reagan administration's determination to challenge the universalization of social benefit programs had very limited success. The 1981 reconciliation bill, for example, established a "needs test" for guaranteed student loans. The Higher Education Act of 1965 had authorized guaranteed, interest-subsidized loans for college students whose family income fell below a specified level. In 1978, the Middle Income Assistance Act removed family income limits for the program, leading to an immediate increase in participation rates and costs.[71] Because the federal government was required to pay the full interest on student loans while the beneficiary was in college (and to subsidize the interest rate), outlay costs had risen sharply. By FY 1982,

[71] Dennis S. Ippolito, *Hidden Spending: The Politics of Federal Credit Programs* (Chapel Hill: University of North Carolina Press, 1984), 30–33.

the nearly $3 billion cost of the program accounted for nearly one-half of total federal spending for higher education.

As part of its credit budget reform initiative, the Reagan administration proposed a new income test that would limit "loans to a student's remaining financial need after all other financial assistance and expected family contribution have been counted."[72] It also called for "eliminating the 9% interest subsidy now provided to students while they are in school." Congress rejected the latter, although it did approve an origination fee for new borrowers that would be applied against the interest subsidy. The needs test that Congress established was less sweeping than the administration had recommended, covering only those families with incomes of more than $30,000 annually. The expected savings from the new income test and related provisions were estimated at $2.8 billion over three years.[73]

The need criterion was extended to a number of other relatively small programs. New and lower-income eligibility standards for federally subsidized meals for school children were designed to reduce subsidies "to school children from middle- and upper-income families" by almost 40 percent.[74] Veterans' burial benefits were limited to veterans eligible for need-based pensions or disability compensation. The 1981 reconciliation bill also replaced the semiannual COLAs for federal civilian and military retirees with an annual adjustment, reversing a policy that had been in place since 1976.

Social Security and Medicare, however, presented more difficult policy challenges, because these programs served an enormous, politically potent population. The large Social Security benefit increases from 1969 to 1972 had been across-the-board, and the indexing of benefits adopted in 1972 applied to all retirees regardless of need. Even as Social Security spending greatly outpaced the growth in other programs, Congress was reluctant to take any action that could be portrayed as cutting benefits. Under the indexing "reform" of 1972, which was coupled to a 20 percent benefit increase, the first COLA was scheduled for 1975. The following year, however, Congress twice approved ad hoc benefit increases – a 5.9 percent increase for June 1974, which was then superseded by a two-step increase of 7 percent for March 1974 and an additional 4 percent in June.[75] In 1977, with the Social Security trust funds facing serious solvency problems, Congress eliminated an overcompensation flaw in the program's initial benefit formula but exempted all current retirees and individuals close to retirement from the change.

With Medicare, the "windfalls" to beneficiaries had been extremely large during the 1970s, and the ratio of expected lifetime benefits to Medicare tax

---

[72] Office of Management and Budget, *Fiscal Year 1982 Budget Revisions*, 67.

[73] Congressional Quarterly, *Congressional Quarterly Almanac, 1981*, 493.

[74] Ibid., 497.

[75] R. Kent Weaver, *Automatic Government: The Politics of Indexation* (Washington, D.C.: Brookings Institution, 1988), 78–79.

payments was more than 14:1 by the early 1980s.[76] For Medicare Part B, premiums were supposed to cover 50 percent of program costs under the 1965 legislation that established Medicare, but Congress limited premium increases beginning in 1972. By the end of the decade, the premiums paid by beneficiaries covered only about 25 percent of costs, with the remainder financed by general revenues. For both Part A and Part B, federal subsidies for beneficiary healthcare had no relationship to need.

The Reagan administration's initial foray into Social Security reform created a political backlash that had a lasting effect on Reagan. After 1981, the administration became quite protective of benefit commitments. With Medicare, the administration and Congress agreed on very limited benefit savings in 1981, but Congress soon made it clear that any means-testing of Medicare benefits was unacceptable.

The Social Security changes that Reagan proposed in 1981 included elimination of the minimum benefit, an increased penalty for early retirement, a revised benefit formula for future retirees, and stricter eligibility criteria for the disability benefit program. The minimum benefit proposal affected two groups – individuals with very low earnings over many years and retired government workers with a limited Social Security work history who also qualified for government pensions. Congress addressed this problem indirectly in 1977 by freezing the minimum benefit for new retirees while raising and indexing it for low-income retirees. The Reagan administration called for ending "windfall benefits" entirely for those on government pensions and providing low-income retirees with equivalent benefits from the SSI program. The congressional battle over this proposal was fierce, with Congress finally agreeing to eliminate the minimum benefit as part of the 1981 reconciliation bill and then voting to restore the benefit later in the year.

The early retirement penalty was even more controversial. Under current law at that time, individuals who retired at sixty-two years of age received 80 percent of the benefits they would have received at the normal retirement age of sixty-five. The Reagan administration proposal would have reduced the early retirement benefit to 55 percent. Other benefit reductions, such as a temporary adjustment to correct the overindexing that occurred during the 1970s, were quickly caught up in the furor over the minimum benefit and early retirement penalty. Even the three-month COLA delay that the administration had included in its reform package did not survive in Congress, despite the substantial savings it would have produced. According to Paul Light, both the magnitude of the proposed budget cuts in the Reagan plan and their immediate phase-in made them politically untenable – "almost 36 million retirees would have lost benefits immediately on the three-month COLA delay; another 18 million would have lost 10 percent of their benefits on a technical change in

---

[76] Marilyn Moon, *Medicare: A Policy Primer* (Washington, D.C.: Urban Institute Press, 2006), 53.

the basic formula; still another 7 million would have lost up to a third of their benefits under the early retirement cuts."[77]

The Social Security rescue plan that passed in 1983 included some benefit cuts. A six-month COLA delay was implemented, and the Social Security benefits received by upper-income retirees were made taxable. Changes in the retirement age from sixty-five to sixty-seven years for twenty-first century retirees represented a major long-term benefit cut as well. Much of the rescue plan, however, depended on higher Social Security taxes to solve short-term solvency problems in the trust funds and provide a reserve to help fund long-term commitments. The payroll tax rates for employers and employees were raised from 6.7 percent to 7.51 percent from 1983 to 1989, the payroll tax rate for the self-employed was raised to match the employer and employee rate, and, for the first time, Social Security benefits were made taxable as regular income for individuals and couples above certain income thresholds. Finally, Congress decided to remove Social Security from the unified budget in 1992 – a change that would presumably insulate it from the annual debates over spending and deficits.

The Reagan administration's acceptance of higher Social Security taxes in 1983 and its pledge to protect future benefits meant that Social Security spending continued to grow at rates that had been considered excessive in 1981. After 1983, Reagan refused to support COLA delays, Congress exempted Social Security COLAs from GRH, and the so-called COLA "trigger" – the requirement for a price increase of at least 3 percent over a twelve-month period to trigger an automatic COLA – was eliminated in 1986. In practical terms, the large portion of the budget accounted for by Social Security was shielded from budget-cutting efforts after 1983. With Medicare, which was smaller than Social Security but faster growing, repeated attempts to restrain spending growth were undertaken but with limited success. In the 1981 reconciliation bill, Congress raised deductibles for both Part A and Part B beneficiaries and reduced reimbursement formulas for hospitals and home health agencies. The following year, Congress again trimmed reimbursement formulas and raised the premium for Part B beneficiaries to cover 25 percent of the program's cost.

Congress made clear, however, that it had no interest in challenging the universalization of benefits, at least with respect to Medicare. Reports that the Reagan administration was considering a means test for Medicare as part of its FY 1984 spending reductions triggered sharp criticisms from congressional Democrats. A sense-of-Congress resolution opposing the reported plan was easily passed in both chambers and added to the fiscal 1983 continuing resolution adopted in the fall. The continuing resolution stated that Congress would

---

[77] Paul Light, *Artful Work: The Politics of Social Security Reform* (New York: Random House, 1985), 121–122.

reject "any proposal to impose a 'means test' on eligibility for the Medicare program or benefits provided by the Medicare program."[78]

In 1983, Congress agreed to change the hospital reimbursement system, in large part because the Hospital Insurance trust fund that financed the Part A program was expected to be insolvent within just a few years. The Reagan administration submitted its proposals for Medicare reform in February, and the basic thrust of the administration's plan was incorporated into the Social Security bill that Congress passed in April. The major change was that payments to hospitals would be converted to fixed rates for the treatment of specified medical conditions. The new "prospective" reimbursement system was to be phased in over three years, with the expectation that hospitals would have clear incentives to develop more efficient treatment protocols that would hold down Part A costs.

For Part B, Congress included a fifteen-month freeze on payments to physicians as part of the deficit-reduction bill that passed in 1984. In addition, Congress extended for three years the requirement that Part B premiums be raised to cover 25 percent of Part B spending. However, a proposal to index the Part B deductible payment for beneficiaries was not approved by Congress.

Medicare returned to the legislative agenda during Reagan's second term. The fiscal 1986 reconciliation bill extended the freeze on physicians' payments. It also provided hospitals with an additional year to complete their transition to the prospective reimbursement system approved in 1983. At that point, the switch to a fixed ratio of payment for inpatient treatment of various medical conditions (itself based on nearly 500 "diagnostic related groups," or DRGs) was to be fully implemented by participating hospitals. In 1987, Congress approved a limited increase in Part A deductibles, while also relaxing the controls that had been imposed on hospital and physician reimbursements.

Perhaps the most illuminating episode about the politics of Medicare was the short-lived Medicare Catastrophic Coverage Act of 1988. This additional protection was designed to shield Medicare's thirty-two million beneficiaries from the extremely costly medical expenses that might be incurred in the treatment of serious acute illnesses. It capped the Medicare deductibles paid by beneficiaries at $2,000 annually, with Medicare then fully covering allowable healthcare expenses above this amount. Congress also enacted, over administration objections, similar coverage for prescription drugs. The prescription drug benefit, which was fully effective in 1991, set a $600 annual deductible limit for beneficiary out-of-pocket expenses, with Medicare then paying 50 percent of additional costs in 1991, 60 percent in 1992, and 80 percent thereafter.

The financing of this new benefit program was an innovative and, as it turned out, failed experiment in means-testing. Unlike the heavy taxpayer subsidies in the original Part A and Part B programs, catastrophic coverage was designed

[78] Congressional Quarterly, *Congressional Quarterly Almanac, 1982*, 474.

to be self-financing through beneficiary premiums. Premium amounts, more-over, were based on income. For most beneficiaries, whose low incomes meant little or no income tax liability, the scheduled premiums would be uniform. For others, additional premiums would be required, with the specific amount determined by income tax liability. These "surtax" premiums would, in turn, be automatically adjusted each year to ensure that 60 percent of catastrophic coverage costs were covered. This Medicare "tax" proved to be spectacularly unpopular among the elderly, and their protests led Congress to repeal the catastrophic coverage just one year later. Repealed as well were new Medicare benefits that had been included in the catastrophic coverage bill.

Social Welfare, Taxes, and Balanced Budgets

The social welfare budgets of the Reagan years were a major disappointment for conservative critics of big government. Reagan's bold plans for domestic retrenchment appeared to have enormous momentum in 1981, but growing congressional and public resistance soon forced the administration to scale back those plans, particularly for Social Security and Medicare. During the 1980s, for example, real defense spending increased by 45 percent, but Social Security and Medicare constant dollar spending increased by 40 percent.[79] Over this period, the combined GDP share for Social Security and Medicare rose to 6 percent, which was considerably higher than it had been during the 1970s and roughly double Great Society levels.

The Medicaid program likewise managed to survive early budget-cutting efforts, and Congress eventually expanded the program in ways that inflated long-term costs. The Medicaid-GDP share was 0.6 percent when Reagan took office and 0.6 percent when he left. Other means-tested entitlements also fared reasonably well after 1981, with stable real funding for even the controversial AFDC program. In addition, Reagan's Tax Reform Act of 1986 included a major expansion of the EITC, a program that would continue to have a significant impact on long-term public assistance spending. The welfare state was, by most measures, more entrenched at the end of the Reagan presidency than it had been during the supposedly halcyon days of the 1970s.

On taxes, by comparison, Reagan's impact was undeniable. The 1981 tax cuts validated, at least for Republicans, the supply-side arguments about low marginal rates and economic growth that have been at the party's core ever since. The Tax Reform Act of 1986 remains the most important structural tax policy initiative of the modern era, and the enactment of this "deficit-neutral" reform in the face of extremely large deficits was a major victory for the administration.

In terms of budget policy, however, the Reagan years further weakened the balanced-budget principle by attaching it to a "smaller government" vision

[79] Office of Management and Budget, *Historical Tables, Fiscal Year 2011*, 142, 157–158.

that was largely illusory. By the end of the Carter presidency, the Democratic Party's version of a balanced budget assumed future revenue levels that most Democrats, to say nothing of their Republican critics, would never support. For Democrats, balancing the budget at more realistic revenue levels would have meant sacrificing the domestic spending gains the party had achieved during the Great Society and the 1970s.

By the end of the Reagan presidency, most congressional Republicans were equally adamant that low taxes (and, correspondingly, low revenue levels) were much more important than balanced budgets. Although Republicans supported tax increases in 1982–1984, these increases sought to lower deficits to "tolerable" levels rather than balance the budget. The net revenue cuts from ERTA remained quite large, especially for individual taxpayers. The balanced-budget promises of Reagan's second term were never taken seriously, because even Republicans had repeatedly refused to make the domestic spending cuts that Reagan continued to promise. For both parties, balanced-budget rhetoric was divorced from fiscal realities, and the 1988 election results reinforced this partisan standoff on budget policy.

5

The Clinton Strategy – Balancing High

During the early 1990s, the deficit problem appeared to have grown worse. The FY 1990 deficit of $221 billion matched the largest deficit of the Reagan years, and the $290 billion FY 1992 deficit set a new record. In fact, a dramatic fiscal turnaround was soon underway, as a nearly three-decade-long streak of consecutive deficits ended in 1998. Two years later, the budget surplus was more than $236 billion, and the Congressional Budget Office (CBO) budget outlook projected surpluses of more than $4.6 trillion over the next decade.[1]

The policy key to this reversal was contained in two multiyear reconciliation bills. The Omnibus Budget Reconciliation Act of 1990 (OBRA 1990), passed by a Democratic Congress and signed by President George H. W. Bush, was a nearly $500 billion deficit-reduction package of tax increases, spending cuts, and budget enforcement provisions. The Omnibus Budget Reconciliation Act of 1993 (OBRA 1993), engineered by President Bill Clinton, was unanimously opposed by congressional Republicans. It, too, increased taxes and by considerably more than the 1990 budget agreement. OBRA 1993 also included spending cuts and budget enforcement provisions as part of its approximately $500 billion in deficit reduction for fiscal years 1994–1998.

A very different version of reconciliation surfaced after the Republican takeover of Congress in the 1994 midterm elections. After barely failing to pass a balanced-budget constitutional amendment, Republican congressional leaders turned to reconciliation as a way to combine massive tax increases and even more massive spending cuts. Republicans hoped to put in place the kind of balanced budget that had eluded Reagan. The Republican version of a balanced budget amounted to a sweeping retrenchment of domestic programs, including entitlements the Great Society had established. Stymied by a

---

[1] Congressional Budget Office, *The Budget and Economic Outlook: Fiscal Years 2002–2011* (Washington, D.C.: Congressional Budget Office, 2001), xv.

Clinton veto of their budget reconciliation bill and chastened by the political fallout from a protracted government shutdown over domestic appropriations in 1995, Republicans were forced to settle for a very different balanced-budget plan two years later.

The 1997 balanced-budget agreement between the Clinton administration and congressional Republicans was supposed to balance the budget in 2002. When the reconciliation bills that implemented this agreement were enacted in the fall of 1997, however, the budget was already moving toward balance more quickly than expected, because Reagan-era priorities had been erased. The revenue-GDP levels that helped generate the surplus budgets of the late 1990s were the highest since World War II. On the spending side, defense-GDP dropped to its lowest level since the late 1940s. By comparison, domestic spending–GDP – both social welfare and discretionary – was higher than it had been at the end of the Reagan presidency.

The end of the Cold War made it possible to cut defense during the 1990s, and the unusually strong economy over much of the decade helped accelerate revenue growth. Nevertheless, solving the deficit problem required significant and politically difficult policy changes, particularly on the tax side of the budget, where the revenue gains of the 1990s were largely the result of individual income tax increases that shifted tax burdens to upper-income households. President Bush was deserted by many congressional Republicans when he signed the 1990 increase. President Clinton barely held his party together on the 1993 increase, and some Democrats attributed the party's midterm election losses the next year to that decision.

The partisan divide over tax policy deepened over the decade, as the Clinton administration and congressional Republicans fought over income tax cuts after the budget had been balanced. Because many Republicans believed that the deficits of the 1980s had been caused by Democratic spending programs, their advocacy of balanced budgets was predicated on domestic spending cuts. When tax increases were used instead, their enthusiasm for balanced budgets dimmed considerably. For Democrats, however, the threat that balanced budgets posed for the party's spending priorities disappeared during the late 1990s. Rather, with high revenue levels, balanced budgets provided fiscal protection to the "welfare state."

From GRH to OBRA 1990: The Bush Tax Increase

The Gramm-Rudman-Hollings (GRH) deficit ceilings had very little impact during Reagan's second term. After the Supreme Court invalidated the key enforcement provisions of the original GRH bill, the revised version passed in 1987 extended the six-year period for balancing the budget until 1993.[2] GRH

---

[2] The new deficit-reduction schedule was as follows: FY 1988, $144 billion; FY 1989, $136 billion; FY 1990, $100 billion; FY 1991, $64 billion; FY 1992, $28 billion; FY 1993, zero. A

II also limited any sequestrations for 1988 and 1989, which meant that serious deficit reduction would be postponed until Reagan left office. The 1987 GRH bill therefore established the National Economic Commission to recommend a bipartisan plan for balancing the budget.

As it turned out, the independent commission's report underscored the impasse over taxes. Eight members of the fourteen-member commission, two of whom had been added by President-elect Bush in late 1988, concluded that the deficit could be erased without a major tax increase, but they did not offer detailed recommendations on how to do so beyond urging "more 'restraints' on spending."[3] The commission's minority report argued that ruling "out any discussion of additional revenue" would lead "nowhere."

George Bush had already made his position clear, with the famous "no new taxes" pledge to the Republican convention. He then highlighted that pledge along with his commitment to the other pillar of the Reagan budget program – increased defense budgets to support strategic and conventional force modernization – during his campaign. Bush distanced himself from Reagan, although not in a way that would make deficit reduction any easier. Rather, he promised a greater openness to spending initiatives for education, environmental protection, social programs, and healthcare.

When President Bush addressed Congress about his budget program on February 9, 1989, he promised a new spirit of cooperation. Bush declared, "My team and I are ready to work with the Congress, to form a special leadership group, to negotiate in good faith, to work day and night . . . to meet the budget target, and to produce a budget on time."[4] It was necessary, he emphasized, to launch "an attack on the deficit" but with "no new taxes." With a Democratic-controlled Congress, however, Bush found that deficit reduction without increased revenues would be next to impossible.

The Limits of Bipartisanship

The GRH deficit ceiling for FY 1990 was $100 billion, and the Bush administration estimated that less than $30 billion in deficit-reduction savings would be needed to meet that target. On April 14, after a nine-week "budget summit" between administration officials and congressional leaders, Bush announced that agreement had been reached on a $28 billion package roughly apportioned between spending cuts and revenue increases. The discretionary spending levels in the agreement incorporated a cut in real defense spending but full inflation adjustments for domestic programs. Beyond defense, spending cuts were largely

---

$10 billion "cushion" was provided for all years except FY 1993. Automatic cuts for FY 1988 were limited to $23 billion, and the FY 1989 limitation was $36 billion.

[3] Congressional Quarterly, *Congressional Quarterly Almanac, 1989* (Washington, D.C.: Congressional Quarterly, 1990), 83.

[4] Ibid., 10-C.

limited to "one-time windfalls and accounting gimmicks with little bearing on long-term fiscal policy."[5]

The revenue side of the agreement was even more problematic. The $14 billion in new revenues included nearly $9 billion that technically met the "no new taxes" test – farm and housing loan sales, user fees, and tax compliance reforms. Approximately $5 billion, however, was in the form of an unspecified "revenue plug," with both sides ultimately agreeing to disagree over whether this might require new taxes. Democrats were not pleased with this compromise. House Speaker Jim Wright commended the administration for "a very good start in the direction of better cooperation" but sharply criticized the administration's no-tax stance.[6] Democrats also feared that Bush was expecting to raise most of the additional revenues with a capital gains tax cut. The administration had proposed a 15 percent maximum tax rate on capital gains from stocks, bonds, and other investments that it claimed would raise an additional $4.8 billion in FY 1990 and a roughly equivalent amount the following year. Signaling their displeasure with this supply-side rationale, the Democratic chairmen of the Ways and Means and Finance committees, both of whom had participated in the budget summit, declined to attend the White House announcement.

Congress adopted its FY 1990 budget resolution without great difficulty, in part because the reconciliation instructions that it included were deliberately vague on the tax issue. The Ways and Means and Finance committees were given wide latitude in determining how the $5 billion "revenue plug" was to be filled, and it was assumed that these committees would work with the White House on a mutually acceptable revenue package. Despite the seemingly small amount at issue, these negotiations were repeatedly delayed by Bush's insistence that a capital gains tax be part of any revenue compromise and by House-Senate differences over tax preferences.

When the reconciliation dispute dragged on past October 1, Bush was forced to issue a $16.2 billion sequestration order to comply with the $100 billion GRH deficit ceiling for FY 1990.[7] Under the GRH formula, these automatic spending cuts were apportioned equally between defense and non-exempt domestic spending. When the reconciliation bill finally cleared Congress on November 22, it included some of these automatic cuts, along with minor entitlement savings and an estimated $6 billion in additional revenues. The administration failed to get its capital gains tax cut but succeeded in blocking what it defined as "new taxes." Among the revenue increases that were approved were accelerated tax payments, extension of the excise tax on airline

---

5 Ibid., 85.

6 Ibid.

7 The final calculation of the estimated deficit for the upcoming fiscal year was reported by the OMB several weeks before the fiscal year began on October 1. When that report was issued for FY 1990, $16.2 billion was required to meet the GRH deficit ceiling, not the $28 billion that had been estimated earlier in the year.

tickets, and a higher Social Security wage base that included employee contributions to tax-deferred retirement plans.[8]

The first year of the Bush presidency produced little progress on the deficit, despite the rhetoric about presidential-congressional cooperation. The administration's willingness to accept defense cuts and discretionary domestic spending increases did little to ease the stalemate over taxes and entitlements. As a result, the deficit outlook at the end of 1989 was essentially unchanged. According to the CBO, the net effect of FY 1990 budget-related legislation – appropriations, reconciliation and sequestration, and the repeal of Medicare catastrophic health insurance – was a $12 billion reduction in the FY 1990 baseline deficit.[9] Unfortunately, what the CBO termed "technical reestimates" wiped out almost all of these savings, leaving the FY 1990 deficit at $138 billion. Moreover, the CBO reported that "without spending cuts or tax increases, the deficit in 1993 is likely to be no lower than in 1990."[10] Since the GRH deficit ceiling for 1993 was zero, the compliance challenge was going to be formidable even if the economy cooperated.

The Bush Retreat

The Bush administration's FY 1991 budget, submitted to Congress on January 29, 1990, sounded an unusually self-congratulatory note. A fourteen-page introduction from Bush's budget director, Richard G. Darman, declared that "This year's budget meets the responsibility to be serious ... giving a more complete and balanced perspective on both the present and the future than has previously been characteristic."[11] Darman was especially proud that the administration had adopted economic assumptions that were "plausible and achievable" but had also included "alternative economic scenarios" for assessing the president's policy recommendations.[12] None of these scenarios pointed to a serious deficit problem in 1991. The "President's Policy Deficit" for 1991 ranged from $54.6 billion under the high-growth scenario to $77.5 billion under the low-growth assumptions, with the administration's plausible and achievable growth assumptions yielding a deficit just below the $64 billion GRH ceiling.[13] In 1993, when GRH required a balanced budget, only the low-growth assumptions forecast a deficit, but at a hardly alarming $27.2 billion.

In line with these forecasts, the administration's budget did not include "major legislative action" to cut the deficit. Rather, it allowed overall spending

---

[8] Congressional Quarterly, *Congressional Quarterly Almanac, 1989*, 103.
[9] Congressional Budget Office, *The Economic and Budget Outlook: Fiscal Years 1991–1995* (Washington, D.C.: Congressional Budget Office, 1990), xvii.
[10] Ibid., xiii.
[11] Office of Management and Budget, *Budget of the United States Government, Fiscal Year 1991* (Washington, D.C.: Government Printing Office, 1990), 21.
[12] Ibid., 12.
[13] Ibid., 10–12.

to increase by approximately 3 percent over FY 1990, while estimating that revenues would grow by 9 percent "on the strength of economic growth" and without any tax increase. The revenue-GNP level for FY 1991 was estimated at 19.9 percent – the highest since the Reagan tax cuts had been enacted – and revenue projections through the mid-1990s were similarly elevated.[14] The Bush budget pointed to future fiscal problems, notably the "rising budgetary claims" of entitlement programs, but the administration was not ready to propose major entitlement reforms.

This reassuring picture did not last for long. In March, the CBO reported that the various economic assumptions in the administration's budget were much too optimistic, that revenue growth had been wildly overestimated, and that spending for interest on the debt and other fixed obligations had been seriously underestimated.[15] If Congress somehow enacted all the president's spending proposals for the FY 1991 budget, which was unlikely, the CBO still forecast a deficit of $130 billion. By the time the CBO updated its budget outlook in July, the fiscal 1991 baseline deficit had risen to more than $230 billion, with even larger deficits as the GRH balanced-budget deadline approached in 1993.[16] Enforcing the GRH deficit limits under these circumstances was not a realistic option. The sequestrations in 1991, for example, would have amounted to an approximately 25 percent cut in defense and an even larger percentage reduction in domestic programs, with additional sequestrations needed in 1992 and 1993.

With the deficit outlook having changed so quickly, President Bush concluded that it was necessary to replace GRH with a more feasible deficit-reduction plan, but congressional Democrats were reluctant to participate in another "budget summit" without some reassurance that tax increases would be considered. At a White House meeting with leaders of both parties on May 6, Bush agreed the budget talks would proceed with "no preconditions."[17] When a number of House and Senate Republicans complained that Bush was abandoning his "no new taxes" pledge, a White House official assured them that the administration would oppose any tax increases that Democrats might offer.

The budget summit officially convened on May 15, but the deadlock over taxes stalled progress for almost six weeks. The nearly two dozen administration and congressional representatives who participated were able to agree on a deficit reduction target of $50 billion in FY 1991 and $500 billion over five years, but Democratic negotiators insisted that the administration acknowledge

---

[14] Ibid., A-282.
[15] Congressional Budget Office, *An Analysis of the President's Budgetary Proposals for Fiscal Year 1991* (Washington, D.C.: Congressional Budget Office, 1990), 1–10.
[16] Congressional Budget Office, *The Economic and Budget Outlook: An Update* (Washington, D.C.: Congressional Budget Office, 1990), xiii.
[17] Congressional Quarterly, *Congressional Quarterly Almanac, 1990* (Washington, D.C.: Congressional Quarterly, 1991), 130.

that tax increases as well as spending cuts would have to be included in the final deficit-reduction plan. That acknowledgement came on June 26. In a written statement issued after meeting with congressional leaders of both parties, Bush conceded that "the size of the deficit problem and the need for a package that can be enacted" meant that "tax revenue increases," as well as spending cuts and budget process reforms, would be required.[18]

Democrats responded by agreeing to include entitlement reforms in the deficit-reduction talks, but congressional Republicans, particularly in the House, were unmoved. On July 18, the House Republican Conference approved a resolution opposing any tax increases, and their opposition did not waver as deficit projections continued to mount. Meanwhile, congressional Democrats reignited the debate over tax equity by demanding that marginal rates be raised for high-income taxpayers. Democrats were less united, however, on the Medicare and other entitlement savings that had been added to the deficit-reduction agenda.

On August 2, Iraq invaded Kuwait, and the United States responded with a massive troop deployment to the Persian Gulf. On September 11, President Bush addressed a joint session of Congress on the U.S. response but also called for a quick resolution of the budget talks. Bush was anxious to "avoid the ax of sequester – deep across-the-board cuts that would threaten our military capacity and risk substantial domestic disruption" and was "hopeful – in fact confident – that Congress will do what it should."[19] The budget talks produced an agreement on September 30, but what followed was a stunning defeat for Bush.

On October 5, the House rejected, by a 179–254 margin, the budget resolution that represented the first step in implementing the budget agreement. Bush had lobbied individual Republicans to support the resolution and had also appealed for public support in a nationally broadcast speech on October 2. Neither effort helped. A majority of House Republicans, led by Minority Whip Newt Gingrich, voted against the resolution and the tax increases it contained. An overwhelming majority of House Democrats also refused to endorse the agreement, although their complaints focused on entitlement cuts and the failure to raise tax rates for high-income taxpayers. As one Democrat explained, the budget agreement "locked in for five more years . . . the cruel and discredited policies of Reaganomics."[20] While hyperbolic, this assessment was not far off the mark. The September 30 budget agreement included two tax increases affecting high-income taxpayers – limits on deductions and an increase in the Medicare payroll tax wage base from $51,300 to $73,200 – but Bush managed to protect the marginal rates that Reagan had put in place. Neither the size of the tax increase in the agreement nor the types of taxes it raised differed

[18] Ibid., 31.
[19] Ibid., 133.
[20] Ibid., 136.

TABLE 5.1. *Omnibus Budget Reconciliation Act of 1990 (P.L. 101-508): Major Provisions and Deficit Savings (in billions of dollars)*

	Fiscal Years 1991–1995
Revenue Provisions[a]	
High-income tax rates; limits on deductions and exemptions; AMT; Medicare payroll tax	– $67
Gasoline, telephone, tobacco, alcohol, and other excise taxes	– 66
Social Security coverage	– 9
Business and other (net change)	– 16
	– 158
Spending Provisions	
Discretionary defense and nondefense	– $190
Mandatory	– 75
Medicare	(– 43)
Federal employee retirement	(– 14)
Deposit insurance	(– 9)
EITC	(+17)
Other	(– 26)
Debt service	– 59
	– 324
Total Deficit Savings	– $482

[a] The total represents net changes for fiscal years 1991–1995.
Source: Congressional Budget Office, *The Economic and Budget Outlook: Fiscal Years 1992–1996* (Washington, D.C.: Congressional Budget Office, 1991), 66–68.

substantially from deficit-reduction tax increases that Reagan had signed, but Bush was still pilloried by many Republicans.

The next stage of the 1991 budget process was firmly controlled by Democrats, and the outcome proved even less palatable to Republican conservatives. In less than three weeks, Congress adopted a revised budget resolution, passed the accompanying reconciliation bill, and completed action on all thirteen FY 1991 appropriations bills. The reconciliation bill that Bush signed into law on November 5 replaced the GRH deficit ceilings with a five-year, $482 billion deficit-reduction package that included tax increases, spending cuts, and budget enforcement controls (see Table 5.1).

The largest share of income and payroll tax increases in OBRA 1990 affected high-income taxpayers. The top marginal rate on individual income was raised from 28 percent to 31 percent, personal exemptions were phased out and deductions were limited at high income levels, and the Medicare payroll tax wage base was raised to $125,000. These provisions accounted for more than 40 percent of the total revenue increase, with a roughly equivalent amount from the broad-based gasoline and excise tax additions and extensions. In terms of relative revenue levels, OBRA 1990 was expected to raise revenue-GNP by 0.5 percent annually from 1992 to 1995, but this increase did not "greatly alter the GNP shares of the major tax sources that were projected for this period before the act."[21]

The policy components of OBRA 1990, particularly the tax increases, clearly favored congressional Democrats. The budget enforcement provisions, however, allowed the administration to claim that it had tightened controls over spending. This claim had some merit, but the strongest controls only affected discretionary spending, with annual appropriations limits $190 billion below baseline levels.[22] In an attempt to provide some protection for defense, the administration insisted on separate limits for defense and discretionary domestic spending for the first three years, with a prohibition on transfers between categories. Nevertheless, most of the mandated spending reductions were in the defense category, and the 1994 and 1995 reductions were expected to fall heavily on defense as well.[23]

The mandatory spending controls, by comparison, did not limit actual spending. The so-called PAYGO limits meant that legislative increases in entitlement program spending had to be offset with other entitlement reductions or revenue increases. (A similar requirement for deficit neutrality applied to legislated tax cuts.) Increases in entitlement spending caused by unexpected economic or demographic changes, however, were permissible. OBRA 1990 therefore left in place high rates of automatic growth in major entitlement programs and accentuated the imbalance between discretionary and mandatory spending growth.

With his skillful handling of the Middle East crisis in the fall of 1990 and the unexpectedly rapid victory in the Gulf War that began the following January, President Bush's public approval ratings soared. The postwar euphoria quickly faded as the economy struggled to recover, and the deficit outlook grew worse, seemingly despite OBRA 1990. The budgetary impact of a weak economy masked OBRA's policy effects, which did prevent the deficit from becoming even larger.[24] Unfortunately for Bush, this modest achievement paled next to OBRA's political backlash among conservative Republicans, and it made the task of defending tax increases to the public considerably more difficult as well.

The Post-1990 Stalemate

The last two years of the Bush presidency featured prolonged disputes over relatively trivial amounts of spending. It took six months, for example, for the administration and Congress to agree on a $5.3 billion extension of unemployment benefits in 1991. Bush had signed the extension in August but then

[21] Congressional Budget Office, *The Economic and Budget Outlook: Fiscal Years 1992–1996* (Washington, D.C.: Congressional Budget Office, 1991), 114.

[22] This estimate included enacted appropriations for FY 1991 that reduced spending by $46 billion over five years. The additional discretionary reductions totaled an estimated $144 billion over the same period. Ibid., xvii.

[23] Ibid., 65.

[24] Ibid., 16–17.

refused to issue the employment emergency declaration needed to release the funds. When a second extension passed in September, Bush vetoed it, insisting that Democrats find an offset consistent with PAYGO rules. Congressional Republicans then prevailed on Bush to bow to political necessity, and a compromise was reached in November. A revenue offset was included, primarily from requiring high-income taxpayers to accelerate the payment of their estimated taxes, but the administration was forced in turn to accept a more expensive benefit extension.

With mandatory spending for FY 1992 projected at nearly $700 billion and the deficit approaching $300 billion, the $5.3 billion cost of the unemployment bill was clearly not a critical fiscal issue. The administration's dogged defense of PAYGO under those circumstances made no sense even to congressional Republicans who otherwise took a hard line on domestic spending. In the end, Bush maintained that he had supported an unemployment bill all along, which made the episode even more puzzling.

Bush scored a minor victory on domestic spending in 1992. When he was renominated at the Republican convention in August, Bush threatened to veto any domestic spending bill that exceeded his budget request. Congressional Democrats then decided to avoid any confrontation that might be turned to Bush's advantage and passed appropriations bills that complied with the administration's unilateral "spending freeze." Discretionary domestic spending, however, still continued to increase, and Bush's last-minute attack on a federal government that "is too big and spends too much" did not appear to improve his standing with conservatives in his party.[25] Bush was also unable to reorder domestic priorities. His FY 1992 budget included cuts or terminations in nearly 350 domestic programs, nearly all of which Congress ignored.[26] The administration called for means-testing in a number of entitlement programs, but its advocacy of entitlement reform was half-hearted, perhaps because the prospects for congressional cooperation were nonexistent.

On defense policy, the administration's record was stronger. With the collapse of the Soviet Union, the administration quickly garnered congressional support for its post–Cold War defense plan. The "Base Force" that the administration proposed combined reduced force levels and lower, but stable, defense budgets. Despite complaints from liberal Democrats that the Bush cuts did not go far enough, Congress did not attempt to capture any "peace dividend" by slashing the administration's defense budget requests.[27]

Bush's national security leadership, however, was overshadowed by his record on taxes. At the Republican National Convention in August, Bush

---

[25] Congressional Quarterly, *Congressional Quarterly Almanac, 1992* (Washington, D.C.: Congressional Quarterly, 1993), 75–A.

[26] Ibid., 55.

[27] See Dennis S. Ippolito, *Why Budgets Matter: Budget Policy and American Politics* (University Park: Pennsylvania State University Press, 2003), 254–255.

admitted to having "made a bad call on the Democrats' tax increase" and to underestimating "Congress' addiction to taxes."[28] He had learned the "hard way" on taxes and asked the American people to trust him as "the candidate who has raised taxes one time and regrets it." To complete his repentance, Bush called for an across-the-board income tax cut and lower capital gains taxes after the election, but with Democrats maintaining heavy majorities in the House and Senate and winning the presidency in 1992, tax policy was about to move in a different direction.

Clinton and the Democrats: The OBRA 1993 Tax Increase

When the Clinton administration took office, the deficit outlook was bleak. The CBO cautioned that even the "onset of economic expansion will bring no relief from recordbreaking budget deficits...near $300 billion for the next few years and...even higher in the second half of the 1990s."[29] In addition, recovery from the economic recession in 1991 had been "extremely weak," with unemployment continuing to rise for more than a year, and economic growth was expected to remain relatively low.

The issue for Clinton, and for the heavily Democratic Congress, was how to reconcile the party's commitment to "public investment" (i.e., spending to create jobs and promote economic growth) with deficit reduction. The Clinton campaign had managed to finesse the problem by claiming that measures to accelerate growth would solve much of the deficit problem, and Clinton had carefully avoided any deficit-reduction commitments that might be politically problematic.[30] Entitlement reform was ignored, as was domestic retrenchment generally. Further, the potential costs of universal healthcare, a new entitlement that Clinton promised to deliver, were never specified. The defense budget cuts that Clinton discussed were also extremely modest, because they were based on the so-called Force C option developed by House Armed Services Committee chairman Les Aspin. This Democratic defense plan endorsed the post–Cold War defense strategy of the Bush administration but concluded that the strategy could be supported with slightly lower force levels and budgets.[31]

On taxes, Clinton was equally circumspect. The Democratic platform called for tax relief for "middle-class Americans" and "families with children," and it proposed to provide this relief by "forcing the rich to pay their fair share."[32] While middle-class tax cuts and an expanded earned-income tax credit (EITC)

---

[28] Congressional Quarterly, *Congressional Quarterly Almanac, 1992*, 76-A.

[29] Congressional Budget Office, *The Economic and Budget Outlook: Fiscal Years 1994–1998* (Washington, D.C.: Congressional Budget Office, 1993), xv.

[30] Iwan W. Morgan, *The Age of Deficits* (Lawrence: University Press of Kansas, 2009), 163–165.

[31] Dennis S. Ippolito, *Budget Policy and the Future of Defense* (Washington, D.C.: Institute for National Strategic Studies/National Defense University Press, 1994), 84–97.

[32] Congressional Quarterly, *Congressional Quarterly Almanac, 1992*, 61-A.

were staples of the Clinton campaign, there was considerably less clarity as to what defined "the rich" or what constituted their "fair share."

The Clinton Budget Program

Clinton's economic advisers remained divided on the relative priorities of public investment and deficit reduction after the election. These internal debates continued for several months, with Clinton finally, and apparently reluctantly, deciding that the economic case for deficit reduction was paramount. On February 17, 1993, Clinton appeared before a joint session of Congress to outline his economic and budget program. The specifics were ambitious and wide-ranging: more than $700 billion in deficit savings over five years, with approximately two-thirds of this amount targeted at deficit reduction and the remainder directed toward long-term "investment" programs. Clinton also recommended a short-term stimulus package of $16.3 billion in the form of a supplemental appropriation for FY 1993. Congressional Democrats decided to defer action on this last request until the deficit-reduction and investment proposals were incorporated into the upcoming budget resolution.

The tax increases that Clinton proposed were estimated at $328 billion over five years and included higher marginal rates and Medicare payroll taxes for high-income taxpayers and a higher tax rate for large corporations.[33] Middle-income taxpayers also faced a new, broad-based energy tax (the "Btu tax") that accounted for more than one-fifth of the total tax increase. The tax portion of the Clinton program drew predictably strong criticism from congressional Republican leaders. House Minority Leader Robert H. Michel, who delivered the official Republican response to Clinton's address, contrasted candidate Clinton – "Tax only the super-rich" – with President Clinton – "If you earn more than $30,000, your taxes are going up."[34] Michel advised the American people "to remember when you hear a Democrat call for taxes, do not ask for whom the tax rises – it will rise for you."

The proposed Clinton tax increases also troubled many Democrats, who were concerned that the party's "tax and spend" reputation was about to resurface. Their concerns were reinforced by the administration's apparent retreat from its earlier promise that a 2:1 ratio of spending cuts to tax increases would guide deficit-reduction efforts.[35] The administration's final recommendations for spending cuts and tax increases were roughly equivalent. Of the projected $345 billion in spending cuts, approximately one-third came from defense, a much larger decrease than had been promised during the campaign.

[33] Congressional Quarterly, *Congressional Quarterly Almanac, 1993* (Washington, D.C.: Congressional Quarterly, 1994), 85.
[34] Ibid., 13-D.
[35] At his confirmation hearings in January, Clinton's OMB director, Leon E. Panetta, had argued for the 2:1 ratio. Ibid., 86.

The entitlement reductions, estimated at $115 billion over five years, primarily affected Medicare reimbursement formulas and Part B premiums rather than actual benefits. The third-largest spending change, an estimated $73 billion cut in nondefense discretionary programs, included federal civilian workforce reductions and "management efficiencies."

The Fiscal Year 1994 Budget Resolution
As Congress took up the Clinton program, any hopes for bipartisan deficit reduction quickly vanished. Republican leaders in Congress denounced the tax increases and vowed to block Clinton's proposed spending stimulus. Republicans also criticized the defense cuts that Clinton had proposed and warned that Democrats would inevitably slash defense even further in order to provide additional funding for domestic programs. House and Senate Democrats, however, quickly passed the FY 1994 budget resolution based on the Clinton plan, setting the stage for the reconciliation bill that would make the tax and spending legislative changes to implement the plan.

The budget resolution stripped some of the investment spending that Clinton had recommended but still contained a rough balance between tax increases and spending cuts. In the House, Republican deficit-reduction plans based exclusively on spending cuts were easily defeated. A substitute offered by House Budget Committee Republicans, for example, contained $500 billion in deficit reduction from cuts in almost 160 domestic programs. It was rejected on a 135–295 vote. In the Senate, Republican attempts to eliminate specific tax increases were defeated, although usually by narrow margins. House-Senate differences were quickly resolved in conference at the end of March, and both chambers proceeded to pass the conference version of the FY 1994 budget resolution with no Republican votes and few Democratic defections.

Republicans were more successful in attacking Clinton's $16.3 billion supplemental appropriations request. After this measure passed the House with only three Republican votes, Senate Republicans mounted a filibuster against it on the Senate floor. In order to end the filibuster, Democrats needed the support of at least four Republicans in addition to unanimous support from their own party members but fell well short of the sixty-vote cloture requirement. On three successive cloture votes in early April, no Republican voted to end debate, and a number of conservative Democrats defected. At that point, the Democratic leadership agreed to delete more than $12 billion of the stimulus spending, leaving only $4 billion for extended unemployment benefits. This stripped-down bill then was approved by both chambers, but the polarization over the budget resolution and supplemental appropriations bill resurfaced on the critical reconciliation bill. While reconciliation legislation was immune to filibusters or filibuster threats, the likelihood of Democratic defections on tax increases and deficit reduction posed a potential threat to Clinton's program.

OBRA 1993: The Tax Controversies

The reconciliation instructions in the FY 1994 budget resolution applied to more than two dozen House and Senate committees with jurisdiction over revenues and entitlement programs; discretionary spending bills handled by the Appropriations committees were subject to spending limits set by the budget resolution. Within these limits, the Appropriations committees made allocations to the thirteen appropriations bills considered by the House and Senate. The reconciliation instructions, by comparison, established deficit-reduction savings for each committee, with committees then determining how these savings were to be achieved. The Ways and Means and Finance committees were responsible for the largest portion of the reconciliation package, and they faced the added burden of writing tax bills that could keep the fragile Democratic majorities from splintering.

The Ways and Means Committee began its markup on May 6 and reported out its portion of the reconciliation bill on a party-line vote one week later. The $250 billion in revenue increases approved by the committee included most of what Clinton had requested, including the higher income tax brackets, Medicare and Social Security tax changes, and increased corporate tax rate. Clinton's Btu energy tax was modified, but his investment tax credit incentives were eliminated. Ways and Means also reported out the approximately $50 billion in Medicare savings that constituted by far the largest component of the entitlement cutbacks to be included in the reconciliation bill. Other House committees completed their reconciliation work with little difficulty.

When the House Budget Committee brought the reconciliation package to the House floor, the Ways and Means tax increases threatened to bring down the entire measure. In addition to their general disquiet about what one Republican called "the biggest tax increase in the history of the world," Democrats from energy-producing states were worried about the new energy tax.[36] Concerns were also raised about the impact the energy tax might have on industrial and agricultural users, and many Democrats feared that they were being asked to take a huge political risk in voting for a tax increase the Senate might then reject. The administration then undertook an intense lobbying campaign, with President Clinton, Vice President Al Gore, and cabinet members seeking to persuade nervous Democrats to support what had become a politically explosive reconciliation bill. The administration agreed to modify the energy tax when the measure moved to the Senate, but the vote to send it there was still extremely close. With thirty-eight Democrats joining a unified Republican opposition, the House version of OBRA 1993 passed by a 219–213 vote.

The Senate Finance Committee struggled for two weeks to put together a tax increase that could make it out of committee. With an 11–9 majority, Democrats could not afford any defections and were forced to drop the Btu

[36] Ibid., 109.

tax to placate David L. Boren, an Oklahoma Democrat. The revenue loss from eliminating the Btu tax was more than $70 billion, which committee Democrats proposed to offset with higher taxes on gasoline and transportation fuels, additional cuts in Medicare, and reduced tax incentives and preferences. During the committee markup, all Republican amendments were defeated, and the Finance Committee's part of the reconciliation package was reported out on a strict party-line vote. While eleven other committees had contributed to the reconciliation bill the Senate took up on June 24, the Finance Committee's tax proposals dominated the eighteen-hour debate that ended at 3:00 A.M. the following day. The vote was 49–49, with Vice President Gore then casting the tie-breaking vote. As in the House, all Republicans voted against the reconciliation bill, and six Democrats opposed it as well.

The conference that followed involved more than 200 conferees and lasted more than two weeks. Despite the literally hundreds of provisions in the House-passed and Senate-passed reconciliation bills, the major sticking points were their tax and entitlement provisions. The conference committee adopted the Senate's fuel tax to replace the Btu tax the House had approved, and restored some of the Medicare cuts the Senate had passed. Compromises were reached on the EITC expansion and small business tax preferences, and the income threshold for the Social Security benefits tax was increased by an additional 10 percent to provide more revenues. Once again, administration lobbying for the deficit-reduction program was intense, with Clinton appealing for public support in a nationally televised speech on August 3. Two days later, the House passed the reconciliation bill by a 218–216 margin, with forty-one Democrats and all Republicans voting no. The Senate voted 50–50 one day later, and Vice President Gore cast the fifty-first vote that sent OBRA 1993 to the president for his signature.

OBRA 1993: Policy Effects
The Clinton administration estimated that more than $500 billion in deficit reduction had been achieved with passage of the reconciliation bill.[37] According to the CBO, which issued an independent estimate in its September budget update, the savings were $433 billion.[38] Most of the difference stemmed from a technical disagreement over whether the discretionary spending savings for 1994 and 1995 that had already been mandated under OBRA 1990 should also be credited to OBRA 1993.[39] On the more important and controversial part of the 1993 reconciliation bill – the tax increases – the CBO calculated the five-year increase in revenues at $240.6 billion, less than $10 billion below

---

[37] Ibid., 108.
[38] Congressional Budget Office, *The Economic and Budget Outlook: An Update* (Washington, D.C.: Congressional Budget Office, 1993), 28–29.
[39] There were additional differences regarding debt service savings from lower deficits and a Treasury plan to refinance a portion of the debt at lower interest rates.

TABLE 5.2. *Omnibus Budget Reconciliation Act of 1993 (P.L. 103-66): Major Provisions and Deficit Savings (in billions of dollars)*

	Fiscal Years
Revenue Provisions[a]	1994–1998
High-income tax rates; limits on deductions and exemptions; AMT; Medicare payroll tax; Social Security benefit tax	− $169
Corporate income tax rate	− 16
Gasoline and fuel excise taxes	− 31
Business and other	− 24
	− 240
Spending Provisions	
Discretionary defense and nondefense	− $69
Mandatory	− 77
Medicare	(− 56)
Federal employee retirement	(− 12)
Medicaid	(− 7)
EITC, Food Stamp	(+22)
Other	(− 24)
Debt service	− 47
	− 193
Total Deficit Savings	− $433

[a] Some revenue provisions produced minor revenue losses. The total represents net changes for fiscal years 1994–1998.
Source: Congressional Budget Office, *The Economic and Budget Outlook: An Update* (Washington, D.C.: Congressional Budget Office, 1993), 28–31.

the administration's figure, and both sides agreed that high-income taxpayers would account for at least two-thirds of the total revenue increase (see Table 5.2).

Approximately $115 billion of the tax increase for high-income individuals was the result of the new 36 percent and 39.6 percent income tax brackets (and related changes in the alternative minimum tax [AMT]), along with the permanent extension of limits on deductions and exemptions. Nearly $30 billion of additional revenue was expected from the Medicare payroll tax increase. Earnings subject to the Medicare tax had been raised to $125,000 in 1990 and indexed thereafter. OBRA 1993 repealed this limit, which had risen to $135,000, and made all wage and salary income subject to the tax. The Social Security benefits tax, which raised the percentage of benefits subject to the income tax for taxpayers above certain income thresholds from 50 percent to 85 percent, accounted for an additional $25 billion. Since taxpayers with very high incomes were disproportionately affected by the corporate tax changes – both the higher tax rate and the deductibility of business and entertainment expenses – their effective tax rates were expected to increase to pre-Reagan levels.[40]

For low-income taxpayers, the expansion of the EITC included higher benefits for families with two or more children, liberalized income eligibility, and new coverage for families without children. For families in the lowest income quintile (based on adjusted family income), after-tax income under OBRA 1993 was expected to increase by more than 2 percent, taking into account not just income and payroll taxes but the estimated effect of excise and corporate income tax increases as well.[41] When the EITC changes were fully phased in by 1996, effective tax rates for this low-income group would fall to the lowest levels since the mid-1970s and to approximately half the level prior to the Tax Reform Act of 1986.

OBRA 1990, OBRA 1993, and Taxes

The 1990 and 1993 reconciliation bills were fairly similar in their spending policy provisions. Discretionary spending caps accounted for a large portion of spending savings in each bill – an estimated $190 billion (including FY 1991 enacted appropriations) for OBRA 1990 and $69 billion for OBRA 1993.[42] Net entitlement and mandatory spending savings totaled $75 billion in 1990 and $77 billion in 1993. In both cases, the Medicare program accounted for most of the deficit-reduction savings, primarily through reduced reimbursements to healthcare providers. The EITC was expanded by an estimated $17 billion in 1990 and $18 billion in 1993.

The important policy differences between the 1990 and 1993 bills were on the revenue side. The estimated five-year revenue increase in OBRA 1993 was more than $240 billion, 50 percent higher than in 1990. The differential for high-income taxpayers was especially striking. In 1990, the income tax and Medicare payroll tax increases for high-income taxpayers totaled less than $70 billion.[43] Under OBRA 1993, the income tax increase alone was $125 billion, and the Medicare wage cap repeal accounted for an additional $30 billion.[44] In addition, the limits on deductions and phase-out of personal exemptions for high-income taxpayers were temporary under OBRA 1990, with a scheduled expiration date of 1995. OBRA 1993 made these changes permanent. As the CBO noted in its assessment of OBRA 1993, estimates of future revenues were "more uncertain," given the relatively small number of taxpayers affected by the high-income tax provisions.[45] As it turned out,

---

[40] Congressional Budget Office, *The Economic and Budget Outlook: An Update* (1993), 29–31.
[41] Ibid.
[42] Congressional Budget Office, *The Economic and Budget Outlook: Fiscal Years 1992–1996*, 66; Congressional Quarterly, *Congressional Quarterly Almanac, 1993*, 133.
[43] Congressional Budget Office, *The Economic and Budget Outlook: Fiscal Years 1992–1996*, 67.
[44] Congressional Quarterly, *Congressional Quarterly Almanac, 1993*, 133.
[45] Congressional Budget Office, *The Economic and Budget Outlook: An Update* (1993), 31.

revenues in FY 1994 were $40 billion higher than estimated, and the deficit fell by more than $50 billion. Since the deficit remained at more than $200 billion, however, congressional Republicans assailed Clinton's budget program and tax increases.

When House Republicans unveiled their "Contract with America" six weeks before the 1994 midterm elections, their first pledge was a constitutional balanced-budget amendment. Of the remaining nine items, four featured tax cuts, including "middle-class tax cuts" as part of the American Dream Restoration Act, lower capital gains rates, and the repeal of the 1993 increase in Social Security benefit taxes. The "Agenda for the Republican Majority" that Minority Leader Robert Dole and other Senate candidates presented on September 21 echoed the theme of lower taxes and small government.

Congressional Democrats had feared that the 1993 tax increases would be politically costly. The 1994 midterm results confirmed these fears as Republicans took control of both the House and Senate for the first time in fifty years. In the House, where Republicans gained fifty-two seats, twenty-eight of the thirty-four Democratic incumbents who were defeated had voted for OBRA 1993. Before the final vote on OBRA 1993, House Speaker Thomas S. Foley had told wavering Democrats that "Tonight is the time for courage."[46] On November 8, 1994, Foley became the first sitting House speaker to be denied reelection since 1862. Foley's replacement, Newt Gingrich, had led the Republican opposition to George Bush's tax increase in 1990. He and Robert Dole, the new Republican majority leader in the Senate, had managed to unite every House and Senate Republican in opposition to the Clinton tax increase in 1993. As the 104th Congress convened in January 1995, the "tax wars" quickly heated up.

Clinton versus the Republicans: Vetoes and Shutdowns

To describe the budget process during 1995 as tumultuous would be an understatement. The Republican challenges to the Clinton administration began with a balanced-budget constitutional amendment that passed the House on January 26. The year ended with a government shutdown that lasted three weeks and furloughed 284,000 federal workers. In between were protracted fights over domestic appropriations, the debt limit, and a nearly $900 billion Republican reconciliation bill – vetoed by Clinton in December – that would have combined large tax cuts and massive domestic spending reductions. When the year began, a solid majority of Americans believed that congressional Republicans would deal with the deficit more effectively than President Clinton.[47] By summer,

---

[46] Congressional Quarterly, *Congressional Quarterly Almanac, 1993*, 122.

[47] An ABC News poll in January showed a 55–32 percent edge for congressional Republicans when the public was asked, "Who do you trust to do a better job on the issue of reducing the federal budget deficit?" A CBS News/*New York Times* poll in April asked, "Who do you think has better ideas about reducing the federal budget deficit?" In this case, 47 percent supported

as the Republican balanced-budget plan took shape, public opinion shifted toward Clinton. After the November and December government shutdowns, Clinton's advantage was unmistakable.[48]

The Balanced-Budget Amendment

The first constitutional balanced-budget amendment was proposed in 1936, but it took almost fifty years for an amendment to reach the House and Senate floor.[49] In 1982, the Senate passed a balanced-budget amendment, but the measure fell well short of the required two-thirds majority in the House. Neither the House nor Senate acted favorably on proposed balanced-budget amendments over the next decade. In 1994, majorities in both chambers supported proposed amendments, but the two-thirds requirement proved insurmountable. The first priority of the Contract with America that House Republicans then adopted was passage of a constitutional amendment to require the president and Congress to balance the budget.[50] The Contract version, however, included an unusual and controversial provision on taxes. Once the balanced-budget amendment came into effect, a three-fifths vote of the House and Senate would be required for any tax increase.

When the 104th Congress convened on January 4, 1995, balanced-budget constitutional amendments were immediately introduced by House and Senate Republican leaders. While the House version included the supermajority tax increase requirement, the proposal introduced by Senate Majority Leader Robert Dole did not. Senate Republicans were convinced that the tax increase provision would never be adopted by the Senate and were not at all certain that the amendment would pass even without it. As it turned out, House Republicans were able to pass a balanced-budget amendment fairly easily, but only after the supermajority tax increase requirement was dropped. House Republicans had problems with Social Security protections and "truth in budgeting" proposals sponsored by Democrats but were able to circumvent these. In the Senate, however, Democrats used these same issues to delay and ultimately to defeat the amendment.

The House Judiciary Committee dutifully reported out the Contract version of the balanced-budget amendment after a day-long markup on January 11. It rejected Democratic amendments, including proposals to drop the

---

congressional Republicans and 36 percent favored Clinton. *National Journal*, October 27, 2007, 40.

[48] Republicans were overwhelmingly blamed for the shutdown. Clinton's plans for balancing the budget also received more support than did Republican plans. Ibid., 41. Clinton's approval ratings improved significantly during and after the shutdown, while Gingrich's plummeted. See Morgan, *The Age of Deficits*, 187.

[49] Congressional Quarterly, *Congressional Quarterly Almanac, 1995* (Washington, D.C.: Congressional Quarterly, 1996), 2-35.

[50] The requirement was to be effective in 2002 or two years after ratification by the states. Ibid., 2-34.

supermajority tax limitation and to include within the amendment a specific exclusion for Social Security. The committee also defeated a truth in budgeting proposal, supported by the Clinton administration, that would have required Congress to adopt a detailed balanced-budget plan before sending the balanced-budget amendment to the states for ratification.

When the measure reached the House floor on January 25, the truth in budgeting amendment was again rejected, but the House overwhelmingly adopted a nonbinding resolution that promised to protect Social Security when the balanced-budget amendment was actually implemented. It also became clear that Republicans would have to drop the tax increase restriction if they hoped to pass the amendment. The House adopted a substitute, without the supermajority tax increase requirement, on January 26, by a vote of 300–132 (R 228–2; D 72–129; I 0–1).[51] A threatened revolt by conservative Republicans who were wedded to the original Contract's tax limitation was averted, but Republican leaders had to promise that a constitutional amendment with that tax restriction would be brought up in 1996.[52]

In the Senate, Judiciary Committee Republicans reported out the balanced-budget amendment with minimal difficulty, but Democrats were able to prolong floor debate for several weeks. As in the House, Democrats wanted to add the truth in budgeting requirement as a precondition for ratification by the states, and they were insistent that explicit protections for Social Security be incorporated into the text of the amendment. Unlike the House, Senate Republicans could not foreclose amendments or end debate by majority vote. A cloture vote on February 16 failed by three votes and gave Democrats the opportunity to introduce and debate additional amendments. Nearly two dozen amendments were offered over the next two weeks, one of which – a prohibition against federal courts hearing cases involving the balanced-budget amendment unless authorized by Congress – was adopted. By February 28, when the final vote on passage was scheduled, it appeared that the amendment would fail by one vote. Of the fifty-three Republicans, only Senator Mark O. Hatfield of Oregon, chairman of the Appropriations Committee, was opposed, which meant that fifteen Democratic votes were needed to reach the sixty-seven-vote threshold. Dole postponed the vote until March 2 to try to pick up the fifteenth vote but failed.[53]

---

[51] This substitute was sponsored by Charles W. Stenholm, a Texas Democrat, and Dan Schaefer, a Republican from Colorado. The Judiciary Committee had rejected the Stenholm-Schaefer proposal by a 30–4 vote. The substitute that the House adopted did require that "No bill to increase revenue shall become law unless approved by a majority of the whole number of each House by a roll-call vote." It also included two-thirds majority requirements for increasing the public debt limit or for allowing a "specific excess of outlays over receipts" in any fiscal year. Congressional Quarterly, *Congressional Quarterly Almanac, 1995*, 2-38.

[52] Ibid., 2-37.

[53] The vote was 66–34. Dole then switched his vote to "no," making the official vote 65–35. This maneuver allowed him to call for a revote at a later time, which he finally (and unsuccessfully)

With the balanced-budget amendment having come to an unexpected dead end, Republican leaders pressed ahead with a more direct and immediate challenge to Democratic budget priorities. The FY 1996 budget resolution that the House and Senate adopted on June 29, with no Democratic votes in the Senate and only eight in the House, was described as "a manifesto of the Republican version of a federal government that was far smaller, much cheaper, and far less intrusive than the one that existed in 1995."[54] The budget resolution provided the truth in budgeting blueprint for balancing the budget that Democrats had called for during the debate on the balanced-budget amendment, and it proved to be even more polarizing than the amendment.

The Republican blueprint for a balanced budget in 2002 included $900 billion in spending cuts, partly through discretionary domestic savings but mostly through mandatory spending cutbacks. The former translated into spending limits for fiscal years 1996–2002 on the annual appropriations bills. The latter required another reconciliation bill. Unlike the 1990 and 1993 bills, however, the 1995 reconciliation plan called for massive cuts in entitlements, especially Medicare, Medicaid, and public assistance programs.

The proposed domestic appropriations and entitlement cuts were especially large, because Republicans had decided to exempt defense spending and Social Security. The Republican plan provided for small increases in defense spending over seven years and excluded Social Security from the deficit-reduction package. Republicans had been obliged to promise that Social Security would not be affected by the balanced-budget amendment, and the reconciliation exclusion confirmed the special political status that Social Security enjoyed.[55] The gamble that Medicare (or the various welfare programs for the poor) did not enjoy similar status was a risk that Republicans were willing to take, in part because they had little choice. By carving out Social Security and defense spending from their budget-balancing formula, and with interest on the debt foreclosed as well, less than half the budget had to absorb all projected spending cuts.[56] This task was made even more difficult by what was arguably the most provocative part of the Republican plan – the largest tax cut since 1981.

The tax cut in the House's budget resolution was more than $350 billion. The Senate's plan included a tax cut roughly half that size, and the Senate made its tax cut contingent on the CBO certifying that any deficit-reduction

---

did before leaving the Senate in June 1996 to pursue his presidential bid. An effort by pro-amendment Republicans to remove Hatfield as Appropriations Committee chairman did not succeed, but the recriminations among Republicans continued for some time.

[54] Congressional Quarterly, *Congressional Quarterly Almanac, 1995*, 2-20.

[55] According to Morgan, Gingrich intended to deal with Social Security eventually but believed that "everything else" had to be dealt with first. *The Age of Deficits*, 179.

[56] Beyond the mathematics, however, many Republicans were intent on "defunding" the welfare state. These Republicans objected to the philosophy as well as the cost of the large entitlement programs, and their philosophical objections were even stronger for some of the less costly public assistance entitlements.

plan Congress passed would actually balance the budget in 2002. The budget resolution that the House and Senate finally adopted included that contingency requirement but also raised the allowable tax cut to $245 billion, well above the Senate's original $170 billion limit.

The tax compromise was worked out in private by House Speaker Gingrich and Majority Leader Dole.[57] For Gingrich, and most House Republicans, tax cuts were inseparable from and, in fact, more important than their balanced-budget goal. This fervor was not matched in the Senate, where Dole, Budget Committee chairman Domenici, and other senior Republicans had initiated deficit-reduction tax increases in 1982 and 1984. Nevertheless, Dole's presidential ambitions gave him no leeway on taxes in 1995, and Senate Republicans followed his lead in supporting a tax cut that made the task of balancing the budget fall exclusively on domestic spending programs.

Congressional Democrats could do little to block the Republican budget plan beyond criticizing its unfairness in using entitlement cuts affecting the elderly and poor to finance tax cuts for the wealthy. The Clinton administration made the same argument and weighed in with a new budget plan in June that extended the balanced-budget timetable until 2005, scaled back the spending cuts that Republicans had proposed, and provided for much smaller and targeted tax cuts. While Republicans quickly dismissed Clinton's proposal, it did provide a useful alternative for Democrats as the budget reconciliation bill took shape over the next several months.

The parameters of the budget resolution were daunting. The Medicare "cut" was $270 billion over seven years, while the Medicaid reduction was $182 billion.[58] Other entitlements, including farm subsidies, student loans, unemployment benefits, and numerous public assistance programs were to be reduced by $175 billion, with nearly two-thirds of this amount targeted at AFDC, SSI, EITC, food assistance, and other "welfare" programs. In addition, domestic discretionary spending cuts totaled $190 billion, although these were to be implemented by appropriations bills rather than reconciliation legislative changes. The tax-cut "allowance" of $245 billion did not provide specific instructions for the Ways and Means and Finance committees, but it was generally understood that capital gains taxes, estate taxes, and business taxes would be reduced, that a $500 per-child tax credit would be enacted, and that "marriage penalty" tax relief would be provided as well.

---

[57] Congressional Quarterly, *Congressional Quarterly Almanac, 1995*, 2-32.

[58] The word *cut* gave rise to one of the many arcane arguments that arose as this process unfolded. According to some Republicans, such as House Budget Committee chairman John R. Kasich, Medicare was not being cut, since it was actually growing. According to Kasich, "We're sick and tired of having a five percent increase described as a cut. This is frankly about language." Of course, the 5 percent increase was well below the baseline growth measured from existing law. Kasich's counterpart, ranking Democrat Martin Olav Sabo, responded, "I understand the political point you're trying to make, but I don't think a soul knows what this means." Ibid., 2-23.

Budget Reconciliation

The process of translating the budget resolution blueprint into the legislative language of a reconciliation bill involved twelve House committees and eleven Senate committees. The major responsibilities, as in 1993, fell on the Ways and Means and Finance committees, which had jurisdiction over Medicare, most large public assistance entitlements, and, of course, tax cuts. The Senate Finance Committee also had jurisdiction over the Medicaid program. The House committees, including Ways and Means, completed their work in mid-October, and the House passed its budget reconciliation bill on October 26. The conference that followed finished its work in mid-November, and the measure was cleared for the president on November 20. In both chambers, Democratic support was almost nonexistent. Only five Democrats voted for the reconciliation bill in the House, and none supported it in the Senate. But with only one defection in the House and one in the Senate, Republicans easily prevailed.

Provisions. The budget reconciliation bill that Congress adopted contained major entitlement program changes. The Medicare reductions, for example, depended heavily on reimbursement savings affecting healthcare providers, but a considerable portion of the estimated $270 billion in savings involved Part B premiums, which were to be maintained at 31.5 percent of program costs (rather than the 25 percent scheduled under existing law). In addition, Part B premiums were to be means-tested – based on the incomes of beneficiaries – as opposed to the equal premium-per-beneficiary formula that had been in effect for three decades.

The Medicare "reforms," however, were not merely fiscal. Additional provisions in the reconciliation bill were meant to encourage beneficiaries to switch from Medicare to private health insurance plans. Beneficiaries who enrolled in health maintenance organizations or chose medical savings accounts and high-deductible insurance coverage were exempted from potential reimbursement limits on healthcare services, and the expectation was that additional healthcare options would be made available in the future to lower program costs.

With Medicaid, the reconciliation bill converted the program into a block grant. This change limited the federal government's payments to the states to a fixed amount, rather than an open-ended entitlement obligation, and it also gave the states much greater control over eligibility, benefits, and program administration. States were required to provide coverage for children and pregnant women who met national income eligibility standards, but Medicaid cost control was otherwise transferred to the states. The block grant approach was carried over to public assistance programs, including AFDC and various childcare programs. States were given the option, under certain conditions, of converting their food stamp funding into a block grant as well. While the ostensible purpose of block grants was to provide states with greater control over programs in exchange for fixed federal funding, the reconciliation bill mandated work requirements and lifetime limits for most recipients of cash benefits, and states were expected to restrict additional benefits for children born to mothers already receiving cash benefits.[59] The other cash assistance program for low-income families, the EITC, was scaled back significantly in terms of eligibility and benefits. The combined savings in all public assistance programs, including the EITC, was estimated at more than $110 billion over seven years.[60]

Numerous other entitlements, ranging from agriculture to student loans to veterans' programs, were affected by the 1995 reconciliation bill, although projected savings in these programs were considerably smaller. Some changes, such as the new limits on subsidized rental payments for low-income families, were reasonably straightforward. The agriculture and student loan program changes, however, envisioned a greatly reduced federal role over time. Other than Social Security, few entitlements emerged unscathed from the reconciliation process.

The tax cuts that Congress adopted included both individual and corporate reductions. The $500 per-child tax credit was provided for families with adjusted gross incomes less than $110,000, a much lower income limit than the House had originally established. Capital gains taxes were reduced through a new 50 percent exclusion that effectively cut the maximum capital gains tax rate to less than 20 percent, and tax-favored individual retirement accounts (IRAs) were expanded. A smaller reduction for corporations was included, along with a lower AMT and expanded tax preferences.

The House had originally hoped to pass a $350 billion tax act, but the reconciliation bill complied with the $245 billion limit set by the FY 1996 budget resolution. The House nevertheless managed to secure a very large tax cut that was "funded" in large part through the economic benefits that the balanced-budget plan would provide. The CBO estimated that the Republican plan might increase economic growth and lower interest rates, resulting in a "fiscal dividend" of approximately $170 billion for fiscal years 1996–2002.[61] Republicans maintained that this fiscal dividend would be fully realized, as would other deficit-reduction savings, because a large tax cut would otherwise add substantially to the deficit problem.[62] Most Republicans, however, did not appear terribly concerned that the budget would actually be balanced by the

---

[59] Similar provisions would be incorporated into the 1996 welfare reform bill that was enacted in August. The Personal Responsibility and Work Opportunity Reconciliation Act converted AFDC into a block grant, and it also placed new restrictions on food stamps, SSI, and childcare assistance programs.

[60] Congressional Quarterly, *Congressional Quarterly Almanac, 1995*, 2-60.

[61] Congressional Budget Office, *The Economic and Budget Outlook: An Update* (Washington, D.C.: Congressional Budget Office, 1995), xvii.

[62] Republicans also downplayed the post-2002 revenue losses from the tax cut, which were expected to grow very rapidly – a point that President Clinton emphasized in his veto message.

2002 deadline, because future deficits would provide the rationale for further reducing domestic spending.

The Clinton Vetoes

On December 6, President Clinton vetoed the FY 1996 budget reconciliation bill, citing his "profound differences with the extreme approach the Republican majority has adopted."[63] The veto message focused on the allegedly "devastating" Medicare and Medicaid cuts the Republicans had approved and on the tax cuts for "the most well-off" that they had passed. But Clinton also sharply attacked the welfare provisions in Title XII of the reconciliation bill that, along with the EITC changes, accounted for such a large share of the Republicans' deficit-reduction plan.

Clinton's veto of the budget reconciliation bill had been preceded by a series of related vetoes that began in June. The common theme in all of these was the determination of congressional Republicans to force Clinton to abandon Democratic spending priorities and, in the process, to weaken his presidency. Years earlier, the Democratic-controlled Congress had pursued this same goal with George H. W. Bush, but the Republican effort in 1995 was more aggressive and more far-reaching. It also proved, in the end, to be less successful.

Round One: Rescissions

The first Clinton veto was announced on June 7 in response to a Republican attempt to cancel more than $16 billion in domestic spending that had been appropriated by the previous, Democratic-controlled Congress. Robert L. Livingston, the new chairman of the House Appropriations Committee, spearheaded this effort in close consultation with Speaker Gingrich. Upon assuming the chairmanship, Livingston had warned, "It is very, very important that people understand . . . we're not fooling around. We are committed to cutting back the role of government."[64] The FY 1995 rescissions bill that Congress passed in May was the first installment in what Livingston and Republican leaders expected be much deeper retrenchments in the domestic spending bills for the upcoming fiscal year.

Since domestic discretionary spending for FY 1995 was approximately $250 billion, the $17-plus billion in rescissions the House approved amounted to a nearly 7 percent cut in spending. Republicans did not, however, apply these cuts across the board. Rather, they targeted the cuts at programs that Clinton and congressional Democrats strongly supported, including housing, education, and job training programs for the poor. House Republicans also attached

---

[63] Congressional Quarterly, *Congressional Quarterly Almanac, 1995*, D-37.
[64] Livingston had been selected by House Republicans over several more senior Republicans on the committee, who were considered less conservative and less likely to control the appropriations agenda accordingly. Ibid., 11-96.

policy riders curtailing environmental regulations to the bill. Within the Appropriations Committee, and later on the House floor, Democratic efforts to scale back and reallocate the cuts were defeated, usually by near-party-line votes.[65]

In the Senate, Democrats had greater success, aided by their threats to filibuster and by a less partisan Appropriations Committee. The Senate bill, debated on the floor for seven days, was reshaped by a last-minute compromise negotiated by Dole and Minority Leader Tom Daschle. As a result, the Senate cuts were smaller, less targeted, and less objectionable to Democrats. The two-week conference that followed tempered some of the more severe House cuts, but a number of social programs were reduced well below levels that the Senate had proposed. Despite repeated veto threats from the Clinton administration, the House quickly approved the conference report. Then, when talks between administration officials and Republican leaders on another compromise collapsed, the Senate cleared the bill, which was then vetoed.

In his veto message, Clinton raised no objections to the amount of deficit reduction that Congress had approved but criticized the proposed cuts in "education, national service, and the environment" rather than in "wasteful" or "unnecessary" spending for highways, building projects, and "pork."[66] Declaring his support for the "bipartisan" compromise embodied in the Senate-passed bill, Clinton agreed to sign a rescissions bill that would reduce "the deficit by at least as much as this [vetoed] bill" but with different priorities. Over the next several weeks, administration representatives and congressional leaders worked out another $16.3 billion rescissions package that reordered spending cuts, provided more than $7 billion in new disaster relief and emergency spending, and softened environmental regulation provisions. This legislation cleared Congress on July 21 and was then signed by the president.

Round Two: Appropriations and the Debt Limit

The five-month battle over rescissions did not dissuade House Republicans from stepping up their challenges to Clinton, particularly since Clinton had conceded their case for deficit reduction. The domestic appropriations bills for fiscal 1996 that the House proceeded to pass contained much larger cuts than were required by the budget resolution, and the policy riders attached to them included abortion restrictions, regulatory cutbacks, school vouchers, and other Republican priorities. This appropriations agenda proved to be predictably contentious in the House, with even some Republicans occasionally wavering. The House-passed bills then encountered strong resistance in the Senate, and reconciling House-Senate differences turned out to be much more arduous

---

[65] The House approved its rescissions package, which also contained more than $5 billion in new disaster relief spending, by a 227–200 vote on March 16. Only six Democrats supported the bill, and an equal number of Republicans voted against it.

[66] Congressional Quarterly, *Congressional Quarterly Almanac, 1995*, D-19.

than anyone had anticipated. As the October 1 deadline for enacting FY 1996 appropriations loomed, only two of the thirteen bills had cleared the House and Senate.[67] A six-week continuing resolution was passed by the House on September 28, cleared by the Senate the next day, and signed by the president on September 30. It included reduced funding levels for many domestic programs and agencies but did not contain policy riders or program terminations.

When the first continuing resolution expired on November 13, the Agriculture, Energy and Water Development, and Military Construction bills had been cleared and signed. Clinton had vetoed the Legislative Branch appropriations bill on October 3, and Congress had failed to pass any of the remaining eight bills. Along with another continuing resolution to keep the affected agencies and programs operating, Congress also was preparing a debt-limit increase the Treasury had requested.[68] In drafting both measures, Republicans attached conditions designed to narrow Clinton's options on the budget reconciliation bill that was about to be approved by the House-Senate conference committee.

The new continuing resolution included the Medicare savings provisions from the budget reconciliation bill along with spending cuts and riders that were drawn from the unfinished appropriations bills. The debt-limit increase contained a "snapback" provision, raising the debt limit to approximately $5 trillion for one month, after which it would drop to $4.8 trillion – $100 billion below the existing ceiling. The short-term extension was coupled to new restrictions on the Treasury Department's authority to circumvent the debt ceiling by "disinvesting" trust fund securities, a maneuver that had been used to deal with a similar debt-limit problem in the mid-1980s.[69] These provisions were initiated by the House, which also included regulatory restrictions, a requirement that the president agree to a seven-year balanced-budget plan, and the elimination of the Commerce Department in its debt-limit legislation. The Senate removed these and other "add ons," but the snapback provision and Treasury borrowing restriction were retained. The revised Senate bill was approved November 9, cleared by the House on November 10, and vetoed by Clinton three days later.

Secretary of the Treasury Robert E. Rubin set the stage for Clinton's veto by taking administrative actions that allowed the Treasury to borrow additional funds without technically exceeding the debt limit. Rubin was able to continue these maneuvers for several months, until Congress finally approved a permanent debt-limit extension in March 1996. The immediate effect, however, was to frustrate the Republican plan for making the budget reconciliation bill "veto-proof." Gingrich and House Republicans assumed that with Treasury

---

[67] The Legislative Branch appropriations bill had been passed on September 22, as had the Military Construction bill.

[68] The most recent increase, to $4.9 trillion, had been enacted in 1993, and the debt was expected to reach that ceiling by late fall.

[69] Congressional Quarterly, *Congressional Quarterly Almanac, 1995,* 2-64.

borrowing authority running out, Clinton would have no choice but to accept a temporary extension. Then, with only a thirty-day respite before the debt ceiling was lowered automatically, he would have to sign the budget reconciliation bill (which contained a permanent extension of the debt ceiling to $5.5 billion), come to an agreement with Republicans on a balanced-budget plan, or risk a government default.[70]

The condition-laden continuing resolution that Congress sent to Clinton was likewise intended to narrow his choices. Signing it would mean accepting in advance controversial provisions in the pending budget reconciliation bill and domestic appropriations bills. Vetoing it meant a government shutdown affecting most departments and agencies and some 800,000 "nonessential" federal workers. Three days after Clinton's veto triggered the shutdown, the House and Senate approved a new continuing resolution that dropped the Medicare provisions but included a balanced-budget deadline as well as economic assumptions and budget-scoring estimates that Clinton opposed.

With Democratic support for Clinton's position beginning to weaken, House Speaker Gingrich made the extraordinary admission that he had attached the arbitrary conditions to the vetoed continuing resolutions because of personal resentment toward Clinton.[71] This widely publicized revelation gave an immediate boost to Clinton and led to a compromise continuing resolution that reopened the government through December 15. This new extension required Clinton and Congress to develop a plan to balance the budget over seven years, while somehow ensuring adequate funding for a list of protected programs including Medicare, Medicaid, and various other domestic programs. The budget talks that ensued predictably went nowhere. Clinton vetoed the budget reconciliation bill on December 6 and vetoed three more appropriations bills that Congress cleared. The second government shutdown began when the December 15 deadline passed. This time, nearly 300,000 federal workers were affected, and the shutdown lasted three weeks.[72]

Senate Republican leaders tried to avert this shutdown, but House Republicans were adamant that it would continue until Clinton agreed to a balanced-budget plan. The House Republican Conference overwhelmingly approved a resolution to that effect, with Conference Chairman John A. Boehner stating, "This is the most defining moment in 30 years in this town, and the question is, is it going to be business as usual, or are we going to do the right thing

---

[70] Ibid.

[71] Clinton's alleged offense was a personal snub to Gingrich during a flight on Air Force One to the funeral of Yitzhak Rabin, the assassinated Israeli prime minister.

[72] By mid-December, seven FY 1996 appropriations bills had been enacted. Three more – Commerce, Justice, State, Judiciary; Interior; and Veterans Affairs, Housing and Urban Development, Independent Agencies – were vetoed by Clinton in December. The remaining three – Foreign Operations; District of Columbia; and Labor, Health, and Human Services, Education – were still locked up in Congress.

for our children?"[73] Congress agreed to keep the District of Columbia government running and allowed government agencies to process benefit checks for veterans and public assistance recipients, but the general shutdown remained in place as the congressional recess began.

The public responded angrily to this shutdown and was overwhelmingly critical of the Republicans for having caused it. When Congress reconvened in January, the government was promptly reopened, but spending conflicts between the administration and Congress continued. Nine additional continuing resolutions were enacted between January 3 and April 25, when an omnibus appropriations bill finally consolidated the remaining appropriations bills for FY 1996.

The Clinton administration's political resurgence during the 1995–1996 budget battles produced important victories on taxes and spending. The Republicans' tax-cut initiative was successfully blocked, as was their assault on domestic spending. Discretionary domestic appropriations for FY 1996, after two government shutdowns, multiple continuing resolutions, and an appropriations process that dragged on for months, were actually higher than under the previous Congress.[74] Congressional Republicans wound up abandoning many of the controversial policy riders that they had proposed, and they failed to achieve any major program terminations as well. More important, Republicans were unable to reshape federal budget policy to reflect their vision of a balanced budget.[75]

With the 1996 election approaching, the Clinton administration demanded increased spending for domestic programs, particularly for departments and agencies that Congress had previously tried to cut or, in some cases, terminate. Funding for elementary and secondary education, job training and employment, public health, and environmental protection rebounded during the FY 1997 appropriations cycle, as did total discretionary domestic outlays. Controversial policy riders were largely absent, because the Senate removed many of those proposed by the House, and the administration insisted that the remaining

---

[73] Congressional Quarterly, *Congressional Quarterly Almanac, 1995*, 11-6. In 2011, as House Speaker, Boehner would again challenge a Democratic president over appropriations, government shutdowns, and the debt limit.

[74] Actual spending for discretionary domestic programs was $248.4 billion, less than $3 billion below FY 1995 and more than $10 billion above FY 1994. By comparison, defense outlays, presumably a Republican priority, totaled $266 billion in FY 1996, a decrease of more than $16 billion in two years.

[75] In addition, one of the heralded budget reforms the Republicans did pass – the line-item veto – was far narrower than House Republicans had hoped. The so-called enhanced rescission authority authorized the president to cancel certain enacted appropriations, tax preferences, and particular types of entitlement spending. Congress could then block these proposed rescissions through a disapproval bill, subject to a presidential veto and the two-thirds override requirement. Congress finally passed this measure in April 1996 but postponed its effective date until January 1, 1997. It was then challenged in the courts and deemed unconstitutional by the Supreme Court the following year.

ones also be dropped. Indeed, the administration used the appropriations process to rewrite an immigration bill that Congress had passed earlier in the year.

Republicans were able to salvage some of the welfare reforms that had been part of their 1995 reconciliation bill. The AFDC welfare entitlement was converted into a scaled-back block grant under the welfare reform bill that President Clinton signed on August 22, 1996, and funding for food stamps, SSI, and other public assistance programs was reduced as well. The new cash benefit program – Temporary Assistance to Needy Families (TANF) – gave the states more control over eligibility and benefits but with national standards imposing time limits and work requirements. The broader Republican plan for comprehensive welfare reform, however, did not survive the determined opposition of congressional Democrats and the Clinton administration. Congress was forced to drop the Medicaid restrictions in its initial welfare bill, and the EITC program remained intact.

In sum, the 104th Congress had virtually no impact on the largest and fastest-growing entitlement programs. The Republican leadership had exempted Social Security at the beginning, and any lingering hope that it could eventually be "reformed" was extinguished by the twin failures of the constitutional balanced-budget amendment and budget reconciliation bill. Medicare and Medicaid, which had been targeted for major retrenchments, instead continued their long-term rise in spending. The EITC program grew by almost 50 percent from 1995 to 1997. Total real spending for mandatory programs had increased by more than $53 billion during the 103rd Congress. The increase under the 104th was virtually the same.

Finally, the Republicans passed a tax cut in 1996, but it bore no resemblance to the $350 billion tax cut the House approved in early 1995 or the $245 billion tax cut included in the vetoed budget reconciliation bill. The 1996 bill included slightly more than $10 billion in tax cuts over a five-year period, primarily from new small business tax preferences, but in order to move their legislation through the Senate, Republicans had to couple it to a minimum wage increase insisted on by Democrats. The Republican platform in 1996 promised to repeal the 1993 tax increases, but that promise would not be fulfilled either.

The Balanced-Budget Agreement: Tax Cuts and Spending Cuts

Divided government remained in place after the 1996 elections. President Clinton won reelection by a comfortable margin, and the Republican majorities in Congress were almost unchanged. When the 105th Congress convened, the deficit outlook was more favorable than it had been in several years, with the FY 1997 baseline deficit estimated at less than $125 billion.[76] The CBO

---

[76] Congressional Budget Office, *The Economic and Budget Outlook: Fiscal Years 1998–2007* (Washington, D.C.: Congressional Budget Office, 1997), xviii.

warned, however, that deficits could more than double over the next decade if current budget policies remained in place.

The Clinton administration's FY 1998 budget declared that "much of the hard work" of reaching the Republicans' balanced-budget deadline of 2002 had already been accomplished and called on Congress "to help . . . finish the job."[77] By May, a general agreement on a balanced-budget plan had been reached between Republican congressional leaders and the administration's negotiating team. Over the next two weeks, specific spending and tax policy changes were worked out, and a twenty-four-page balanced-budget plan was approved by both sides on May 15. Congress then proceeded to pass its FY 1998 budget resolution incorporating the agreement on June 5. The resolution mandated two reconciliation bills – one dealing with taxes and the other with spending law changes – and these were cleared by Congress at the end of July and signed into law by Clinton on August 5.

The key 1997 budget bills moved through Congress fairly quickly, but partisan complaints were widespread. Conservative Republicans were upset that the net tax cuts amounted to only $80 billion through 2002, and they were less than enthusiastic about what they perceived as the paucity of domestic spending cuts. Meanwhile, the Clinton administration was criticized by liberal Democrats for the tax and entitlement concessions that it had made. Congressional Democrats were also upset about their virtual exclusion from the balanced-budget negotiating talks.

Complicating these intraparty tensions were competing claims of victory from both sides. When the May budget accord was finalized, one Clinton official claimed, "We got 98 percent of what we needed or wanted."[78] The Republican leadership's rebuttal was a document titled "What the President Did Not Get From This Agreement," which explained, among other things, that they had succeeded in forcing Clinton to accept much larger tax cuts than he had wanted and to scale back his "insatiable appetite for more government spending programs." In fact, Clinton had managed to gain the advantage during the May negotiations, and he used repeated veto threats to extend that advantage as the tax and spending reconciliation bills went to conference in July.

The Tax Bill: Cuts without Policy
The deficit-reduction total that had guided the spring budget negotiations was roughly $200 billion – approximately $80 billion in net tax relief and $280 billion in net spending cuts.[79] The decision to split reconciliation legislation into separate tax and spending bills was dictated by the White House in the belief

---

[77] Office of Management and Budget, *Budget of the United States Government, Fiscal Year 1998* (Washington, D.C.: Government Printing Office, 1997), 3, 7.

[78] Congressional Quarterly, *Congressional Quarterly Almanac, 1997* (Washington, D.C.: Congressional Quarterly, 1998), 2-23.

[79] Ibid., 2-20.

TABLE 5.3. Taxpayer Relief Act of 1997 (P.L. 105-34): Major Provisions and Revenue Effects (in billions of dollars)

	Fiscal Years
Revenue Reductions	1998–2002
Child tax credit	–$73
Hope and Lifetime Learning tax credits and other education incentives	–39
Capital gains rate reduction	–2
Estate and gift tax reductions	–6
Corporate AMT reductions	–8
IRA expansions	–2
Other	–10
	–140
Revenue Increases	
Air transportation excise taxes	+$33
Tobacco and other excises	+6
Federal unemployment surtax	+6
Other and timing	+15
	+60
Total Revenue Changes	–$80

Source: Congressional Budget Office, The Economic and Budget Outlook: An Update (Washington, D.C.: Congressional Budget Office, 1997), 36–39.

that Clinton and congressional Democrats would have greater leverage over a freestanding tax bill. From the beginning, Republicans had pressed for cuts in capital gains and estate taxes, child tax credits, and expanded tax advantages for IRAs. The Democratic priority, in addition to limiting the size of the tax cut, was to target tax relief on low- and middle-income families.

The Joint Committee on Taxation estimated the total tax reductions in the Taxpayer Relief Act of 1997 at $140 billion for fiscal years 1998–2002, with offsetting revenue increases of more than $60 billion over the same period.[80] No coherent policy guided either the tax cuts or tax increases. Nearly 80 percent of the overall tax cut was accounted for by the new child tax credit and eleven new tax preferences for education (see Table 5.3). The income eligibility ceiling for the full child tax credit was set fairly high ($75,000 in adjusted gross income for single taxpayers and $110,000 for couples) in accordance with Republican demands, but Clinton secured a refundable credit for low-income families with no income tax liability.[81] The education tax incentives, notably the Hope and

---

[80] Congressional Budget Office, The Economic and Budget Outlook: An Update (Washington, D.C.: Congressional Budget Office, 1997), 35.

[81] The child tax credit was then phased out for families above these income levels, with the phase-out schedule based on the number of children in the household.

Lifetime Learning tax credits, also conformed in large part to administration proposals.

On capital gains, the change from current law was less sweeping than Republicans had hoped. The top rate was reduced from 28 percent to 20 percent, but the holding period to qualify for the preferential rate was extended from twelve months to eighteen months. In addition, Republicans failed to index long-term capital gains, which greatly reduced capital gains revenue losses and the benefits for high-income taxpayers. The estate and gift tax provisions that were adopted fell well short of repeal. The unified credit, which had been at $600,000 since 1987, was raised to $1 million, but most of this increase was postponed for several years. Unlike capital gains, indexing was applied to the unified credit and related provisions, with implementation delayed until 2006. The corporate AMT, which Republicans tried to eliminate, was instead modified to cover depreciation for investments beginning in 1999 and had only a minimal effect on long-term corporate tax payments.

Tax increases were likewise cobbled together from multiple sources. The excise taxes to support the Airport and Airway Trust Fund had been scheduled to expire in 1997 but were instead extended and, in some cases, raised. Cigarette and tobacco excises were increased by more than 50 percent. A number of business tax increases affected the timing of tax payments, not their amounts.

The Spending Trade-Offs

The Balanced Budget Act of 1997 – the spending reconciliation bill – contained discretionary spending savings estimated at slightly less than $90 billion over five years and a net reduction in mandatory spending of more than $105 billion.[82] The discretionary spending cuts amounted to a 12 percent reduction in real spending by 2002, but most of these cuts did not take effect until 2001.[83] The mandatory spending savings primarily affected Medicare payments to healthcare providers.[84] Only about 10 percent of the estimated $112 billion in Medicare cuts directly affected beneficiaries, in the form of increased Part B premiums. The Medicaid program savings, which totaled approximately $7 billion, were similarly base provider payments, in this case state reimbursements to hospitals serving disproportionately high Medicaid caseloads.

The spending reconciliation bill also included more than $45 billion in new or expanded entitlements. The largest new program, with an estimated cost of

---

[82] Congressional Budget Office, *The Economic and Budget Outlook: An Update* (1997), 40.

[83] The overall cap for 1998 was $556 billion, rising to $566 billion in FY 2000. The cap then fell to $561 billion in 2002. For three years, separate caps were set for defense and nondefense spending. Ibid., 30.

[84] The second-largest mandatory "reduction" was over $21 billion in estimated receipts from expanded Federal Communications Commission commercial auctions of the electromagnetic broadcasting spectrum. As the CBO noted, these estimated savings were "very uncertain" because of volatile market conditions and changing technologies. Ibid., 42.

$20 billion over five years, was the Clinton administration's State Children's Health Insurance initiative. This entitlement program was expected to provide healthcare coverage to two million children in low-income households that did not qualify for Medicaid. Increased funding was also provided to restore some of the public assistance benefits, including SSI and food stamps, that had been restricted by the welfare reform bill in 1996. An additional $11.6 billion represented the costs of the refundable tax credits for low-income families in the Taxpayer Relief Act.

The Balanced Budget Act of 1997 did not seriously retrench entitlement programs or domestic spending generally, and the Taxpayer Relief Act of 1997 was limited in its fiscal and programmatic effects. As a result, the key question was whether an improved budget outlook would enable Republicans to enact larger tax cuts. House Republicans had been especially disappointed with the size of the 1997 tax cut, but were promised that more tax cuts were on the way. "We're just warming up," vowed Ways and Means Committee chairman Bill Archer.[85] It was Clinton and congressional Democrats, however, who wound up controlling the tax policy agenda and expanding the scope of domestic spending.

Controlling Surplus Budgets

The budget that Bill Clinton sent to Congress on February 2, 1998, trumpeted the first "balanced Federal budget in 30 years," but Clinton warned Congress that he would not "spend a budget surplus for any reason until we have a solution to the long-term financing challenges facing Social Security."[86] Clinton's stated goal was to bolster Social Security by reserving projected surpluses for debt reduction.[87] He was also intent, however, on neutralizing the Republican demands for tax cuts, and he continued to oppose these cuts even as surpluses soared to much higher levels. In 1999 and 2000, when non–Social Security spending and revenues moved into balance for the first time since 1960, Clinton managed to expand domestic spending while blocking large tax cuts. This high-revenue version of balanced budgets accommodated, rather than threatened, Democratic spending priorities and was therefore anathema to conservative Republicans in Congress. As a result, the bipartisanship that produced the 1997 budget agreement did not survive for long.

---

[85] Congressional Quarterly, *Congressional Quarterly Almanac, 1997*, 2-38.

[86] Office of Management and Budget, *Budget of the United States Government, Fiscal Year 1999* (Washington, D.C.: Government Printing Office, 1998), 3. In fact, the FY 1998 budget would turn out to be in surplus by nearly $70 billion, and the FY 1999 surplus climbed to more than $125 billion.

[87] The argument was that lowering the publicly held debt would make it easier to cover the projected shortfall between Social Security revenues and benefits beginning approximately in 2012. Ibid., 232.

The Republican Challenge

On June 5, 1998, the House of Representatives narrowly approved a FY 1999 budget resolution that called for $100 billion in tax cuts over five years and an equivalent cut in domestic spending. The latter would have reduced discretionary domestic spending below the caps agreed on in 1997. According to Clinton administration officials, these appropriations cuts were a "direct violation" of the budget agreement, and Senate Republican leaders also criticized the House plan.[88] House-Senate differences over taxes and spending could not be resolved, and Congress failed to pass a budget resolution for the first time since the 1974 Budget Act had gone into effect.

The lack of a budget resolution eliminated the reconciliation option that would have made it easier for House Republicans to implement their budget plan. The House nevertheless passed a scaled-back $80 billion tax cut in September on a largely party-line vote. The threat of a Clinton veto, however, convinced Senate Republican leaders that it was futile to bring a tax cut to the Senate floor. Spending disputes between the House and Senate also delayed action on FY 1999 appropriations. Only one appropriations bill – Military Construction – was passed by the September 30 deadline. Clinton then threatened to veto an omnibus appropriations bill covering the remainder unless Congress agreed to add funds for administration priorities. Instead of reducing discretionary spending below the caps, as the House had intended, the new "emergency spending" raised outlays above the caps. The omnibus appropriations measure that was finally enacted incorporated a tax cut, but it too bore no resemblance to the original House blueprint. Instead, Congress settled for noncontroversial business tax credit extensions that had minimal revenue effects.

Clinton managed to dominate the budget policy debate in 1998 despite the accumulating personal scandals that led to his impeachment by the House in December. Republicans had failed to increase their House and Senate majorities in the November midterm elections, and the disappointing results contributed to the ouster of Speaker Newt Gingrich by House Republicans.[89] When the 106th Congress convened in January, Clinton easily survived a Senate impeachment trial and went on to set the new parameters of surplus budgeting.

---

[88] Congressional Quarterly, *Congressional Quarterly Almanac, 1988* (Washington, D.C.: Congressional Quarterly, 1989), 6-8.

[89] The chairman of the House Appropriations Committee, Robert L. Livingston, had decided to challenge Gingrich for the Speaker's position. Gingrich announced his resignation on November 6. In December, Livingston confessed to extramarital affairs, withdrew his candidacy for the speakership, and declared that he would resign from Congress within six months. That same day, the House voted two articles of impeachment against Clinton. The House Speaker for the 106th Congress was J. Dennis Hastert, a senior Republican whose low-key style and temperament differed markedly from Gingrich's.

Back to the Veto

Clinton's FY 2000 budget again promised to "save Social Security first" but also called for drawing on rapidly increasing surpluses to bolster Medicare along with "military readiness, education, and other critical domestic priorities."[90] For Republicans, however, the most critical domestic priority was an across-the-board tax cut. With projected surpluses having grown so large, the House and Senate readily approved a budget resolution that incorporated the largest tax cut since 1981.

As his committee began its markup of an $864 billion, ten-year tax cut, Ways and Means chairman Bill Archer declared that taxes were "the defining difference between Republicans and Democrats."[91] The committee went on to approve, by a party-line vote, a package of income tax rate cuts, capital gains and inheritance tax reductions, and "marriage penalty" correctives, along with expanded retirement and education savings options. On July 24, the House passed a slightly smaller $792 billion reconciliation tax cut, with only six Democrats voting for the measure.

The Senate bill that passed a week later totaled $792 billion as well, but its major provisions differed from the House-passed tax cut. In particular, the income tax rate cut was limited to the lowest income bracket, and the capital gains and inheritance tax reductions were less generous. The Senate bill also included a sunset provision that limited the tax cut to ten years.[92] As in the House, the Senate tax cut received only a handful of Democratic votes. House and Senate Republicans were able to conclude conference negotiations quickly, and the tax reconciliation conference report was approved by both chambers with almost no Democratic support. As expected, President Clinton vetoed the Taxpayer Refund and Relief Act of 1999 on September 23, and House Republicans did not attempt an override.

With across-the-board tax cuts effectively stymied, Republicans turned to much smaller targeted cuts. A number of expiring tax credits, including a research and development tax credit for business, were extended in November under an agreement reached with the administration. The ten-year net cost of the measure was less than $20 billion. In 2000, Republicans used reconciliation to pass another tax cut for married couples, but Clinton vetoed it and the House failed to override. A second Republican priority – repeal of the estate tax – was also successfully vetoed.

---

[90] Office of Management and Budget, *Budget of the United States Government, Fiscal Year 2000* (Washington, D.C.: Government Printing Office, 1999), 14–16.

[91] Congressional Quarterly, *Congressional Quarterly Almanac, 1999* (Washington, D.C.: Congressional Quarterly, 2000), 21-11.

[92] A number of other provisions expired after nine years, in order to keep the size of the tax cut at $792 billion.

Other tax initiatives, including a repeal of the telephone excise tax and increased tax incentives for retirement savings, attracted bipartisan support but were caught up in disputes between Congress and the administration on unrelated fiscal issues. The most significant tax measure that did pass was the repeal of a 1986 tax preference for export businesses. This repeal had been requested by the administration to avert trade sanctions threatened by the European Union over alleged unfair trading practices. House Republicans had hoped to attach the repeal proposal to a broader tax-cut package, but Congress finally passed a freestanding repeal measure in a postelection session.

The spending vetoes that Clinton cast in 1999 and 2000, and the numerous veto threats issued by the administration, protected administration priorities as well. Four appropriations bills were vetoed in 1999, necessitating another omnibus spending measure that included more than $5 billion in additional funding demanded by the administration. Two more vetoes in 2000 led to an even larger increase in programs that Republicans had previously promised to cut.

Clinton's leverage over the appropriations process was reinforced by growing Republican support for new spending. With the budget in surplus and a deadlock over tax cuts, Republican appropriators joined the administration in raising domestic spending well above the spending caps enacted in 1997. Excess spending in FY 2000 was more than $50 billion above the caps, and the differential in FY 2001 was nearly $80 billion.[93] In both instances, domestic spending rose much more rapidly than did defense.

The PAYGO limits on entitlements, like the discretionary spending caps, remained technically in effect but were ignored in practice. Medicare reimbursement rates that had been sharply reduced under the 1997 Balanced Budget Act were raised in 1998, 1999, and again in 2000. With hospitals and other healthcare providers lobbying intensely for Medicare "givebacks," payments were increased by an estimated $50 billion over five years.[94] Other entitlements, including military retiree healthcare, veterans' benefits, and children's health programs, were also expanded. In 2000, the House agreed to add prescription drug coverage to the Medicare program, but Senate Democrats blocked action on what they criticized as an inadequate Republican plan.

The Medicare, Medicaid, and public assistance "reforms" that Republicans had called for in 1995 were conspicuously absent in 2000. Republicans did propose, albeit halfheartedly, adding private retirement accounts to Social Security, but Clinton and congressional Democrats were strongly opposed to this approach to Social Security reform. Similarly, Clinton's plans to

---

[93] The caps for 2000 and 2001 were approximately $565 billion. Actual discretionary outlays totaled $615 billion in 2000 and nearly $650 billion in 2001.

[94] Congressional Quarterly, *Congress and the Nation, 1997–2001* (Washington, D.C.: Congressional Quarterly, 2002), 461.

TABLE 5.4. *Revenues, Spending, and Deficit Reduction, Fiscal Years 1990–2000 (in billions of dollars and percentage of GDP)*

	Fiscal Year 1990	Fiscal Year 2000	Change
Total Revenues	18.0%	20.6%	+2.6%
Total Outlays	21.9	18.2	−3.7
Total Deficit/Surplus	−3.9	+2.4	+6.3
	(−$221)	(+$236)	(+$457)
Revenues	18.0%	20.6%	+2.6%
Individual income	(8.1)	(10.2)	(+2.1)
Corporate income	(1.6)	(2.1)	(+0.5)
Social insurance	(6.6)	(6.6)	(0.0)
Other	(1.6)	(1.6)	(0.0)
Outlays	21.9%	18.2%	−3.7%
Discretionary defense	(5.2)	(3.0)	(−2.2)
Discretionary nondefense	(3.5)	(3.3)	(−0.2)
Mandatory programmatic[a]	(9.0)	(9.7)	(+0.7)
Deposit insurance	(1.0)	(0.0)	(−1.0)
Net interest	(3.2)	(2.3)	(−0.9)

[a] Excluding deposit insurance.

Source: Office of Management and Budget, *Historical Tables, Budget of the United States Government, Fiscal Year 2011* (Washington, D.C.: Government Printing Office, 2010), 22–25, 35, 146.

dedicate debt reduction savings to the Social Security trust funds were ignored by Congress. Nevertheless, the publicly held debt was reduced by more than $450 billion from 1997 to 2001, and net interest on that debt dropped by almost $40 billion. As a result, the long-term solvency problem facing Social Security became less severe, and Social Security benefit commitments were considerably easier to defend.

Taxes and Domestic Spending

During the 1990s, the shift from chronic deficits to large surpluses was dramatic. As shown in Table 5.4, most of this shift was the result of individual income tax increases and defense spending cuts. In FY 2000, the individual income tax–GDP level was 10.2 percent, some 20 percent above Reagan-era levels and even higher than the World War II peak. Defense-GDP in 2000 was 3 percent – half of what it had been during the 1980s and the lowest level since 1948.

The tax law changes that produced these elevated revenue levels included the higher marginal rates enacted in 1990 and 1993, along with the limits on deductions and exemptions for high-income taxpayers. By the late 1990s, effective individual income tax rates for high-income taxpayers were much higher than they had been during the 1980s and early 1990s.[95] The share of individual income tax liabilities for the top 1 percent of households rose from less than 25 percent in 1990 to nearly 37 percent in 2000.[96] For the top 10 percent, the corresponding increase was from 54 percent to 67 percent. In addition, the increase in corporate income–GDP levels during the 1990s disproportionately affected high-income households. In contrast to the 1980s, tax policy during the 1990s had a distinctly Democratic cast.

The spending outcomes during the 1990s provided little solace to Republicans whose support for balanced budgets had been predicated on domestic spending retrenchments. Discretionary domestic spending–GDP levels decreased only marginally during the 1990s, while mandatory programmatic spending–GDP rose appreciably. Moreover, much of this increase took place in the Medicare and Medicaid programs that congressional Republicans had targeted for large cuts. The domestic role of the federal government was actually larger and more entrenched in 2000 than it had been when Clinton took office.

In 1981, Reagan had tried to shrink the government through tax cuts, and his failure to do so produced large deficits. Once the 1990 and especially the 1993 tax increases took hold, it was possible to erase those deficits while accommodating high domestic spending levels. The 1997 balanced-budget agreement between Clinton and congressional Republicans was almost entirely irrelevant to the changed fiscal outlook. Its domestic spending constraints were ignored, and its impact on revenue policy and revenue levels was minor.

The defining budget battle of the 1980s and 1990s – whether budgets should be balanced at low revenue levels or high revenue levels – was ultimately won by Clinton and congressional Democrats. The key to that victory was the 1993 tax increase, which congressional Democrats approved by the barest margin and for which they paid a political price. That victory, however, would not have been possible without the reconciliation process. Indeed, the 1990 and 1993 deficit-reduction initiatives of the Bush and Clinton administrations demonstrated how the reconciliation process could reshape budget policy. Because Republicans made large tax cuts the centerpiece of the 2000 elections, they hoped to implement a very different fiscal program. Given their victory in the presidential and congressional races, reconciliation would again prove indispensable.

---

[95] Congressional Budget Office, *Historical Effective Tax Rates, 1979 to 2005* (Washington, D.C.: Congressional Budget Office, 2008), Table 1.
[96] Ibid., Table 2.

6

Bush, Obama, and Fiscal Deadlock

When George W. Bush took office, the projected surplus for the next decade was $5.6 trillion.[1] His administration's first budget offered what it called "a new vision of governing for our nation."[2] As expected, the budget included "fair and reasonable tax relief" but within the context of a measured and cautious fiscal plan. The president's budget message assigned higher priority to additional spending for important defense and domestic needs, retiring $2 trillion in publicly held debt – "the fastest, largest debt reduction in history" – and reserving $1 trillion for "additional needs and contingencies." "Tax relief," Bush stated, would be limited to the "remaining . . . roughly one-fourth" of the projected surplus.

However, the Bush fiscal plan was riskier and more politically problematic than it appeared. On the spending side, it showed the relative size of the federal government falling to its lowest levels since the 1950s.[3] Because tax cuts were expected to accelerate economic growth, revenue levels would remain relatively high, albeit below the Clinton-era peaks.[4] The large surpluses in the Bush budget plan, along with the debt retirement and contingency reserves, were thus predicated on unusually low defense and domestic spending levels and optimistic assumptions about the revenue productivity of large tax cuts.

---

[1] Congressional Budget Office, *The Budget and Economic Outlook: Fiscal Years 2002–2011* (Washington, D.C.: Congressional Budget Office, 2001), xiii.
[2] Office of Management and Budget, *Budget of the United States Government, Fiscal Year 2002* (Washington, D.C.: Government Printing Office, 2001), 3.
[3] By FY 2006, spending-GDP was projected at 16.6 percent, approximately the same level as 1956. Office of Management and Budget, *Historical Tables, Budget of the United States Government, Fiscal Year 2002* (Washington, D.C.: Government Printing Office, 2001), 23–24.
[4] The projected average revenue-GDP level for fiscal years 2002–2006 was nearly 19.5 percent. Ibid.

One year later, the large tax cuts enacted in 2001, increased defense and domestic spending after the September 11 terrorist attacks, and an economic recession had erased some $4 trillion of the projected surpluses.[5] The rest quickly disappeared as the deficit rose to more than $400 billion in 2004, but the 2001 tax cut remained in place and was followed by additional tax cuts over the next several years. While Republicans had control of the House and Senate from 2003 to 2007, they did not retrench the domestic role of the federal government but rather raised discretionary spending, expanded Medicare, and ignored Social Security reform.

The Bush presidency marked a unique chapter in federal finance. In previous wars, including Vietnam, taxes had been increased, but they were repeatedly cut during the wars in Afghanistan and Iraq. Despite unexpectedly large deficits after 2001, there were no deficit-reduction tax increases or domestic retrenchments as there had been under Reagan, Bush I, and Clinton. Under Bush II, budget reconciliation was used for tax cuts, not deficit reduction. Instead of reducing the debt to its lowest share of the economy since the 1920s, the Bush administration added more than $2.5 trillion in publicly held debt between 2001 and 2008.

The Great Recession that took hold of the American economy in 2008 then triggered an unparalleled federal fiscal response that exacerbated these deficit and debt problems. Spending stimulus in the form of financial assistance to individuals and families, state and local governments, corporations, and financial institutions quickly raised spending-GDP to almost 25 percent from 2009 to 2011. Tax-cut stimulus and a weak economy lowered revenues to less than 15 percent. In just three years, the publicly held debt soared to nearly 70 percent of GDP, and concerns about the size, cost, and economic impact of high debt levels that had once been distant and vague suddenly became immediate and urgent.

When the Obama administration took office in 2009, it inherited a confluence of fiscal challenges without modern precedent. A slow and halting economic recovery clouded the short-term fiscal outlook. Postrecovery projections were even gloomier. Continued large fiscal gaps appeared virtually certain over the next decade without major adjustments to control spending and raise revenue levels. Longer-term spending posed an even more difficult control problem, given the accelerating growth of retirement and healthcare entitlements. Unless meaningful and reasonably timely policy adjustments were made, accumulating deficits and debt would impose a severe and potentially dangerous burden on the economy.

These new fiscal challenges failed to narrow partisan divisions over budget policy. In particular, the tax cuts that George W. Bush had put in place continued to frame debates over budget policy long after his presidency had come to

[5] Congressional Budget Office, *The Budget and Economic Outlook: Fiscal Years 2003–2012* (Washington, D.C.: Congressional Budget Office, 2002), xiii.

an end. The issue was no longer whether to balance the budget at high or low revenue levels but rather how to reduce deficits to "sustainable" levels. Despite this less demanding standard, the "tax wars" continued.

Taxes and Spending: The First Bush Term

The 2000 Republican Party platform stated that "Budget surpluses are the result of over-taxation of the American people."[6] The $1.6 trillion tax cut featured by the Bush campaign reprised the economic incentives and growth rationale that Reagan had introduced twenty years earlier, and it was similarly tied to limiting the size of government.[7] In Bush's case, the argument was that large surpluses would inevitably be used to support new domestic spending. Balancing the budget at low revenue levels had stymied Reagan, who could never achieve the required spending cuts. Even though Bush's task appeared much easier, his tax-limited balanced budget turned out to be similarly elusive. The tight control over spending Bush initially promised was essentially abandoned during his first term. Ironically, the importance assigned to tax cuts then became greater as the disconnect between spending and revenue levels grew larger.

The Republican Tax Agenda

The most important item on the tax-cut agenda for the 107th Congress was the lowering of individual income tax rates, particularly the top marginal rate of 39.6 percent that Democrats had set in 1993. Republicans also included tax cuts that Democrats would find less objectionable, such as "marriage penalty" tax relief and more generous child and family tax credits. A third priority, repeal of the estate tax, had become "a matter of Republican orthodoxy" during the 1990s and was viewed by conservatives as a critical part of a broader contest over progressive taxation.[8]

Support for these and other tax policy changes was especially strong among House Republicans, whose commitment to lower taxes closely mirrored that of the Bush administration. Reservations about their fiscal impact and policy effects were much more evident in the Senate, which forced Bush to scale back his tax-cut plans in 2001. That scaling back, however, did not last for

---

[6] Congressional Quarterly, *Congressional Quarterly Almanac, 2000* (Washington, D.C.: Congressional Quarterly, 2001), D-23.

[7] The exact size of the Bush tax-cut program was not always clear, particularly because there were disputes about whether to include the interest costs associated with lower surpluses. The administration's FY 2002 budget, however, specified "tax relief" amounting to "$1.6 trillion over 10 years." Office of Management and Budget, *Budget of the United States Government, Fiscal Year 2002*, 7.

[8] Michael J. Graetz and Ian Shapiro, *Death by a Thousand Cuts* (Princeton: Princeton University Press, 2005), 4.

long. In 2003 and 2004, Congress expanded the initial cuts and approved additional individual and corporate tax reductions. These tax cuts in Bush's first term were not separate initiatives but rather a coordinated effort to reverse the individual income tax increases of the 1990s while making Democrats defend those increases. The tax-cut agenda thus had an important political goal, as Bush and congressional Republicans tried to build a new Republican majority.

The 2001 Tax Cut The Bush administration's original tax cut totaled $1.6 trillion over ten years. The Economic Growth and Tax Relief Reconciliation Act that Bush signed into law on June 7, 2001, was estimated at $1.35 trillion, including nearly $100 billion in refundable tax credits and an additional $40 billion in 2001 tax rebates that Bush had not originally proposed.[9] The 2001 tax cut was appreciably smaller than Bush had hoped. More important, it was not permanent. Both its reduced size and the scheduled expiration of all its provisions by the end of 2010 were the result of the unusual path it took through the Senate. During the rest of his first term, Bush managed to erase that reduction but was unable to achieve permanence.

Despite their slim nine-seat majority, House Republicans quickly passed a series of tax cuts that closely followed Bush's lead. In early March, the House approved $960 billion in marginal rate reductions.[10] The House bill cut the top bracket to 33 percent (from 39.6 percent) and created a new low-income bracket of 10 percent. These new rates were to be phased in more quickly than the administration had recommended, and the revenue costs of the House measure were higher as well. Republicans unanimously voted in favor of this tax cut when it reached the House floor, but only ten Democrats supported it.

The dearth of Democratic support was not unexpected, because Ways and Means Republicans had made no pretense of trying to fashion a bipartisan bill. Democrats also criticized the Republican leadership for circumventing the budget process, because there was no budget resolution in place when this first tax-cut bill was reported out of committee and passed by the House. The House Budget Committee did not send a budget resolution to the floor until March 21. By the time the House adopted its FY 2002 budget resolution one week later, it had passed a $400 billion package of tax relief for married couples (the so-called marriage penalty reform) and increased child tax credits for families.[11] The House was also poised to pass a $185 billion reduction in estate and gift taxes and a $52 billion increase in tax benefits

---

[9] Congressional Budget Office, *The Budget and Economic Outlook: An Update* (Washington, D.C.: Congressional Budget Office, 2001), 5.

[10] Congressional Quarterly, *Congress and the Nation, 2001–2004* (Washington, D.C.: Congressional Quarterly, 2006), 92.

[11] Ibid.

for retirement savings that had been drawn up by the Ways and Means Committee.[12]

Senate Republicans could not pass the Bush tax cuts, even in modified form, without the procedural protection against Democratic filibusters afforded by the reconciliation process. The 50–50 party division in the Senate had resulted in an unusual power-sharing arrangement. Standing committee seats were equally divided between Republicans and Democrats, although Republicans held all of the chairmanships, and the Republican leader, Trent Lott, was designated as Majority Leader.[13] The Senate Budget Committee, divided 11–11, was unable to reach agreement on a budget resolution. Republicans therefore had to delay action until April 1, when Senate rules allowed the leadership to bypass the committee and bring a draft resolution directly to the Senate floor. Several Republican moderates then joined Democrats in a successful effort to amend the leadership proposal, in particular by reducing the size of the tax cut by almost $450 billion.[14] Multiple amendments restored only about $100 billion to the Senate's ceiling on tax cuts. Although the House and the Bush administration were strongly committed to a minimum $1.6 trillion cut, they eventually accepted the smaller Senate cut that was also limited in its duration.

The budget resolution the Senate adopted included a reconciliation tax cut, despite Democratic objections that reconciliation could only be used for deficit-reduction purposes.[15] The drawback, however, was that this interpretation of Senate rules meant that reconciliation tax-cut legislation was limited to the time period covered by the budget resolution. The budget resolution covered a ten-year period, which meant that the reconciliation tax cut could not be extended beyond 2010. This "sunset" limitation was not considered to be critical, because the administration expected to be able to make the cuts permanent at a later time. There was greater concern that Congress would make the tax cut conditional, with its multiyear implementation tied to future surpluses. Federal Reserve chairman Alan Greenspan had come out in favor of this restriction, and a number of senators in both parties had agreed to support its inclusion in the tax bill.[16] Bush, however, insisted that any conditions attached to future tax relief would undercut its economic benefits, and Senate Republican leaders were able to defeat the various "trigger" proposals.

---

[12] Ibid., 93.

[13] Since Vice President Dick Cheney could cast tie-breaking votes, Republicans had the advantage on any organizing resolution for the Senate.

[14] Congressional Quarterly, *Congress and the Nation, 2001–2004*, 51–52.

[15] See Lance T. LeLoup, *Parties, Rules, and the Evolution of Congressional Budgeting* (Columbus: Ohio State University Press, 2005), 187–188.

[16] Within the administration, Secretary of the Treasury Paul H. O'Neill was a strong advocate for conditional tax cuts. His tenure did not last very long. See Iwan Morgan, *The Age of Deficits* (Lawrence: University Press of Kansas, 2009), 224.

The conference version of the budget resolution was worked out in early May and passed by both chambers shortly thereafter. The White House agreed to the smaller tax cut, with Bush stating that the "dynamics have shifted in this debate" from the "ideological to the practical."[17] House Republicans went along, although they would later try to ease the Senate's restrictions as the actual tax legislation was written. On May 16, the House repassed its original $960 billion income tax rate reductions, including the top 33 percent marginal rate, as part of the new reconciliation tax package. According to a senior Republican, the House had acted quickly to demonstrate to the Senate that the 33 percent rate was "critically important to the House."[18] The Senate Finance Committee, however, had spent several weeks putting together a tax bill that could pass the closely divided Senate, and the top rate it settled on was 36 percent. The marriage penalty and child tax credit provisions in the Finance Committee bill were less expensive than the House had approved, and the estate and gift tax reductions were less sweeping as well. Four of the Finance Committee's ten Democratic members voted to report out the reconciliation tax bill, as did all ten Republicans.

The Finance Committee bill then encountered numerous challenges on the Senate floor. Minority Leader Tom Daschle and other senior Democrats charged that the bill was fiscally irresponsible, because it depended on long-term surplus projections that were highly uncertain. Most Democrats also supported an amendment offered by Republican Senator John McCain to cut the top marginal rate by only one percentage point and to provide greater tax relief for low- and middle-income taxpayers. The amendment failed on a 49–49 vote, as did a similar version the following day on a 50–50 tie. The Senate finally passed a slightly amended version of the Finance Committee's tax bill on May 23, setting up a potentially contentious conference with the House.

The Senate's leverage was then strengthened by the surprise defection of Republican Senator James M. Jeffords, recently elected to his third term from Vermont. On May 24, Jeffords announced that he was changing his affiliation to Independent but would caucus with the Democrats and vote with them to organize the Senate. Jeffords explained that his switch would take effect when the impending House-Senate conference on the tax bill had been concluded and the conference report approved and sent to President Bush. With Republican control of the Senate about to end, the Bush administration persuaded House Republicans to act quickly. The conference bill did cut the top rate to 35 percent, one percentage point less than the Senate had approved, but the size of the tax cut, its phase-ins, offsets, and 2010 repeal followed the Senate version. The House and Senate ratified the conference agreement on May 26. House Republicans unanimously supported it, joined by twenty-eight Democrats. In

---

[17] Congressional Quarterly, *Congress and the Nation, 2001–2004*, 52.
[18] Ibid., 93.

the Senate, two Republicans voted against it, but twelve Democrats joined the remaining Republicans to provide a decisive majority.

The Economic Growth and Tax Relief Reconciliation Act of 2001 (EGTRRA) contained approximately $1.35 trillion in "surplus reduction" over ten years, with $1.26 trillion in tax cuts and $92 billion in spending for refundable tax credits.[19] Among the individual income tax changes, the new marginal rate structure provided the largest share of tax relief (see Table 6.1). The 10 percent and 15 percent brackets took effect in 2001. The cuts in other rates – down to 25, 28, 33, and 35 percent – were to be phased in from 2001 to 2006. Thus, the tax cuts for lower-income groups were proportionally greater during the first five years covered by EGTRRA. Over ten years, however, the distribution of tax relief was roughly equal between taxpayers in the new 10 percent bracket and higher-income taxpayers.

In order to stay within the revenue ceiling in the budget resolution, phase-ins were used for most tax law changes. Marriage penalty relief, which involved raising standard deductions and income brackets for taxpayers filing jointly, was scheduled from 2005 to 2009. The deduction and exemption limits affecting high-income taxpayers were reduced beginning in 2006 and entirely repealed in 2010. The new, higher limits on tax-advantaged retirement savings and expanded tax benefits for education expenses had varying implementation schedules, and the existing $500 child tax credit did not reach $1,000 until 2010. The exemption amounts and tax rates for estate and gift taxes were adjusted over an extended period, with major revenue effects beginning in 2007. In addition, the "fix" provided for the alternative minimum tax (AMT) was temporary, taking effect in 2001 and expiring in 2004.

The Bush administration and House Republicans may have been disappointed with the size of the 2001 tax cut, but the notion that it was funded out of budget surpluses was quickly dispelled. As Steuerle notes, the "administration downplayed budget concerns" in pressing forward with its tax-cut program, and, as in 1981, "White House projections proved too optimistic, partly because a recession soon followed."[20] The Bush administration, however, did not retreat from its drive to cut taxes, despite the enormous deficits that it soon faced.

The Stimulus and Growth Tax Cuts With the economy going into recession in the last quarter of 2001 and job losses mounting, House Republicans passed a $99.5 billion package of individual and business tax cuts that included a capital gains tax cut and an accelerated phase-in of the 25 percent tax rate

[19] Congressional Budget Office, *The Budget and Economic Outlook: An Update* (2001), 5.
[20] C. Eugene Steuerle, *Contemporary Tax Policy* (Washington, D.C.: Urban Institute Press, 2008), 200.

TABLE 6.1. *Economic Growth and Tax Relief Reconciliation Act of 2001 (P.L. 107-16): Major Provisions and Estimated Revenue Effects, Fiscal Years 2001–2011 (in billions of dollars)*

		(Revenue Loss:
INDIVIDUAL INCOME TAXES		−$1,349 billion)
Tax Rates	New 10 percent marginal rate bracket.	−$421
	Expanded 15 percent bracket; reduced marginal rates to 25 percent, 28 percent, 33 percent, and 35 percent (phased-in 2001–2006).	−$421
Child Tax Credit	Tax credit increased from $500 to $1,000 by 2010; refundable credits of 10–15 percent (phased-in 2001–2010).	−$172
Married Couples	Increased standard deduction and expanded 15 percent bracket (phased-in 2005–2009).	−$63
Estate and Gift Taxes	Reduced estate tax rates and increased exemptions; reduced gift tax rates (phased-in 2001–2010).	−$138
Retirement Savings	Increased contribution limits on IRAs and other retirement accounts (phased-in 2001–2006); low-income tax credit.	−$50
Deductions and Exemptions	Reduced limits on itemized deductions and exemptions for high-income taxpayers (phased-in 2006–2010).	−$33
Education Incentives	New education expense tax deduction; increased education IRA limit; extended employer-provided education assistance income exclusion; new qualified tuition plan earnings exclusion.	−$29
AMT	Increased income exemption limits for AMT (2001–2004).	−$14
Other		−$8

Source: Congressional Budget Office, *The Budget and Economic Outlook: An Update* (Washington, D.C.: Congressional Budget Office, 2001), 8–11.

for individuals.[21] Senate Democrats countered with a $66.4 billion measure that reduced the business tax benefits in the House bill, eliminated the capital gains and income tax rate cuts, and provided extended unemployment benefits and tax breaks. Six months later, after a series of compromise efforts failed, Congress passed a stripped-down bill that extended unemployment benefits and contained noncontroversial tax breaks for business. The Job Creation and Worker Assistance Act of 2002 had an estimated ten-year cost of slightly more than $38 billion.[22]

House Republicans then spent a good deal of time passing bills to make various provisions in the 2001 tax cut permanent. In April, the House voted to repeal the scheduled expiration of individual rate cuts, child tax credits and marriage penalty relief, and estate tax repeal. It followed with bills on the marriage penalty, estate tax, and tax incentives for pension and retirement savings. On a procedural vote, the Senate rejected the estate tax repeal and simply ignored the other measures passed by the House. In October, House Republicans made a final effort to provide tax relief – this time to individual investors affected by the continued decline in the stock market – but an intraparty dispute over unrelated provisions kept the bill from moving to the floor.

Despite the deteriorating deficit outlook in 2002, neither the Bush administration nor the congressional Republican leadership considered delaying, much less canceling, the 2001 tax cuts. Indeed, Bush promised to balance "the budget by 2005 without endangering the war against terrorism . . . and without raising taxes."[23] When Republicans managed to pick up a handful of House seats and regain control of the Senate in the 2002 midterm elections, Bush renewed the call for tax cuts, in this case for economic stimulus.

The administration's FY 2004 budget conceded that the "re-emergence of deficits is not welcome news" but claimed that current deficits "are modest and manageable."[24] The road back to a balanced budget, according to the president, required "a sustained period of strong economic growth" that would produce the necessary "increases in federal receipts." In order to achieve that growth, the budget highlighted a "jobs and growth package," the main components of which were the acceleration of scheduled tax cuts enacted in 2001 and a new exclusion for corporate dividend income received by individuals. Along with an increased exemption in the individual AMT, expanded small business tax incentives, and new reemployment assistance

[21] Congressional Quarterly, *Congress and the Nation, 2001–2004*, 101–102.

[22] Gerald Auten, Robert Carroll, and Geoffrey Gee, "The 2001 and 2003 Tax Rate Reductions: An Overview and Estimate of the Taxable Income Response," *National Tax Journal*, 61 (September 2008), 362.

[23] Office of Management and Budget, *Budget of the United States Government, Fiscal Year 2003* (Washington, D.C.: Government Printing Office, 2002), 8.

[24] Office of Management and Budget, *Budget of the United States Government, Fiscal Year 2004* (Washington, D.C.: Government Printing Office, 2003), 25.

for the unemployed, the cost of the president's program was estimated at $418 billion for fiscal years 2003–2008.[25] The Joint Committee on Taxation then reported to Congress that the ten-year cost would be more than $725 billion.[26]

Republicans once again took advantage of the procedural protection afforded by the reconciliation process. The budget resolution needed to initiate that process led to a replay of the 2001 dispute between the Bush administration and House Republicans on one side and Senate Republicans on the other. On March 20, House Republicans pushed through a budget resolution that incorporated the full Bush tax cut by a narrow 215–212 margin. Republican support for the tax-cut provision was strong but not universal, as a small number of Republicans objected to the increased deficits and debt that would ensue. In the Senate, these objections had greater resonance, with several Republican moderates forcing a scaling-back of reconciliation tax cuts to a maximum of $350 billion.[27] In all, forty-four amendments to the Senate Budget Committee's proposed budget resolution were adopted, which then passed by a 56–44 vote on March 26.

The conference report on the FY 2004 budget resolution contained a compromise $550 billion reconciliation tax cut, but the reconciliation directive for the Senate included a $350 billion point of order limitation.[28] Under the budget resolution's complicated provisions, the $350 billion Senate limitation did not apply to any future reconciliation tax bill, which led House Republicans to believe that a larger tax cut could eventually be negotiated. Senate Finance Committee chairman Charles E. Grassley assured the Senate, however, that he would block a "growth package with a number greater than $350 billion in revenue reductions."[29] Even with that assurance, the budget resolution passed the Senate by a bare 51–50 margin on April 11, with Vice President Cheney casting the tie-breaking vote.

House Republicans still proceeded as if a larger tax cut was possible. The Ways and Means Committee approved a $550 billion tax-cut package on May 5, dropping Bush's dividend exclusion proposal and replacing it with lower tax rates on dividends and capital gains, along with business tax incentives that had not been part of the president's proposal. The Ways and Means bill barely survived Democratic efforts to return the bill to committee. One recommital motion directed Ways and Means to include a provision delaying

---

[25] In 2003, the administration announced that it would limit its forecasts to five years, because the ten-year forecasts initiated in the mid-1990s proved to be unreliable. For large tax cuts, such as those proposed in the FY 2004 budget, the reduced time frame greatly lowered the revenue cost.

[26] Congressional Quarterly, *Congress and the Nation, 2001–2004*, 105–106.

[27] Ibid.

[28] Bill Heniff, Jr., *Congressional Budget Actions in 2003* (CRS Report for Congress, August 5, 2003), 13.

[29] Ibid., 14.

implementation of the tax cut until the budget was balanced. It was defeated by a 202–218 vote. Then, on May 9, the Ways and Means bill was passed by a 222–203 House vote.

In the Senate, the Finance Committee reported out its proposal by a 12–9 vote on May 8. The Finance Committee bill included a complicated and partial dividend exclusion, left capital gains tax rates unchanged, and provided for business tax increases to offset revenue losses as part of a $300 billion tax cut. The remaining $20 billion in the Finance Committee measure consisted of federal financial assistance to states. The delicate balance in the Senate was demonstrated during floor debate. The administration succeeded in restoring its dividend exclusion proposal, with the Senate agreeing to a 50 percent cut in individual income taxes on dividends in 2003 and full repeal of dividend taxes from 2004 to 2006. This amendment, sponsored by Budget Committee chairman Don Nickles, was adopted after Vice President Cheney voted to break another 50–50 tie. The revised Finance Committee bill then passed the Senate by a 51–49 vote on May 15, with three Democrats providing the margin of victory after three Republicans refused to support the tax cut.

What could have been a protracted and contentious House-Senate conference was then averted. The president agreed to accept the $350 billion Senate limit and called on the conferees to resolve their policy differences quickly. The compromise that followed provided the House with an important policy victory, as the conference agreed to the reduced 15 percent rates for dividends and capital gains rather than the Senate's dividend exclusion plan. The House bill's business tax incentives, notably accelerated depreciation for small businesses, also made it into the conference bill. In order to keep the revenue losses from those and other provisions within the $350 billion ceiling, the 2003 tax cut used multiple phase-ins rather than the offsetting tax increases in the Senate-passed measure. Passage of the conference report by the House was on a mostly party-line vote, while the vice president once again had to cast the tie-breaking vote in the Senate.

As shown in Table 6.2, the reductions in dividend and capital gains tax rates to 15 percent accounted for nearly half of the estimated revenue loss from the Jobs and Growth Tax Relief Reconciliation Act of 2003 (JGTRRA). These cuts, which included a 5 percent rate for lower-income taxpayers, took effect in 2003 and expired at the end of 2008. The accelerated individual income tax rate reductions applied to changes previously scheduled for 2004 and 2006. Along with the increased standard deduction for married taxpayers, which was also moved up to 2003, these tax rate changes reduced revenues by more than $120 billion. These revenue losses added, in effect, to the size of the 2001 individual tax cut. The business tax cut in 2003, particularly the special depreciation allowances, included sunset provisions

TABLE 6.2. *Jobs and Growth Tax Relief Reconciliation Act of 2003 (P.L. 108-27): Major Provisions and Estimated Revenue Effects, Fiscal Years 2003–2013 (in billions of dollars)*

INDIVIDUAL INCOME TAXES		(Revenue Loss: −$319 billion)
Capital Gains and Dividends	Reduced capital gains and dividend tax rates (15%/5%) for 2003–2007 and (15%/0%) for 2008.	−$148
Tax Rates	Accelerated phase ins of expanded 10 percent bracket and reduced marginal rate brackets to 2003.	−$86
Married Couples	Accelerate increase in standard deduction and expanded 15 percent bracket to 2003.	−$35
Child Tax Credit	Accelerate increase in child tax credit to $1,000 to 2003.	−$32
AMT	Increased exemption limits for AMT (2003–2004).	−$18
CORPORATE INCOME TAXES		(Revenue Loss: −$10 billion)
Depreciation and Expensing	Increased first-year depreciation deduction for qualified property and increased deduction for immediate expensing (2003–2005).	−$10
OUTLAYS		(Revenue Loss: −$10 billion)
State Fiscal Relief Fund	Temporary fund to provide additional $20 billion to states for Medicaid programs and essential government services.	−$20
TOTAL COST		($349 billion)

Source: U.S. Congress, Joint Committee on Taxation, *Summary of Conference Agreement on H.R. 2, The "Jobs and Growth Tax Relief Reconciliation Act of 2003,"* 108th Cong., JCX-54–03, May 22, 2003.

that produced revenue losses for 2003–2005 but increased revenues thereafter. The $20 billion state fiscal relief fund, equally apportioned between Medicaid and "essential governmental services," went into effect in 2003 and expired at the end of 2004. The multiple phase-ins and sunsets in the 2003 tax bill allowed the Bush administration to achieve many of its policy goals despite the $350 billion ceiling. In particular, the rate cuts for high-income taxpayers in 2003 were offset by temporary extensions for low- and middle-income tax relief that the administration would soon call on Congress to renew.[30]

"Bipartisan" Tax Relief In his 2004 State of the Union Address, President Bush acknowledged that the budget would not be balanced anytime soon and called on Congress to work with him in cutting the "deficit in half over the next 5 years."[31] The Bush version of deficit reduction, however, was based entirely on cuts in discretionary spending. Rather than increasing taxes, Bush asked Congress to "complete some unfinished business" by making its previous tax cuts permanent. House Republicans were eager to highlight election-year tax cuts, and many House Democrats were reluctant to oppose them. In late May and early April, the House quickly passed several tax bills that extended expiring tax cuts through 2010 and made the 2001 tax cuts permanent. Each of the measures drew substantial support from Democrats, and Republicans hoped that electoral pressures would compel Senate Democrats to cooperate as well. Senate Republicans, however, helped derail the permanent tax-cut drive, but the temporary cuts were overwhelmingly approved.

The House-Senate split surfaced with the FY 2005 budget resolution. The Senate insisted on reviving the pay-as-you-go rule that had been in place during the 1990s and that required offsets for tax cuts. The PAYGO inclusion in the Senate budget resolution came on a Democratic-sponsored amendment that gained the support of several Republicans. The House refused to accept the PAYGO restriction during conference, because it made any tax cuts more difficult and permanent tax cuts impossible. With no budget resolution in place, the Senate ignored the permanent extensions that had passed the House. Finally, Senate leaders in both parties agreed to extend expiring "middle class" tax-cut provisions enacted in 2003 without revenue offsets. The House and Senate then passed the Working Families Tax Relief Act of 2004 by large bipartisan majorities.

The 2004 tax cut extended the $1,000 child tax credit for five years, the marriage penalty tax provisions for four years, the expanded 10 percent income bracket through 2010, and the increased AMT exemption for one year.[32] The individual income tax cuts in 2004 were estimated at $133 billion, with an additional $13 billion in business tax preferences that were extended as well. Democratic presidential nominee John Kerry endorsed the tax-cut extension, and many congressional Democrats who had opposed the original Bush tax cuts also wound up supporting the extension, as electoral pressures proved more compelling than arguments about fiscal responsibility.

[30] Marc Labonte and Andrew Hanna, *The Impact of Major Legislation on Budget Deficits, 2001–2009* (CRS Report for Congress, March 23, 2010), 10.

[31] George W. Bush, *Public Papers of the Presidents of the United States: George W. Bush, 2004* (Washington, D.C.: Government Printing Office, 2007), 86.

[32] Congressional Quarterly, *Congress and the Nation, 2001–2004*, 114.

The final pre-election tax bill of 2004 was the Jobs Creation Act that cleared Congress in mid-October. This legislation was yet another attempt to restrict export tax subsidies that the World Trade Organization had ruled in violation of international trade agreements, and it led once again to an expansion of unrelated corporate tax preferences. Described by a House Democratic leader as "an appalling orgy in self-indulgence," the estimated $137 billion in targeted tax preferences was ostensibly revenue-neutral, because it contained equivalent offsets from restrictions on existing corporate preferences.[33] Despite serious questions about these offsets and the possibility that the legislation would actually increase deficits by as much as $80 billion, dozens of House and Senate Democrats joined the overwhelming majorities of Republicans in passing the final tax bill of Bush's first term. Even without the Jobs Creation Act, however, the tax cuts during George Bush's first term totaled nearly $1.9 trillion – considerably more than he had originally proposed. Moreover, these tax cuts were enacted along with wholesale expansions of domestic spending.

War, Spending, and Deficits

George Bush's first budget called for curbing the "recent explosive growth in discretionary spending," particularly for nonpriority domestic programs.[34] The administration recommended an increase of approximately $40 billion over 2001 discretionary outlays, with subsequent increases of roughly $20 billion annually.[35] The congressional budget resolution for FY 2002 was slightly more generous, as Republicans struggled to reconcile their support for popular domestic programs with their party's "official" commitment to reduce federal spending.

The importance assigned to deficit reduction in the 1990s had led Congress to adopt multiyear discretionary spending caps, but compliance with these caps ended when the budget moved into surplus. Whether Republicans could revive spending discipline given the projected surpluses in early 2001 was uncertain, but they soon faced the presumably easier challenge posed by soaring deficits. Neither the administration nor Congress, however, made a serious effort to cut discretionary domestic spending to reduce deficits or to offset the increases in defense spending after September 11. The administration and Congress also approved multiple entitlement spending increases during Bush's first term, notably the Medicare Part D prescription drug benefit in 2003. Reducing the domestic role of the federal government was, at least in practice, not a real priority for Republicans. When increased defense spending became

---

[33] Ibid.
[34] Office of Management and Budget, *Budget of the United States Government, Fiscal Year 2002*, 7.
[35] Ibid., 230.

a necessity after September 11, the implications for overall budget policy were deliberately obscured.

War and Defense Spending The pre–September 11 Bush defense program was surprisingly modest, given the strong criticism that he and other Republicans had directed at alleged underfunding under Clinton. For FY 2002, Bush requested a nearly $20 billion increase in defense spending, but the projected outyear increases were much smaller.[36] By FY 2005, defense spending–GDP was projected at 2.7 percent, substantially below the levels of the late 1990s. After September 11, defense spending followed a very different trajectory. In 2002, actual defense outlays were nearly $30 billion higher than Bush's initial budget request. In 2006, the differential was almost $170 billion. Instead of falling, the defense-GDP level rose to 3.3 percent in 2002 and to 4 percent three years later. Much of this additional funding directly supported the military operations in Afghanistan and Iraq and other costs of the War on Terror. According to the Congressional Budget Office (CBO), estimated appropriations for these purposes rose from less than $20 billion in 2002 to $120 billion in 2006.[37]

While there was no serious congressional opposition to these increased defense budgets, the administration continued to rely on emergency supplemental funding even after the wars in Afghanistan and Iraq were well under way. The Johnson administration had used a similar tactic during the early stages of the Vietnam War, leading critics to charge that the real costs of the war were being hidden. In Bush's case, the potential costs of the war in Iraq were seriously underestimated at the outset, and the assessment of ongoing costs improved only marginally over time.[38]

In October 2002, for example, Congress approved a $355.1 billion appropriations bill for the Department of Defense. The following March, President Bush announced that Operation Iraqi Freedom had commenced and one week later requested $74.7 billion in supplemental funding for FY 2003, including $62.4 billion for military operations in Iraq and other military spending.[39] The administration requested that virtually all of the latter be allocated to a Defense Emergency Response Fund rather than to specific appropriations accounts. In April, Congress cleared a 2003 defense supplemental for all of the requested funding but restricted it to conventional appropriations accounts.

---

[36] Office of Management and Budget, *Historical Tables, Budget of the United States Government, Fiscal Year 2002*, 123–126.

[37] These are estimates, as the CBO explains, because "determining exactly how much ... budget authority has been spent is difficult." Congressional Budget Office, *The Budget and Economic Outlook, Fiscal Years 2008–2017* (Washington, D.C.: Congressional Budget Office, 2007), 6–7.

[38] See Steven A. Bank, Kirk J. Stark, and Joseph J. Thorndike, *War and Taxes* (Washington, D.C.: Urban Institute Press, 2008), 158–164.

[39] Congressional Quarterly, *Congress and the Nation, 2001–2004*, 329.

Congress then turned its attention to the FY 2004 budget. Three months after signing the $330 billion JGTRRA tax cut into law, the president submitted an $87 billion supplemental request just as Congress was about to complete action on a $368.7 billion FY 2004 defense appropriations bill.[40] The supplemental's cost, which included $65 billion for military operations and more than $20 billion for Iraq reconstruction, took lawmakers in both parties by surprise. Democrats then attempted to defray these costs by repealing the tax cuts for high-income taxpayers, but the $87.5 billion FY 2004 supplemental that Congress cleared in early November contained no tax increases. Congress then enacted a $417.5 billion defense appropriations bill for 2005 that included additional emergency funding.[41] When Congress completed action on the $146 billion Working Families Tax Relief Act of 2004, an $82 billion emergency supplemental was requested to cover another shortfall in war operations.[42]

The funding underestimates associated with the wars in Iraq and Afghanistan were not substantially worse than the cost escalations in prior wars. What was unusual, however, was the Bush administration's refusal to adjust its budget program in the face of growing costs and large deficits. World War II and Korea had produced multiple tax increases, particularly in individual income taxes, and significant domestic spending retrenchments. The Johnson administration had tried to avoid tax increases for the Vietnam War but eventually bowed to fiscal necessity and supported individual and corporate income tax increases as well as excise tax extensions. As a result, revenue-GDP in 1969 rose to its highest level since World War II, and the wartime budget deficit was erased.

The 2001 Bush tax cut was enacted well before the wars in Afghanistan and Iraq began, but the administration never considered postponing or scaling back the scheduled tax cuts once the wars were well under way. Instead, it simultaneously pressed for large emergency war supplementals and accelerated tax cuts. In 2003 and 2004, revenue-GDP was slightly more than 16 percent – the lowest level since the late 1950s. The budget deficits for these years totaled more than $790 billion. As one study concluded, "However one feels about the Bush-era tax cuts, they plainly constitute an extraordinary episode in the history of American war finance."[43]

Discretionary Domestic "Economies" The first post–September 11 Bush administration budget warned against repeating the "mistakes" of the 1960s, when the Johnson administration "refused to adjust its spending to account for

---

[40] Ibid., 345.
[41] Ibid., 354.
[42] Congressional Quarterly, *Congress and the Nation, 2005–2008* (Washington, D.C.: Congressional Quarterly, 2010), 348–349.
[43] Bank, Stark, and Thorndike, *War and Taxes*, 164.

the costs of the war in Vietnam."[44] "Having both 'guns and butter'" had caused prolonged inflation and "four recessions, including two of the most severe in modern times." The Bush budget approvingly cited the "wiser choices" of the Roosevelt administration in World War II, when "expenditures not related to the war effort were reduced by more than 20 percent," preparing "the way for almost a quarter-century of robust economic growth." The president called on Congress to strengthen its budget process controls over spending and "to maintain overall spending discipline" so that "deficits will be both small and temporary."[45]

Instead, neither Congress nor the administration seriously considered reinstituting the spending controls of the 1990s or, more important, cutting politically popular domestic programs. With divided control of the House and Senate for most of the 107th Congress, these domestic retrenchments might not have been feasible. After Republicans regained control of Congress, however, the Vietnam era's guns and butter example was repeated. Discretionary domestic spending, for example, increased by more than $60 billion from 2000 to 2002, while defense spending rose by less than $55 billion.[46] Some of this domestic spending was in the form of reconstruction assistance and homeland security improvements, notably the emergency spending appropriations bill that Congress unanimously approved after September 11, but "regular" domestic appropriations increased as well. Despite occasional hints that President Bush might veto domestic appropriations that exceeded his recommendations, the administration agreed to congressional add-ons in education, social programs, energy and water development programs, and economic development.[47] The bipartisan allure of domestic spending was especially notable in the Veterans Affairs–Housing and Urban Development appropriations bill that contained a then-record 1,600 earmarks for projects the administration had not requested.

The FY 2003 appropriations process repeated this pattern. The House and Senate failed to pass an FY 2003 budget resolution, primarily because of disagreements over discretionary spending limits. An effort to revive statutory discretionary spending caps failed in the Senate, where appropriators then proceeded to exceed the president's domestic spending requests by $13 billion.[48] When House Republican leaders attempted to enforce the president's spending limits, the appropriations process ground to a halt. With continuing resolutions funding most domestic programs for more than four months, the new 108th Congress finally passed an omnibus appropriations bill in

[44] Office of Management and Budget, *Budget of the United States Government, Fiscal Year 2003*, 13.

[45] Ibid., 39.

[46] Congressional Budget Office, *The Budget and Economic Outlook, Fiscal Years 2011–2021* (Washington, D.C.: Congressional Budget Office, 2011), 139.

[47] Congressional Quarterly, *Congress and the Nation, 2001–2004*, 54–56.

[48] Ibid., 62.

February 2003 that contained modest increases over the president's budget requests.

Republican control of the House and Senate produced an FY 2004 budget resolution, but the discretionary spending limits it set were almost an afterthought. Much more important, and certainly more controversial, were the $726 billion tax cut and $400 billion Medicare prescription drug program that it authorized. In addition, while the discretionary spending totals that Congress did approve were $2 billion less than Bush had requested, the prolonged appropriations process, which included an omnibus appropriations bill that did not pass until January 2004, led once again to congressional add-ons in numerous domestic programs.

In the final year of Bush's first term, Congress failed to adopt a budget resolution, and nine of the thirteen appropriations bills for FY 2005 were not passed until a lame-duck session after the election. The domestic discretionary spending increase for 2005 was ostensibly 1 percent – the smallest increase in almost a decade – but disaster relief and other "emergency" spending raised actual outlays by nearly 7 percent.[49] Although the growth in defense spending outpaced discretionary domestic spending after 2002, the latter continued to grow at a healthy rate, which was hardly a guns versus butter fiscal approach.

The Bush record on discretionary domestic spending contrasted sharply with Reagan's. For fiscal years 1981–1985, discretionary domestic spending increased by less than $10 billion, and its spending-GDP level fell from 4.5 percent to 3.5 percent.[50] The increase for 2001–2005 was $115 billion, as discretionary domestic spending–GDP increased from 3.1 percent to 3.5 percent. During the first stage of the Vietnam War, a similar increase in discretionary domestic spending had taken place, and the Vietnam-era expansion of entitlements was also repeated under Bush.

Protecting Entitlements Given the surplus outlook in early 2001, it is not surprising that the Bush administration ignored entitlement reform. With the abrupt return of deficits, however, the administration continued to avoid the retrenchment theme that Reagan had sounded in 1981 and congressional Republicans had revived in the mid-1990s. Neither the administration nor the congressional Republican leadership proposed using the reconciliation process to cut major entitlements, and efforts to restore PAYGO controls on entitlements were blocked by Republicans who feared that these controls would affect tax cuts. In the most obvious example of electoral calculations driving entitlement policy, the Bush administration and congressional Republicans enacted the largest Medicare expansion since 1965. It contained no cost-control reforms of any consequence and was passed when Iraq war costs and deficits

---

[49] Congressional Budget Office, *The Budget and Economic Outlook, Fiscal Years 2011–2021*, 139.

[50] Ibid., 139–140.

were soaring.[51] It also followed another electorally driven policy reversal, the Farm Security and Rural Investment Act of 2002, which scrapped the administration's free-market agricultural program and substantially increased farm subsidies.[52]

President Clinton had been unable to overcome partisan differences over the design and cost of a Medicare prescription drug program, and a similar impasse initially occurred under Bush. The administration's first budget included a $153 billion Medicare "modernization" program featuring "a prescription drug benefit for all Medicare beneficiaries."[53] In 2002, House Republicans approved a Medicare bill that provided federal subsidies for private insurance drug plans at an estimated cost of $350 billion over ten years. Democrats in both the House and Senate supported a much more costly program administered through the Medicare program rather than private insurers. Bipartisan compromises could not be reached in either chamber.

With Republicans back in control of both the House and Senate in 2003, the Bush administration made the prescription drug benefit a legislative priority, and the FY 2004 budget resolution contained a $400 billion allocation for the new program. The Senate Finance Committee reported out a bipartisan bill on June 12, as most Democrats recognized that costlier alternatives were no longer an option. In order to keep costs within the $400 billion ceiling, the Finance Committee bill contained a coverage gap (the so-called doughnut). The federal subsidy for prescription drug costs would cover a beneficiary's annual expense up to a certain threshold, be suspended for additional out-of-pocket expenses up to another threshold, and reinstated (at a higher level) for all additional costs. Beneficiaries who chose to participate in the program were required to pay annual premiums to obtain coverage and to meet annual deductibles as well. Liberal Democrats attacked this coverage gap during floor debate, while conservative Republicans criticized the $400 billion cost. The measure nevertheless attracted broad bipartisan support, passing by a 76–21 margin.

The cost issue proved more troublesome in the House. Many Republicans refused to support a $400 billion expansion of a program that they were unenthusiastic about to begin with, while Democrats were unwilling to accept the benefit limitations that the $400 billion ceiling imposed. The House version of the Medicare bill was reported out of the Ways and Means and Energy and Commerce committees on party-line votes, and most Democrats opposed the bill when it came to the floor. The House leadership was finally able to

---

[51] The $400 billion cost was, according to some analysts, seriously understated. See Morgan, *The Age of Deficits*, 233–234.

[52] For cost estimates associated with this policy change, see Labonte and Hanna, *The Impact of Major Legislation on Budget Deficits, 2001–2009*, 13.

[53] Office of Management and Budget, *Budget of the United States Government, Fiscal Year 2002*, 107.

put together a 216–215 majority after holding the vote open for nearly an hour.

The conference bill that emerged after four months of negotiations reinforced conservatives' complaints about costs. It included a modified version of the coverage gap, along with premiums and deductible offsets, that purportedly kept costs within the $400 billion ceiling. Cost estimates also depended, however, on related savings in the Medicaid and Medicare programs. These savings were highly uncertain, particularly since conferees had approved legislative overrides on hospital and physician payment reductions scheduled to take effect in 2004 and 2005 and $25 billion in additional payments to hospitals and healthcare providers in rural areas.[54]

The House passed the conference report by 220–215 on November 22, but only after holding the vote open for nearly three hours. When the electronic tally showed Republicans losing 216–218, House leaders, assisted by phone calls from President Bush, pressed dissenting Republicans to switch their votes. When several votes switched, the Republican leadership finally had their majority and announced the official vote. The Senate cleared the bill by a 54–44 vote on November 5, with Democratic support having slipped because of health savings accounts and Medicare competition plans that had been added during conference. On December 8, President Bush signed the Medicare Prescription Drug, Improvement, and Modernization Act of 2003, calling it "the greatest advance in health care coverage for America's seniors since the founding of Medicare."[55]

The Bush administration had also pledged to strengthen Social Security by using all of its projected $2.6 trillion in surpluses over the next decade "to reduce debt held by the public until Social Security reform is enacted."[56] Acknowledging the need for long-term improvements in Social Security's financing, Bush had emphasized that reform "must not change existing benefits for current retirees or near-retirees, and it must preserve the disability and survivors' components." But by the time the administration took up Social Security reform in 2005, the plan for reserving Social Security surpluses had been abandoned, and Social Security quickly disappeared from the legislative agenda.

Public assistance entitlements were largely unchanged during Bush's first term, and the few changes that did occur were expansionary. In 2002 and again in 2003, Congress liberalized retirement and disability benefits for veterans – in particular, ending the restrictions on the "concurrent receipt" of retirement and disability benefits that had been in place since 1891.[57] The ten-year cost of

[54] Congressional Quarterly, *Congress and the Nation, 2001–2004*, 500.
[55] Ibid., 501.
[56] Office of Management and Budget, *Budget of the United States Government, Fiscal Year 2002*, 117.
[57] Congressional Quarterly, *Congress and the Nation, 2001–2004*, 530.

the 2003 dual benefit program was estimated at $22 billion. In 2003, Congress approved a package of new healthcare benefits for veterans that also involved significantly increased funding.

The Medicare prescription drug program in 2003 augmented Medicaid by providing full premium subsidies for "dual eligibles" who qualified for both programs. Medicaid spending increased more rapidly under Bush than it had under Clinton, as did spending for virtually all of the cash and in-kind programs serving the poor. The 2001 tax cut, for example, expanded the earned-income tax credit (EITC) by raising the phase-out income levels for married couples. Extended unemployment benefits were approved in 2002, and the Bush administration persuaded congressional Republicans to pass a second extension in 2003. Although disputes between the House and Senate over work requirements and benefits for legal immigrants forced Congress to settle for temporary reauthorizations of the 1996 welfare reform law, funding for cash assistance childcare grants was unaffected.

Mandatory programmatic spending–GDP had been essentially flat in the two decades before Bush took office. Under Bush, the relative spending levels for most entitlement programs increased. With entitlements and domestic programs generally, the Bush administration and congressional Republicans routinely expanded spending to buttress their electoral support. That strategy appeared to pay off in 2004, but it also made it much more difficult to reconnect spending and taxes in Bush's second term.

Deficits and Debt: The Second Bush Term

Along with George W. Bush's reelection in 2004, Republicans increased their Senate majority to 55–45 and raised their margin in the House to 232–202–1. Republican hopes for a "permanent majority," however, quickly faded. Bush's political standing eroded as the wars in Iraq and Afghanistan dragged on, and the bungled response to Hurricane Katrina – one of the worst national disasters in the nation's history – accelerated that decline. Meanwhile, a series of congressional scandals further undermined the party's electoral support, and the Democratic Party gained control of both the House and Senate in the 2006 midterm elections.

During the early months of 2005, however, the Bush administration was optimistic about "working closely with the Congress...to cut the deficit in half by 2009," but its deficit-reduction program was entirely based on domestic spending cuts.[58] Bush's newfound commitment to domestic spending retrenchments produced disappointing results. House and Senate Republicans were

---

[58] Office of Management and Budget, *Budget of the United States Government, Fiscal Year 2006* (Washington, D.C.: Government Printing Office, 2005), 2.

reluctant to attack popular domestic programs, and any prospect of Democratic cooperation in cutting spending was ruled out by the administration's refusal to consider tax increases.

Midway through Bush's second term, the deficit gap narrowed, but the improvement was short-lived. Even with strong economic growth, post–tax-cut revenues never reached the levels the administration had promised, and domestic spending levels remained well above those that Bush had inherited. When the economy slowed and then nearly collapsed in 2008, the structural imbalance between revenues and spending was magnified. In 2008, the deficit nearly tripled, rising to slightly less than $460 billion. In 2009, it exploded to more than $1.4 trillion.

"Permanent Tax Relief"

The Bush presidency had begun with a $1.35 trillion tax cut. Four years and more than $1.1 trillion in deficits later, the administration called for another large tax cut with a ten-year cost estimated at $1.3 trillion.[59] Approximately $1.1 trillion of this total represented the cost of making the 2001 and 2003 tax cuts permanent, with individual income tax rate reductions accounting for more than $500 billion and estate and gift tax modifications accounting for an additional $255 billion. Among the new or expanded tax cuts requested by the administration were healthcare tax credits, tax-free retirement savings accounts, and corporate research and development tax credits.

The congressional appetite for tax cuts, however, had waned, particularly in the Senate. The budget resolution that Congress adopted in April 2005 included only $70 billion for reconciliation tax legislation. The House and Senate then proceeded to pass different tax-cut packages. The House bill focused on capital gains and dividend tax rates. Under the 2003 tax law, the preferential 15 percent rates on capital gains and dividends expired after 2008, and the House approved a two-year extension of these rates that took up most of the $70 billion reconciliation allowance. The bill that passed the Senate in November was geared toward "middle-class" tax relief in the form of higher exemptions from the AMT. Temporary AMT "patches" had been enacted in 2001, 2003, and 2004, with the most recent of these expiring at the end of 2005. Unless Congress agreed to another extension, the number of taxpayers subject to the AMT, and therefore to higher income taxes, was expected to increase from 3.6 million in 2005 to 19 million in 2006.[60] While House Republicans supported an AMT extension, they hoped to pass it as separate legislation not subject to the $70 billion reconciliation ceiling.

---

[59] Congressional Quarterly, *Congressional Quarterly Almanac, 2005* (Washington, D.C.: Congressional Quarterly, 2006), 4-4.
[60] Ibid., 15-3.

These House-Senate differences could not be resolved in 2005. After more than two months of conference committee negotiations in the spring of 2006, agreement was reached on a combined AMT/capital gains and dividend tax cut with a ten-year revenue cost of $90.9 billion.[61] In order to keep the net cost of the Tax Increase Prevention and Reconciliation Act of 2005 (TIPRA 2005) within the $70 billion budget resolution limit, more than $20 billion in revenue-raising "offsets" had to be included. These included new withholding tax requirements on government payments for services and property and revised individual retirement account (IRA) conversion rules – neither of which was a "tax increase" according to Republicans.

TIPRA 2005 was the third reconciliation tax cut that Congress had enacted since 2001. The importance of reconciliation protection for Republican tax bills was underscored by their inability to pass freestanding estate tax cuts. In April 2005, the House passed a permanent estate tax repeal. Senate Republicans, however, could not overcome a Democratic filibuster that kept the measure from reaching the Senate floor. A cloture vote was scheduled before the Senate's August recess but was not held. Ten months later, a cloture vote took place but fell three short of the sixty-vote threshold. The House then passed a bill that permanently reduced but did not repeal the estate tax. This measure never made it to a cloture vote in the Senate. A third House attempt, which combined estate tax reductions, corporate tax preference extensions, and an increase in the minimum wage, also was blocked by Senate Democrats.

Having failed to secure "permanent tax relief" with the Republican 109th Congress, President Bush proposed an even larger package of permanent tax cuts in 2007.[62] At that point, the ten-year costs of permanent income tax rate cuts and estate tax repeal had ballooned to nearly $1.25 trillion, and the revenue loss from the entire proposal was estimated at more than $1.85 trillion. This total included only a one-year AMT "fix," because a permanent solution to this problem would have cost an additional $870 billion over ten years.[63] The deficit outlook had improved in 2007, which President Bush attributed to "tax relief [that] helped the economy to recover and grow, resulting in record-high revenues."[64] But with Democrats in control of the House and Senate, the kind of permanent tax relief that Bush was seeking was clearly out of the question. At the same time, congressional Democrats were unable to reinstate budget process controls on tax cuts or to redistribute tax burdens.

---

[61] Congressional Quarterly, *Congressional Quarterly Almanac, 2006* (Washington, D.C.: Congressional Quarterly, 2007), 19-5.

[62] Office of Management and Budget, *Budget of the United States Government, Fiscal Year 2008* (Washington, D.C.: Government Printing Office, 2007), 163–167.

[63] Congressional Quarterly, *Congressional Quarterly Almanac, 2007* (Washington, D.C.: Congressional Quarterly, 2008), 7-10.

[64] Office of Management and Budget, *Budget of the United States Government, Fiscal Year 2008*, 1.

At the beginning of the 110th Congress, Democrats adopted a FY 2008 budget resolution with a PAYGO provision that required the cost of any AMT extension to be fully offset by other tax increases. The House then passed a $50.6 billion AMT extension as part of an $82.5 billion package of "extenders" that included individual and business tax preferences that were due to expire. The offsets the House approved to make its tax bill revenue-neutral included higher taxes affecting private-equity firms, hedge funds, and multinational corporations.[65] House Republicans argued against the offsets and unanimously opposed the House bill. Senate Republicans offered the same criticism and, given Senate rules, were able to block action on the AMT extension. In December, Democrats agreed to abandon the PAYGO requirement and pass a "clean" AMT extension.

In 2008, Congress approved another AMT extension, along with additional tax extenders that had lapsed after 2007 and pending energy tax incentives that had been stalled by the dispute over offsets. By the time this legislation passed in October, the economic downturn had grown much more severe, and the deficit outlook had turned sharply negative. Nevertheless, Senate Republicans were again able to prevent the House-passed bill that included full offsets from coming to a vote, and the Senate bill that was approved contained only partial offsets. Of the approximately $150 billion in individual and corporate tax reductions in the Senate bill, only about $40 billion was offset.[66] The larger of these revenue offsets, estimated at more than $25 billion, affected deferred compensation rules for executives in multinational corporations. After months of sparring between the House and Senate over PAYGO rules and offsets, the Senate finally prevailed by attaching its tax bill to the emergency financial services rescue bill that Congress passed in October.

The economic crisis had also spawned a stimulus bill in early 2008 that included an estimated $150 billion in individual tax rebates and small business tax deductions for FY 2008. The Bush administration and congressional leaders of both parties had agreed to expedite action on this legislation in January. For Democrats, the key provisions included refundable tax credits for low- and middle-income taxpayers, including those who paid no income taxes, and phase-outs for high-income taxpayers. The trade-offs for Republicans and the Bush administration included accelerated depreciation rules and other tax benefits for small businesses as well as the exclusion of spending stimulus, including extended unemployment benefits. In this case, no revenue offsets were considered.

[65] The "carried interest" provision, for example, would have taxed certain profits received by managers of private-equity firms as ordinary income rather than at the 15 percent capital gains rate then in effect.

[66] Congressional Quarterly, *Congressional Quarterly Almanac, 2008* (Washington, D.C.: Congressional Quarterly, 2009), 4-11.

As the 2008 election approached, President Bush took steps to preserve his tax-cut legacy. In his 2008 State of the Union Address, he had dismissed the argument that "letting tax relief expire is not a tax increase."[67] He warned that "unless Congress acts, most of the tax relief ... over the past seven years will be taken away" and "116 million American taxpayers ... would see their taxes rise by an average of $1,800." Bush managed to keep Democrats on the defensive regarding taxes. In his acceptance speech at the Democratic National Convention, Barack Obama avoided any discussion of tax increases and instead promised to "cut taxes for 95 percent of all working families" and to "eliminate capital gains taxes for small businesses and start-ups."[68] A return to Clinton-era tax policy was not on the Democratic agenda, particularly during a severe economic downturn. As the debate over postrecovery tax policy began to take shape, however, the Bush tax cuts continued to present serious problems for the Obama administration and congressional Democrats.

The Entitlement Deadlock

In the mid-1990s, congressional Republicans had tried to pay for tax increases with entitlement cuts and, after a successful Clinton veto and negative public response, soon abandoned that approach. During George W. Bush's first term, that separation between taxes and entitlements remained in place, even as deficits mounted. In 2005, however, Bush attempted to make domestic spending cuts, including entitlements, the foundation of his deficit-reduction program. The administration did not include Social Security in its deficit-reduction proposals but did present a highly touted reform plan designed to lower long-term costs.

Democratic opposition to entitlement retrenchments was, as expected, fierce from the beginning, but congressional Republicans also failed to embrace Bush's reform program. Social Security quietly disappeared from the congressional agenda in 2005, and the short-term entitlement savings that Congress approved the following year fell well short of the reductions that Bush had proposed. House Republicans endorsed the abstract principle of paying for tax cuts with entitlement cuts, but they had great difficulty in applying that principle to programs like Medicare. Among Senate Republicans, there was considerable uneasiness over the principle itself, particularly as Democratic criticisms about fairness gained traction.

The entitlement program savings that the Bush administration presented to Congress in 2005 targeted Medicaid but included agriculture subsidies and student loans.[69] The combined five-year reductions as estimated by the administration totaled approximately $67 billion, and the ten-year savings were slightly

---

[67] Ibid., D-3.
[68] Ibid., D-20.
[69] Office of Management and Budget, *Major Savings and Reforms in the President's 2006 Budget* (Washington, D.C.: Government Printing Office, 2005), 178–180.

less than $150 billion. The FY 2006 budget resolution that Congress approved in April included reconciliation instructions for less than $35 billion in entitlement reductions over five years.

The Deficit Reduction Omnibus Reconciliation Act of 2005 that passed nine months later contained net savings estimated at $38.8 billion.[70] The Medicaid cuts that Congress approved were much smaller than Bush had proposed but still generated strong opposition, particularly in the Senate. Congress enacted reductions in agriculture subsidies and student loan programs, but these too were below the administration's savings targets. While Congress extended its reconciliation initiative to include Medicare, benefits were fully maintained. Instead, Congress reduced reimbursements for certain services, such as home healthcare, and moved up the scheduled increase in Part B premiums for high-income beneficiaries. Net Medicare savings, however, were reduced by yet another legislative suspension of scheduled reductions in payments to physicians. Finally, nearly one-third of the estimated savings in the 2005 reconciliation bill were relatively painless. More than $7 billion was accounted for by revenues from spectrum auctions to television broadcasters and nearly $4 billion from increased employer premiums for federal pension insurance. Congress still found it difficult to curb entitlements. The Senate vote on the final version of the reconciliation bill was 50–50, with Vice President Cheney then casting the deciding vote. The House vote, which took place on February 1, 2006, was 216–214.

President Bush hailed the Senate vote as "a victory for taxpayers, fiscal restraint, and responsible budgeting [that] will keep us on track to cut the deficit in half by 2009."[71] However, Congress was also about to complete action on a second reconciliation bill at the end of 2005 – in this case, a $70 billion five-year tax cut. In order to balance this revenue loss, the administration proposed a second, and larger, package of entitlement reforms in 2006. These entitlement savings, estimated at more than $71 billion over five years and nearly $180 billion over ten years, primarily affected Medicare.[72] The administration's recommended savings, however, were difficult to assess because they depended on unspecified improvements in "productivity and efficiency," program "integrity," and unspecified competition.[73]

Congress ignored this second round of entitlement reforms. The House adopted a FY 2007 budget resolution with reconciliation instructions for less than $7 billion in entitlement savings that exempted Medicaid, Medicare, and student loans. The Senate's budget resolution did not include any entitlement reductions and was well above the House ceiling on discretionary domestic

---

[70] Congressional Quarterly, *Congress and the Nation, 2005–2008*, 81.

[71] Ibid., 85.

[72] Office of Management and Budget, *Major Savings and Reforms in the President's 2007 Budget* (Washington, D.C.: Government Printing Office, 2006), 165–166.

[73] Ibid., 165.

spending. Republican leaders could not resolve these differences, and the House and Senate failed to adopt any budget resolution in 2006.

Faced with a Democratic congressional majority in 2007, President Bush renewed the call for entitlement cuts but significantly raised his savings targets. The administration's new goal was a balanced budget in 2012, and it proposed to reach that goal by making its tax cuts permanent while cutting domestic spending. The entitlement share of domestic "spending restraint" was more than $95 billion in savings over five years and more than $300 billion over ten years.[74] More than two-thirds of these savings were to come from unspecified reforms in Medicare. The Bush budget was sharply attacked by congressional Democrats. The juxtaposition of tax cuts and entitlement cuts was especially troublesome, even for Democrats who were willing to consider the latter. When administration representatives met with the Senate Budget Committee, chairman Kent Conrad complained, "I am prepared to get savings out of long-term entitlement programs. What I don't hear from your side, ever, is that you are prepared to do anything on your side except more tax cuts."[75]

Indeed, the administration soon found itself fending off entitlement expansions. The FY 2008 budget resolution included $70 billion for expansions in children's health programs and agriculture subsidies.[76] In September, Congress approved a $35 billion expansion of the State Children's Health Insurance Program (SCHIP), a Clinton-era initiative designed to provide healthcare to children from low-income families that did not qualify for Medicaid.[77] The SCHIP expansion that Congress authorized was seven times larger than the administration had requested, and Bush vetoed the measure on October 3. A second SCHIP bill, with slightly more restrictive income eligibility standards, was passed in November and again vetoed by Bush. Neither veto was overridden. In December, Congress passed a measure that extended baseline funding for the program for fifteen months and coupled it to yet another suspension of scheduled reimbursement cuts in Medicare payments to physicians. The president signed this bill on December 29.

The FY 2009 congressional budget resolution simply ignored the administration's proposed cuts in Medicare and Medicaid and authorized additional funding for agriculture subsidies. The five-year farm bill that Congress cleared in May provided much more generous subsidies than the administration had recommended, and it also included a revenue offset in the form of increased user fees and accelerated tax payments for businesses. Bush vetoed the bill on

---

74 Office of Management and Budget, *Major Savings and Reforms in the President's 2008 Budget* (Washington, D.C.: Government Printing Office, 2007), 139–140.

75 Congressional Quarterly, *Congressional Quarterly Almanac, 2007*, 4-3.

76 Congressional Quarterly, *Congress and the Nation, 2005–2008*, 109.

77 SCHIP funding was in the form of matching grants to the states, and Democrats hoped to increase coverage by raising income eligibility levels that individual states had established. The additional federal funding was offset by an increase in the federal cigarette tax.

June 18, citing its lack of "program reform and fiscal discipline."[78] The House and Senate easily overrode the president's veto. Because of a clerical error, Congress then had to repass the measure. Bush vetoed the new farm bill on June 18, and Congress overrode his veto that same day.

Congress also overrode the president's veto of the Medicare Improvements for Patients and Providers Act of 2008. This measure suspended scheduled cuts in Medicare payments to physicians through 2009, with the estimated $94 billion six-year cost offset by cuts in funding for Medicare Advantage plans.[79] Medicare Advantage provided federal subsidies for private health insurance alternatives to traditional Medicare coverage, and congressional Democrats had tried unsuccessfully to restrict these plans in the past. Bush's veto on July 15 criticized the new restrictions on private health plan options, which he claimed would significantly decrease Medicare Advantage enrollments. Congress overrode the veto that same day.

In addition, Congress approved increased education benefits for post–September 11 veterans. Federal payments for college tuition and stipends to cover living expenses were raised to cover 40 percent to 100 percent of actual costs, depending on the length of active-duty service. The administration opposed this measure, but Congress added it to an emergency war supplemental that the president signed on June 30. The cost of this new entitlement was estimated at more than $60 billion over ten years. At the insistence of congressional Republicans, it contained no offsets.[80]

Discretionary Spending and Deficits
The Bush administration's deficit-reduction program was predicated on major cuts in discretionary programs. Its FY 2006 budget, for example, included more than 150 proposed reductions and terminations.[81] Many of these had previously been rejected by Congress, but the administration nevertheless hoped to impose the "tightest such restraint . . . since the Reagan administration" on the discretionary domestic portion of the budget.[82] It also expected to be able to reduce defense spending, as the wars in Iraq and Afghanistan wound down and large war funding supplementals were no longer needed. By 2009, total

---

[78] Congressional Quarterly, *Congressional Quarterly Almanac, 2008*, D-12.

[79] Ibid., 9-13.

[80] Ibid., 6-8. The House also included a surtax on high-income taxpayers to fund this new entitlement. Senate Republicans successfully blocked this provision in the Senate bill, and the Senate version ultimately prevailed.

[81] Office of Management and Budget, *Major Savings and Reforms in the President's 2006 Budget*, 9.

[82] Office of Management and Budget, *Budget of the United States Government, Fiscal Year 2006*, 5.

discretionary spending–GDP was projected at 6.3 percent – the lowest level since 2000.[83]

The path that discretionary spending actually followed during Bush's second term was quite different, in part because additional funding was needed for domestic disaster relief and for the war in Iraq. In the fall of 2005, more than $90 billion in disaster relief was enacted, primarily for Hurricane Katrina.[84] Over the next three years, additional disaster relief supplementals totaling more than $43 billion were approved. The Iraq war "surge" that President Bush announced in January 2007 then raised defense spending–GDP to more than 4 percent.

In addition, Congress rejected most of the domestic policy cutbacks the administration proposed, even when Republicans controlled the House and Senate. In FY 2007, discretionary domestic spending was cut, but the reduction was less than $2 billion (from a discretionary domestic budget of more than $460 billion). Apart from this one-year reduction, discretionary domestic spending growth during Bush's second term was relatively high. Discretionary domestic spending–GDP remained well above the levels of the late 1990s – quite apart from the economic emergency spending enacted during 2008.

The congressional appropriations process over this period demonstrated the difficulties in trying to reduce deficits solely through spending cuts. In 2005, for example, Republican congressional leaders were able to pass a budget resolution that incorporated the tight spending limits the administration had proposed, and all of the regular appropriations bills were passed on schedule and within these limits. During 2005, however, Congress also approved more than $200 billion in emergency supplementals for disaster relief, veterans' healthcare, and war expenses that raised spending well above these limits.[85]

Disputes over discretionary spending between the House and Senate kept Congress from adopting a budget resolution in 2006 and delayed action on all domestic appropriations bills well past the beginning of the fiscal year. The funding for domestic departments and agencies was provided by a series of continuing resolutions, the last of which was passed by the new Democratic-controlled 110th Congress that convened in 2007. While this measure nominally complied with the administration's spending ceiling, it used unobligated balances and other technical adjustments to provide additional funding for Democratic domestic priorities.[86]

The 2007 budget cycle featured repeated veto threats and two critical vetoes. On May 1, Bush vetoed an emergency war supplemental appropriation that

---

[83] Office of Management and Budget, *Historical Tables, Budget of the United States Government, Fiscal Year 2006* (Washington, D.C.: Government Printing Office, 2005), 128.

[84] Labonte and Hanna, *The Impact of Major Legislation on Budget Deficits, 2001–2009*, 22.

[85] Congressional Quarterly, *Congress and the Nation, 2005–2008*, 72.

[86] Ibid., 108.

included deadlines for withdrawing troops from Iraq and also contained funding for disaster relief and for a number of domestic programs that Democrats wanted to expand. After a failed override attempt, Congress agreed to delete the Iraqi war provisions and to reduce the domestic add-ons, and President Bush signed the revised emergency supplemental on May 25.

The budget resolution that Congress adopted in May included higher discretionary domestic spending limits than the administration had proposed. The administration then threatened to veto domestic appropriations bills that contained additional funding. The House ignored these threats, but action on most domestic bills stalled in the Senate, which necessitated another series of continuing resolutions. When Congress cleared the Labor, Health and Human Services, Education appropriations bill in November, it included approximately $10 billion in added funding and was vetoed by the president. After the House failed to override the veto, the remaining fiscal 2008 appropriations bills were packaged into an omnibus measure that cleared on December 19. The fiscal 2008 omnibus appropriations bill complied with the administration's discretionary domestic spending ceiling and also included emergency supplementals for military operations in Iraq and Afghanistan, disaster relief, and veterans' programs.[87]

In 2008, Congress again adopted budget resolution levels for discretionary domestic spending that were well above the administration's requests, but Democratic leaders decided to postpone final action on FY 2009 appropriations bills until a new, presumably Democratic, administration took office. A continuing resolution that cleared Congress in September provided funding for domestic departments and agencies at FY 2008 levels for six months. Along with three defense-related appropriations bills, a $23 billion emergency appropriations bill for disaster relief, and a $25 billion loan program for U.S. automakers, the continuing resolution was signed into law on September 30.

If not exactly irrelevant, these disputes over nondefense appropriations were dwarfed by the massive economic emergency spending the Bush administration requested in 2008. The Housing and Economic Recovery Act of 2008, signed into law on July 30, effectively nationalized the Federal National Mortgage Association and Federal Home Loan Mortgage Corporation. These government-sponsored enterprises owned or guaranteed nearly half of the $12 trillion in residential mortgages in the United States, and the abrupt collapse of the housing market threatened their solvency. The Housing and Economic Recovery Act authorized the Secretary of the Treasury to purchase their assets, including mortgage holdings and other securities, and it also established a new federal regulatory agency to assume legal control and oversight of these previously private agencies. While the costs to the government of this takeover were

[87] Ibid., 112.

TABLE 6.3. *Revenues, Spending, and Surplus/Deficit, Fiscal Years 2001–2009 (in billions of dollars and percentage of GDP)*

	Fiscal Year 2001	Fiscal Year 2005	Fiscal Year 2009
Total Revenues	19.5%	17.3%	14.9%
Total Outlays	18.2	19.9	25.0
Total Surplus/Deficit	+1.3	−2.6	−10.0
	(+$128)	(−$318)	(−$1,413)
Revenues	19.5%	17.3%	14.9%
Individual income	(9.7)	(7.5)	(6.5)
Corporate income	(1.5)	(2.2)	(1.0)
Social insurance	(6.8)	(6.4)	(6.3)
Other	(1.4)	(1.3)	(1.2)
Outlays	18.2%	19.9%	25.0%
Discretionary defense	(3.0)	(4.0)	(4.7)
Discretionary domestic	(3.1)	(3.5)	(3.8)
Discretionary other	(0.2)	(0.3)	(0.3)
Mandatory programmatic	(9.9)	(10.6)	(14.8)
Net interest	(2.0)	(1.5)	(1.3)

Source: Congressional Budget Office, *The Budget and Economic Outlook: Fiscal Years 2011–2021* (Washington, D.C.: Congressional Budget Office, 2011), 133–142.

uncertain, the CBO estimated that credit subsidies and related costs could total as much as $240 billion in FY 2009.[88]

The Emergency Economic Stabilization Act of 2008, enacted two months later, authorized the Secretary of the Treasury to spend up to $700 billion to purchase mortgages and other assets held by private financial institutions. The Troubled Asset Relief Program (TARP), which was opposed by a majority of House Republicans, was then used by the Bush administration to purchase stock in troubled banks and financial institutions, as well as U.S. automakers and their financing affiliates. Here again, potential costs were highly uncertain, but initial estimates of budgetary effects for the multiyear TARP program ranged as high as $190 billion.[89]

As shown in Table 6.3, the Great Recession depressed revenues, generated huge amounts of emergency spending, and raised the deficit to nearly 10 percent of GDP. The underlying structural deficit that had taken hold during the Bush administration was already quite substantial but had little to do with discretionary domestic spending. At the FY 2005 midpoint, for example, the surplus to deficit reversal amounted to nearly 4 percent of GDP, with tax cuts

---

[88] Labonte and Hanna, *The Impact of Major Legislation on Budget Deficits, 2001–2009*, 24.

[89] Ibid., 26. Actual costs have thus far been much lower. See Congressional Budget Office, *Report on the Troubled Asset Relief Program* (Washington, D.C.: Congressional Budget Office, November 2010).

and war costs accounting for more than 80 percent of this change and mandatory programmatic spending accounting for much of the remainder. Even if the Bush administration had succeeded in cutting the relative level of discretionary domestic spending to Reagan-era lows, large deficits would have remained. Paying for tax cuts with discretionary domestic cuts was clearly unrealistic, but the Bush administration continued to claim otherwise, as did congressional Republicans after Bush left office.

The Obama Budget Program: The Battle over Spending

Along with Barack Obama's decisive victory in the 2008 presidential election, the Democratic Party also strengthened its control of the House and Senate. The Democratic majorities in the 111th Congress were nearly identical to those at the beginning of the Clinton administration – a margin of almost eighty seats in the House and a 59–41 advantage in the Senate.[90] The budget and economic situation that Obama inherited, however, was considerably more challenging than Clinton's, and his priorities differed accordingly.

In 1993, the Clinton administration had confronted a weak but recovering economy. The recession that had begun in the third quarter of 1990 had been relatively mild in comparison to the previous post–World War II recessions, although the pace of the subsequent recovery had been slow, and the unemployment rate continued to rise during 1992. Still, the economy was expected to grow, albeit moderately, without significant fiscal stimulus.[91] While the Clinton administration's initial budget program included a stimulus and investment component, very little of it managed to make its way through Congress. Instead, the centerpiece of the 1993 session was the deficit-reduction program that was enacted in August and that brought the budget into balance five years later.

The recession that began in 2007, by comparison, was the deepest and most protracted since the 1930s. In January 2009, the CBO forecast a "marked contraction in the U.S. economy" over the next twelve months, with the unemployment rate rising to more than 9 percent and continued "turmoil in the housing and financial markets."[92] For the Obama administration, the overriding priority at the outset was economic stimulus – particularly spending – and

---

[90] The Senate lineup was not settled until June 30, when Democrat Al Franken was finally declared the winner of the disputed Minnesota Senate election. The official party lineup at that point included fifty-eight Democrats, two Independents who caucused with the Democrats, and forty Republicans. In April, Arlen Specter, a Pennsylvania Republican, had switched to the Democratic Party. When Franken was sworn in on July 7, Democrats had the 60–40 margin needed for cloture, assuming of course that all Democrats cooperated. *CQ Weekly* 67 (July 6, 2009), 1586.

[91] Congressional Budget Office, *The Budget and Economic Outlook, Fiscal Years 1994–1998* (Washington, D.C.: Congressional Budget Office, 1993), xiii.

[92] Congressional Budget Office, *The Budget and Economic Outlook, Fiscal Years 2009–2019* (Washington, D.C.: Congressional Budget Office, 2009), 1.

that priority remained in place for the next two years despite enormous deficits and greatly increased debt.

The Obama administration also had an ambitious domestic agenda, notably the expansion of health insurance coverage to the nation's estimated forty-five million uninsured, as well as increased federal investments in education, infrastructure, and renewable energy. Its first budget called for reversing "a legacy of misplaced priorities," whereby "prudent investments" in domestic programs had been "sacrificed for high tax cuts for the wealthy and well-connected."[93] The president's budget message conceded that recovery and investment initiatives would mean continued deficits but promised to "begin the process of making the tough choices necessary to restore fiscal discipline, cut the deficit in half by the end of my first term in office, and put our nation on a sound fiscal footing."[94]

The Obama program was attacked by congressional Republicans at the outset, and the attacks grew harsher over time. Emergency spending was opposed because it increased deficits and debt, but Republicans also criticized new domestic spending – particularly the Democratic Party's health insurance initiative – that was supposedly deficit-neutral. For most congressional Republicans, and certainly for House Republicans, the battle over spending was also a battle over taxes. If new spending expanded the permanent size and role of government, Republicans feared that higher taxes would inevitably be needed to control deficits and debt.

The fate of the Bush tax cuts was an immediate concern, but Republican antitax sentiments were much broader. As the Tea Party phenomenon took hold in 2009, the Republican Party's opposition to new taxes of any kind was amplified, and bipartisan compromises on budget policy became virtually impossible. The partisan confrontations over spending began in earnest with the administration's emergency stimulus plan in February 2009 and continued for the remainder of the 111th Congress. When Republicans gained control of the House for the 112th Congress, the attacks on domestic spending escalated.

The Stimulus Battle

Planning for an economic stimulus package began soon after the 2008 election, as congressional Democrats and economic policy advisers to President-elect Obama drafted legislation that could be acted on quickly by the new Congress. The House Democratic leadership introduced an $825 billion stimulus plan on January 15, legislative details were worked out by House committees the following week, and the House passed an $819.5 billion measure on January 28. While the administration had hoped to gain some bipartisan backing for

---

[93] Office of Management and Budget, *Budget of the United States Government, Fiscal Year 2010* (Washington, D.C.: Government Printing Office, 2009), 5.
[94] Ibid., 3.

its first major initiative, House Republicans unanimously opposed the stimulus bill when it reached the floor.

The floor vote was not surprising. Republican members of the House Appropriations Committee had rejected an invitation from the Democratic chairman, David R. Obey, to help write the committee's portion of the stimulus package.[95] The ranking Republican on the committee, Jerry Lewis, reportedly told Obey, "I've simply got my instructions. We can't play." The Ways and Means tax section was likewise opposed by all of the committee's Republican members.

The prospects for bipartisanship in the Senate were not much brighter, as evidenced by the Republican effort to block the release of TARP funds for the incoming administration. On January 12, President Bush asked Congress to release the remaining $350 billion of the TARP authorization enacted in 2008. Bush's request, which followed discussions with the president-elect, quickly led to the introduction of a Republican-sponsored disapproval resolution in the Senate. Despite Barack Obama's personal assurance that the need for the TARP authorization was "imminent and urgent," only six Republicans joined with Democrats in rejecting the disapproval resolution.[96]

Because Congress had been asked to move so quickly on the stimulus plan, there was no budget resolution to provide procedural protection in the Senate. At some point, Democrats would need Republican votes to impose cloture and waive points-of-order, and this gave a handful of Senate Republicans, along with moderate Democrats, leverage in cutting back the spending stimulus in the House bill and expanding its tax-cut portion. House Democrats had decided to deal with the recurring AMT exemption problem through separate legislation. The Senate's stimulus bill was $40 billion smaller than the House had approved, and it also included a one-year AMT "patch" with an estimated cost of $70 billion. As a result, the new spending authorized by the Senate bill was well below the level that the House and the Obama administration had hoped to secure. Nevertheless, only three Senate Republicans joined a unanimous bloc of Democrats in invoking cloture on February 10 and then proceeding to pass the stimulus bill.[97] House Speaker Nancy Pelosi had denounced the Senate cuts as "very dangerous," but the Senate prevailed during abbreviated conference committee negotiations.[98] The conference report was adopted by the House on February 13, in the face of unanimous Republican opposition. Three Republicans again provided the pivotal votes in the Senate's 60–38 vote that same day.[99]

[95] Susan Davis, "A Different Place," *National Journal* 42 (October 16, 2010), 8.

[96] Congressional Quarterly, *Congressional Quarterly Almanac, 2009* (Washington, D.C.: Congressional Quarterly, 2010), 7-12.

[97] The three Republicans were Susan Collins and Olympia Snowe, both from Maine, and Arlen Specter of Pennsylvania.

[98] Congressional Quarterly, *Congressional Quarterly Almanac, 2009*, 7-5–7-6.

[99] Senator Edward M. Kennedy, the Massachusetts Democrat, was undergoing medical treatment and was unable to vote. Kennedy died on August 25, and Democrat Paul G. Kirk, Jr., was

The CBO estimated the total cost of the American Recovery and Reinvestment Act of 2009 (ARRA) at $787.2 billion.[100] The revenue provisions in ARRA totaled nearly $212 billion, with outlays for refundable tax credits accounting for an additional $70 billion. From the Republican perspective, the size of the stimulus tax cuts in ARRA was too small, and the individual tax relief was too targeted. The new "Making Work Pay" refundable tax credit, for example, was the largest individual tax cut in ARRA, providing a maximum credit of up to $800 (for joint filers) in 2009 and 2010 but with an income phase-out for high-income taxpayers. The AMT exemption increase – effective only for 2009 – was set at $70,950 for joint returns. Temporary increases in the EITC and refundable child tax credit were also restricted in terms of income eligibility, as was the expanded tuition tax credit. There was no "broad-based" individual tax relief in ARRA, and the business tax cuts – more generous depreciation and net operating loss rules – were minor.

New discretionary domestic appropriations in ARRA totaled almost $310 billion, with more than half of this spending scheduled beyond FY 2010. Republicans claimed that this spending was not aimed at economic recovery but rather was a Democratic ploy to advance long-term spending commitments. Similar objections were raised about state fiscal relief and other mandatory spending that would extend beyond 2010. In his address to a joint session of Congress on February 24, President Obama praised the "quick action" on ARRA and predicted that it would "save or create 3.5 million jobs" over the next two years.[101] He cautioned that ARRA was "just the first step" in getting the "economy back on track." The administration's upcoming budget would extend the economic recovery program and, at the same time, move forward with healthcare reform and "end tax breaks for the wealthiest 2 percent of Americans."[102] The partisan lines that had been so sharply drawn over the stimulus bill, however, remained firmly in place.

Spending and Healthcare

The Democratic congressional leadership had postponed final action on FY 2009 domestic appropriations until the spring of 2009. After the stimulus package was enacted, the House quickly passed an omnibus appropriations bill that included the expected $20 billion increase in domestic programs, but action in the Senate was delayed by Republican attacks over earmarks

---

appointed as his interim replacement in September pending a special election on January 19, 2010.
[100] Congressional Budget Office, *Estimated Cost of the Conference Agreement for H.R. 1, the American Recovery and Reinvestment Act of 2009* (Washington, D.C.: Congressional Budget Office, February 13, 2009), 5.
[101] Congressional Quarterly, *Congressional Quarterly Almanac, 2009*, D-5.
[102] Ibid., D-8.

and excess spending. A second continuing resolution was necessary before the Senate invoked cloture on March 10 and proceeded to pass the omnibus bill that the House had approved.

Republican attacks on the Democrats' spending program then shifted to the 2010 budget. The FY 2010 budget resolution was unanimously opposed by House and Senate Republicans, who objected to the new domestic spending the Democrats had authorized. According to House Minority Leader John A. Boehner, the Democratic spending program was "nothing short of an audacious move to a big socialist government in Washington, D.C."[103] Republicans were also upset that Democrats had included an option for a reconciliation healthcare measure, even though the budget resolution required that it be deficit-neutral. Indeed, the requirement added to Republican concerns about tax increases. In addition to possible new taxes to fund healthcare benefits, the budget resolution mandated that pre-Bush tax rates be restored for households with earnings of more than $250,000.

The remainder of 2009 was dominated by partisan fights over domestic appropriations bills and especially the Obama administration's new healthcare program. The administration had outlined a general proposal with a ten-year cost of approximately $900 billion. In an effort to avoid the problems the Clinton administration's "top-down" direction of healthcare reform had encountered, the Obama legislative approach accorded wide discretion to the congressional and committee leaderships. Although the president periodically intervened as the legislative process dragged on, the lack of clear administration direction allowed Republicans to exploit the divisions among congressional Democrats over the financial and regulatory provisions that were being decided. Republican attacks on spending and federal control were relentless, and Democrats finally had to resort to a highly unusual use of the reconciliation process to salvage a legislative effort that had become politically treacherous. Although Republicans ultimately failed to block what they derisively called "Obamacare," they used the healthcare issue to resurrect their offensive against "tax and spend" Democrats.

With the House leadership exercising tight control over the drafting of the several committee bills that contained the new health insurance program and its related regulatory and revenue provisions, committee action was completed by July 31. House Republicans could not block the House from acting on these proposals, but there was a split among Democrats over the scope of the House bill, particularly the leadership's decision to include a government-sponsored health insurance plan (the so-called public option) and to impose an income tax surcharge on taxpayers with very high incomes. After months of internal party negotiations, the House barely managed to pass its healthcare bill on November 7. With 39 Democrats defecting

[103] Ibid., 4–9.

and 176 of 177 Republicans voting no, H.R. 3962 was approved by a 220–215 vote.[104]

The Senate process was even more protracted. Senate Democrats had initially agreed to forego the reconciliation option for a measure as momentous and contentious as healthcare reform, but, as the hopes for bipartisan cooperation faded, this left the leadership with the task of garnering sixty votes for the cloture vote that would eventually be needed. While the Democrats enjoyed a 60–40 majority after the disputed Minnesota Senate election was finally settled, intraparty disagreements led to weeks of bargaining and trade-offs over the same issues that had proved troublesome in the House as well as provisions that several senators demanded to benefit their states.

The Senate's Health, Education, Labor, and Pensions (HELP) Committee reported out its portion of the healthcare bill on July 15. The committee's month-long markup produced a proposal that contained the public option the House had approved and generally reflected the policy priorities of liberal Democratic senators. The Finance Committee had tried and failed to put together a bipartisan plan, but the proposal that the committee reported out on October 13 did not include a public option, and its funding mechanism – an excise tax on high-priced employer-sponsored health insurance plans and fees on drug companies and health insurance firms – was a further departure from the bill that House Democrats were assembling.

The Senate Democratic leadership then tried to merge the HELP and Finance committees' bills into a measure that would satisfy the entire Democratic caucus. Majority Leader Harry Reid introduced an official leadership compromise on November 19, and, as Senate debate continued over the next month, Reid continued to bargain with individual Democrats. In the end, Reid's bill dropped the public option, retained the Finance Committee's tax and fee proposals, and included a number of provisions granting financial relief to particular states. In a series of votes from December 22 to 24, Reid secured sixty Democratic votes to invoke cloture on the bill and finally to pass it. In each case, Republicans were unanimous in their opposition.

At this point, House-Senate differences could not be easily bridged. In addition, the extended and often messy legislative process in the Senate allowed Republicans to mount a public opinion offensive against healthcare reform that had gained considerable traction by the end of the year. Democrat disquiet over Republican attacks on their fiscal record then forced the House and Senate leaderships to abandon plans for a $1.8 trillion debt-limit increase the Treasury had requested. Instead, the Democrats were only able to secure a short-term $290 billion increase that guaranteed the issue would resurface in 2010.

---

[104] House approval was complicated by the inclusion of anti-abortion restrictions demanded by conservative Democrats. See Congressional Quarterly, *Congressional Quarterly Almanac*, 2009, 13-13.

The healthcare debate was further muddled when Republican Scott P. Brown won an upset victory in a Massachusetts special Senate election on January 19, 2010. House Democrats had been insistent that the Senate's version of the healthcare overhaul was unacceptable, but any revised measure would have to be passed again in the Senate. With forty-one Republicans now determined to block the Senate from acting on any new proposal, healthcare reform was at an impasse. After weeks of internal discussions and a presidential healthcare "summit," Democratic leaders decided that the House would pass the original Senate bill and then approve a reconciliation bill incorporating the changes the House had demanded. At that point, the limited-debate rule governing reconciliation would allow the Senate to vote on these changes. After a last-minute dispute over abortion funding was resolved, the House cleared the Senate bill by a 219–212 vote and the companion reconciliation measure by a 220–211 margin on March 21. The Senate passed the reconciliation bill 56–43 on March 25.[105]

The estimated ten-year cost of the Patient Protection and Affordable Care Act and the Reconciliation Act of 2010 was $938 billion, with most of this new spending funding expanded coverage of the Medicaid and Children's Health Insurance programs and subsidies for individuals purchasing private health insurance from state exchanges.[106] These provisions were expected to reduce the number of uninsured persons by about thirty-two million when the new laws were fully implemented.[107] In addition, the healthcare bill eliminated the coverage gap in the original Medicare Part D prescription drug program.

Among the numerous federal regulatory changes contained in the health-care reform, the requirements that individuals purchase insurance (individual mandates) and that large employers provide adequate coverage were especially controversial. The fiscal effects of the expanded federal healthcare role, how-ever, were the focus of Republican objections. According to CBO estimates, the costs of the new insurance coverages would be more than offset by new taxes and fees and by savings in Medicare and Medicaid reimbursements to healthcare providers.[108] Indeed, the CBO projected a net $143 billion decrease in deficits as a result of these offsets over the next decade. For Republicans, these new taxes were unacceptable. House and Senate Democrats had agreed to forego an income surtax in favor of an increased Medicare payroll tax rate on individuals with more than $200,000 in wage and salary income and an addi-tional Medicare tax on their investment income. These Medicare taxes would

---

[105] Most Republican objections to reconciliation provisions were dismissed by the Senate parlia-mentarian. In a few instances, however, the Senate was required to delete provisions in the House bill that violated Senate rules on reconciliation. Another House vote was then necessary on this amended reconciliation bill. The process was finally completed on March 27.

[106] Congressional Budget Office, *Cost Estimate, Final Health Care Legislation* (Washington, D.C.: Congressional Budget Office, March 20, 2010), Table 4.

[107] Ibid., 9.

[108] Ibid., Table 1.

take effect in 2013 and provide $210 billion in additional revenues through 2019. New fees on health insurance companies, drug companies, and manufacturers of certain medical devices were expected to generate approximately half that total.[109] A new excise tax on high-premium employer-sponsored health insurance plans would take effect in 2018 and provide additional revenues of more than $30 billion over two years. Altogether, net revenue increases of the healthcare reform bill totaled $420 billion.

Spending savings, by comparison, were much larger, exceeding $510 billion over ten years. The Medicare and Medicaid reductions included more than $170 billion in the Medicare Advantage Program and in special payments to hospitals for treating disproportionate numbers of the uninsured. Nearly $200 billion, however, was tied to reduced Medicare payments to healthcare providers based on productivity efficiencies. These projected savings were criticized by Republicans as highly unrealistic and, perhaps contradictorily, as posing a threat to the future delivery of expensive Medicare services for the seriously ill.

The Republican Party's wide-ranging critique of Obamacare reflected long-standing concerns about the appropriate federal role in the delivery of healthcare services. At issue as well were substantive health policy issues such as the potential impact of coordinated care and technological innovation on costs. The most persistent theme, however, related to how this new spending would make it even more difficult to control deficits and debt. While Democrats could argue that healthcare reform was, according to official estimates, deficit-neutral at worst, they were clearly on the defensive about spending. The halting economic recovery and high unemployment rate in 2010 made the nearly $800 billion stimulus bill a convenient Republican target, and a $900-plus billion healthcare bill did nothing to assuage public anxieties about "runaway" spending.

Spending and Taxes

The Democratic Party's dilemma over spending was compounded by divisions over taxes. In 2009, Democrats could not agree on revisions in the estate tax, which was scheduled to expire in 2010 and then return to its pre-Bush levels the next year. In December, the House passed an extension of expiring business research and development tax credits and other "extenders" that had been routinely approved in the past. Senate Republicans and some Democrats, however, objected to the revenue offsets in the House bill, notably a higher tax on carried interest, and the Senate did not take up the House bill.

In February 2010, Congress passed a $1.9 trillion increase in the debt limit that included pay-as-you-go rules requiring legislative changes in tax laws or

---

[109] Ibid., Table 2.

entitlement programs to be deficit-neutral.[110] Republicans had opposed previous efforts to include revenues in the PAYGO process and continued to argue that tax cuts be exempted. Many Democrats, however, were also concerned about PAYGO restrictions on tax cuts. As a result, the new PAYGO rules exempted any extension of the expiring Bush tax cuts for all but the wealthiest taxpayers, AMT exemption increases, estate tax revisions, and legislative overrides of scheduled reductions in Medicare reimbursements to physicians. The growing Democratic unease over fiscal issues was underscored by legislative maneuvering on the debt-limit increase. In order to shield their members from having to vote directly on the increase, House leaders instead resorted to a self-executing rule for floor debate. Once adopted, the rule automatically incorporated the debt-limit increase.

During debate on the debt limit in the Senate, there appeared to be bipartisan support for an independent commission that would recommend a deficit-reduction plan that Congress would be required to consider under expedited procedures. That requirement, however, was ultimately rejected by Republicans, who were concerned that tax increases would be harder to defeat as part of a deficit-reduction package. President Obama then created a commission by executive order on February 18, naming former Republican Senator Alan K. Simpson and Clinton White House Chief of Staff Erskine Bowles as its co-chairmen.[111] The commission's charge was "to bring the budget into primary balance (balance excluding interest costs) in 2015 and to meaningfully improve the long-run fiscal outlook." Its reporting deadline was scheduled after the midterm elections.

The immediate deadlock over budget policy, however, continued as the House and Senate failed to adopt a budget resolution for FY 2011. Democrats were unable to bridge internal disagreements, much less overcome Republican opposition, regarding tax increases, new stimulus spending, and even routine domestic appropriations. With the economy continuing to lag and unemployment still high, the stimulus bill and healthcare bill votes were seen as an electoral handicap by many Democrats, particularly House members from marginal districts, and they were not anxious to create additional problems with controversial tax and spending votes. As a result, no action was taken on the expiring Bush tax cuts, and none of the domestic appropriations bills had been passed when Congress adjourned for the elections in early October.

---

[110] The general PAYGO approach allowed Congress to cut certain taxes below baseline levels for a fiscal year as long as other taxes were raised or entitlements cut by an equivalent amount. Similarly, an increase in an entitlement program would have to be offset with an equal cut in other entitlements or an increase in taxes.

[111] The president appointed six members, including the co-chairmen, with twelve members selected by the Republican and Democratic leaders in the House and Senate.

The Republican message for the midterm elections was straightforward. In September, House Republicans issued their "Pledge to America" agenda, which began with the permanent extension of all Bush tax cuts and a new tax deduction for small business to promote job creation and economic recovery.[112] The next item on the agenda was spending, and Republicans promised to cancel future stimulus spending, terminate the TARP program, and "roll back government spending to pre-stimulus, pre-bailout levels." Future spending would then be capped and limited. The target then shifted to healthcare, with a call for "immediate repeal of major portions" of the legislation that Democrats had enacted in March.

With Tea Party organizations having constantly promoted the anti-tax/antispending message in Republican primaries, numerous Tea Party–backed candidates had been nominated. In addition, advocacy groups such as Americans for Tax Reform and business interest groups reinforced the pressure on all Republican candidates not to deviate from the low tax, small government theme. This orthodoxy emerged from the midterm elections even stronger, as Republicans proceeded to gain control of the House, picking up sixty-three seats, and to narrow the Democrats' Senate margin to 53–47. Virtually all Republicans had subscribed to a campaign pledge opposing any tax increases. In the postelection congressional session that followed, Republicans won a clear victory on taxes and made certain that they would have an early opportunity in the 112th Congress to confront the Obama administration and congressional Democrats over spending.

The Lame-Duck "Truce"

The President's Fiscal Commission issued its report on December 1. The nearly $4 trillion deficit-reduction plan, which included spending cuts and revenue increases, was endorsed by eleven of the commission's eighteen members. While this fell three votes short of the fourteen-vote threshold that had been established for an "official" recommendation to be submitted to Congress, the more serious problem was the tepid support the plan received from all sides, including President Obama. While the Simpson-Bowles report, as it was christened, would serve as a useful benchmark for future deficit-reduction proposals, its immediate impact was minimal.

The Bush tax cuts were scheduled to expire on December 31, and congressional Republicans had promised to block any extension that did not include high-income taxpayers. On December 6, President Obama announced that an agreement had been reached with Senate Republicans to extend the 2001 and 2003 tax cuts for all income levels through December 31, 2012. In addition, the administration accepted Republican proposals for a two-year estate tax revision. Included as well in the tax-cut package were a one-year AMT patch,

[112] *CQ Weekly* 68 (September 27, 2010), 2231.

a one-year reduction in the Social Security payroll tax rate, extended child and tuition tax credits, and business tax credits. Finally, the administration was able to secure Republican support for a thirteen-month continuation of federal unemployment benefits.

The tax deal immediately came under fire from House Democrats, who denounced the income tax and estate tax concessions the administration had made. In the Senate, a mini revolt occurred as well, but the tax-cut compromise was passed on an 81–19 vote on December 15. After a series of failed attempts to change the estate tax provisions in the Senate bill, the House finally cleared the measure on December 17. House Democrats were also forced to accept a short-term extension of FY 2011 appropriations. On December 8, the House passed a continuing resolution to fund domestic programs and agencies through the end of the fiscal year. When Senate Democrats tried to bring this measure to the floor, Republicans blocked the move. Republicans wanted to postpone final action on FY 2011 appropriations until the new Congress, when they would have greater control over spending decisions. With a December 18 deadline under the expiring continuing resolution, Democrats agreed to a temporary extension through March 4, 2011.

The two-year extension of the Bush tax cuts gave Republicans firm control over the debate on tax policy in the new Congress. In addition, they would have an immediate opportunity to cut domestic spending when the FY 2011 continuing resolution expired in March and additional opportunities with other must-pass legislation such as the debt-limit increase and regular appropriations bills. There had been some bipartisan successes during the lame-duck session. The Obama administration was able to win Senate approval of a nuclear arms treaty with Russia, and Congress also cleared legislation repealing the ban on openly gay persons serving in the military. In both cases, Republican support for cloture votes had been needed in the Senate, and thirteen Republicans joined Democrats in ratifying the START treaty. The partisan lines on taxes and spending, however, held firm.

The Divided Government Stalemate

With more than $2.7 trillion in deficits during 2009 and 2010, deficit reduction was ostensibly a bipartisan priority for the 112th Congress. However, the return of divided government further strained an already fractured budget process. Instead of enacting comprehensive deficit-reduction agreements as in 1990 and 1993, Congress struggled to avert government shutdowns and debt defaults. Efforts to restrain entitlement spending encountered stiff resistance from congressional Democrats, and Republican opposition to tax increases was unyielding. As a result, deficit-reduction policy focused almost exclusively on discretionary spending, and the limits of that approach were demonstrated once again.

Averting a Shutdown

The first budget "crisis" began in February, as House Republicans demanded more than $60 billion in domestic appropriations cuts in order to keep the government from shutting down when the FY 2011 continuing resolution expired in early March. A series of stopgap measures then were approved until a final agreement was reached between the Obama administration and House and Senate leaders and cleared by Congress on April 14. The spending package that Congress passed contained nearly $40 billion in spending cuts, but most of this reduction was spread out over several years. In terms of actual spending during 2011, the CBO estimated that the reduction was only $352 million.[113] Although a substantial portion of the outyear reductions involved domestic programs that the Obama administration had previously designated as low priority, a majority of House Democrats voted against the final agreement. On the Republican side, there was considerable dissatisfaction with the size and types of cuts that their leaders had managed to secure, and fifty-nine Republicans also voted no.

For Republicans like House Speaker John Boehner, who had witnessed first-hand the political backlash from the Clinton-era shutdowns, the 2011 deal was a necessary compromise. For newer members of the House, particularly the several dozen in the Tea Party Caucus, an actual shutdown was a desirable outcome, and the leadership's failure to exploit this threat more effectively was not well received. Thus, with the budget resolution and debt-limit ceiling moving onto center stage, House Republicans began to stake out more ambitious goals for cutting spending and reducing the size of the federal government, and they were joined by an aggressive group of conservative Senate Republicans.

The budget resolution the House adopted in April set forth unambiguous Republican policy goals with regard to spending. Largely shaped by Paul D. Ryan, chairman of the House Budget Committee, the Republican plan called for more than $6 trillion in spending cuts over ten years and a massive scaling back of long-term entitlement commitments. Medicaid was to be converted into block grants to the states, while Medicare was to be transformed into a private insurance program supported by federal subsidies. The Medicaid proposal had been put forth by Republicans in 1995, but the Medicare reforms were more far-reaching than anything Republican leaders had endorsed in the past. While the healthcare proposals attracted most of the attention from Democratic critics in 2011, House Republicans also proposed major cutbacks in other entitlements such as food stamps, agriculture subsidies, higher education aid, and rental assistance. Deficit reduction in the House plan was entirely dependent on spending cuts because Republicans promised future tax cuts, notably a cut in the top marginal rate on individual income from 35 percent to 25 percent.

---

[113] *CQ Weekly* 69 (April 18, 2011), 862.

The long-term Republican goal was to have the smallest federal government since the 1950s.

The House plan had no chance in the Senate, which the Democratic leadership highlighted by bringing the measure to the floor for a predictable defeat. Because of the hugely controversial Medicare provisions in the original House budget plan, only forty of the Senate's forty-nine Republicans supported it.[114] Meanwhile, Democrats were unable to pass an alternative resolution, because they remained divided over taxes. The budget policy debates in the spring of 2011 included a heavy dose of symbolic votes and political theater, but the upcoming debt-limit extension was a much more serious matter. According to the Treasury, the federal government would reach its $14.3 trillion statutory limit on borrowing in early August, and Congress would have to raise that limit beforehand to avoid any financial disruptions, including an actual default.

Debt Ceiling Politics

Congress had raised the debt limit seven times under George W. Bush and three times under President Obama. While debt-limit votes were usually partisan, especially in the House, Congress had never missed a deadline. Congress had, however, attached debt-limit increases to deficit-reduction plans on a number of occasions, most notably the 1990 and 1993 reconciliation acts. In 1995, congressional Republicans had tried to use another debt-limit increase to force the Clinton administration to accept their nearly $900 billion spending-cut/tax-cut reconciliation bill. That attempt had failed, but Republicans were determined to use the 2011 debt-limit increase to advance an even more ambitious spending retrenchment. Since many Democrats also saw the political necessity of combining the debt-limit increase with some type of deficit-reduction plan, the Obama administration initiated what turned out to be several months of negotiations with congressional leaders on a bipartisan solution. The parameters of these talks, initially led by Vice President Joseph R. Biden, Jr., continually changed. The general goal was to couple an immediate debt-limit increase with deficit-reduction savings over an extended period of ten to twelve years. The amount of potential savings, however, depended on whether entitlements and revenues were included in a final agreement.

Republican leaders had announced at the outset that any tax increases would be unacceptable, but the White House hoped that a deficit-reduction package with a high ratio of spending cuts to tax increases would attract Republican support. The Biden-led talks, however, eventually foundered on the tax issue, and President Obama then became directly involved in negotiations with House and Senate leaders in July. By that point, however, Republican demands had

[114] On May 24, Democrats had captured a traditional Republican seat in New York in a special House election. This upset was interpreted by Democratic leaders as a referendum on the Republican Medicare reform proposal, and they hoped to make it a defining issue again in 2012.

grown more extreme. Republican leaders did not explicitly threaten a default, but many rank-and-file Republicans insisted that they would not support any increase in the debt ceiling that did not include equivalent spending cuts. Several dozen Senate Republicans, for example, insisted that multitrillion-dollar spending cuts and Senate passage of a constitutional balanced-budget amendment were preconditions for their support of an increase in the debt limit. Many House Republicans favored similar preconditions and an additional stipulation that future tax increases were completely off limits. For congressional Democrats, domestic spending cuts without tax increases were equally unacceptable, and after the Obama administration agreed to discuss entitlement "reforms," they were even more adamant that taxes for high-income earners and corporations would have to be raised. In the end, the president's hopes for a multitrillion-dollar "grand bargain" came to nothing. Congress managed to avoid any default, but the debt-limit agreement was a gimmick-laden compromise that satisfied no one.

When Congress took up consideration of debt-ceiling bills in July, the House first passed a "Cut, Cap, and Balance" plan that incorporated the major demands of conservative Republicans and was easily defeated in the Senate. Senate Democrats then proposed a much narrower bill that raised the debt ceiling through 2012 in exchange for largely unspecified spending cuts. This proposal was rejected by House Republicans, who then passed a short-term increase in the debt limit as part of a package that included $1.2 trillion in spending cuts and the balanced-budget amendment requirement. After this House measure was defeated in the Senate, a Republican filibuster blocked floor action on the Democratic alternative proposed by Majority Leader Harry Reid.

As the August 2 deadline approached, congressional leaders from both parties also continued to meet with President Obama and Treasury representatives, and an agreement was finally reached on a debt-limit extension package that passed the House by a 269–161 vote on August 1 and the Senate by a 76–24 margin the following day. The agreement included a debt-limit increase to cover expected borrowing through 2012, a nonbinding provision concerning a balanced-budget amendment, discretionary spending savings of more than $900 billion over ten years, and a requirement for additional savings of at least $1.2 trillion over the same period. President Obama then signed the agreement into law just hours before the borrowing authority ceiling would have been reached.

The key provision in the Budget Control Act of 2011 was an immediate increase of $400 billion in the statutory debt ceiling and authorization for additional increases of up to $1.7 trillion as these became necessary. Upon certifications by the president that these increases were needed, Congress would have the opportunity to enact joint resolutions of disapproval within fifty days. If no disapproval resolutions were passed, the debt ceiling would increase automatically by $500 billion for the first certification and by $1.2 trillion for the second. In the unlikely event that a disapproval resolution made it through the House and Senate, the president could veto it, and two-thirds votes in both chambers would be needed to override the veto. The Obama administration could, therefore, be reasonably confident that the Treasury would have adequate borrowing authority through 2012 even if Republicans continued to raise strong objections.

In order to placate conservative Republicans in both chambers, the Budget Control Act also required the House and Senate to vote on passage of a constitutional balanced-budget amendment by the end of 2011. Tea Party Republicans had initially insisted that both chambers actually pass an amendment before Congress agreed to raise the debt limit and only reluctantly agreed to what was, in effect, a face-saving compromise. The Budget Control Act did not specify a particular version of the amendment to be voted on, did not suspend Senate rules that would allow amendment opponents to mount a filibuster, and did not impose any penalty if either the House or Senate failed to vote on an amendment by the required deadline. However, the act provided for an additional $300 billion debt ceiling increase if both chambers somehow managed to pass an amendment.

On November 24, all but four House Republicans dutifully voted for their version of a constitutional balanced-budget amendment, but the proposal fell well short of the two-thirds majority needed for passage. Among the Republican dissenters was Paul Ryan, the Budget Committee chairman who had designed the controversial House budget plan in the spring. Ryan was skeptical that Congress had the spending discipline to enforce a balanced-budget amendment, particularly in light of the announcement several days earlier that the widely heralded Joint Select Committee on Deficit Reduction had failed to reach agreement on the second stage of the deficit-reduction plan mandated by the Budget Control Act.

Section 101 of the Budget Control Act imposed statutory ceilings (caps) on discretionary spending for fiscal years 2012–2021. Estimated savings from these caps would be $917 billion if enforced for the entire period.[115] As with previous versions of discretionary spending caps, particularly those in place during the 1990s, automatic spending cuts, or sequesters, would be applied whenever the annual appropriations limits were exceeded. Certain emergency spending, however, was excluded from the caps, notably funding for Overseas Contingency Operations and the War on Terror.[116] For fiscal years 2012 and 2013, separate caps were set for security and nonsecurity spending, after which a single cap applied to all discretionary spending.

The Budget Control Act also required additional deficit reduction of at least $1.2 trillion over this same ten-year period and created a new House-Senate

---

[115] Bill Heniff, Jr., Elizabeth Rybicki, and Shannon M. Mahan, *The Budget Control Act of 2011* (CRS Report for Congress, August 19, 2011), 2.
[116] Ibid., 12–13.

committee to write a bill that would achieve these savings. The twelve-member Joint Select Committee on Deficit Reduction – the so-called Supercommittee – included equal numbers of Republicans and Democrats from both chambers to be appointed by their party leaders. The committee had no restrictions on the policy options that it could recommend but did have a reporting deadline. Any committee proposal submitted to the House and Senate by November 23 would be protected against amendments and considered under expedited procedures ensuring an up-or-down vote within one month. Shortly before the deadline, the committee announced that it was hopelessly deadlocked, with Republican members blaming Democratic intransigence on entitlement reforms and Democrats singling out Republican fealty to the Bush tax cuts.

The failed supercommittee experiment triggered yet another provision of the Budget Control Act, in this case $1.2 trillion in automatic deficit reduction from fiscal years 2013–2021. Under the statutory formula specified by the act, this $1.2 trillion included $216 billion in debt service savings and $984 billion in spending cuts divided between defense and nondefense programs. The automatic cuts within each category would fall almost exclusively on discretionary spending programs, because exemptions were provided for Social Security, Medicaid, federal civilian and military retirement programs, and most low-income assistance programs.[117] In addition, Medicare reductions were limited to a maximum of 2 percent annually.

These automatic cuts would not take effect, however, until FY 2013 and would then be apportioned equally over the next eight years. Congress and the president could at any point cancel the automatic cuts by enacting an alternative deficit-reduction program or by suspending, modifying, or canceling them entirely. Otherwise, the discretionary spending caps under the Budget Control Act combined with the additional automatic spending cuts would reduce baseline spending by $1.9 trillion through 2021, a significant sum but less than half the deficit reduction that the Simpson-Bowles Fiscal Commission and independent experts had concluded was needed to stabilize the budget.

The Aftermath

The brinksmanship that House Republicans brought to the government shutdown negotiations in the spring of 2011 and to the debt-ceiling talks in the fall produced disappointing results. In the context of the enormous deficits that were at issue, short-term appropriations cuts made very little difference, and the Budget Control Act promised only limited and uncertain long-term relief. In addition, Republicans could scarcely be pleased with the prospect of more than $450 billion in defense reductions under the spending caps and an additional $500 billion in automatic cuts by 2021. If, as leaders of both parties repeatedly claimed, the fiscal crisis caused by the Great Recession provided a unique

[117] *CQ Weekly* 68 (August 8, 2011), 1754.

opportunity to stabilize the budget, that opportunity had been squandered, and it was hard not to conclude that tax increases were the major stumbling block.

In the aftermath of the Supercommittee debacle, Congress had to deal with pending spending and tax bills for 2012, and House Republicans made one final attempt to assert themselves. None of the regular FY 2012 appropriations bills had been enacted by October 1, and several continuing resolutions then provided continued funding. When the third of these expired on December 16, nine appropriations bills were still outstanding, and appropriators agreed to combine these into a consolidated bill that could be enacted quickly.

Senate Democrats and Republicans had also reached an understanding that the consolidated appropriations bill would include a one-year extension of the Social Security payroll tax cut that was due to expire on December 31 and a shorter extension of federal unemployment benefits. House Republicans, however, insisted that the payroll tax cut then be voted on separately and vowed to block any extension that was not fully offset by spending cuts. This threat worked about as well as previous ones. President Obama expertly attacked House obstructionism, Senate Republicans were unsympathetic, and the public responded negatively as well. At the last minute, yet another face-saving compromise was announced that temporarily extended the payroll tax cut (and unemployment benefits) without any offsets and with the clear understanding that the full extension would be acted on in early 2012.

The degree to which fiscal battles dominated the agenda in 2011 was reminiscent of those between the Clinton administration and the Republican-controlled Congress in 1995. In the earlier case, Clinton was defending the tax increases and deficit-reduction plan that had been enacted two years earlier, and the Republicans' failure to implement their own plan did not arrest progress toward a balanced budget. The year-long standoff between the Obama administration and Congress in 2011 meant that there was no credible plan in place to stabilize a budget that was in much worse shape than it was in 1995, and neither was there any prospect for such a plan until after the 2012 election. At that point, the newly elected president and Congress would have to decide the fate of the Bush tax cuts and the future direction of budget policy.

7

Reconnecting Taxes and Budgets

The last major reform of the federal tax system took place in 1986. Much of that reform has since been erased by proliferating tax preferences for individuals and corporations. The percentage of individual income not subject to taxation, for example, has increased to its highest level since the early 1980s.[1] The economic distortions of the current tax system are, according to most experts, substantial. Its complexity imposes costly compliance burdens on individuals and corporations, and the noncompliance "tax gap" has been estimated at more than 15 percent of total tax liability.[2] While fairness is an elusive concept, few would argue that the tax system has become noticeably fairer over recent decades.[3] More important in terms of budget policy, the federal tax system suffers from a problem that predates the Tax Reform Act of 1986. It does not raise sufficient revenues to finance the defense and domestic programs in the federal budget.

Despite the often intense debates over taxation during our early history, budgets were usually balanced. From 1789 to 1930, deficits were routinely incurred during wars and financial upheavals, but nearly 70 percent of annual budgets were in surplus. The Great Depression and World War II produced a long series of consecutive deficits, but the balanced-budget standard was revived in the late 1940s and 1950s. With only a handful of exceptions over the past half-century, however, budget deficits have been the norm, and this fiscal imbalance is unlikely to improve anytime soon. Indeed, the urgent task

---

[1] *CQ Weekly* 69 (September 26, 2011), 1982.
[2] Eric J. Toder, "What Is the Tax Gap?" *Tax Notes* 123 (October 2007), 1–12.
[3] See Congressional Budget Office, *Historical Effective Federal Tax Rates: 1979 to 2005* (Washington, D.C.: Congressional Budget Office, 2007).

for the federal government is to keep deficits and debt at "sustainable" levels in the decades ahead.[4]

Part of the ongoing discussion about taxation focuses on tax policy reform. This agenda includes changing the current tax system to reduce economic distortions and compliance costs and to improve tax administration. Tax policy reform also extends to new types of taxation, such as consumption or value-added taxes, that might accomplish these same purposes. In assessing various tax reform proposals, prescriptive principles such as fairness (horizontal equity, vertical equity, individual equity), economic and administrative efficiency, and simplicity are widely accepted as "useful guides for policymaking."[5] While Democrats and Republicans disagree about how best to satisfy or balance these principles, few would reject them as irrelevant.

The more contentious part of the debate over taxation involves budget policy and principles. As Steuerle has stated, "Revenue raising is probably more a goal than a principle, but its primacy cannot be overstated.... At stake is nothing less than the government's ability to achieve its purposes and run its functions."[6] Unless revenue raising is sufficient to "pay for what society needs," the government faces the economic costs of excessive deficits and debt.

This seemingly straightforward goal of revenue raising, however, has been at the heart of budget policy disputes for many years. The disconnect between revenue levels and spending levels that currently exists is much greater than in the past, but it did not arrive suddenly or unexpectedly. It is the latest iteration of a long-standing argument over whether decisions on taxes should ultimately be governed by revenue-raising requirements or by competing economic policy goals, spending retrenchment strategies, and even electoral calculations. These competing considerations have gained considerable force over the past several decades, substantially weakening the revenue-raising goal of taxation.

Taxes and Spending: The Unraveling

For nearly two decades after World War II, taxes and spending were tightly connected. Under Truman and Eisenhower, budgets were frequently balanced, and by 1961, publicly held debt was nearly $4 billion less than it had been after World War II. With deficits rigorously controlled and the economy expanding,

---

[4] *Sustainable* is usually defined as keeping public debt from growing faster than the economy. The more ambitious deficit-reduction plans aim at reducing the federal publicly held debt from current levels of approximately 70 percent. More limited plans look to stabilize it. See Jane G. Gravelle, *Addressing the Long-Run Budget Deficit: A Comparison of Approaches* (CRS Report for Congress, August 25, 2011).

[5] C. Eugene Steuerle, *Contemporary Tax Policy* (Washington, D.C.: Urban Institute Press, 2008), 10–15.

[6] Ibid., 15.

the publicly held debt–GDP level fell from nearly 110 percent to 45 percent. This fiscal discipline owed a great deal to executive budget policy leadership. Both Truman and Eisenhower successfully fought congressional pressures for large tax cuts and calibrated their spending programs to keep budgets at or near balance.

Inflation and Defense

Truman and Eisenhower shared the widely held belief that balanced budgets enhanced economic stability, particularly by helping to control inflation. Their annual budgets were replete with warnings about deficits and inflation, and while neither rejected the need for deficit stimulus during recessionary periods, they did not view tax cuts as a routine prescription for economic growth. In effect, the Truman-Eisenhower period appears to be an example of "tax smoothing," with taxes and spending in balance over the long term but with temporary deficits in response to economic or other emergency shocks.[7]

Finally, neither Truman nor Eisenhower viewed tax cuts as an instrument for shrinking the size of government. When the Republican-controlled 80th Congress adopted that strategy, Truman managed to protect New Deal domestic programs, aided by Republican disagreements over specific spending cuts. In any case, the transition to Cold War defense budgets defused much of the partisan conflict over spending during Truman's second term.

Eisenhower rejected entreaties from conservative Republicans to "repeal" the New Deal, just as he resisted Democratic efforts to expand it. The priority accorded to defense spending under Truman continued after the Korean War. Although Eisenhower imposed budget ceilings on defense, defense outlays accounted for more than half of total spending – and approximately 10 percent of GDP – from 1955 to 1961. Tax policy was explicitly subordinated to the financing demands of a Cold War defense program and a moderate federal domestic role during Eisenhower's presidency, and the result was a rough balance between taxes and spending.

Economic Growth and Domestic Spending

Passage of the Revenue Act of 1964 marked a basic change in the balanced-budget constraint on taxes.[8] According to Kennedy, tax cuts would spur economic growth, leading to higher revenues that would erase any immediate deficits. With Lyndon Johnson embracing that same rationale, Congress

---

[7] From 1947 to 1961, there were eight deficits, only one of which – FY 1959 – was more than 2 percent of GDP. See the discussion of tax smoothing in William R. Keech, *Economic Politics* (New York: Cambridge University Press, 1995), 155.

[8] Ibid., 178.

enacted a large tax cut at a time when deficits had been high for several years. Revenues did indeed surge after the 1964 tax cut, but deficits were never entirely erased.

Kennedy and Johnson were also intent on raising domestic spending, which meant that either defense transfers or higher revenues would eventually be needed to keep budgets reasonably close to balance. Johnson's simultaneous pursuit of his Great Society program and Vietnam War commitment raised the revenue stakes even higher. In a sharp departure from the Korean War financing model, Johnson delayed wartime taxation until 1968 and refused to curtail his domestic spending agenda until Congress forced his hand. The budget returned to balance in 1969, but the revenue-GDP level that year was the highest since World War II.

The Kennedy and Johnson presidencies loosened the connection between revenues and spending. Inflation control was no longer the paramount fiscal policy goal, with the economic growth benefits of deficits gaining considerable support. In addition, revenues increased after the 1964 tax cut, which suggested to some that tax cuts would pay for themselves whenever there was slack in the economy. Both the Reagan and Bush II tax cuts, for example, incorporated revenue projections that proved to be wildly optimistic.

The balanced-budget standard remained in place during the 1960s, but the new fiscal policy emphasis on growth gave more leeway to policy-makers. The Johnson administration's introduction of the unified budget in 1967 provided additional flexibility. Previously, executive branch budgets had measured deficits or surpluses in terms of the administrative budget, which excluded the Social Security trust funds. By the mid-1960s, Social Security had become a significant component of the annual budget, and the unified budget's inclusion of its large trust fund surpluses improved Johnson's deficit projections. Without the nearly $4 billion Social Security surplus in 1969, the much-heralded balanced budget that year would have been in deficit. When Social Security surpluses disappeared in the late 1970s, Congress approved two large tax increases. By the mid-1980s, large and growing trust fund surpluses had returned, helping once again to lower deficits in the rest of the budget. In effect, the mandated fiscal discipline of the Social Security program allowed a less disciplined approach to the rest of the budget.

The balanced-budget constraint on taxes and spending was further weakened during the 1970s. Congress continuously expanded domestic spending but also enacted a series of individual and corporate tax cuts. Much of this domestic expansion was financed by defense budget cuts that slashed real spending by more than 30 percent between 1970 and 1979. At the end of the decade, the defense budget share had dropped to less than 25 percent, yet total spending–GDP had climbed to levels previously reached during the Korean and Vietnam wars.

On the tax side of the budget, high rates of inflation raised average income tax rates for all income groups, and individual income tax revenues continued to rise despite periodic tax cuts.[9] For upper-income households, marginal tax rates rose from 25 percent in 1970 to more than 40 percent in 1980, helping fuel the "tax revolt of the late 1970s" aimed, in large part, at the federal income tax.[10] Inflated revenues, however, still failed to keep pace with the growth of domestic spending.

Deficits during the 1970s were much larger than those of the preceding two decades, averaging approximately 3 percent of GDP from 1975 to 1981. Jimmy Carter may have been deeply committed to a balanced budget, but he was unable to provide the policy leadership needed to solve the deficit problem. His failures on tax policy were especially glaring, as Congress ignored revenue requirements, pursued piecemeal tax relief for individuals and corporations, and refused to adjust nondefense spending. When Congress was forced to raise Social Security taxes in 1977, it rejected even modest benefit cuts. As a result, Social Security trust fund deficits were not erased, and a much larger tax increase was needed in 1983.

The enormous "welfare shift" of the 1970s was engineered by congressional Democratic majorities that were not terribly concerned with the negative impact on defense budgets and military capabilities. With congressional challenges to executive budget policy leadership now routine, and stagflation having undermined what remained of the balanced-budget rule, fiscal discipline was not a high priority. Facing up to the revenue requirements of a domestic spending program that had taken shape since the Great Society was difficult for Democrats, particularly with the 1980 election looming. When Jimmy Carter unveiled a 1984 balanced-budget goal in his election-year budget, his revenue target was nearly 23 percent of GDP – a level that had not been reached even in World War II.[11] This revenue target received no support from Carter's fellow Democrats and was quickly abandoned. Republicans nonetheless made low taxes a defining issue in the election, with the party's platform setting forth the Republican version of a balanced budget: "The Republican Party believes balancing the budget is essential but opposes the Democrats' attempt to do so through higher taxes. We believe than an essential aspect of balancing the budget is spending restraint . . . and higher economic growth, not higher tax burdens."[12]

---

[9] Income brackets were affected, along with the value of personal exemptions and other tax provisions. C. Eugene Steuerle, *The Tax Decade* (Washington, D.C.: Urban Institute Press, 1992), 22–26.

[10] Ibid., 25–26.

[11] Office of Management and Budget, *Budget of the United States Government, Fiscal Year 1981* (Washington, D.C.: Government Printing Office, 1980), 612–614.

[12] Congressional Quarterly, *Congressional Quarterly Almanac, 1980* (Washington, D.C.: Congressional Quarterly, 1981), 59-B.

The Reagan Legacy

The Economic Recovery Tax Act of 1981 was much larger than the Kennedy-Johnson tax cut of 1964 but had the same economic growth objective. In ceding the responsibility for dealing with inflation to the Federal Reserve, Ronald Reagan removed one of the conventional objections to tax cuts. His plan for shrinking the domestic role of government, notably the Great Society expansions, loosened the revenue-raising constraint. However, congressional support for Reagan's domestic retrenchments quickly waned, and the resulting deficits exceeded even the most pessimistic predictions. The publicly held debt was slightly more than 25 percent of GDP in 1980. When Reagan left office, it had climbed to more than 40 percent and would rise to nearly 50 percent in 1995.

The connection between taxes and spending was not completely ignored during the 1980s. Corporate taxes were raised in 1982 and 1984, when it became clear that deficits could not be substantially reduced through spending cuts. Reagan refused, however, to reverse any part of his individual tax-cut program and even managed to extend these cuts in the Tax Reform Act of 1986. The Gramm-Rudman-Hollings deficit ceilings enacted in Reagan's second term exempted revenues entirely from its automatic deficit-reduction provisions.

The Reagan presidency firmly established the economic growth justification for low income tax rates, especially among Republicans. It also demonstrated that a healthy economy with low inflation outweighed any public concerns about deficits. Walter Mondale's pledge to increase taxes during his 1984 presidential campaign was not the only cause of his landslide defeat, but it cemented the Republican Party's belief in the electoral appeal of tax cuts. Reagan, of course, paid no electoral price for a deficit record that would have occasioned bipartisan outrage in the not-too-distant past.

The other lesson of the Reagan years was less persuasive to Republicans. Despite Reagan's considerable efforts, tax cuts did not "starve the beast." Domestic spending levels remained high during Reagan's presidency, as the growth in mandatory programs more than offset cuts in discretionary domestic programs. Reagan managed to check the sharp rise in total domestic spending–GDP that had occurred during the 1970s, but the increased GDP shares for defense and interest payments raised overall spending–GDP well above prior levels. Reagan and many Republicans continued to insist that budgets could be balanced at low revenue levels, but the domestic spending cuts needed to accomplish this never stood a serious chance of being enacted.

Taxes and Balanced Budgets

Reagan was able to avoid major deficit reduction challenges in his second term, as economic growth boosted revenue levels and brought deficit-GDP to less than 3 percent in 1989. George H. W. Bush was not so fortunate. When the economy reversed course in 1990 and deficits rapidly spiraled upward, Bush made the fateful decision to support tax increases. A balanced multiyear deficit-reduction plan of spending cuts and tax increases was scuttled by House Republicans, at which point Bush was forced to accept a Democratic alternative that was predictably less aligned with Republican priorities.

The Bush episode underscored how antitax attitudes among congressional Republicans had hardened since the early 1980s, when Senate Republicans helped convince Reagan that deficit-reduction corporate tax increases were necessary. With an equally serious deficit problem in 1990 and a much higher level of publicly held debt, Bush was deserted by most of his party. He was also excoriated by conservative Republicans for breaking his "no new taxes" pledge, which did not improve his chances for reelection.

With Bill Clinton, Republican opposition to deficit-reduction tax increases was unanimous, and the Omnibus Budget Reconciliation Act of 1993 barely survived Democratic defections. Clinton's program for economic recovery highlighted the connection between deficit reduction and low interest rates, which was hardly a new or novel argument. Republican critics, however, dismissed this argument and pointed instead to the growth-destroying effect of tax increases. Republicans went on to exploit the tax issue in the 1994 midterm elections, just as congressional Democrats had feared, and were able to gain control of both the House and Senate for the first time in four decades.

Despite Republican claims, the balanced budgets in Clinton's second term were not a bipartisan accomplishment. Instead, they resulted from individual income tax increases that Republicans had denounced, a surge in economic growth they predicted could not occur because of those increases, and post–Cold War defense cuts. From 1990 to 2000, defense spending–GDP dropped by 2.2 percentage points; mandatory programmatic and discretionary domestic–GDP actually increased slightly.[13] In 2000, individual income tax–GDP was 10.2 percent, the highest level since the modern income tax was established. The lowest defense-GDP levels of the post–World War II period and the highest income tax levels ever were not Republican priorities by any definition, and Clinton's balanced budgets incorporated domestic spending commitments that congressional Republicans opposed as well.

The electoral benefits of balanced budgets, however, were questionable. Clinton was reelected while deficits were still high, and congressional Democrats remained in the minority after the budget was balanced. In 2000, George W. Bush and congressional Republicans campaigned for large tax cuts, taking advantage of the accumulating budget surpluses under Clinton. Once in office, Bush's first priority was the largest tax cut since Reagan.

---

[13] Dennis S. Ippolito, *Why Budgets Matter: Budget Policy and American Politics* (University Park: Pennsylvania State University Press: 2003), 11.

The Bush II Disconnect

Budget policy under Bush, especially tax policy, was not a replay of the 1980s. Taxes were repeatedly cut despite massive deficits, costly wars, and domestic spending expansions. Vice President Cheney's famous quip that "deficits don't matter" came after Republicans had taken control of the House and Senate in the 2002 midterm elections. Nearly $800 billion in deficits over the next two years did not derail George W. Bush's reelection or reduce the Republican majorities in Congress. In addition, neither inflation nor interest rates appeared to be a problem, and the slow pace of economic growth was interpreted by the administration as an argument for more tax cuts.

Democrats routinely deplored Bush's deficit record and recalled the halcyon days of Clinton's balanced budgets. They did not, however, advocate restoring the tax policies that had helped produce those balanced budgets. Rather than repealing the Bush tax cuts, the 2004 Democratic platform promised to protect "98 percent of Americans" by increasing taxes only for the wealthy (in this case, families with annual incomes of more than $200,000).[14]

Where taxes were concerned, balanced budgets were not a priority for Democrats or, of course, for Bush. Neither side was willing to support the major tax increases needed to eliminate revenue shortfalls. Instead, Bush promised unspecified spending cuts, and Democrats pretended that high-income tax increases would suffice. This bipartisan avoidance of fiscal discipline was possible because the pre–Great Recession fiscal situation was not all that unusual. Bush had squandered massive budget surpluses, which set him apart from his predecessors, but he otherwise managed to keep deficits and debt reasonably close to levels over the previous several decades.

Deficits, Debt, and Defense

With the possible exception of the Reagan-era deficits, the levels of federal debt over the past half-century did not trigger widespread concerns about fiscal sustainability.[15] Instead, the deficit issue was typically argued in terms of direct effects on inflation, interest rates, or economic growth rather than "unsustainable" debt burdens. Moreover, because the size of deficits over this period usually lagged behind economic growth, debt burdens fell. In 1960, publicly held debt was slightly more than 45 percent of GDP. In 2008, it was approximately 40 percent.

Despite frequent claims of "runaway spending," spending levels were actually quite stable, averaging a little more than 20 percent from the 1960s through

---

[14] Congressional Quarterly, *Congressional Quarterly Almanac, 2004* (Washington, D.C.: Congressional Quarterly, 2005), 32-B.

[15] When sustainability was discussed with respect to public debt, it was usually in terms of the entitlement financing problems of the 2020s and thereafter. See Congressional Budget Office, *The Long-Term Budget Outlook* (Washington, D.C.: Congressional Budget Office, 2003), 1–18.

2008. From 2000 to 2008, the spending-GDP average was 19.5 percent. What kept total spending relatively flat over this extended period was the long-term decline in defense budgets that funded much of the growth in domestic programs. Policymakers were able to finance this growth without raising taxes by drawing down the defense "cushion" inherited from Truman and Eisenhower. The 1970s, for example, would have produced a more dramatic escalation in deficits if Congress had moderated its defense budget cuts. Instead, Congress financed its wholesale expansion of domestic programs not by raising taxes but by cutting defense. The result was a widely acknowledged deterioration in military capabilities, but Congress was able to avoid politically risky tax increases.

The Reagan deficits, by comparison, were amplified by a defense buildup that redressed these 1970s deficiencies. If defense spending–GDP levels under Reagan had matched those under Carter, average deficit levels would have been only marginally higher.[16] It is also important to recognize, however, that Reagan's defense budgets were still much smaller than those of the 1950s and 1960s in terms of budget and GDP shares. The balanced budgets of the late 1990s were then made possible on the spending side by the lowest defense GDP and budget shares since before World War II. These defense spending levels naturally rose with the Afghanistan and Iraq wars, but even these increases raised the defense budget share to only 20 percent, well below Reagan or even Carter levels.

Defense cutbacks helped keep deficits at tolerable levels much of the time, but higher revenues were needed to erase those deficits entirely. In 1968, Congress approved a temporary individual income tax surcharge, along with corporate and excise tax increases, to meet the rising costs of the Vietnam War and the Johnson administration's domestic program commitments. The next two individual income tax increases occurred in 1990 and 1993, both as part of multiyear deficit-reduction plans. These were permanent tax increases, unlike the Revenue and Expenditure Control Act of 1968, but the Bush tax cuts in 2001 and 2003 technically suspended them through 2010. That suspension then was extended for an additional two years after the 2010 midterm elections.

The average revenue level from Johnson through Bush II was approximately 18.5 percent of GDP. Relatively modest revenue increases would, therefore, have balanced most of the budgets over this period. In the 1974 Budget Act, Congress had revised its budget process to highlight the coordination of revenue and spending policy. This coordination was rarely in evidence in the decades that followed, but deficits and debt levels remained within tolerable limits. Today's policymakers, however, do not have the benefit of the favorable and

---

[16] Defense spending–GDP under Carter averaged 4.8 percent, with an average deficit-GDP of 2.5 percent from 1977 to 1980. Under Reagan, the defense average was 5.9 percent, while deficit-GDP averaged 4.1 percent.

forgiving fiscal equilibrium that allowed their predecessors to avoid difficult choices between spending cuts and tax increases.

The New Fiscal Paradigm

As the Bush presidency entered its final year, the Congressional Budget Office (CBO) described the fiscal outlook as "relatively sanguine."[17] With the Bush tax cuts scheduled to end in 2010, the CBO projected a rough balance between spending and revenues over the next decade and a steady decline in the publicly held debt–GDP level. If the tax cuts were continued and wartime spending remained high, modest deficits could be expected, but public debt levels would be stable. Even under supposedly "pessimistic" policy projections at that time, spending, revenue, deficits, and debt would be close to their long-term historical averages.

The CBO warned of future problems balancing spending and revenues when entitlement costs would begin to escalate in the 2020s, but these warnings were hardly new. The budget outlook was certainly less favorable than it had been in 2000, but the nation's fiscal problems still appeared to be quite manageable. The Great Recession, however, soon destroyed the relative equilibrium the United States had enjoyed for more than half a century.

The new fiscal paradigm – huge cyclical deficits, soaring debt levels, and protracted economic uncertainties – was not confined to the United States. The economic downturn and financial crisis that began in 2008 affected the global economy, and other industrialized democracies responded with costly stimulus measures that resulted in the sharpest increases in government debt since World War II.[18] From 2002 to 2011, publicly held debt–GDP doubled to more than 70 percent in the United States. In Western Europe and Great Britain, the increases were similar, while the public debt level in Japan rose from 80 percent to 130 percent of GDP.[19] The economic impact of this globalization of debt is unknown but unlikely to be entirely benign. Thus, the United States and the other advanced democracies will be pursuing their individual fiscal policy consolidations in an unusually volatile and uncertain international economic environment.

The Debt Problem

When the disconnect between spending and revenues took hold in the 1960s, concerns about federal debt were almost nonexistent. Debt-GDP levels were

---

[17] Congressional Budget Office, *The Budget and Economic Outlook: Fiscal Years 2008–2018* (Washington, D.C.: Congressional Budget Office, 2008), vi.
[18] Joseph E. Gagnon and Marc Hinterschweiger, *The Global Outlook for Government Debt over the Next 25 Years* (Washington, D.C.: Peterson Institute for International Economics, 2011), 3.
[19] Ibid.

low, and most of that debt was held within the United States. In 1970, for example, foreign investors accounted for only 5 percent of the publicly held debt.[20] Two decades later, that percentage was still less than 20 percent, and virtually all of this was held by central banks and financial institutions in Europe and Japan. At that time, the credit of the United States was unquestioned, and it remained so even as public debt levels nearly doubled in the 1980s and early 1990s.

Rising debt levels certainly buttressed the case for deficit reduction in 1990 and 1993, but the predominant concern at the time was the negative effect that large deficits would have on interest rates and growth. In any case, whatever anxieties there might have been about the public debt were quickly dispelled by the successful deficit-reduction agreements under Bush I and Clinton. Indeed, policymakers soon found themselves facing a very different problem. When projected surpluses "threatened" to retire the entire public debt, Congress was cautioned that the Federal Reserve would find it more difficult to conduct effective monetary policy.[21]

The debt problem has since taken a very different form. Publicly held debt–GDP is expected to climb to more than 70 percent in 2012 – its highest level in more than 60 years. Nearly half of this debt is now held abroad, with the largest share owned by China.[22] In addition, the credit rating of the United States is no longer unquestioned. The protracted deadlock in Congress over raising the debt limit in 2011 led the Standard and Poor's rating agency to downgrade Treasury securities below Triple-A for the first time in 70 years.[23] Thus far, international confidence in the safety of United States debt has not been affected by this downgrade, but the fact remains that the heavy reliance on foreign investors and foreign governments to finance that debt at favorable interest rates indefinitely cannot be taken for granted.[24]

The financing of the existing public debt, however, is only part of the problem. When the economy is growing at a healthy rate and interest rates are relatively low, the debt level can be stabilized simply by maintaining a primary budget balance – that is, revenues equal spending minus net interest payments. Since the Great Recession was caused by a financial crisis, however, the pace of economic recovery has been slow and may remain halting for an

---

[20] Office of Management and Budget, *Analytical Perspectives, Budget of the United States Government, Fiscal Year 2012* (Washington, D.C.: Government Printing Office, 2011), 73.

[21] Alan J. Auerbach and William G. Gale, "The Economic Crisis and the Fiscal Crisis: 2009 and Beyond," *Tax Notes* 125 (October 5, 2009), 101.

[22] China's holdings represent 21 percent of the debt held by foreign investors, with Japan at 20 percent and the United Kingdom at 11 percent. Office of Management and Budget, *Analytical Perspectives, Fiscal Year 2012*, 74.

[23] *Washington Post* (August 25, 2011), A1.

[24] Marc Labonte, *The Sustainability of the Federal Budget Deficit: Market Confidence and Economic Effects* (CRS Report for Congress, June 28, 2011), 7–8.

unusually extended time.[25] Low interest rates cannot be simply assumed, particularly given U.S. dependence on foreign-held debt. The variable that can be controlled – future budget policy – has become so politicized and arguably irrational that even primary balances may prove to be elusive. Unfortunately, the gap between spending and revenues that must be closed over the next decade is extremely large, and it will almost certainly grow larger thereafter.

Fiscal Uncertainties

Budget projections are greatly affected by economic assumptions regarding growth and other variables.[26] The recent recession was much more severe than other post–World War II downturns, so there is added uncertainty about economic and budget forecasts.[27] Even under highly optimistic economic assumptions, however, difficult policy choices will be needed to control deficits and debt over the next decade. These short-term budget forecasts are tied to the fate of the Bush tax cuts and, to a lesser extent, on whether Congress allows planned reductions in spending to take effect. As forecasts shift to the 2020s and beyond, revenues and entitlements dominate the deficit-reduction agenda.

Future Spending The starting point in analyzing the current budget policy challenge is spending. From 2012 to 2021, spending-GDP levels are expected to fall as stimulus programs expire and the economy recovers. The CBO's current law baseline projects spending-GDP at approximately 22 percent for fiscal years 2012–2021, compared to more than 24 percent from 2009 to 2011.[28] The CBO has warned, however, that the current law baseline probably underestimates the course of future spending.

Under current law, for example, Medicare payment rates for physicians would be reduced by nearly 30 percent in 2012 and by smaller amounts thereafter in accordance with the Sustainable Growth Rate (SGR) payment system enacted in 1997. Since 2003, Congress has blocked every scheduled SGR reduction, and there is bipartisan support for actually increasing physician payment rates when Congress revisits its annual "Doc Fix." The cost of maintaining current rates, however, is substantial, totaling nearly $300 billion over ten years, with an estimated $50 billion in additional debt service payments required as well.[29]

Projected healthcare savings from the Patient Protection and Affordable Care Act of 2010 are also included in current law baseline projections but

[25] Ibid.
[26] For a discussion of how budget projections are affected by different economic assumptions, see Congressional Budget Office, *The Budget and Economic Outlook: Fiscal Years 2011–2021* (Washington, D.C.: Congressional Budget Office, 2011), 115–119.
[27] Congressional Budget Office, *The Budget and Economic Outlook: An Update* (Washington, D.C.: Congressional Budget Office, 2011), 35.
[28] This includes all of the discretionary spending cap reductions and the additional $1.2 trillion in automatic cuts under the Budget Control Act of 2011. Ibid., 5.
[29] Ibid., 26.

may be unrealistic. The Community Living Assistance Services and Support (CLASS) program, for example, was expected to reduce net healthcare spending by nearly $85 billion in its first decade of operation, because beneficiary premiums would exceed benefit payments.[30] In October 2011, however, the Obama administration announced that the program would not be financially viable and canceled its scheduled implementation. Total healthcare spending is estimated at nearly $12.9 trillion from 2012 to 2021, but numerous other provisions of the 2010 healthcare reform, such as health insurance subsidies and exchanges, have yet to take effect.[31] Even if healthcare policy remains unchanged, actual costs could be substantially higher, or lower, than expected.

The course of future discretionary spending presents major forecasting problems. If Congress complies with the discretionary caps in the Budget Control Act of 2011, discretionary spending–GDP would drop by one-third, to approximately 6 percent by 2021.[32] Further reductions are mandated under the additional $1.2 trillion in deficit reduction that will take effect beginning in 2013. If these reductions are enforced, discretionary spending–GDP could fall as low as 5.5 percent by 2021.

While discretionary spending will almost certainly decline from current levels, it may not be possible to achieve these kinds of savings. The end of combat operations in Iraq and Afghanistan will lower defense budgets, but the War on Terror continues, and the core defense budget must be supported as well. Congressional Republicans have vowed to block the mandated future cuts in defense funding, and many Democrats may join them. Given the strong support for national security imperatives in Congress, it is highly doubtful that defense spending–GDP will return to its post–Cold War low of 3 percent anytime soon.

It is equally improbable that the entire burden of deficit reduction will be placed on discretionary domestic programs. Congressional Democrats would be strongly opposed, and it is not at all clear that most Republicans would support the draconian cuts in domestic programs needed to do so. Domestic and international discretionary spending has averaged more than 3.5 percent of GDP over the past fifty years. Neither the Reagan cutbacks of the 1980s nor the spending caps of the 1990s brought nondefense discretionary spending appreciably below this level, and it is difficult to imagine that the future nondefense spending trajectory could somehow be returned to pre–Great Society levels.

These and other reservations have led the CBO and other forecasters to construct alternative baselines that incorporate the spending policies likely to remain in place. These "plausible" baselines are generally much higher than the official current law estimates, which means that entrenched policy

---

[30] Congressional Budget Office, *The Budget and Economic Outlook: Fiscal Years 2011–2021*, 63.
[31] Ibid., 58.
[32] Congressional Budget Office, *The Budget and Economic Outlook: An Update* (2011), 20.

commitments would have to be changed in order to limit actual spending. The Simpson-Bowles Fiscal Commission, for example, estimated that nearly $2.5 trillion in mandatory and discretionary spending cuts would be needed to lower spending-GDP to 22 percent from 2012 to 2020.[33] Deficit-reduction plans issued by the Bipartisan Policy Center and the Committee for a Responsible Federal Budget have proposed multitrillion-dollar spending cutbacks with similar spending-GDP targets of 22 percent to 23 percent.[34] Obama administration spending projections have been within this range as well.[35] House Republicans managed to pass a budget resolution in 2011 that promised to cut spending-GDP to 20 percent, but the Senate easily defeated it. The future prospects for the House Republican plan, or something similar, would appear to be nonexistent.

The starting point in projecting future budgets is that an enormous amount of spending discipline will be needed to come reasonably close to the current law baseline, and that spending will still be much higher than the levels in place from the 1960s through the early 2000s.[36] Over that earlier period, revenues were generally inadequate to balance spending. These "historical" revenue levels will be even less adequate given the higher spending that almost certainly lies ahead.

Future Revenues Over the past decade, legislated tax cuts and uneven economic performance resulted in unusually low revenue levels.[37] From 2009 to 2011, revenues dropped to less than 15 percent of GDP – their lowest levels since 1950. When the economy fully recovers, revenues will rebound, but the extent of that rebound will depend on the fate of the Bush tax cuts and how Congress handles the recurring alternative minimum tax (AMT) problem. There are also dozens of corporate and excise tax reductions expiring between 2013 and 2015. While allowing these temporary provisions to end will raise additional revenues, the revenue effects are relatively small compared to those tied to individual tax rates.

The current law revenue baseline projects a return to 1990s tax law and revenue levels over the next few years. It assumes that the Bush tax cuts – particularly the Economic Growth and Tax Relief Reconciliation Act of 2001 and the Jobs and Growth Tax Relief Reconciliation Act of 2003 – will not be extended past 2012, that the AMT will be allowed to take full effect

---

[33] *The National Commission on Fiscal Responsibility and Reform* (Washington, D.C.: The White House, 2010).

[34] Gravelle, *Addressing the Long-Term Budget Deficit*, 22.

[35] Ibid.

[36] For fiscal years 1968–2008, outlays-GDP averaged 20.6 percent. Congressional Budget Office, *The Budget and Economic Outlook: Fiscal Years 2008–2018*, xiv.

[37] For fiscal years 2002–2011, tax cuts reduced baseline revenues by an estimated $2.8 trillion, but economic (and technical) factors contributed to an additional $3.4 trillion in revenue losses. Congressional Budget Office, *Changes in CBO's Baseline Revenue Projections Since January 2001* (Washington, D.C.: Congressional Budget Office, May 12, 2011), 1–2.

at that time, and that Congress will not renew other temporary tax relief measures. Under this current law baseline, the revenue-GDP level quickly rises to more than 20 percent by FY 2014 and reaches nearly 21 percent by 2021.[38]

An enormous amount of deficit reduction could be realized if these scheduled tax law changes actually take effect, but Congress is unlikely to cooperate. There is strong bipartisan support for continuing to limit the reach of the AMT and for keeping in place the child tax credits, marriage penalty relief, and other low- and middle-income tax reductions enacted under Bush. Neither party supports a wholesale reversal of the income tax rate cuts that have been in place since 2001, and even the estate tax is unlikely to revert to the low exclusions and high rates of the 1990s.

The revenue gains (or losses) from these provisions are substantial, totaling an estimated $4.7 trillion from 2013 to 2021.[39] Indexing the AMT for inflation, which seems inevitable, would reduce these future revenues by nearly $700 billion. Combining AMT relief with the full extension of the Bush income tax rates and a modified estate and gift tax raises that revenue loss to $3.9 trillion. Extending other individual and corporate tax preferences could cost as much as $800 billion in reduced revenues.

There are widespread concerns that any near-term tax increases might impede the pace of economic recovery, and the stagnation in real income gains for many taxpayers in recent years adds a further complication. The basic fiscal problem, however, is that the 18-plus percent revenue-GDP levels of the past fifty years will not come close to matching the spending commitments of the next ten years. Making the Bush tax cuts permanent for all taxpayers, as Republicans have demanded, would effectively limit revenues to that fifty-year average.

The Democratic alternative, raising rates on high-income taxpayers while shielding low- and middle-income taxpayers from any tax increase, would result in only moderately higher revenue levels. Reinstating the 36 percent and 39.6 percent brackets for married couples with incomes of more than $250,000 (and single taxpayers with more than $200,000 in income) would raise nearly $365 billion in revenues over ten years.[40] Other changes affecting high-income taxpayers, including limits on itemized deductions, phase-outs of personal exemptions, and higher tax rates on capital gains and dividends would add an additional $315 billion. Nevertheless, limiting tax increases to high-income taxpayers would leave in place much of the revenue loss from the 2001 and 2003 tax cuts.

---

[38] Congressional Budget Office, *The Budget and Economic Outlook: An Update* (2011), 5.

[39] Ibid., 26.

[40] Nonna A. Noto, *Raising the Tax Rates on High-Income Taxpayers: Pros and Cons* (CRS Report for Congress, November 5, 2010), 5.

There is a long-standing partisan debate over the economic impact of increased tax rates for high-income taxpayers, including the possible disincentives affecting the formation and growth of small businesses.[41] It is also possible that high-income taxpayers would find ways to avoid higher rates by shifting compensation to nontaxable fringe benefits or other forms of income taxed at lower rates. The 1990 and 1993 tax increases, however, were followed by an extended period of strong economic growth, and the revenue gains from these tax increases were actually much higher than expected.[42]

It is also the case that the 1990 and 1993 tax increases were not confined to high-income taxpayers, although they were disproportionately affected. The need for additional revenues at that time meant increased tax burdens for middle-income families, retirees, and even corporations. Since the deficit and debt problems now being faced are even greater than those of the early 1990s, the corresponding revenue requirements are also higher, and increased taxes for high-income taxpayers alone would not satisfy these requirements.

Spending versus Revenues The unsettled economic and political situation makes it difficult to determine "plausible" baselines for budget policy. Nevertheless, certain policy choices are likely to determine whether budgets can be stabilized at sustainable deficit levels. At least for the next decade, entitlements are not a principal concern. Mandatory programmatic spending–GDP is not expected to increase significantly even if all currently scheduled benefits remain in place. The real challenge will be enforcing the multiyear defense and nondefense discretionary cuts enacted in 2011. An even more important policy choice, however, involves taxes.

As shown in Figure 7.1, current law baseline deficits fall well below sustainable levels by 2014 and would remain relatively low thereafter. A few deviations from current law constraints, however, would raise projected deficits to much higher levels indefinitely. The most likely entitlement policy change – canceling the scheduled reductions in payment rates for physicians – would have only a modest impact. Relaxing the limits on discretionary spending would have a somewhat greater effect. A permanent extension of expiring tax cuts, however, would change the deficit outlook dramatically. The defining fiscal policy choices for the next decade are not limited to entitlements and taxes. At stake as well will be the pace and depth of defense budget cuts that the president and Congress will allow to take effect and the willingness of elected officials and the public to accept major retrenchments in discretionary domestic programs.

---

[41] Many small businesses are organized as pass-through entities, with income taxed at individual rather than corporate tax rates. Ibid., 14–16.

[42] Ippolito, *Why Budgets Matter*, 285.

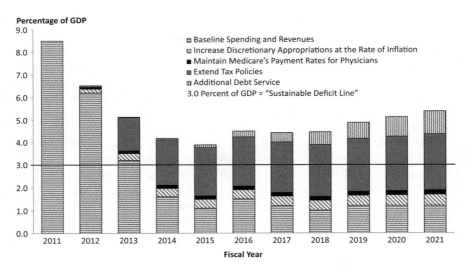

FIGURE 7.1. Baseline Deficits and Deficits Assuming a Continuation of Certain Policies, Fiscal Years 2011–2021 *Source:* Adapted by the author from Congressional Budget Office, *The Budget and Economic Outlook: An Update* (Washington, D.C.: Congressional Budget Office, 2011), xii, 5, 26.

The Long-Term Cost of Entitlements

As the costs of entitlement programs begin to escalate in the 2020s, reconciling overall spending and revenue levels will become much more difficult. The federal government now finances, in whole or in part, some two dozen entitlement programs for the elderly, the poor, the unemployed, and other beneficiary groups. Entitlement spending, however, is heavily concentrated in just three programs – Social Security, Medicare, and Medicaid. This concentration will become even greater over time, with nearly 80 percent of total entitlement spending accounted for by these programs in 2020 and a rising share thereafter.[43]

More important is the projected increase in spending-GDP for Social Security, Medicare, and Medicaid. From 2010 to 2020, spending for these programs is expected to increase from 10.3 percent of GDP to slightly more than 12 percent.[44] The current policy projection then climbs to 15 percent in the 2030s and to 20 percent by 2050. That level would roughly equal spending-GDP for the entire federal government over the past half-century, and unless

[43] Congressional Budget Office, *The Budget and Economic Outlook: Fiscal Years 2011–2021*, 58–59.
[44] The healthcare portion of this spending includes Medicare, Medicaid, the Children's Health Insurance Program (CHIP), and private health insurance subsidies. Congressional Budget Office, *CBO's 2011 Long-Term Budget Outlook* (Washington, D.C.: Congressional Budget Office, 2011), 80.

future spending for defense and other domestic programs disappears entirely, it would amount to the biggest increase in the size of government since the New Deal–Cold War era.

The higher costs of retirement and healthcare entitlements over the next decade are primarily the result of programmatic rather than demographic factors. Automatic cost-of-living adjustments and higher per-beneficiary costs account for more than 70 percent of the Social Security, Medicare, and Medicaid spending increase over this period.[45] The expanding caseloads for these programs – that is, the larger populations eligible for benefits – generate less than 30 percent of the additional costs. Demographic pressures do intensify over time, but programmatic factors remain an important determinant of costs, particularly for Medicare and Medicaid.

Social Security

After the 1983 Social Security rescue plan was enacted, the program's trust fund accumulated a surplus that reached nearly $2.6 trillion in 2010.[46] Since then, benefit payments have exceeded Social Security tax collections, with the shortfall being covered by interest payments on the special government securities in which the trust fund surplus is invested. In about ten years, however, these interest payments will no longer be sufficient to bridge the gap between benefit payments and tax revenues. It will then be necessary to draw down the program's reserve funds by redeeming those securities. Current estimates are that the reserve will be entirely depleted by the late 2030s, at which point the Social Security taxes being collected would cover only about 75 percent of the benefits mandated by law.[47]

The pending insolvency of the Social Security trust funds, however, is not the principal fiscal concern, because it can be resolved by increasing taxes, reducing benefits, or some combination of these options. More important is Social Security's budgetary impact – how it affects overall spending and revenues. If the spending-GDP level for Social Security increases significantly over the next several decades, higher taxes, cutbacks in other spending programs, or additional borrowing will be necessary.

With the benefit formulas and eligibility criteria currently in place, Social Security spending–GDP is expected to rise from 4.8 percent in 2011 to 6.1 percent in 2035 and to stabilize at approximately that level thereafter. The payroll taxes that fund the program, however, are projected to remain at less than 5 percent of GDP for the next several decades.[48] Large payroll tax

---

[45] Congressional Budget Office, *The Budget and Economic Outlook: Fiscal Years 2011–2021*, 70.

[46] This total includes the Old Age and Survivors Insurance Fund and the Disability Insurance Trust Fund. Office of Management and Budget, *Historical Tables, Budget of the United States Government, Fiscal Year 2012* (Washington, D.C.: Government Printing Office, 2011), 323.

[47] Congressional Budget Office, *CBO's 2011 Long-Term Budget Outlook*, 53–54.

[48] Congressional Budget Office, *Social Security Policy Options* (Washington, D.C.: Congressional Budget Office, 2010), 6.

increases would, therefore, be needed to close the Social Security fiscal gap if no action is taken to cut mandated benefits.

There are a number of revenue options that would supply these additional revenues.[49] The payroll tax rate can be raised for workers and employers, and the taxable maximum on earnings subject to Social Security taxes can be raised or eliminated entirely. It would also be possible to extend Social Security taxes to capital gains or dividend income, as opposed to the existing wage and salary income coverage. The latter two changes would primarily affect those workers with higher incomes, because more than 90 percent of current workers fall below the maximum earnings limit.[50]

As with income taxes, neither party endorses broad-based payroll tax increases to erase the Social Security fiscal gap. Republicans have opposed higher payroll taxes of any kind, while Democrats would prefer to limit any increase to high-income taxpayers. The latter would provide appreciable revenues only if the definition of high-income is broad enough to include many middle-class workers and if benefits are not allowed to increase along with taxable earnings.[51]

The Social Security spending path can be lowered, however, by revising benefit formulas and cost-of-living adjustments or raising the retirement age. Under current law, the initial benefit for a retiree is based on that retiree's taxable earnings adjusted for changes in average annual wages for the entire labor force. This wage indexing is much more costly than price indexing, and substituting the latter in determining initial benefits for future retirees would keep Social Security spending–GDP levels essentially unchanged over the next several decades.[52]

A revised cost-of-living adjustment formula would also yield substantial, if lesser, savings over time. The consumer price index that has been used for calculating the annual increase in Social Security benefits possibly exaggerates the inflation that actually affects retirees.[53] A less generous but presumably more accurate adjustment would lower the Social Security–GDP level over the next decade and slow its rise thereafter. The normal retirement age for Social Security has already been raised to sixty-six years and will increase to sixty-seven years between 2021 and 2027. Future retirement age increases that take into account lengthening life expectancy would reduce spending by cutting the number of years during which retirees receive benefits.

In 2005, the Bush administration proposed a "partial privatization" scheme that combined benefit reductions for future Social Security retirees with individual investment-based retirement accounts. According to the administration, the

---

[49] Ibid., xi.
[50] Ibid., 18.
[51] Ibid.
[52] Ibid., 23.
[53] Ibid., 31–32.

income from these private accounts would more than compensate for the reduction in Social Security benefits, but the privatization proposal made little headway in 2005. The substantial transition costs needed to fund it (increased borrowing to make up for the diversion of payroll taxes to fund private accounts) preclude its consideration today.

Benefit retrenchments in Social Security have been rare. The 1983 legislation that raised the retirement age also scaled back early retirement benefits. It then made Social Security benefits taxable, which effectively cut the benefits received by retirees above certain income thresholds. The taxable portion of Social Security benefits was later increased by the Omnibus Budget Reconciliation Act of 1993. Neither these benefit adjustments nor tax increases, however, have permanently solved the Social Security financing problem. Future changes will be necessary to bring the program's spending and revenues into balance, but these changes cannot be divorced from the remainder of the budget. If individual income taxes are significantly increased in order to control deficits and debt over the next decade, higher payroll taxes for Social Security would be harder to enact. Limiting the long-term growth in Social Security spending through benefit cuts would reduce the need for additional revenues, and it would also provide more flexibility with regard to other spending programs. Social Security presents reasonably manageable financing problems when considered in isolation from the rest of the budget, but its size and future growth need to be integrated into a comprehensive fiscal plan for the federal government.

Medicare and Medicaid

Over the past several decades, healthcare spending in the United States has grown much faster than the economy. Medicare and Medicaid costs have risen at roughly the same rate as healthcare spending generally, from a combined spending-GDP share of 2.2 percent in 1985 to 5.5 percent in 2010.[54] Past spending growth for Medicare and Medicaid has been driven partly by expanding beneficiary populations for both programs, and this demographic effect will become even more pronounced in the future. Over the next decade, the number of Medicare beneficiaries is expected to grow by more than 35 percent, while Medicaid coverage will expand by 45 percent.[55] By 2021, combined enrollment in the Medicare and Medicaid programs would exceed 160 million.

The primary factor affecting past federal healthcare spending, however, has been rising per beneficiary costs. For Medicare and Medicaid, costs per beneficiary have exceeded per capita GDP growth for several decades.[56] This "excess cost growth" for the Medicare program averaged 2.4 percent annually from

---

[54] Congressional Budget Office, *CBO's 2011 Long-Term Budget Outlook*, 35.
[55] Congressional Budget Office, *The Budget and Economic Outlook: Fiscal Years 2011–2021*, 61–62.
[56] Congressional Budget Office, *CBO's 2011 Long-Term Budget Outlook*, 42.

1975 to 2007, while the average rate for Medicaid was slightly lower. Over the next twenty-five years, beneficiary population increases and excess cost growth are each expected to account for about one-half of the increase in Medicare and Medicaid spending. Beyond the mid-2030s, however, excess cost growth is likely to be by far the more important determinant of federal healthcare spending.[57] If excess cost growth were to continue at past rates, Medicare and Medicaid spending could exceed 20 percent of GDP by 2050.[58]

An increase of that magnitude is inconceivable, but more optimistic assumptions about controlling healthcare costs still project greatly elevated levels of spending. The CBO, for example, bases its long-term forecast on an excess cost growth rate of 1.7 percentage points, which it believes more accurately reflects the effectiveness of ongoing efforts to lower Medicare and Medicaid costs.[59] Nevertheless, the CBO estimates that spending–GDP for Medicare and Medicaid will increase from 5.5 percent in 2010 to nearly 9.5 percent in 2035 and to 12 percent in 2050.[60] If excess cost growth were somehow eliminated entirely, Medicare and Medicaid spending–GDP levels would still increase, but roughly on par with Social Security.

Effective healthcare cost controls will be needed to keep the size of federal budgets from spiraling ever upward, but potential Medicare and Medicaid reforms lack the simplicity and predictability of Social Security policy options. An increase in the eligibility age for Medicare, for example, might simply transfer the government's costs to the subsidized private insurance that will soon be available. Lowering the federal government's share of Medicaid spending to the states would reduce its costs but might also affect access to healthcare. In addition, the 2010 healthcare act contains a number of "provider-value" reforms intended to lower Medicare and Medicaid costs without impairing access or quality of care, but these reforms are largely untested, and their long-term budgetary impact is highly uncertain.[61]

It would be possible to control the federal government's Medicaid costs by converting the program into a block grant and giving the states greater discretion over coverage and benefits. Annual Medicare budgets would also cap federal costs by providing, for example, defined subsidies for individuals to purchase private insurance or imposing greater cost-sharing responsibilities on beneficiaries. These mechanisms could stabilize Medicare and Medicaid budgets, but they would fundamentally change the federal government's long-standing commitment to the elderly and poor. Changes of this magnitude may

---

[57] Ibid., 10.
[58] Congressional Budget Office, *The Long-Term Budget Outlook* (Washington, D.C.: Congressional Budget Office, 2005), 32.
[59] Congressional Budget Office, *CBO's 2011 Long-Term Budget Outlook*, 42.
[60] Ibid., 80.
[61] See Peter R. Orszag, "How Health Care Can Save or Sink America," *Foreign Affairs* 90 (July/August 2011), 42–56.

ultimately be necessary, but they are unlikely to be accomplished quickly or easily.

The political and policy challenges associated with the Medicare and Medicaid programs are formidable. The beneficiary populations for both programs are expanding, and if excess cost growth remains high, the spending needed to support them will require levels of taxation that are unprecedented or borrowing that is unacceptable. Closing the gap between the benefits promised today and the resources available in the future will likely require a level of bipartisan realism that has been sorely lacking for a very long time and seems unlikely to resurface anytime soon.

Dependency Ratios

The financing problems of retirement and healthcare entitlements are underscored by projections of population aging in the United States. As the large baby-boom generation reaches retirement age, the number of future retirees will grow rapidly. Life spans for these retirees are expected to continue to lengthen as well, with the sixty-five years of age and older share of the population reaching approximately 20 percent by mid-century.[62] At the same time, the growth rate of the labor force is expected to fall abruptly even if future immigration is taken into account.

Population aging will, therefore, change the relative number of workers versus retirees. The dependency ratio – that is, the number of workers for each retiree – averaged roughly 5:1 during the latter part of the twentieth century, making it possible to finance entitlement expansions fairly easily. Current ratios are lower, and future ones are expected to be much less favorable, falling to approximately 3:1 by 2030 and below 2.5:1 by 2050.[63] If current benefit commitments remain in place, future workers will face greatly increased tax burdens. Some of this increased burden would be offset by high rates of economic growth and real income gains, but these would depend in turn on substantial and sustained gains in worker productivity. While population aging in the United States is not as severe as in other industrialized democracies, it adds a further complication to the debate over entitlement policy.

Fiscal Consolidation and Revenue Raising

During the 1990s and early 2000s, a number of democratic governments adopted fiscal consolidation programs to reduce deficits and stabilize public debt levels. Spending controls and other macrobudgetary rules were widely used to keep these programs on track and proved to be helpful in many instances. Regardless of the particular rules that various countries employed, however, fiscal consolidation required a combination of concrete revenue increases and spending cuts.

---

[62] Congressional Budget Office, *The Long-Term Budget Outlook* (2005), 9.
[63] Ibid., 21.

According to an Organization for Economic Cooperation and Development (OECD) study of the these fiscal consolidation programs, revenue increases typically accounted for a large share of deficit reductions, in many cases a larger share than spending cuts.[64] In the United States, approximately 40 percent of the deficit reduction from 1990 to 2000 was accounted for by higher revenue levels, especially individual income tax revenues, with an additional 35 percent contributed by defense cuts.[65] The remaining deficit reduction was provided by interest savings and other nondomestic spending. Cuts in domestic programs – discretionary and mandatory – played almost no part in the decade-long transition from deficits to surpluses.

In the United States and elsewhere, fiscal consolidation was undertaken despite reservations about short-term contractionary effects on growth, but an International Monetary Fund (IMF) analysis has concluded that these effects were generally less than anticipated and in some cases entirely absent.[66] Over an extended period, fiscal consolidation was expected to have a positive impact on growth by reducing government borrowing and improving the macroeconomic environment. While the timing of future fiscal consolidation efforts in the United States cannot ignore possibly negative short-term effects – that is, whether tax increases and spending cuts will abruptly reduce the demand for goods and services and lower economic growth – there is universal agreement that the next round of fiscal consolidation is not optional. Unless deliberate steps are taken to reduce deficits and limit additional borrowing, long-term economic growth will be at serious risk.

The critical question facing the United States and other countries in similar fiscal straits is the form that fiscal consolidation will take. Given past experience with fiscal consolidation programs and the spending dynamics now in place in the United States, it is difficult to imagine that substantial revenue increases can be avoided. If these increases stand any chance of being enacted, however, myths and exaggerations regarding taxation will have to be corrected.

Taxes and Growth

The standard Republican argument against higher taxes is based on an economic principle, namely that low tax rates encourage work, savings, and investment that, in turn, spur higher growth. This supply-side rationale drove the Kennedy-Johnson tax cut of 1964 and the Reagan tax cuts of the 1980s, and the strong economic growth that followed both helps to explain why many other countries decided to lower individual and business tax rates beginning in

[64] James K. Jackson, *Limiting Central Government Budget Deficits: International Experiences* (CRS Report for Congress, July 19, 2011), 12.

[65] Ippolito, *Why Budgets Matter*, 11.

[66] Jackson, *Limiting Central Government Budget Deficits*, 9.

the 1980s.[67] It is generally accepted today that low tax rates reduce distortions within an economy and improve its global competitiveness. Far from settled, however, is that tax rates alone determine how an economy grows or that higher rates are a prescription for low growth.

In the United States, the connection between tax cuts and economic growth is much less clear-cut than Republicans admit. There is the extended success of the 1964 and 1981 tax cuts, the abbreviated success of the 1986 tax reform and rate cuts, and the highly questionable success of the 2001 and 2003 Bush tax cuts. Equally as important given the current fiscal impasse, the 1990s tax increases did not harm economic growth. From 1993 to 2002, the top marginal rate on individual income was 39.5 percent, and the rate of real GDP growth was 3.68 percent.[68] Lower tax rates were in effect during the late 1980s and early 1990s and from 2003 to 2007, but economic growth over both periods was well below this level. These differences do not imply that higher taxes cause higher growth but do suggest that many factors besides tax rates affect the health and growth of the economy. The singular Republican focus on marginal tax rates also diverts attention from effective tax rates, which are the real concerns of taxpayers and businesses and presumably have a greater impact on their economic behavior.

From the standpoint of budget policy, there is little evidence for claims that tax cuts are somehow self-financing; that is, that the revenue loss from tax cuts is largely offset by feedback effects from higher growth.[69] Both the Reagan and Bush II tax cuts were followed by revenue declines that were much larger than initially projected, while the revenue gains from the 1990 and 1993 tax increases were much greater than expected. It has also been argued that certain types of tax cuts, such as capital gains or corporate rate cuts, have especially large feedback effects, but recent studies suggest that these effects are actually quite modest.[70]

Many factors contribute to the health of the economy besides the budget. Legal and regulatory systems play an important role, as does technological innovation and penetration, along with a well-educated work force. In today's unsettled international economic environment, however, it would be hard to overstate the need for a government to manage its finances responsibly. The deficit and debt problems confronting the United States are undeniably serious, and the federal government must soon close the gap between spending and revenues. There should be an informed debate over the most economically

---

[67] Organization for Economic Cooperation and Development, *Tax Reform in OECD Countries* (Centre for Tax Policy and Administration, February 17, 2011), 2–3.
[68] Jane G. Gravelle and Donald J. Marples, *Tax Rates and Economic Growth* (CRS Report for Congress, December 5, 2011), 6.
[69] Ibid., 9.
[70] Ibid.

efficient way to raise revenues, but the need for higher revenues simply cannot be met using the tax rates and tax base that have been in place since 2001.

Taxes and Fairness

The Democratic Party accepts the need for higher revenue levels but has claimed that sufficient revenues can be raised without a broad-based tax increase. Instead, President Obama and congressional Democrats have called for raising tax rates on high-income taxpayers while maintaining reduced rates and other benefits for low- and middle-income taxpayers. As discussed earlier in this chapter, something very close to the revenue-GDP levels of the late 1990s will be needed to keep deficits and debt at acceptably safe levels over the next decade. A tax increase that only affects the top 1 percent or 5 percent of taxpayers will fall well short of that requirement.

Democratic complaints about the unfairness of the tax system are also misleading. The share of individual income taxes paid by high-income earners, for example, has increased fairly steadily over the past three decades. The top 1 percent of taxpayers accounted for about 20 percent of individual income tax liabilities and 15 percent of total federal tax liabilities in 1980.[71] By the mid-2000s, despite the Bush tax cuts, these shares had nearly doubled. Parallel trends over the same period have affected the top 5 percent and top 10 percent income groups. In 2006, the top 10 percent of taxpayers supplied nearly 73 percent of individual income taxes and more than 55 percent of all taxes.[72]

The problem with today's individual income tax is not a lack of fairness but rather inadequate revenues, and this revenue shortfall cannot be remedied simply by concentrating tax burdens on the affluent. The effective individual income tax rate for high-income taxpayers is less than 20 percent, and it is less than 10 percent for most middle-income earners.[73] Higher effective tax rates for both middle-class taxpayers and the affluent are perfectly compatible with progressivity and other fairness principles. They are also necessary if we expect the individual income tax to generate sufficient revenues.

While nearly half of American households do not pay income taxes, most of these are low-income working families and retirees. Many of the former do pay Social Security and Medicare taxes, and it is estimated that only about 1 percent of the population with annual incomes of more than $20,000 pays neither income nor payroll taxes.[74] Both parties, however, have supported the increased standard deductions and exemptions that have eliminated income

---

[71] Dennis S. Ippolito, "Equity, Growth, and Balanced Budgets," in *The Political Economy of the Public Budget in the Americas*, eds. D. Sanchez-Ancochea and I. Morgan (London: Institute for the Study of the Americas, University of London), 222–223.

[72] Congressional Budget Office, *Historical Effective Tax Rates: 1979 to 2006* (Washington, D.C.: Congressional Budget Office, 2009), 4.

[73] Ibid.

[74] *The Fiscal Times* (August 31, 2011), 4.

tax liabilities for the working poor, and there has also been bipartisan support for the various tax credits that benefit low-income families. Considerations of fairness do apply here, which makes it even more essential to ensure adequate revenue raising from middle- and upper-income households through higher tax rates or reduced tax preferences.

Tax Preferences and Reform

The revenue productivity of the tax code is greatly reduced by the numerous tax preferences (or tax expenditures) that benefit individual and corporate taxpayers. Tax preferences lower the tax liability for an individual or corporation by allowing special exclusions, exemptions, deductions, credits, and rates. While estimates of revenue losses from these provisions are far from precise, it is generally accepted that the impact is substantial.[75] For 2012, the revenue loss from the fifteen largest tax preferences is estimated at nearly $825 billion, and dozens of others raise the total to approximately $1.2 trillion.[76] With FY 2012 budget receipts estimated at only $2.6 trillion, this broad array of costly tax preferences offers multiple opportunities for raising additional revenues.

Eliminating or restricting tax preferences can also enhance the fairness and economic efficiency of the tax system. The Tax Reform Act of 1986, for example, broadened the tax base by eliminating the capital gains deduction, two-earner married couple deduction, and investment tax credit and by modifying a number of other individual and corporate tax preferences. The 1986 act also lowered individual and corporate tax rates. These trade-offs reduced economic distortions and enhanced individual equity while keeping the overall revenue changes deficit-neutral.

The 1986 reform model was embraced by the Simpson-Bowles Fiscal Commission, which recommended the wholesale elimination of tax preferences in exchange for lower tax rates. Similar plans were proposed during the debt-limit negotiations in 2011, but Republicans refused in the end to support tax law changes that, like Simpson-Bowles, combined tax reform with a net increase in revenues. Combining tax reform and revenue raising was also problematic for some congressional Democrats who simply prefer higher tax rates and a stricter reallocation of tax burdens.

Tax reform poses other political problems.[77] Many of the largest individual tax preferences, such as the health insurance exclusion and mortgage interest deduction, distribute benefits broadly and enjoy strong public support. Their outright repeal is unlikely, and the revenue gains from more limited changes might be too small to generate widespread interest in a reform initiative. There are similar difficulties with changes in corporate taxation. Corporate tax rates

---

[75] See Office of Management and Budget, *Analytical Perspectives, Fiscal Year 2012*, 240.

[76] Ibid., 252–255.

[77] The special interest politics and skewed benefits of the tax preference system, particularly its housing and healthcare subsidies, are provocatively analyzed in Suzanne Mettler, *The Submerged State* (Chicago: University of Chicago Press, 2011).

in the United States are high when compared with those of other countries, but a host of corporate tax preferences reduces effective tax rates for many corporations and eliminates tax liabilities entirely for some. As a result, navigating a base-broadening and rate-reducing reform package through Congress has made little headway over the course of many years. In addition, corporate income taxes account for a relatively small share of federal revenues. While this share could be marginally increased, the potential revenue gains from what would undoubtedly be a protracted corporate tax battle would be limited.

New Tax Sources
Many industrialized nations rely heavily on consumption taxes to fund their central governments. The U.S. federal government does not utilize a value-added tax or other broad-based consumption taxes. These types of taxes are, according to most economists, more economically efficient than income taxes, and they can also generate substantial revenues. Carbon taxes and higher gasoline excise taxes have also been proposed, both to raise additional revenues and to advance environmental policy goals.

There are, then, a number of tax policy options that could be incorporated within a deficit-reduction plan. The Bipartisan Policy Center's Debt Reduction Task Force, for example, proposed a national sales tax along with individual income tax reform to raise additional revenues. The President's Fiscal Commission took a different approach, focusing solely on individual income tax reform. Whatever the economic policy merits of these and other plans might be, Congress first has to decide how much additional revenue must be raised. Once the dimensions of the revenue challenge are acknowledged, the need for new revenue sources may be apparent.

Restoring Fiscal Responsibility

The 2012 elections will determine whether Barack Obama has a second term and which party controls the House and Senate. The winners will then have to revisit the deficit-reduction agenda left unresolved by the 112th Congress. As over the past few years, there will be no shortage of plans for stabilizing the budget, but reconnecting taxes and spending will not be possible without difficult and perhaps highly unpopular changes in policy.

Restoring fiscal responsibility is also going to require an honest debate about the budget. For decades, both parties have indulged the public. Democrats have pretended that costly domestic programs did not require higher taxes. Republicans have offered a competing vision of tax cuts financed by pain-free spending cuts. This bipartisan flight from reality began with the Johnson administration's assurance that the nation could afford the Vietnam War and the Great Society without a timely and permanent increase in taxes. It was bookended fifty years later when the George W. Bush administration insisted that its version of "guns and butter" required even less sacrifice. In fact, taxes could actually be cut for everyone.

There was an occasional interruption in this unprecedented aversion to tax increases. When deficits grew too large in the early 1990s, Presidents Bush and Clinton signed major tax increases, and budgets were balanced. Otherwise, budget policy has been tailored to fit the electoral interests of both parties for most of the past half-century.

The current situation differs little. If anything, Republicans are even more adamant that tax increases will not be needed to finance the defense budgets that they favor or Social Security, Medicare, and other programs that their constituents demand. Meanwhile, Democrats assure voters that their expanded domestic agenda will only require higher taxes for the very, very few.

It is theoretically possible to stabilize deficits and debt at the low revenue levels that Republicans are committed to and the modestly higher ones that Democrats support, but the spending cuts needed to do so would be enormous over the next decade and even greater thereafter. Holding the line on taxes in the vague hope that spending cuts will materialize has never worked in the past, and it is an especially dangerous strategy given the fiscal exigencies the nation now faces. At some point – preferably soon – political leaders will have to heed George Washington's advice and gain the public's "spirit of acquiescence in the measures for obtaining revenue" by offering "a candid construction of the conduct of the government." Continued pandering in tax cuts and entitlement promises is probably not what Washington had in mind.

Index

Page numbers in *italics* indicate tables.